Introduction to Western Philosophy: Pre-Socratics to Mill

Introduction to Western Philosophy:
Pre-Socratics to Mill

George L. Abernethy
Davidson College

Thomas A. Langford
Duke University

Dickenson Publishing Company, Inc., Belmont, California

L. C. Cat. Card No.: 72–103034

Printed in the United States of America

1 2 3 4 5 6 7 8 9 10 –– 73 72 71 70

To
Robert and Jean
Andy, Jay, Tim, and Hugh

Contents

Preface

Philosophy cannot be understood apart from its own history. Indeed Western civilization cannot be fully understood without a knowledge and appreciation of the history of philosophy. The invitation to study the history of western philosophy is an invitation to examine the ideas and criticisms which have influenced, both positively and negatively, one's own mind and the cultural context within which he lives.

There is no end to the appearance of new textbooks on the history of philosophy, for the subject may be approached from many different perspectives, at various levels of complexity, and with more or less detail. A student or teacher may, then, select a text in terms of his interests, needs, and abilities. Our text is designed primarily to help the beginning student in a typical undergraduate course in the history of philosophy, but we hope it may also prove useful in introductory courses in which historical materials are stressed and in providing orientation for the general reader who has become interested in philosophy long after his own college days.

This history of philosophy has not been designed to replace either the instructor or the reading of source materials. By presenting summaries of historical and biographical material and the exposition of major topics, it frees the instructor to give his class hours to the discussion of key issues and the clarification of difficulties the student encounters in assigned collateral readings. Thus it provides for considerable flexibility in the instructor's program. Although it has been planned to accompany the authors' book of readings, *History of Philosophy—Selected Readings*, this textbook may be used effectively with any standard anthology. The bibliographies at the end of each chapter contain a large number of paperback titles to make it easier for the instructor to assign additional readings in sources or in critical studies when he wishes to place greater emphasis on a particular philosopher. A textbook that really fulfills its function reinforces the student's motivation to gain greater familiarity with the original sources, critical studies or commentaries, and the more technical histories of philosophy.

Any work of this size must employ rigorous selectivity. Perhaps few will quarrel with the inclusion of the philosophers we have selected. More likely, readers will join the authors in lamenting that other interesting and significant philosophers could not have been included. The decision to conclude the volume with Kierkegaard and Mill stems from practical considerations. It was important to keep the volume to a reasonable length and to keep in mind what a typical class can cover effectively in two semesters. There is much disagreement among philosophy teachers as to what should be emphasized in the last one hundred years of philosophy, especially when it has to be covered in the final weeks of a semester. Since twentieth-century philosophy deserves a full semester of its own, it did not appear to us wise to select arbitrarily a few recent philosophers for discussion or to provide capsule summaries of a great many recent thinkers. Excellent anthologies and paperbacks dealing with twentieth-century philosophy are available to the instructor who has time to use them in his course.

We acknowledge with gratitude the careful reading of portions of the manuscript by the following persons: Earl R. MacCormac, Daniel D. Rhodes, Raymond F. Martin, Robert Osborn, and Don Anderson. Any errors that remain are the responsibility of the authors.

G.L.A.
T.A.L.

Introduction to Western Philosophy: Pre-Socratics to Mill

Chapter One

The Pre-Socratics

Thales

The ancient Greeks invented, among other things, philosophy, science, and mathematics in the sense of first applying the principles of deductive reasoning from general premises. These first scientific and philosophical thinkers lived chiefly in two areas that began as colonies of the Greek mainland: the Ionian cities of Asia Minor, especially Miletus; and southern Italy and Sicily.

Miletus, the cradle of Ionian philosophy, was at the beginning of the sixth century B.C. an important seafaring power and a highly civilized community. Its colonies were spread along the shores of the Black Sea, and it had established the earliest Greek settlements in Egypt. Miletus was allied with the kingdom of Lydia, which had cultural relations with Babylonia. In an important sense Miletus was at the commercial and cultural crossroads of the Mediterranean.

There are special difficulties in determining the nature and development of Milesian philosophy. Most obvious is the lack of firsthand documentary sources. Such knowledge as we have of Thales, the earliest of the known Milesian philosophers, is limited to a few references in Herodotus and Aristotle, and to a series of anecdotes, perhaps apochryphal, preserved by Diogenes Laertius. Other difficulties arise from the fact that these early Milesian thinkers were working in a time when clearcut distinctions were not drawn between the problems of religion, philosophy, and science, or between history and myth. This explains why we must characterize the Milesian thinkers as both scientific and philosophical innovators, and why we must try to avoid reading into their work our own contemporary distinctions.

Herodotus reports that Thales suggested the practical idea of forming a federation of Ionian states with a capital at Teos. He also reports that Thales successfully predicted an eclipse, which we know by other evidence was visible in Asia Minor in May, 585 B.C. It is not suggested that he knew the true cause of eclipses. Thales has been referred to as the "father of geometry." He did travel in Egypt, where he probably encountered valuable Egyptian methods of land measurement. It appears that he knew how to calculate the distance of a ship at sea from observations taken at two points on shore. It is likely that later Greek thinkers, rather than Thales, actually developed the notion of deductive proof in geometry.

In the *Metaphysics* (983 b6) Aristotle attributes to Thales the belief that water is the material from which everything else is originally produced. Aristotle speculated that Thales may have arrived at this conclusion through reasoning that "the nutriment of all things is moist, and that heat itself is generated from the moist and kept alive by it . . ., and from the fact that the seeds of all things have a moist nature, and water is the origin of the nature of moist things"; and observing that, in the older theology, Ocean and Tethys were the parents of creation and that the water of the Styx was even used in the ritual of the oath of the gods. But Aristotle does not really know how Thales came to his conclusion. It may have been that Thales was influenced, in part, by the observations in nature of the phenomena of dew and rain, of evaporation and freezing, and of the influence of water on vegetation. In any case, it is significant that Thales assumed the existence of a coherent world and raised the question of precisely what constituted its underlying nature.

In *De Anima* Aristotle also attributes to Thales the statement that all things are full of gods, that the magnet has a soul because it moves iron. It is difficult to interpret such sayings. They may represent the continuance of earlier animism, or they may be later attributions. In any event, they do not permit us to describe Thales as a pantheist or to entertain a specific hypothesis as to the kind of "life" which he believed animated the magnet.

Anaximander

Anaximander, a younger contemporary of Thales and the second philosopher of the Milesian school, was born about 610 B.C. He was the first of the Greeks to write a book in prose on his philosophical theories. This book, although now lost, was available in the time of Theophrastus, to whom we are indebted for information about Anaximander. Anaximander engaged in practical scientific pursuits, made a map probably for Milesian sailors in the Black Sea, and even led a colony to Apollonia.

Anaximander accepted the assumption of Thales that there must be one primary substance underlying existence. But he rejected the notion that it could be any one particular kind of matter, such as water. If change—birth and death and decay—is to be explained as the result of conflict in which one element overcomes another, then it would be difficult to see why, in a world where reality is ultimately water, everything in time has not become water. Since we experience so many different kinds of determinate matter, Anaximander reasoned that the basic substance was "neither water nor any other of the so-called elements," but "a substance different from them, which is boundless." In other words, to be the origin of everything, the basic substance must transcend any particular limitation or determination. To underscore this, Anaximander calls the basic substance the *apeiron*, the boundless or the infinite. Thus it is eternal, unbegotten, and indestructible.

The *apeiron*, or boundless, is pervaded by two kinds of motion. (1) A to-and-fro motion results in a separation of opposites—hot and cold. The cold in turn separates into "air" or vapor or earth. (2) These are caught up in whirling motion so that the heavy gathers at the center while the lighter goes to the periphery. Consequently, we have a body of earth at the center surrounded by a blanket of air and water, with fire at the outermost parts. Our earth has the form of a cylinder with its diameter three times its depth. The earth was in the beginning blanketed with a coat of mud, according to Anaximander, and was subsequently subjected to the intense heat of a cloak of fire and developed explosive pressure. He explains the origin of heavenly bodies in similar terms.

In these speculations of Anaximander we see that the Milesians thought without sharp distinctions between philosophy and science. Anaximander reveals a shrewd and imaginative mind, for after finding fossils in mine quarries he conjectured that the land was once covered by water and that human life could not have begun on earth in its present form, because human beings with a long infancy could not have survived. He therefore suspects that man is descended from a fish-like ancestor.

Anaximander's cosmology rests on the basic assumption that "into that from which things take their rise they pass once more, for they make reparation and satisfaction to one another for their injustice according to the ordering of time." This is the principle of *dike*, righteousness, and *adikia*, unrighteousness, applied to the universe. This conception of justice prohibiting the overstepping of eternally fixed bounds and enforced by natural law or necessity is deeply rooted in Greek religion and mythology. Although his thought may appear to us as basically naturalistic and secular, Anaximander's thinking is still shaped by moral and religious assumptions.

Anaximenes

The third important teacher in the Milesian school was Anaximenes, who appears to have been more admired in antiquity than Anaximander.

We do not have precise dates for him, but it is believed he flourished around 545 B.C. He was a younger associate of Anaximander and also wrote a book, a fragment of which survived.

Anaximenes shares with his predecessors the interest in determining the fundamental substance of which all things are made. He rejects water and *apeiron*, and instead offers air as the fundamental substance. "Just as our soul, being air, holds us together, so do breath and air encompass the whole world." Anaximenes shows his originality in offering the notion of condensation and rarefaction as an explanation of how specific objects are formed from the primary element of air. Air is invisible, but becomes visible in this process of condensation and rarefaction, becoming fire as it is rarefied. It becomes wind, cloud, water, earth, and stone as it is condensed. Thus air is a sort of half-way house between water and the *apeiron*. Its significance lies in its attempt to explain all quality by quantity.

Anaximenes reverts to the earlier view of Thales in holding that the earth is a sort of floating platter or dish. He believes that the clouds are everywhere. He gives a simple naturalistic explanation of the rainbow as caused by the falling of the sun's rays on a thick cloud which it is unable to penetrate.

With the destruction of Miletus in 493 B.C. by the Persians during the Ionian revolt, the Milesian school came to an end. Since Anaximenes was its last representative, the ancients came to identify the teachings of the entire school with him. A vigorous and autonomous school of philosophy disappeared, but its influences were to bear later fruit. The main contribution of the Milesians was the framing of questions about the ultimate nature of things, thus setting in motion the search for answers. The effort to discover a material cause of things in non-mystical terms and the assumption that matter is eternal were important contributions, although they do not make the Milesians "materialists" in our twentieth-century use of the term.

Heraclitus

Heraclitus of Ephesus (*c.* 540–475 B.C.) more or less follows chronologically the philosopher Pythagoras, whom we shall discuss in another connection. Heraclitus is known to us principally through more than 100 extant fragments, many only a sentence in length. The reconstruction of Heraclitus' philosophy from these fragments has resulted in a number of diverse interpretations. Apparently he wrote in an obscure, oracular style with many oblique allusions. It is not surprising that traditionally he was called the "dark" or "weeping" philosopher. He had seen the Persian armies sack the Ionian cities and reduce Miletus to ashes. He expressed bitter contempt for thoughtless people who remained unconcerned about the despotism of these conquered lands and instead spent their time admiring athletes. He declined an invitation to the court of King Darius of Persia to explain his wisdom and to receive honors.

Wisdom, for Heraclitus, is to be found only when one has a formula, or unifying insight, in terms of which one may interpret all of existence. Heraclitus believed that he had the true formula in his philosophy of change, which was succinctly stated in the famous aphorism: "All things flow." This has been commonly interpreted as a denial of permanent substances in nature and as an affirmation that flux alone is real. Nothing is changeless but change. According to tradition, Heraclitus maintained that no one can step into the same river twice, because fresh waters are ever flowing upon him. It was later maintained by Heraclitan extremists that no one can step into the same river once or can remain the same person as he moves, because both the river and the man who takes a step undergo changes during the event. If, in Milesian fashion, one must have a basic stuff or substance in nature, Heraclitus proposes fire, since fire itself is a process and a continuing change from one form to another. Thus we see fire thickening into air or vapor, and vapor becoming water, slime, and solids. The reverse process is always going on. Everything is coming and going, it is and it is not. The death of plants and animals is our own food and life.

In the thought of Heraclitus, universal change and continuous strife are basic ideas. Heraclitus condemns Homer for deploring the wars of men, and Anaximander for talking about the punishment by Fate of the elements which encroach upon their opposites. Heraclitus insists that harmony and disharmony are inseparable. The true or underlying harmony is to be found only in strife and tension. When Homer asks for the end of strife, he is really asking for universal death. Tension sustains existence in perpetual process, which has no meaning apart from opposition.

But the process of tension and change has an order, or structure. There is a law of change and a *logos*, or reason, in the behavior of the universe, which one can know through understanding but not through the deceptive appearances of the senses—a basic distinction which was to have an important role in the long history of philosophy. Since he accepts a law of change and a *logos*, Heraclitus believes nature is a cosmos in which even seemingly unpredictable men and gods are ruled by an ordered existence. Although "Nature loves to hide," our reason can decipher its unities, its reason, and its laws.

Heraclitus wrote two treatises on theology and politics from which a few fragments have survived: "Strife is Justice" and "War is the father and King of all." In the city-state of his time internal peace was an indication that neither the lower classes nor the nobility was sufficiently powerful to seize power in its own interests. Without this tension or balance of opposing powers, peace was impossible. Heraclitus appears to have been a member of the royal house of Ephesus, having aristocratic biases which led him to reject the egalitarian notions of democratic thinkers. One of his fragments declares: "The Ephesians would do well to hang themselves, every grown man of them, and leave the city to beardless lads, for they have cast out Hermodorus, the best man among them, saying, 'We will have none who is best among us; if there be any such, let him be so elsewhere and among others'" (Fragment 114, Burnet). Another fragment declares his contempt for the values of the masses: "Asses would rather have straw than gold." He expressed similar contempt for the religious beliefs of the common man as reflected in the teachings of Hesiod and Homer. "Hesiod is most men's teacher. Men are sure he knew very many things, a man who did not know day or night." He believed that Homer "should be turned out of the lists and whipped." There are, however, fragments in which Heraclitus appears to have identified God with the world process, as when he says: "God is day and night, winter and summer, war and peace, surfeit and hunger; but takes various shapes, just as fire, when it is mingled with spices, is named according to the savour of each" (Fragment 36, Burnet).

If one identifies God with the total process of nature, it then becomes difficult to see how God can have providential care for men or rule nature in terms of cosmic justice as Hesiod, Solon, and earlier Greek thinkers had taught. Good and evil, pleasure and pain are in essence the same thing. One cannot experience pleasure without its opposite pain. Individuals use *good* and *evil* as terms to designate their personal reactions to things as they are experienced. Thus Heraclitus concludes: "To God all things are fair and good and right, but men hold some things wrong and some right" (Fragment 61, Burnet). This would seem to indicate that Heraclitus has a relativistic theory of value. We have here also a stage in the development of the concept of natural law. The older tendency to fuse moral and natural law is being undone by the effort to establish a concept of a neutral and amoral force or process which still remains universal and necessary. This view of the pervasive interrelationship of all things in the natural world prepares the way for the concepts of science which are to develop eventually in the modern world.

The influence of Heraclitus' teachings continues through Plato's time. The philosopher Cratylus, a disciple of Heraclitus, is said to have been the teacher of Socrates. Aristotle reports that Cratylus was the source of "the Heraclitan opinions that all sensible things are continually flowing and there is no knowledge of them," which, among other things, led Plato to formulate his doctrine of unchanging forms (Vide Guthrie, p. 468).

Xenophanes

The view of Heraclitus that *everything* changes was immediately challenged by the Eleatic school, which maintained that *nothing* changes and that existence or being is a unity. In this Eleatic school are included the philosophers, Xenophanes, Parmenides, and Zeno.

Xenophanes of Colophon was born probably during the third or fourth decade of the sixth century B.C. After the Persians had subjugated all the Ionian cities except Ephesus, he fled and eventually took refuge in Elea, a Greek city in southern Italy. Fragments of a poem he wrote are all that have come down to us from his work. These reveal his rejection of Homeric anthropomorphism and his skepticism about the possibility of human knowledge. "Both Homer and Hesiod," he states, "have attributed to the gods all things that are shameful and a reproach among mankind: theft, adultery and mutual deception" (Fragment 11, Freeman). Since his scorn was also directed against human luxury, effeminacy, and drunkenness, he has on occasion been compared with the Hebrew prophets. In an early statement of sophisticated theological criticism, Xenophanes observes that men have created gods in their own image: "Ethiopians have gods with snub noses and black hair, Thracians have gods with grey eyes and red hair," and, if they could, horses and oxen would also create gods in their own image. This criticism does not mean that Xenophanes has rejected religion. He is confident that he has something better than what the old mythologies offered, for he says there really is "one God . . . neither in form like unto mortals nor in thought. . . . He sees all over, thinks all over, and hears all over. . . . Without toil he swayeth all things by the thought of his mind" (Fragment 25, Burnet).

What Xenophanes is offering is a form of philosophical pantheism not unlike that of Heraclitus, for his god is the ultimate reality beyond all limit and variation. However, to characterize him this bluntly is probably to read into the concept too much of subsequent and particularly modern connotations. It is at least an expression of his unqualified conviction of the basic unity of nature. The more systematic analysis and exposition of the philosophical implications of this position were to be worked out by Parmenides, the real head and developer of Eleatic philosophy.

Parmenides

The date of Parmenides' birth is a matter of conjecture, but it seems reasonable to believe that he was born towards the close of the sixth century B.C. He was born in Elea, in the south of Italy, and flourished in the first half of the fifth century B.C.

Usually Parmenides is contrasted with Heraclitus, since he saw a basic problem in the Heraclitan belief in universal flux when compared with Xenophanes' teaching that deity was one and unchanging. It may be that Pythagorean doctrine suggested to Parmenides the contrast between appearance and reality. In any event, Parmenides took his stand for truth and reality on the side of Xenophanes and elaborated with pioneering dialectical skill the doctrine of the one Being as a systematic metaphysics.

Parmenides elaborated his doctrine in a poem *On Nature*, which was divided into three parts: *Prologue*, *Way of Truth*, and *Way of Opinion*. In the *Prologue*, Parmenides uses the literary device of claiming that his knowledge comes from a goddess and that his poem is addressed to her. In the *Way of Truth* he states his famous and characteristic arguments. In his *Way of Opinion* Parmenides provides a summary of opposing views, largely Pythagorean, which Parmenides himself rejected. The two Ways reveal a contrast between truth and opinion, reality and appearance, intellect and sense. This contrast has been a perennial one in the history of philosophy ever since Parmenides' day.

The significance of Parmenides' work is that he invented a form of metaphysical argument based on logic which subsequent philosophers were to employ and develop further. In this type of dialectical argument Parmenides tried to prove an assertion by demonstrating that when anyone denies the given assertion he falls into contradiction, so that his denial is seen to be logically untenable. This approach does not make an appeal to observed facts. Indeed, it contends that the observations of changing sense experience are illusory and hence untrustworthy.

Parmenides' initial argument is a simple one. What *is* is; and nothing else is. If we suppose that what *is not* is, we are obviously involved in a contradiction. Therefore, only what *is* is. Or, again, he argues that what *is* has neither beginning nor end. In other words, it has not come into being nor will it ever pass away. Here he is rejecting Heraclitus' argument that it was doing both at the same instant. If Heraclitus is right in thinking it has come into being, it must have come from what-is or from what-is-not. It could not have come from what-is-not, since what-is-not is not. Nor could it have come from what-is, because it was always what-is. What-is cannot pass away into what-is-not, since that would imply that what-is-not would replace it.

Parmenides also argues that what-is is unchanging and immovable. Let us assume that something changes. Then it no longer is what-is and becomes what-is-not. It is logically untenable to assert that what-is is not what-is. If it is unintelligible, it is clearly false. What-is is immovable as a whole, because it would require a place into which to move—a place other than what-is. Thus what-is cannot move.

Parmenides argues that Being is indivisible; it cannot be divided into parts. Let us assume, for argument, the Being is divided into parts. If Being has parts, then the parts are parts of what-is. This leaves Being homogeneous, continuous, and undivided. If what-is is divided by what-is-not, this is no division at all and hence Being remains indivisible. If it is indivisible, it is one or single. Thus Being remains one, eternal, uncreated, indestructible, and unchangeable on Parmenides' dialectical arguments based on the consequences of denials. What we have here is something quite different from the familiar world of ordinary sense experience. It is a concentration upon one basic fact: is-ness. What-is is one, or unity; and hence we are obliged to be monists when we think clearly and logically about what-is. Parmenides thus challenges the apostles of common sense and all the theories which interpret nature as in process, as both being and not-being. If you believe reality is permanent or eternal, Parmenides is saying, you cannot at the same time believe it to be impermanent. This is to fall into a logical contradiction. Parmenides asserts that reality cannot be a contradiction.

Plato's dialogue *Parmenides* indicates that Parmenides' doctrine was attacked by all sorts of people who felt that the evidence of ordinary sense experience gave indubitable proof that Parmenides was wrong. Zeno, an Eleatic disciple and popularizer, in a very dramatic fashion sought to outflank these critics by taking their assumptions and reducing them to logical absurdities.

Pythagoras

Another influential school of philosophy making its appearance in the Greek cities of southern Italy was that of the philosopher Pythagoras.

The details of his personal background remain unknown to us, although it is believed that he migrated to the west from the island of Samos when the advance of Persian power to the Aegean threatened the liberties of Greeks in Asia Minor. Probably he settled in Croton in southern Italy about 531 B.C. There he founded a religious brotherhood for the practice of asceticism and the study of mathematics. In this connection it should be noted that during the seventh and sixth centuries B.C. a sort of religious revival had taken place in Attica and in the Greek cities in Italy and Sicily. It was largely centered around the worship of Dionysus as a religion of redemption in which there would be a final union with the savior god to compensate for the feelings of frustration and defeat experienced in this earthly life. It organized cults known as "mysteries," which were really exclusive societies with secret rites of initiation guaranteeing final union with the savior god and immortality. Preliminary rites involved fasting and various acts of purification. Often the worshippers of Dionysus, under the influence of intoxicating dances and songs, tore the flesh of living animals from their bones, drank their blood, and danced to exhaustion, when the cultists sometimes claimed they felt the spirit of the god enter their bodies.

Although it was undoubtedly influenced by these mystery cults, the Pythagorean brotherhood raised its practices to a higher intellectual and spiritual level. It is true that the Pythagoreans retained odd prohibitions against the eating of beans, the touching of a white rooster, the stirring of the fire with iron, and the leaving of a bodily impress on the bed after one arose. But they used music to purify the soul, and they enjoined a way of life rather than the routine performance of rites. They believed in the immortality of the soul and its transmigration from the prison of the perishable body. The moral goal of life was, for them, to gain ultimate release from the cycle of birth and death. These ideas were to be influential later in the discussions of Socrates and the teachings of Stoicism and Epicureanism.

The Pythagoreans believed that men fell into three classes like those attending the Olympic Games. Lowest are the "lovers of gain," who come to buy and sell; next are the competitors seeking the honor of winning; highest are the "lovers of knowledge" who stand watching above the vulgar crowd that seeks money and fame. This elevation of the contemplative or philosophical life was something new and was to be developed further, not only by the Pythagoreans, but in the later thought of Plato and Aristotle.

The Pythagoreans were scientists of no mean rank in the fields of mathematics, music, astronomy, and medicine. To them we owe the proof of the Pythagorean theorem in geometry. They recorded important observations on the arithmetical proportions that govern musical harmony. We are indebted to their astronomy for our phrase "the music of the spheres" and the suspicion that the earth is not the center of the universe. In medicine they expressed the belief that health consists of an attunement and harmony of opposites. Thus the body is healthy when it is neither too hot nor too cold—in a mean between two extremes. It is only a short step from this notion to the definition of the good as the mean.

According to Aristotle, the Pythagoreans believed that there are two basic principles: the Limit and the Unlimited. In other words, they were dualists rather than monists like the Milesians or pluralists like Empedocles or Anaxagoras. The Unlimited or "boundless breath" was, they held, indeterminate or indefinite. Opposed to this indeterminate is the principle of Limit, the application of which to the Unlimited maps it out in various things. Thus what distinguishes one sort of thing from another is the amount of the Unlimited that is required to fill a given figure or the number of units contained in its outline. To get the number of anything was to capture its distinctive nature. Consequently, we owe to number the proper measuring out of the Unlimited into a harmonious universe, in which each thing receives its due share.

The later Pythagoreans developed number mysticism to extreme lengths, finding numbers for social and political organizations and even for moral qualities. Thus it was held that the number five, which is the union of the first odd with the first even combination of units, is the essence of marriage.

However difficult it may be to assess the total contribution of the Pythagoreans, several aspects of their thought are significant for the history of philosophy. The doctrine that our universe is the result of the action of the Limit upon the Unlimited influenced Plato and prepared the way for the eventual distinction between form and matter which is so central in Platonic and Aristotelian thought. The insight that things are basically number influenced Plato and anticipated modern science, which wishes to describe everything by mathematical equations.

The Pluralists

The Greeks were baffled by the problem of change in the light of their monistic view of nature. How can the one basic substance change in any way? Heraclitus' philosophy of change seemed to underline the common man's observation of everyday experiences, but it seemed to be undermined in turn by Parmenides' devastating dialectical argument. Thus the next group of philosophers concentrated on ways of avoiding the difficulties Parmenides had raised. Since they believed that change and motion actually do occur, they gave up the Milesian assumption of monism—one basic substance. Instead they asserted that the universe is made up of a number of microscopic elements which retain their basic identity while entering and leaving different complex combinations of microscopic entities. These pluralistic philosophers agreed with Parmenidean notions of universal permanence in that the basic elements retained their identity; they agreed with the Heraclitan doctrine of universal flux and change insofar as they accepted everchanging combinations of permanent elements. In general terms, this was the sort of compromise which the pluralist philosophers worked out. Within this framework they differ as to the number of permanent elements in nature and as to what creates or destroys the various combinations of these elements.

Empedocles

The earliest of the pluralists was the Sicilian philosopher Empedocles of Acragas (modern Girgenti), who lived about 490–430 B.C. He was reputed to be a many-sided thinker interested in biology and chemistry who was in turn a poet, a mystic, a social reformer, and a wonder-worker performing miracles of healing. According to one legend, he died by leaping into the volcanic crater of Etna to prove that he was a god. A more prosaic account reports that he died an exile in the Peloponnesus.

Empedocles followed the Eleatics in believing that Being is eternal and indestructible, but he refused to accept their assertion that Being was unitary and that change and motion are impossible. He held instead that there are four kinds of ultimate particles from combinations of which all things are formed. The four elements or roots of existence he designated as Fire, Air, Water, and Earth. This theory of the four elements dominated chemical science for two thousand years. From these four elements or roots is generated an endless variety of combinations or compounds which constitute the macroscopic things with which we deal in everyday life. Usually we call each combination or compound by the root or element which dominates its makeup. Earth, for example, will then be a single name for what is actually a large number of quite different macroscopic things.

Empedocles believed each of the four elements permanently retained its identity without alteration. In the extant fragments he interprets the process of change or rearrangement of the elements as a "coming together," "scattering," "interchange of place," or "mixing." To account for this change he introduces two opposing powers of cosmic agencies, Love and Strife, which are regarded in some sense as material or substantial like the four elements themselves.

The process of universal change is, for Empedocles, a cyclical one without an absolute beginning. In the first stage of the cycle the four elements are held together in perfect union by Love. Strife next interrupts this Golden Age and drives the elements apart so that in the third stage there is complete isolation of all the elements. But finally this proves unstable and Love returns once more to bring the elements together and restore the earlier cosmic harmony. In the cosmic process worlds arise, dissolve, and reappear in an eternal recurrence. A world such as ours exists as a partial mixture in the intermediate stages, revealing great masses of earth gathered into continents and of water collected as seas, and simultaneously all combinations of various elements which we know as plants and animals. If, then, our world is "in process," the ordinary inhabitant will want to know whether it is moving at the moment in the direction of complete separation or complete mixture.

Some of the extant fragments of Empedocles' writing indicate that his speculations and guesses anticipated modern evolutionary doctrines like the survival of the fittest. At the point when Love begins to contest the dominance of Strife, Love mixes the separated elements so that "heads spring up without necks and arms wander bare and bereft of shoulders. Eyes stray up and down in want of foreheads." As Love advances its sway anatomical members are combined in bizarre and haphazard ways. Many of these random and monstrous combinations are too unsatisfactory to survive, yet other combinations are fruitfully related and survive. Since all of this happens by chance rather than by divine plan, men with their present faculties exist only as the result of accidental mixture or combination of elements.

Empedocles does not deal adequately with the question of why there are only four elements and how the powers of Love and Strife come to be related to them. But he does set the stage for the development of atomism which came to be a fruitful and important theory in Western thought.

Anaxagoras

The first philosopher to take up residence in Athens was Anaxagoras, who remained for some thirty years, from the end of the Persian Wars to the middle of the century. He was born about 500 B.C. in Clazomenae, Ionia, and his interests reflect the Ionian school at Miletus. In Athens he was a member of the enlightened and skeptical circle which gathered around Pericles and Aspasia. Although his great learning and personal dignity won wide recognition, he incurred the hostility of the adherents of the Homeric mythology. He was eventually prosecuted for impiety and convicted. He was specifically indicted for denying the divinity of the sun and asserting that it was merely a white-hot stone somewhat larger than the Peloponnese. He managed to escape from prison with the help of Pericles, and continued his teaching in Lampacus where the local residents took a more enlightened view of his activities. His teachings were set down in a book, fragments of which have survived in other sources.

Anaxagoras developed an involved theory concerning the nature of matter. Scholars are not in agreement as to the correct interpretation of it. As a pluralist Anaxagoras rejects the Eleatic doctrine of the unitary nature of Being. His counter claim is that things are infinitely various both in number and kind. This may be called qualitative atomism or qualitative pluralism.

Instead of taking only four elements, Anaxagoras asserts the number of different elements is beyond man's power of reckoning. He calls them the seeds of existence. He introduces the notion that everything is infinitely divisible and that even the smallest portion of matter contains something of each element. The difference between things is accounted for by the greater preponderance of one of the elements. Everything in the world contains the element of fire, but we call something fire only when the element of fire predominates over all the other elements. The seeds of existence in all their qualitative distinctiveness are eternal and unchanging, but their relations to one another vary continually as they are commingled or separated. This is the world as we know it.

Since the infinitely various seeds of existence left to themselves would constitute only an indiscriminate mass, Anaxagoras introduces mind (*Nous*) as an ordering agency. He maintains that in everything there is a portion of everything except mind, and in addition, certain things contain *Nous*. This *Nous*, infinite and self-ruled, has power over all living things. Sometimes Anaxagoras describes *Nous* as a moving, rotating force which causes the heaviest things to fall to the center and the lightest to go to the periphery. In this way seeds are separated into appropriate combinations and eventually the worlds and systems of worlds come into existence. Thus Anaxagoras saw in nature the consequences of an organizing rational power which replaces Empedocles' Love and Strife. He still considered *Nous* to be a substance, although a very subtle and rare substance which remains pure and unmixed.

Subsequently, both Plato and Aristotle were impressed by his recognition of the sovereignty of mind, but they complained that Anaxagoras
made very little use of the principle after introducing it to start off
the cosmic order, relying mostly on a mechanical explanation for
detailed changes and causality. Of course these criticisms rest on sharper
distinctions and clearer conceptions than were available to Anaxagoras
in his day. The significance of his work does not lie in providing a full
answer to the dialectical argument of Parmenides, for he did not provide one. But he did prepare the way for the later atomists and he did
help to formulate more clearly the basic problem of how we can relate
the changing common-sense world of multiple sense things to ultimate,
qualitatively simple, but quantitatively plural, real things.

Leucippus and Democritus

The origins of atomism are somewhat obscure. Traditionally the
atomic theory has been jointly attributed to Leucippus and Democritus.
So little is known of Leucippus that his existence was doubted by his
great follower Epicurus and even denied by an occasional modern
scholar. Since we have no fragments of Leucippus' writings, the usual
approach has been to identify his teaching with that of Democritus,
from whose work we have fragments and considerably more indirect
evidence. Democritus was a northern Greek, from Abdera in Thrace,
who was born about 460 B.C., and was a younger contemporary of
Anaxagoras. He apparently had a first-rate mind, which was admired
by Aristotle. Democritus worked out not only an atomic theory of
change but also theories of knowledge and ethics.

Atomism in Democritus' work was essentially an attempt to reformulate pluralism in such a way as to avoid some of the difficulties
which Empedocles and Anaxagoras had encountered in dealing with
Parmenides' arguments. The formulation which Democritus gave
atomism persisted in its essentials until the nineteenth century. It
asserted that everything is composed of atoms which are physically
indivisible and indestructible, infinite in number and kind, everlastingly
moving in empty space. There is conflicting testimony as to whether
Democritus believed atoms to be possessed of weight. Qualitatively
atoms were all alike, differing only in size, shape, position, and relation
to other atoms. Democritus held that the qualitative differences we
note in macroscopic objects arise from the manner in which homogeneous atoms happen to assemble. Thus measureable quantitative differences account for the qualitative differences we experience. He placed
this doctrine within the framework of a strictly mechanistic cosmology
and a thoroughgoing materialism. Unlike Empedocles, he located

motion within the atoms themselves so that their actions were spontaneous rather than the results of external or supernatural causes. His
detailed explanations of natural phenomena were not based on observation, but on the systematic development of his speculative or intuitive
insights.

Democritus assumes the existence of empty space in which he
postulates a whirl or a sort of cosmic rain in which the larger atoms
overtake the smaller, resulting in an endless chain of collisions, which
explains the particular and often temporary groupings of atoms into
what we call objects. By extension, human beings are also whirling
masses of atoms in empty space. Democritus seeks to interpret the
mechanical process in every sensation. Yet sense perception gives us
only a knowledge of appearance and of secondary qualities which do
not ultimately exist. It is only through reason that we are led to infer
the truth of the nature of atoms and their combinations moving through
empty space. This raises difficult questions for any mechanistic
explanation of knowledge.

Many of the extant fragments from Democritus' writings are ethical
teachings. These advocated as the aim of conduct a state of well-being,
happiness, tranquility, and moderate pleasures accompanied by
philosophic cheerfulness. Many in antiquity referred to Democritus
as "the laughing philosopher." For him, there was no supernatural
reward and punishment, either present or future; the soul was not
immortal and the gods, although real, were completely indifferent to
the conduct of men. Thus one of the roles of ethical teaching was to
relieve man of needless fears and anxieties.

In Democritus' version of atomism we find brought together a
number of problems and ways of handling them that will engage our
attention repeatedly in the history of philosophy. Thus we may well
postpone any judgment on their significance, relevance, and enduring
qualities.

Conclusion

In looking back over the intellectual interests of the early Greek
philosophers, several of their distinctive characteristics may be clearly
seen. At this juncture in man's interpretation of his world there is the
discovery of nature and of a fresh way of coming to know nature. In
a most direct fashion, the question of the nature of physical reality
comes into focus. Casting aside the earlier attempts to interpret nature
and natural happenings in terms of divine activity, the philosophers
of this period assume that the whole universe is natural and potentially

within the reach of knowledge as ordinary and as rational as our knowledge that fire burns and water drowns. In rather dramatic steps, the conception of nature was extended to incorporate what had been thought to be the domain of the supernatural; the world was secularized and made amenable to human understanding.

Among these thinkers, new questions emerged: What is the original ground of things? How does this reality outlast temporal change? How does this original ground change itself into particular things or change particular things back into itself? Throughout, as we have seen, the chief interest fell on physical questions. The word for nature, *physis*, became the central concept as these early cosmologists sought a more meaningful interpretation of their environment. In contrast to the succeeding period when the character of human nature was to become the basic issue, the men we have looked at in this chapter gave a new footing to scientific thought and provided the base upon which future scientific investigation could take place.

Pre-Socratics: Suggested Additional Reading

Abernethy, George L. and Thomas A. Langford, eds., *History of Philosophy: Selected Readings*. Belmont, Calif.: Dickenson Publishing Company, Inc., 1965, pp. 1–42.*

Ancilla to the Pre-Socratic Philosophers (translation of the fragments in Diels, *Fragmente der Vorsokratiker*). Translated by Kathleen Freeman. Cambridge: Harvard University Press, 1948.*

Burnet, John, *Early Greek Philosophy*, 4th ed. New York: World Publishing Company, Meridian, 1962.

Cornford, Francis M., *Before and After Socrates*. New York: Cambridge University Press, 1962.

Cornford, Francis M., *Principium Sapientiae: A Study of the Origins of Greek Philosophical Thought*. New York: Harper and Row, Torchbook, 1965.

Dodds, E. R., *Greeks and the Irrational*. Berkeley, California: University of California Paperbacks, 1963.

Frankfort, H., H. A. Frankfort, John A. Wilson, and Thorkild Jacobsen, *Before Philosophy*. Baltimore: Penguin, 1963.

Greene, William C., *Moira: Fate, Good and Evil in Greek Thought*. New York: Harper and Row, Torchbook, 1963.

Guthrie, W. K. C., *The Greek Philosophers: From Thales to Aristotle*. New York: Harper and Row, Torchbook, 1960.

Jaeger, Werner, *The Theology of the Early Greek Philosophers*. New York: Oxford University Press, 1967.

Kaufmann, Walter, *Philosophical Classics*. Englewood Cliffs, N.J.: Prentice-Hall, 1961, I, 1–90.*

Kirk, G. S. and J. E. Raven, *Presocratic Philosophers*. New York: Cambridge University Press, 1967.

Lovejoy, Arthur O., *The Great Chain of Being: A Study of the History of an Idea*. New York: Harper and Row, Torchbook, 1960.

Snell, B., *The Discovery of the Mind*. Translated by T. G. Rosenmeyer. New York: Harper Torchbook, 1960.

Warner, Rex, *The Greek Philosophers*. New York: New American Library, Mentor, 1958.

Wheelwright, Philip E., *Heraclitus*. Princeton: Princeton University Press, 1959.*

Zeller, Eduard, *Outlines of the History of Greek Philosophy*. New York: World Publishing Company, Meridian, 1960.

* Indicates hardback books in this and following chapters.

Chapter Two

The Sophists and Socrates

Society is never static, but Greek culture was undergoing un-usually rapid and fundamental changes during the last quarter of the fifth century B.C. Political upheaval was changing the order of Athens and the power structure among the city-states. Increased trade and travel, with a concomitant awareness of variations in religion, politics, and moral codes, brought new questions in regard to cultural mores. In philosophy, the inconclusiveness of the cosmological discussions of the earlier thinkers gave rise to profound skepticism about the possibility of understanding the nature of the world, and many questioned whether trustworthy knowledge of the physical world could be had. But man and his culture were immediately at hand. The distinctively human achievements of social life were coming to be admired, and men were increasingly turning their attention to this area of life. Certainly for many, a clear need was felt for purposeful control of politics and personal activity.

At the same time, the understanding of man and his culture was not to be achieved easily. The conflict of diverse socio-cultural patterns helped to call accepted standards in moral, religious, and political beliefs into question. Thoughtful men urgently asked if there was anything which could be known for certain in the more distinctively human area; is there any certain knowledge? The philosophical formulation of these problems was expressed by a group of itinerant teachers known as Sophists, the "wise ones," who were reputed to be able to teach men how to "make their way" through the maze of uncertainty or at least how to control the changing course of events.

The Sophists taught rhetoric, the art of speech and persuasion, a tool absolutely necessary in the political life of the Greek city-states, and above all in Athens. In the Athenian public assembly, a man could be charged with a crime, found guilty by a majority of those present, exiled, and his property confiscated unless he could persuasively defend himself. There was an additional demand for the instruction of these professors. If a man wanted to become rich he usually did it by lawsuits, and the Sophists claimed they could teach men how to win court decisions, even if the cause was not just. (Perhaps this practice gave rise to Plato's insistence in the *Laws* that the conduct of lawsuits with a view to gain should be punishable by death.) Thus, the Sophists were teachers who took as their task the developing of their pupils' ability to "win friends and influence people." That is, the Sophists trained their pupils to use their powers of persuasion to achieve the goals they personally desired.

But what goals should be desired? This question the Sophists took to be completely relative. For the well-traveled, sophisticated, cosmopolitan Sophist who had observed that standards of conduct varied from place to place, the only norm which could be affirmed was that of convention. Consequently, they accepted the utilitarian principle which said that the end to be sought was that which was conducive to the achievement of each individual's goal in a particular community.

For many of the Sophists, such as Protagoras, Gorgias, Hippias, Callicles, and Thrasymachus, this conclusion meant that the rule of conduct is to be found in an understanding of man's natural interests and motivations. Protagoras speaks for the Sophists when he says, "Man is the measure of all things" (*Cratylus*, 386). Thus in the *Republic* Thrasymachus claims that might makes right, which is another way of saying that the desire and the ability of one man to assert his power over another man is the standard which governs human relationships. Therefore, the most important thing the Sophists can teach is the determination of what one's interests and desires are, and then how to bring about their achievement.

In the last analysis, the norm which is established is not that of the opinion of men in general but only that of the individual man; not mankind, but the one man who is making the decision about what he wants and how he should achieve it, is the measure of all things. The Sophists obviously had little interest in transforming men; they only wanted to instruct men in the achievement of their self-interested ends. They took man as they found him and reinforced his natural tendencies.

One of the major reasons for the strength of the Sophists' influence was the demise of the traditional norms of the Greek religions. The question which they faced, along with most men of their period, was whether anything was universally valid. Since they were convinced that there were no universal principles which should govern man's activity the Sophists were content to teach rhetoric or political persuasion in order to enable individual persons to achieve their own aims.

Two Important Sophists

Protagoras

Protagoras, a native of Thrace, probably came to Athens about the middle of the fifth century B.C. (His exact dates are difficult to establish due to conflicting indications in source materials.) He was, it is clear, a contemporary of Pericles, and lived in Athens during the zenith of its cultural, economic, and political importance. Scarcely a dozen fragments of his writings have come down to us and of these only two are of primary importance.

Probably the most familiar statement of Protagoras is found in the first fragment, "Man is the measure of all of things that are that they are, and of things that are not that they are not." The correct interpretation of this cryptic statement is a matter of debate, and the discussion hinges on the question of whether the "man" mentioned is the individual or mankind. Plato indicates (in his dialogue *Protagoras*) that Protagoras meant the individual, and this would imply that there is no universal truth and that all knowledge is relative to the individual. But in the dialogue *Theaetetus*, it is clear that Protagoras is thinking not only of individual ethical practice, but that he also envisions a living interchange between the individual and his society. Ethical customs vary from one society to another, and each individual is to make his way within his special context. It must be admitted that this position is open to at least two interpretations: either man must become a traditionalist and conform to the orders of his society, or in every society man must be cunningly aware of the environment in order to achieve his own ends. But the more usual interpretation of the Sophists generally follows the second alternative and while it cannot be claimed with certainty, this is probably the most accurate interpretation of Protagoras' statement also.

In his fragment *On The Gods*, Protagoras states that with regard to the deities he "cannot feel sure either that they are, or that they are not, nor what they are like in figure, for there are many things that hinder sure knowledge, the obscurity of the subject and the shortness of human life." This agnosticism is typical of his suspension of final judgment and his willingness to let each man continue his particular tradition or follow his own individual ideas. It is clear that he is recommending a suspension of judgment about the deities, for agnosticism is preferable to false commitment. But again it must be acknowledged that it is not absolutely clear whether Protagoras meant this to be revolutionary or a caution to conformity. In any case, political and moral systems are not to be attributed to the gods, but rather they are to be explained as products of man's civilizing activity.

In a disputed passage, the claim is made that Protagoras was accused of impiety and condemned by a court while in Athens. This seems theoretically possible, but other evidence indicates that he was never so suspected by the Athenians. On the whole he seems to have been well accepted, and his teaching received as a benefit by the majority of the people of the city.

Gorgias

The second most important Sophist mentioned by Plato was Gorgias. Originally from Leontini in Sicily, he was sent as an emissary to Athens in an effort to persuade the Athenians to join with his home city in a battle against Syracuse. He arrived in Athens in 427 B.C., during the waning of the Periclean period, and became so enchanted by the city that he decided to stay. Gorgias was particularly known for his oratorical ability and his great persuasiveness.

In agreement with the other Sophists, Gorgias was antagonistic to the metaphysical speculations of the earlier Greek philosophers. In his fragment *On Nature or the Non-Existent*, he denies that reason has the power to discover what reality exists behind sensory experience. Specifically he makes three thoroughly radical claims. First, he asserts that nothing exists, or that there is no reality. Since Zeno had shown that thought invariably arrives at contradictions, Gorgias contends we must think of reality as both one and many, finite and infinite, and so forth. This means for him that men are obviously attempting to think about *nothing*, and therefore there is no such thing as being. Second, which is another way of putting the same problem, even if something does exist it cannot be known. In addition to our contradictions of thought, we have the further complicating fact that our senses are unreliable, proved by the fact that we can be tricked by illusion or misperception. In truth, Gorgias claims, we tend to reason from our own desires or wants, which we project upon the phenomena of sense awareness. Third, even if we could know reality we could not communicate it to others. The complete isolation of each individual is here affirmed. For instance, every word seems to have a different meaning for each individual, and concepts differ from person to person. Consequently communication is impossible, or at least it is impossible to know if we are communicating. By these arguments Gorgias arrives at complete skepticism. Some interpreters have charged Gorgias with nihilism, but others understand him to be expressing a disaffection for physical speculations in order to prepare the ground for his concentration upon men and society.

Certain positive evaluations may be made of the Sophists. Historically, they were instrumental in turning man's attention from the physical world to himself. Thus it may be claimed that in the Sophists the spirit of humanism became dominant. They took man as they found him and sought for him only goals which seemed achievable in the light of his predispositions and strength.

Moreover there is self-restriction if not humility in their turning philosophical interest away from the cosmos, metaphysics, and religious speculation and their suspension of the need to come to a conclusion about these matters. They also raised the question of the source of ethics and its social embodiment. And, finally, some have claimed that with the Sophists philosophy became more practical and concrete and hence more relevant for man in his actual living. Some philosophers claim to find in these men at least seeds of utilitarianism, pragmatism, and positivism.

The legacy of the Sophists also gave certain unresolved questions to their successors, especially the question of the relativity of moral norms. And it was precisely this question which came to dominate Socrates' interest.

Socrates

Socrates (*c.* 469–399 B.C.) shared the interests of the Sophists. Whereas the earlier philosophers had been primarily concerned with physical nature (*physis*), we find that Socrates, along with the "wise ones," oriented his thinking toward human nature or anthropology. In a famous passage in the *Phaedo* (97–99) Socrates is described as registering his disappointment with the efforts of his predecessors, and especially with Anaxagoras, because they had failed to develop their philosophical interests beyond a consideration of the natural world as perceived by the senses.

Then I heard some one reading, as he said, from a book of Anaxagoras, that mind was the disposer and cause of all, and I was delighted at this notion, which appeared quite admirable, and I said to myself: If mind is the disposer, mind will dispose all for the best, and put each particular in the best place; and I argued that if any one desired to find out the cause of the generation or destruction or existence of anything, he must find out what state of being or doing or suffering was best for that thing, and therefore a man had only to consider the best for himself and others, and then he would also know the worse, since the same science comprehended both. And I rejoiced to think that I had found in Anaxagoras a teacher of the causes of existence such as I desired, . . . These hopes I would not have sold for a large sum of money, and I seized the books and read them as fast as I could in my eagerness to know the better and the worse.

What expectations I had formed, and how grievously was I disappointed! As I proceeded, I found my philosopher altogether forsaking mind or any other principle of order, but having recourse to air, and ether, and water, and other eccentricities . . . (*Phaedo*, 97–98).

With determination Socrates turns from the study of nature and focuses his attention upon man and the unique character of human personality. The reorientation of Socrates' thought brings him to assert in the *Apology* (30) that his effort is to make men look at their own souls, or to that which distinguishes man from the rest of nature and provides man with the possibility of interpreting his ethical responsibility. Plato has him say in the *Phaedo*, "I was afraid that my soul might be blinded altogether if I looked at things with my eyes and tried to apprehend them by the help of the senses. And I thought that I had better have recourse to the world of the mind and seek there the truth of existence" (99). Or again in the *Phaedrus* he says of this change of perspective, "The men who dwell in the city are my teachers, and not the trees or the country" (230).

With the Sophists, also, he was concerned with the question of universally valid norms for action. But his answers were very different from those of his predecessors. Socrates was opposed to the Sophists on two counts: In the first place, he was convinced that there was a universally valid truth which could be found by the proper use of reason. To follow the Sophists meant to become established in the unexamined life; to be content to live by opinion and thereby not forced to go on to the critical examination of that opinion—an investigation which could result in "knowledge" or in genuine enlightenment. And, secondly, he was convinced that this knowledge could be taught, or at least that men could be made aware of truth if they could be led to examine their own distinctive humanity. In addition to these differences, Socrates also refused to accept any pay for his teaching and denounced the Sophists for doing so.

The dates of Socrates can be most accurately ascertained from the time of his death, which can be dated in 399 B.C. Since Plato indicates that he was at least seventy years old, his early life fell within the period of the greatest age of Athenian history. The great architectural achievements of Athenian culture, such as the Parthenon, and the Periclean democratic political establishment had come to fruition during this period.

The main descriptions of Socrates are found not only in Plato's dialogues but also in Aristophanes' play *The Clouds*, Xenophon's *Memoirs*, and Aristotle's writings. Even though Aristophanes is cynical, Xenophon an uncertain reporter, and Plato a creative artist whose characterizations make it difficult to say precisely what is historical and what is not, the portrait left by these men does indicate that Socrates was an unusual person. Physically robust, he was capable of both extreme withdrawal, even to trance-like states, and of warm participation in friendship and social life. But more important for Plato and Xenophon were his intelligence and character. Socrates himself indicates something of his unique character when he reports that he was from youth aware of a special "daemon" or inner voice which gave negative warnings in order to help him avoid certain prohibited acts. This "conscience" was perhaps a fundamental influence in Socrates' lifelong interest in ethics and ethical norms.

It is difficult to distinguish Socrates from Plato in the Platonic dialogues. But if one takes the evidence of Xenophon and Aristotle, then it is possible to say that Socrates' interest is primarily ethical and that while he may have laid the foundations for the later metaphysical, political, epistemological, and legal speculations of Plato, these later developments go beyond his own thought.

In turning his attention to man, Socrates explored the moral consciousness of man, and this was his greatest contribution to the Western philosophic tradition. What he had hoped to find was some inalienable part of human experience which would provide a guide to the understanding of man and of the values by which man should live. This he believed he found in man's sense of moral obligation, thus his famous emphasis upon the need of man to "tend his soul," and to make it "as good as possible."

Socrates disparages previous attempts to explore the beginnings of life in the physical world and turns, rather, to the question of the end of life. The search for ends is a search for norms or values by which man can gauge his life and in the achievement of which he can exert his energy. The prerequisite for such a search is a rigorous self-examination. The celebrated inscription on the temple of Apollo at Delphi, "Know Thyself," is the beginning of wisdom. The first fruits of its application are to clear away ignorance and find true wisdom, which is established upon notions common to all men.

Underlying Socrates' position is a trust in man's rational capacity, for he is convinced that man's intelligence is controlled by or directed toward what is best. He is so completely persuaded of this fact that he is prepared to use this principle as the key to the interpretation of the world. Therefore, man's intelligence and his moral awareness are to be trusted and used as the best guides to the discovery of what is the universal good. This conviction is succinctly expressed: "To act according to intelligence is to act from a decision or choice of what is best" (*Phaedo*, 99a).

A strange experience with the Delphic oracle (Delphi was a religious center) seems to have given Socrates the sense of mission to share his convictions. Chaerephon, a close friend of Socrates, questioned the oracle, asking if there was any man living who was wiser than Socrates. In response he received the answer "No." The experience was related to Socrates, who was puzzled by such a statement. At first he set out to prove Apollo a liar by finding someone wiser than himself. But his search only revealed man's pretension and ignorance. Finally Socrates realized that he was the wisest man in the sense that he recognized the importance of finding a norm for the good life and admitted his ignorance of what this standard was. As against the pretentions of other men, he at least knew he was ignorant.

Convinced that most of the knowledge which men professed was only a matter of opinion, Socrates took as his primary task that of making other men aware of their need to examine carefully their opinions and attempt thereby to arrive at true knowledge. To many, Socrates seemed to be a skeptic who questioned everything, while to others he was a gadfly who was constantly probing and perplexing men by his questions; but a few were convinced that he was seriously engaged in the most important task of life.

Socrates' approach may be described as conversational. He engages someone in discussion and asks a question about some ethical issue, such as what is justice or what is courage. By interrogating the other person carefully and pointing out contradictions and uncertainties he is able to drive the conversation forward and make the pertinent questions clear. These conversations do not establish a conclusive answer— philosophy is never for Socrates the possession of the truth, it is always a love of the truth—but are intended to demonstrate that man has some awareness of ultimate norms of ethical action, that he has a moral sense.

Socrates' Philosophy

Aristotle attributes two advances in science to Socrates: "inductive arguments and universal definitions" (*Metaphysics*, M. 1078 b27–29). The inductive arguments seem to refer to those discussions or dialogues about ethical issues that Socrates would engage in. The effort of these conversations, as we have already said, was to lead to the final end of clarifying the universal definition of concepts such as piety or justice. How far Socrates went in his discussion of these definitions is not clear. Aristotle maintained that it was Plato and not Socrates who attempted to set the definitions within a metaphysical context and made them "Forms" or "Ideas" which are the patterns for all created objects.

In contrast to the Sophists who were relativists and asserted that there was no final standard for judging ways of life, Socrates was convinced that there were absolute norms. Or, to put this in other words, Socrates was convinced that while particular instances may change the universal concept remains the same, and it is this universal concept which the wise man discovers. It is impossible to determine exactly how far Socrates developed his thought on this point, but one may judge that at least in the realm of ethics Socrates believed there are universal definitions or absolute standards which are discoverable and which man can come to know.

Socrates was always a man of practical concern; most scholars do not think of him as being a theoretician. The intention of his philosophical undertaking was to establish the good life, and he was certain that in order for a man to act well he must know what the good life is. His search for ethical norms, therefore, was in the interest of bringing the good life into existence.

The conviction that every man has within him the potential for clarifying these norms of action made him attempt (using his own imagery) to become a "mid-wife" to the birth of understanding. In the *Apology* (36) his task is explained as the attempt "to persuade every man among you that he must look to himself, and seek virtue and wisdom before he looks to his private interests, and look to the State before he looks to the interests of the State; and that this should be the order which he observes in all his actions."

This description of his mission reveals a basic assurance that knowledge is identical with virtue. The reverse means that vice is ignorance or intellectual error; and, in addition, that wrongdoing is always involuntary. Or, in other words, a man has to convince himself that an evil is good before he will do it. Hence it is Socrates' firm conviction that the man who knows what is right will do what is right.

This argument is based upon the assumption that man acts according to what he believes to be in his best interest. Now men may confuse themselves about what their best interest really is, but they are still acting in accordance with this principle. What is needed is a clarification of what is in a person's best interest and then he will act in keeping with that criterion. Aristotle criticizes Socrates for failing to take into sufficient account moral weakness; in other words, man sometimes seems incapable of doing the good he knows, but Socrates himself is convinced that it is not moral weakness, but a confusion of goals which must be dealt with, and to this end he directs his dialectics.

But how is self-knowledge obtained? If one takes the early dialogues of Plato as the best indication of an answer to this question the findings are meager. However, Socrates does imply that the acquisition of knowledge is by way of "recollection" or "recognition" (*anamnesis*). When man looks inward, when he "tends his soul," he is reminded of what he should always have known, though now has forgotten, namely, that there are norms which should direct his living.

Trial and Death of Socrates

In the *Apology* and *Crito* Plato describes the trial and death of Socrates. In 400/399 B.C. he was brought before the Athenian court and was charged on two counts: first, of not worshipping the gods of the state and of introducing strange religious rites, and, second, of corrupting the youth of the city. The first charge is never made explicit, but the second, while not documented, almost certainly referred to the fact that Socrates had been the mentor of Alcibiades, who had deserted to Sparta, and of Critias, who was a tyrannical member of the ruling oligarchy in Athens before its overthrow by the then-existing popular government.

At the trial, Socrates refused to compromise his position and made light of the charges. The jury evidently wanted to provide him with a way of escaping death and asked him what he thought the punishment should be—evidently expecting him to suggest exile—but he showed his contempt for the trial by suggesting that he be given free meals in the Prytaneum and agreed to pay a ridiculously small fine. The jury responded by sentencing him to death by poisoning.

Even after the trial a number of his friends attempted to provide means for escape, but Socrates resolutely refused, and after discussing the immortality of the soul (in the *Crito*) he drank the hemlock and with great courage waited for his death. His life ended in martyrdom, and like some other martyrs he left a large legacy.

The Sophists and Socrates: Suggested Additional Reading

Cornford, Francis M., *Before and After Socrates*. New York: Cambridge University Press, 1962.

Guardini, Romano, *The Death of Socrates*. New York: World Publishing Company, Meridian, 1962.

Gulley, Norman, *The Philosophy of Socrates*. New York: St. Martin's Press, 1968.*

Guthrie, W. K. C., *A History of Greek Philosophy*, vol. I, Cambridge: Cambridge University Press, 1962.*

Kaufmann, Walter, *Philosophical Classics*. Englewood Cliffs, N.J.: Prentice-Hall, 1961, I, 91–117.*

Kraus, Rene, *The Private and Public Life of Socrates*. Translated by Barrows Mussey. New York: Doubleday, 1940.*

Taylor, A. E., *Socrates*. New York: Doubleday, Anchor, 1960.

Untersteiner, Mario, *The Sophists*. Translated by Kathleen Freeman. Oxford: Blackwell, 1954.*

Winspear, A. D. and Tom Silverberg, *Who Was Socrates?* New York: The Cordon Co., 1939.*

Zeller, Eduard, *Socrates and the Socratic Schools*. London: Longmans, Green, 1885.*

Chapter Three

Plato

No other philosopher has been as influential upon Western thought as Plato (*c.* 427–347 B.C.). Heir to the many legacies of Athens, he was also the recipient of special gifts: outstanding qualities of mind and character, aristocratic family, a sense of political responsibility, and, above all, the acquaintance of Socrates.

Plato was born the year after Pericles' death; this means that his own era, though following immediately Athens' most illustrious period, was one of decline and disillusionment. Wars with Sparta and internal strife hastened the civil and cultural dissolution. These factors were especially significant for young Plato. Because he was raised in a distinguished family and from childhood had been actively aware of the political life of the city, he was nurtured with the conviction that it was a high duty to be in the service of his fellows. But now, with the changing conditions, he had to raise the question of how public responsibility could best be discharged.

We know little of Plato's life up to the time of Socrates' martyrdom, an event which prevented his entering honorably into the existing political parties of his city, and forced him into contemplating and writing about philosophical problems and their application. Immediately after Socrates' death, Plato, along with other supporters of the martyr, fled the city; for over twelve years he traveled through other parts of the Mediterranean world. During this time he wrote most of his dialogues.

At approximately age forty (388–387 B.C.) he returned to Athens and founded the Academy, a school for scientific study, and spent most of his remaining energy developing it. Plato's most important activity outside the Academy was his attempt to help educate the ruler of the city of Syracuse, Dionysius II, a task which met with frustration and disappointment. His last years were spent at the Academy, and during this time he completed his final works, the most notable of which was the *Laws*.

Questions of the chronology of the writings and the development of ideas within the dialogues are quite complex. Some scholars, such as A. E. Taylor, claim that Plato simply reflects the thoughts of others and that the various well-known speakers appearing in the dialogues actually present these individuals' ideas. But generally scholars have seen a development of Plato's own thought in the dialogues, beginning with a fundamental dependence upon the influence of Socrates and ending with the statement of his own mature views. The usual arrangement of the dialogues is as follows. The early dialogues in which Socrates' thought is most faithfully rendered are *Apology*, *Euthyphro*, *Crito*, *Charmides*, *Laches*, and *Protagoras*. Also among the early dialogues, but moving slightly beyond the explicit position of Socrates, are *Meno*, *Euthydemus*, *Gorgias*, and *Lysis* (and perhaps *Hippias I*, *Hippias II*, and *Menexenus*). The middle dialogues, which indicate the maturing thought of Plato and manifest original directions, are *Cratylus*, *Symposium*, *Phaedo*, *Republic*, *Phaedrus*, *Theaetetus*, and *Parmenides*. The late dialogues, which explore the cosmological implications of the theories developed in the middle dialogues, are the *Sophist*, *Politicus*, *Philebus*, *Timaeus*, *Critias*, and the *Laws*.

Change and Permanence

The Sophists had forced Socrates and now Plato to raise the question of change and permanence. Is there only continuous movement from one thing to another or are there some things which remain fixed? The Sophists asked this question in terms of ethics and cultural mores and were impressed by the historical relativity which they found. Previously Heraclitus had asked the same question in regard to all reality and had been convinced that "all things are in flux." But Heraclitus had been countered by the diametrically opposed position of Parmenides, who claimed that only permanence is real, and the Sophists had been challenged by Socrates, who claimed that there is a norm for virtue which is applicable to all men.

Plato undertakes the task of dealing with the problem of change and permanence, of the one and the many, as this appears in the varied facets of reality, and his philosophy represents a sustained effort to find a place for both elements in a comprehensive view of reality. Plato's approach to this problem is to postulate the existence of two realms: the realm of sense experience, which is the arena of change and temporality, and the realm of intellectual Ideas or Forms, which is the realm of permanence and most real Being. Plato agrees with Heraclitus that sense experience does reveal a world of continuous change and transformation. Plato is probably well aware of this fact, for Aristotle tells us that as a youth he studied philosophy with Cratylus, a

Heraclitean philosopher. The world we perceive through our senses is one of mutability and flux, and this realm Plato calls "becoming."

But Plato insists that reality is not exhausted by the realm of becoming, for there is also the realm of "being." Beyond the arena revealed to us by our sense impressions, there is a nontemporal reality, a formal reality which Plato designates the realm of "Ideas" or "Forms." This realm has the quality of permanence, for in it is found the formal character of all things, Forms which are even more real than the fact of change. For instance, individual men may come and go, but the Idea of Man is eternal. These Forms are not merely "ideas" in the minds of men, but have an existence of their own apart from man. These "Ideas" are known in part by all men, so that every man knows, for instance, what a circle, a tree, or a man is, even in the imperfect examples which he perceives through his senses, for he has knowledge of the perfect Forms or Ideas of these objects.

The Forms

These universal Forms or Ideas (*eide, ideai*) are objective to man; they are not simply the subjective construction of the individual thinker. But what does it mean to call them "objective"? Primarily it means that they are discovered, not invented or "made up" by man. But "where" do they reside? Do they form some world of their own? How are they related to one another and how are they related to the world of becoming?

Plato's language does at times imply that the Forms exist in a world of their own (a metaphysically independent world), so he is sometimes interpreted to mean that these Ideas do have a "place" of their own beside the world of becoming. In this interpretation the Ideas constitute a world of their own, duplicating the world of sense experience. But one must be careful here, for to describe Ideas as having a separate existence does not necessarily imply that they are spatially separate, since, in fact, they are said to be incorporeal essences.

In his doctrine of the eternal soul, Plato does imply that these Forms are detached from the realm of becoming, but it is not necessary to indicate a place in which they reside. They are in particular objects, "in-forming" them, and they are also independent, not exhausted in existing objects, and ultimately not subject to change. This points to the fact that the Forms or Ideas, while present in all objects, are not known simply through the senses which grasp the mutability of reality, but through the intellect which knows permanent reality.

To illustrate the influence of the Forms, think of a triangle with the Forms at the top. The lines coming from the apex to each of the corners represent the Forms' impression upon the mind of man at one corner and the external world at the other corner. When the external objects are perceived by the mind Form meets Form, the object is recognized, and its identity established.

The sensory world is not wholly illusory, for it "participates" in the Ideas, but it also contains an element of unreality or nonbeing. In *Parmenides* Socrates speaks of the relation of the Ideas to the concrete object as participation and as imitation. But the exact meaning of these terms and their delineation of the more critical problems of bringing the two levels together is not given in this dialogue. Some scholars [1] have suggested that in the late dialogues, such as the *Sophist*, Plato does attempt to answer this problem by arguing that the Forms may themselves be one and many at the same time, so the class concept of "animal" may at the same time contain many subclasses, for example "cat" and "dog." The Forms, therefore, constitute a hierarchy moving from the highest Form, the One, which includes all subclasses, to the atomic Forms which can no longer be divided. For our immediate interest, it is important to note that the process of division from class to subclass does bring the Forms down to "the border of the sensible sphere" (Copleston, *op. cit.*, p. 186). However, the problem of the connection between the Forms and the world of becoming still remains and will be a point of contention, as we shall see, in Aristotle's criticism of Plato's position.

The Divided Line

The relation of these two dimensions of reality to man's knowledge of his world may be illustrated by Plato's use of the analogy of the divided line in the *Republic* (Book VI, 509–511). In spite of some obscurity, the main implications of this illustration are clear. The suggested diagram appears below.

The mind, according to Plato, moves through four stages of development in its discovery of true knowledge. At each level, there is a parallel between the kind of object presented to the mind and the type of thought this object makes possible. Below the center line is the level of opinion, which is based upon perception and interpretation of the visible world; above this line is the realm of knowledge, which is associated with the intelligible world.

Opinion, or an uncritical assumption about the nature of reality, may be true, but as long as it remains uncriticized, it cannot *know* itself to

---

[1] See especially Frederick Copleston, *A History of Philosophy: Greece and Rome* (Garden City: Doubleday, Image, 1962), vol. I, pp. 185–189.

	OBJECTS	MODES OF THOUGHT	
INTELLIGIBLE WORLD	The Good (Ideas or Forms)	Knowledge	KNOWLEDGE
	Mathematical Objects	Thinking	
VISIBLE WORLD	Things	Belief	OPINION
	Images	Imagining	

be true. Knowledge, on the other hand, is the critical, rational perception of essential reality; it is true opinion that has explored and established its foundations. Opinion results from man's concentration upon the world of becoming; knowledge results from man's concentration upon the realm of Ideas or Forms.

A description of the movement up the ladder of knowledge may be helpful in characterizing Plato's epistemology. At the lowest level one finds the most superficial form of mental activity. Here concentration is upon appearances as immediately received through sense perception. These images Plato calls "shadows." These shadows are real, but the person who mistakes shadows for the intelligible world or the perfect Forms is in the state of imagining or illusion. But, for the man who becomes uneasy about the identification of these shadows with a perfect version of reality, there is hope; for the recognition of such a difference is the first step toward knowledge.

The stage immediately above imagining is belief, a state induced by seeing actual objects. The perception of concrete objects carries with it a strong sense of certainty that one is viewing the world as it really is. This is the assurance which the uncritical empiricist possesses. Even in the perception of these visible, tangible objects, there is, however, a possibility of deception. Hence one must constantly reevaluate and change his interpretation of things as they are perceived under particular circumstances. Once again, if a person becomes uneasy as to whether his sense perceptions do convey the objects perceived in their definitive character he may move toward a more thorough understanding and reach for knowledge.

In both levels, opinion is engendered by insufficiently critical appraisal of the objects perceived through the senses. In the realm of sense perception, men may be aware of many imperfect, though often impressive, expressions of the perfect Forms, such as the expression of beauty as it is found in the Parthenon, of justice as demonstrated by written law codes, or of piety as exemplified by worshipful acts. But as long as man's attention is focused upon these representations of ultimate Forms, he can only possess an opinion about the essential quality of the perfect Forms. The confusion of opinion with truth is an error common even to teachers such as the Sophists, but error and ignorance may be overcome by the critical intellect.

The most decisive move of the mind is the going beyond believing to thinking, and transferring the attention from the visible to the intelligible world, from the realm of opinion to the realm of knowledge. This knowledge may come by the deductive reasoning found in mathematics. This type of thinking is characterized by its treatment of visible objects as symbols. Hence, when a mathematician sees the diagram of a triangle, he thinks about triangularity or triangle-in-itself. He distinguishes between the visible triangle and the intelligible triangle. Such abstraction requires our passing beyond what is directly known in sense awareness to the Forms embodied in things which may be perceived.

Another type of thinking is reasoning from hypotheses. A hypothesis, according to Plato, is not a temporary truth or a suggested way of handling objects in order to reach a momentary waystation in the search for knowledge. Rather, a hypothesis is a self-evident truth, but one which still depends upon a higher truth. It is truth, but partial truth. Thus, thinking or reasoning from hypotheses does provide a knowledge of truth, but this knowledge is limited because it isolates one truth from the total interinvolvement of truth. Even when the mind has reached this stage it must remain unsatisfied and feels the urge to push toward more comprehensive knowledge.

Higher than mathematical reasoning is the level of direct apprehension of being. This way of knowing, Plato claims, is intuitive. Such intuition is possible because of the affinity which exists between man's mind and essential being. The whole Platonic theory of knowledge depends upon the fundamental Socratic conviction that the mind of man is cognate with ultimate reality. Knowledge, in this final sense, is found when the mind is completely released from sensible objects. The mind at this level deals with perfect Forms without interference of visible objects, their symbolic function, or hypothetical constructions. Now the unity of all Forms is known directly and comprehensively. The method used to reach this final stage is called dialectics, and we shall return to this means of knowing.

The Myth of the Cave

Perhaps the most familiar story or "myth" in all of Plato's writings is that of the "cave," which is found in the seventh book of the *Republic* and deals with the question of opinion and truth. In this myth, Plato describes man as being a captive in a cave; in front of him is a screen and behind the screen is a fire which throws shadows upon the screen. Men sit with their eyes fixed upon this screen and attempt to interpret the meaning of the shadows. People can become quite adroit in deciphering the meaning of these objects, but there is always a falseness about seeing only shadows and never the real object. Some men, however, escape the cave and do see the real objects (Ideas or Forms). This insight makes it possible not only to interpret each individual object more correctly, but it also enables this man to recognize that previously he was only looking at shadows.

The cave in the myth is, for Plato, the world in which man lives. Our normal vision is what he calls looking at shadows. But men seem to be chained to this one particular way of seeing the world, and they do not want to ask critically whether or not this is the real world. Again, men can become quite adroit in their analysis of this world (this is the contribution of the "scientist") and in developing their opinions (literally) about the world. But some men want to get a "new perspective" upon this world and raise the question of its ultimate meaning, its purpose, and its goal. These men are the philosophers.

Perhaps we might use a different metaphor to make the same point. Imagine a group of people on a large ocean liner. On this ship all of their needs are taken care of; they have recreation, work, food, shelter. For some of the voyagers this is enough, life on the ship is their total context. But others demand answers to questions such as, "Where are we going? Can we find reasons for our actions *en route*? Is life on this ship the realm of true reality?" Still other passengers understand the goal toward which they are heading; for them activity aboard the ship has a purposeful meaning.

Most men are like those who take their particular life for granted and who have opinions about its significance. There are several factors which strengthen the hold of this false orientation of life upon men. First, there is the influence of man's environment upon him. Men are easily persuaded by the opinions of their peers, and when there is concerted agreement about a position it is difficult to deny the validity of group opinion. Thus men in the cave support and reaffirm their opinions through one another, and the strength of this view of the world is reinforced. Secondly, Plato is aware that there is no cure for not seeing except seeing. This is a fundamental problem. For not only are men in need of seeing the light in order to recognize the darkness, but men whose eyes are accustomed to the darkness are unable to look at the light. Finally, there is the stubborn character of human ignorance, that is, the inner refusal to admit that one's ignorance is really ignorance; on the contrary, one attempts to convince himself that he really does know the truth, even if this demands self-deception.[2]

The problem is that men are centered upon the unreal or transitory world and fail to recognize their true rootage in most real being. This misorientation is involuntary in that it is contrary to the mind's original and therefore natural bent toward true being, but it is also voluntary in that the identification of transitory being, or the realm of becoming, with the realm of essential being has been made. This identification is, of course, false, but it does reflect the dominant interest of men. In other words, a lower love replaces a higher love, and man is led into the captivity of the world of becoming by this misdirected affection.

Plato's Anthropology

Before we continue the study of Plato's description of how man moves across the line from opinion to knowledge, we must first understand Plato's analysis of man. According to Plato man is distinct because he possesses a "soul," that is, there is a unique part of every man which has two basic characteristics: indivisibility and eternality. Both characteristics mean that there is an inalienable part of man which persists in the midst of temporal, bodily decay and is in some manner connected with the realm of permanence of being. This latter point is important, for to say that man has a relation to the eternal order of reality is to say that there is in man a potential awareness of the norm whereby things are to be judged wise or foolish, good or evil; and, it is the base upon which Plato builds his doctrine of reincarnation. There is, in the general doctrine of the soul, a connection between the thought of Plato and that of Socrates, but Plato goes even further and describes the soul as being composed of three parts.

At the top level is the intelligence of man (*nous* or *logos*), and combined with this intelligence in man's rational soul is the "spirited" (*thumos*) part which Plato says is attracted to things which are excellent or good. The spirited striving he also identifies as the "love" (*eros*) of man for the Good. Below this rational part of the soul is the emo-

---

[2] See Robert E. Cushman, *Therapeia* (Chapel Hill, N.C.: The University of North Carolina Press, 1956), pp. 140 f.

tional or appetitive aspect (*epithumia*), which distracts man's concentration upon the Good. Perhaps the diagram below will make this tripartite description clear.

$$
\left.
\begin{array}{l}
\text{Intelligence (\textit{nous})} \\
\text{Spirited striving toward} \\
\text{excellence (\textit{thumos})}
\end{array}
\right\} \longrightarrow
\begin{array}{l}
\text{Rational soul} \\
\text{(\textit{logistikon})}
\end{array}
$$

$$
\left.
\begin{array}{l}
\text{Appetitive or emo-} \\
\text{tional (\textit{epithumia})}
\end{array}
\right\} \longrightarrow
\begin{array}{l}
\text{Irrational or nonrational} \\
\text{soul (\textit{alogistikon})}
\end{array}
$$

According to Plato's description of the functioning of the soul, the ideal situation or ordering of the soul has the rational part in control of the irrational or nonrational part. This is proper because there is an affinity between the rational part of the soul and most real being. Every soul originally had an understanding of ("looked upon") the abiding values or Reality; thus one can speak of a primordial conformity between the rational soul and ultimate being. Man should act in obedience to this rational order, but he has been misdirected, or, more precisely, has allowed his soul to become disordered. The appetitive nature has gained control over the rational nature of man; and in this misordering of man's soul is to be found the most fundamental problem for philosophy: namely, how can man be brought back to a properly structured existence? The answer which Plato offers is what he, following Socrates, calls "recollection."

In the dialogue *Meno* we encounter the doctrine of "recollection" for the first time (80c–82a). This doctrine must not be confused with the theory that men come into the world with ideas which are fully formed and which are only waiting to be applied to external reality. While Plato does maintain that all men originally knew the truth or are related to it, he also believes that they have forgotten the truth. Even so, because of his earlier knowledge man can reclaim the truth if he diligently attempts to recall it. The discovery requires sustained effort and hard mental activity. While Socrates does mention that he learned the doctrines of preexistence and reincarnation from the Orphic religious doctrines, he emphasizes the functioning of the mind as it probes its own resources. Knowledge cannot be gained by casually looking inward or by passively receiving impressions from the external world. Rather, knowledge is to be found only in strenuous personal effort initiated by fundamental questions which arouse man to investigate his background and draw forth the formal structures which are imbedded in his mind. Upon this basis it is understandable that Socrates and Plato insist that knowledge can only be won by personal participation in the search and that it cannot simply be handed from one man to another.

In the *Phaedrus* (246) the functioning of the soul is depicted in a myth. Man's soul is described as being like a charioteer driving two winged horses. The charioteer symbolizes man's attempt to control his life. The good horse, the one of honor (the spirited striving toward excellence), tries to pull man upward, while the other horse, the appetitive or emotional, nonrational symbol, attempts to pull man downward and submerge him completely in the world. Note that the orientation of man's life is the result of this inner tension and reflects the person's dominant commitment. Hence, in tending his soul, man prepares himself both for knowledge in the realm of becoming and for the next life.

The Method of Dialectics

When man becomes falsely directed, some transformation must be induced, and some art of persuasion must be found which can alter man's attention and redirect his affection from the world of change and opinion to the realm of being and knowledge. The Sophists' efforts to further inculcate natural propensities, reflecting their attachment to the realm of becoming, is denounced, and a new method of therapy or impulse for change must be found. Plato suggests the use of what he calls dialectics (*elenchos*).

Because of Plato's view of the predicament of man, one of the main themes of his philosophy may be described, as R. E. Cushman [3] has done, as the exploration of a possible therapy. A conversion or transformation of the order of life is necessary, so that man may become truly rational and the higher elements of his soul may rule his life. But how is such a change achieved? This is the central question in Plato's ethical, political, and epistemological discussions.

In developing his dialectical method Plato begins with Socrates' emphasis and makes man's moral experience the fundamental base. He considers man as distinct from nature and finds part of this uniqueness in his awareness of moral values. The essential man, despite the hindrance of life in the cave, does believe, "that doing wrong is worse than suffering it" (*Crito*, 49). He intends to investigate this awareness in order to make the standard of goodness dominant in the life of the investigator.

Plato realizes that not everyone is willing to grant this first premise. But Plato answers that only as men recognize this point of their essential

[3] R. E. Cushman, *op. cit.*

humanity can they explore their true nature as men. This means that one cannot investigate the meaning of the "Good" unless he is already aware of a predisposition toward the Good. But Plato accepts this liability; as Werner Jaeger writes: "There is nothing to which Plato right down to the end of his life was more passionately opposed than the statement that the soul can know what is just without *being* just." [4] Robert E. Cushman has written, "Virtue is quite as much the condition of knowledge as it is also true, and better known, that knowledge is the condition of virtue". [5]

This may be the weakest link in Plato's dialectics—that the very principle of conversion or change assumes a predisposition to change of character. And yet this predisposition is not universal, as is recognized by the obstinate commitment to life in the cave. Consequently, Plato is forced to recognize that what is needed by all will be accepted only by a few. As we have seen in the *Republic*, most men are so fettered by the bondage of the cave that they cannot escape its influence. Philosophy appeals only to those who acknowledge the predisposition to investigate their sense of a moral norm.

There are several conditions which must be met in order to undertake a serious dialectical investigation. First, one must admit that he does not have knowledge and must be willing to seek it. Because of this necessary first step, Plato appreciated Socrates' character as a gadfly attempting to force men to admit that they needed to seek wisdom.

Second, there must be, as we have indicated, a proper disposition of the mind toward true reality. One must admit that he has some awareness of a standard of value or of moral knowledge. Third, the participants in the inquiry must be willing to consent to the guidance of the evidence. In other words a man cannot close his mind to what can or must be found. Rather, at every point in the inquiry he must be ready to admit the truth as he finds it and willing to investigate the implications of that truth. This is probably one of the fundamental reasons Plato wrote dialogues and not philosophical treatises; it is his effort to make the reader an active participant in the discussion, since ultimately the reader is philosophically serious only as he willingly engages in the discussion.

Finally, the end of dialectics requires acknowledgment or personal commitment to the values which have been discovered. The final justification of the argument is in the fact that at the conclusion man experiences an "at-home-ness" or an inner agreement of his affirmation with his intuitive awareness of the nature of ultimate reality.

---

[4] Werner W. Jaeger, *Aristotle* (Oxford: Clarendon Press, 1948, 2nd ed.), p. 23.

[5] Robert E. Cushman, *op. cit.*, pp. 53–54.

But what does Plato mean by personal commitment? What is the intuitive knowledge which he places at the top of the divided line illustration? A central theme in Plato's thought is the role of love in knowledge. While Plato alludes to this theme in such dialogues as the *Phaedo* and *Republic*, only in the *Symposium* and *Phaedrus* does he explore it with great care. We have already said that Plato presupposes that some inclination toward the Good must precede any dialectical movement toward understanding the Good. The aspiring movement of the mind toward the Good Plato calls love (*eros*). Just as love brings about order in the human realm, it also brings about conformity between the mind of man and ultimate reality. Love is the personal inclination which is necessary if true therapy of the human condition is to be achieved.

Plato mentions two kinds of love—a higher love which is generous and which seeks what is Good and True and Beautiful, and a lower or base love which is sensual and calculating. (The *Phaedrus* also mentions a third, intermediate type of love which may be called friendship.) The man who would work for the therapy of the soul must aspire to the elucidation of the nobler type of love. Such love can release man from the bondage of the cave; the tyranny of the love of the cave existence is expelled by the power of the love for the abiding, eternal Good. Thus Plato speaks of *eros* as the author of man's greatest blessing and therefore the chief gift of the gods.

This "love of wisdom" which characterizes the philosopher should be carefully assessed. What distinguishes the true philosopher is not the possession of knowledge but the love of truth; it is not profession of truth, but the aspiration to understand, appreciate, and acknowledge what is truth. In this sense Plato's work might more properly be called "erosophy" than "philosophy," since the love of wisdom which he eulogizes is the passionate, all-consuming *eros* of the Good.

Educational Theory

Again we come to the question: How may this love for the Good be developed, what can activate its latent power? In the *Republic* Plato espouses an educational theory calculated to achieve this end. The details of this pedagogy may be simply described as the teaching of music, humanities, and athletics; but the importance of the theory is to be found only when one asks what he hopes to achieve by propounding this method of education? The answer is that Plato is attempting to induce men to obey the propulsion of *eros* and thereby bring their sensate desires under the control of this nobler quality of the soul.

The pedagogy of Plato, therefore, is an attempt to dispose men toward the truth; it is not an attempt to immediately inculcate men in the truth. Such subjects as music and mathematics are introduced into the curriculum not because these disciplines are ends in themselves; on the contrary, he is convinced that these particular studies are conducive to freeing the mind and the affections from the dominance of the cave mentality. Viable education does not simply pass along accepted truths or information; it is always directed toward transformation of perspective, so that the educated person is able to see himself from a new perspective and begin to investigate the distinctively humane qualities of his life. However, one must realistically acknowledge the differences in human receptivity to this undertaking; this is the major factor in Plato's construction of his political theory.

Ethics and Political Theory

We have already indicated that Socrates rejected the ethical relativism of the Sophists; this is also evident in the writings of Plato. Like his teacher, Plato wants to discover the absolute moral standard which should control man's life. Where is this standard to be found? How is it to be described? He attempts to answer these questions.

As with Socrates, moral values or norms are to be found by examining the distinctive moral awareness of human beings. By looking inward and raising questions about the meaning of courage, justice, and temperance, among others, Plato believes that if one really desires to seek sources and is willing to follow the lead of his *eros*-controlled mind, one can see that underlying all particular moral conceptions is a consciousness or awareness of what is Good.

It must also be clearly stated that for Plato ethics is eudaemonistic —that is, directed toward the attainment of man's highest good, a good which brings happiness to man. When the soul is in its correct state, man is happy. The secret of this good life is the proper balance of life in accordance with the Good. Therefore the happy life is based upon the knowledge of the eternal Ideas and the ordering of life in accordance with this knowledge. Since Plato, like Socrates, holds that knowledge is virtue, then to have the right knowledge is to have the right integration of life.

In the *Protagoras* Plato argues that underlying the several virtues which men admit, such as justice and courage, there is a unifying principle or Idea of the Good. Knowledge is virtue, which is to say, the sounding of the inalienable rational nature of man relating him to ultimate reality leads him to know what is Good and how each individual virtue expresses the Good.

By this approach, Plato denies that morality is simply a matter of expediency or convention. But how is the good to be discovered? How is virtue to be known? The answer is that the Good is found when man comes to recognize his unique and peculiar relation to ultimate reality. And virtue is acting upon the principles which are discovered, principles which can be described in terms of justice, fortitude, courage, and prudence.

The critical problem, from Plato's standpoint, is that virtue cannot simply be handed from one person to another, and in this sense cannot be transmitted at all; if a person is to be virtuous then he must find the resources within himself and learn from this self-knowledge what the good is and how he should pursue it. It is perplexing to Plato that virtuous men often are unable to transmit their virtue to their sons, such as in the case of Pericles (*Meno*, 94). Virtue, then, cannot be taught in the sense of being "handed down"; it must be won by each individual as he struggles to understand his humane distinctiveness and as he accepts the moral requirements as his own. But if virtue cannot be made a public commodity, how is a virtuous society to be established? How is a moral community to be organized?

Plato's description of the ideal state is to be found in his *Republic*, and it has been the cause of much discussion. This is the first attempt in Western culture to depict a utopia (literally "no-place") which can function as the criterion for social organization. After a careful analysis of political change, Plato claims that the state is to be understood in the same way as an individual, for the social community has a "personality" or "type of character" similar to the personality of an individual person. We have discussed Plato's description of the levels or aspects which constitute the human soul, and now he suggests that in a state we find a similar division between individuals. There are three types of people: the best, which may be described as "gold," are the rulers; the second, which may be described as "silver," are the warriors or protectors of the community; and the third, which may be called, "brass," are the workers or the common people.

This division of people within the state forms the basis upon which Plato discusses the proper roles of citizens and the concept of justice. The educational requirements which we have mentioned seem to apply primarily to the guardians or those who are entrusted with government, although it is difficult to know how extensively Plato conceived their application. But it is obvious that the administrative élite are the most important group within the state. In the first place,

the guardians are to be the sole rulers of the community, for government is to be committed into the hands of those with ability to exercise
power justly. To become a guardian may be a matter of birth, for with
his suggestion of rigid birth control (eugenics) Plato thinks that the
guardians will give birth to the more able people; but any person of
unusual promise from one of the lower classes may move into the
guardian class if his ability is demonstrated or detected.

The guardian class is to be communistic in its structure, and all
things are to be held in common such as material goods, wives, and
children. The control of wealth will limit both affluence and poverty,
for Plato is convinced that either will contribute to the eventual ruin
of the political order. The common sharing of wives and children
provides the best control for eugenics and creates a cohesiveness in the
community of the guardians which would otherwise be lacking.

In the guardian class men and women are to receive the same training,
although Plato accepts a distinction in the abilities of males and females.
The censorship and control of the intellectual development of this
group is thoroughgoing. Those who nurture the children are to tell
them only authorized stories; some classics of Greek culture such as
Homer and Hesiod are not to be read because of their corrupting
moral standards; reactions such as laughter are to be controlled;
drama is to be censored so that no bad habits will be inculcated in the
audience, and music is to be rigidly supervised.

The warriors or protectors who comprise the second class are to be
trained primarily for the waging of war and the defense of the community. This means that their education will have special direction toward
the acquiring of those skills which will contribute to this end. The
lowest class, the workers, will receive basic training in trades and
skills which will enable them to contribute to the well-being and total
needs of the state.

This is obviously a rigidly controlled system of social government,
and many have called it a totalitarian form of organization. Because of
its austerity and tight discipline Bertrand Russell has found its most
adequate analogy to be the city of Sparta. And, whatever else may be
said, it is a thoroughly controlled order and is opposed to democracy,
which would give the untrained and ungifted as much voice in the
government as the guardians.

What then does Plato understand by "justice" in this system?
We should first understand that Plato's vision is of an organization
of the city which will promote the good of the whole and not the happiness or privilege of any one class. This means that justice for Plato
means the proper working of the entire community; therefore it is

expressed in the complementary tasks and duties of each group. In other words, a system is just when each man does his own job and leaves every other man free to perform his special task. Injustice would be disorder and would arise, for instance, if a man with guardian capacities were kept from moving into that class or if a person born into the guardian class were allowed to remain there even if he lacked ability.

As an ideal for government, this description is open to attack and has been frequently, and often vehemently, criticized. While it is interesting to discuss the practical implementation of Plato's ideas, it must be noted that the theoretical intention of the state as the context in which therapy may be provided for the human condition does not stand or fall upon Plato's own attempt to apply it. This practical description must be appraised, but other possibilities for social order on the basis of Plato's analysis of man must also be investigated.

Plato's World View

Two different phases in Plato's mature thought may be indicated. Up through the middle dialogues, especially the *Republic*, the concern of this philosopher has been with the healing of man, and for this therapeutic undertaking he finds dialectics the most appropriate way for leading men to the rediscovery of the realm of most real being. But in the later dialogues, especially the *Sophist*, *Philebus*, and *Timaeus*, Plato turns to nature or the world as a whole, as this may be interpreted from the vantage point established in the early dialogues.

Cornford can claim, for instance, "Platonism is what the doctrine of Socrates never was, a system of the world, embracing the whole province of external nature . . ." (*Before and After Socrates*, 56). But unlike the pre-Socratics, Plato finds the key to the understanding of nature not in its origins but in its end. Therefore Plato uses the Idea of the Good to interpret the nature of the world. It may be claimed that in this writing we have the first teleological explanation of the world in Greek philosophy.

To further indicate the change in Plato's attention, we note that in the early dialogues he is attempting to disclose the ultimate principle or object to which the mind of man is inherently related. But in the later dialogues his concern is with the use of this principle for an understanding of the whole world. Thus the Good is not simply some object which is "out beyond" the world, it is the *nous* or mind of the world which the entire cosmos expresses (literally a harmony which is established by the integrative factor of the Good). Thus, the whole world is seeking to exemplify the same values in its existence which the individual attempts to express in his existence.

During this last phase of his writing, Plato attempts to indicate how reality is always a mixture of the Ideas with the realm of becoming, or, in traditional language, how is it possible to bring the One (the Idea of the Good) and the many (the realm of becoming) into relationship. Plato denies that they are only externally related to one another or that they exist as "strangers" only accidentally introduced to one another. Rather, they are always intrinsically related so that the Ideas are never known apart from their particular expression in a concrete object, just as concrete objects are capable of being known only as they are expressions of the Ideas. Aristotle doubts that Plato achieved this goal, but he clearly intends to define the relation of permanence to change.

It may be claimed that in this last phase of his thought Plato is attempting to draw together all of his former discussions. Not only is the social life of man to be described as "the individual writ large" but now we can go on to claim that the universe as a whole is to be understood in the same way. The Idea of the Good which is to be discovered by man's recollection of his true nature also dominates the discovery of the true nature of man's total environment. Hence, in a profound way, the philosophy of Plato ends with the same search with which it began; man's first duty is to tend his soul, and in its furthest implications this means that he is also passionately investigating the soul of the universe.

Plato: Suggested Additional Reading

Abernethy, George L. and Thomas A. Langford, eds., *History of Philosophy: Selected Readings*. Belmont, Calif.: Dickenson, 1965, pp. 43–120.*

Barker, Sir Ernest, *The Political Thought of Plato and Aristotle*. New York: Dover, 1959.

Brumbaugh, R. S., *Plato for the Modern Age*. New York: Macmillan, Collier, paperback, 1962.

Cornford, Francis M., *Plato's Theory of Knowledge*. Indianapolis: Bobbs-Merrill, Liberal Arts Press, 1957.

Cornford, Francis M., *Plato's Cosmology*. Indianapolis: Bobbs-Merrill, Liberal Arts Press, 1957.

Crombie, Ian, *An Examination of Plato's Doctrines*. London: Routledge; New York: Humanites Press, 1962.*

Crossman, R. H. S., *Plato Today*, 2nd ed. rev. New York: Oxford University Press, 1959.*

Cushman, Robert E., *Therapeia.* Chapel Hill, N.C.: University of North Carolina Press, 1958.*

Field, G. C., *The Philosophy of Plato.* New York: Barnes and Noble, 1967.

Friedlander, Paul, *Plato: An Introduction.* New York: Harper and Row, Torchbook, 1967.

Great Dialogues of Plato. Translated by W. H. D. Rouse. New York: New American Library, Mentor, 1956.

Gulley, Norman, *Plato's Theory of Knowledge.* New York: Barnes and Noble, 1962.*

Kaufmann, Walter, *Philosophical Classics.* Englewood Cliffs, N.J.: Prentice-Hall, 1961, I, 118–356.*

Levinson, R. B., *In Defense of Plato.* Cambridge, Mass.: Harvard University Press, 1953.*

More, Paul E., *Platonism.* Princeton, N.J.: Princeton University Press, 1917.*

Plato, *The Dialogues of Plato.* Edited by B. Jowett. Garden City, N.Y.: 1937. (A fourth revision of Jowett's edition was published in 1953, Oxford, by D. J. Allen and H. E. Dale, general editors.)*

Popper, Karl, *The Open Society and its Enemies.* Vol. I. New York: Harper Torchbook, 1963.

Ritter, Constantin, *The Essence of Plato's Philosophy.* Translated by Adam Alles. New York: Dial Press, 1933.*

Shorey, Paul, *What Plato Said.* Abridged. Chicago: University of Chicago, Phoenix, 1965.

Stenzel, Julius, *Plato's Method of Dialectic.* Translated by D. J. Allen. Oxford: Clarendon, 1940.*

Chapter Four

Aristotle

As a young student, Aristotle made his way to Plato's Academy to complete his formal education. Caught up in the school's vigorous intellectual life, he stayed for nearly two decades. Here he laid the foundations for his remarkable achievements as the first systematizer of formal logic, the author of the first systematic treatise on ethics and the first history of philosophy, the student of a collection of 158 constitutions which resulted in his classic work on politics, the author of the first treatise on the principles of literary criticism, and the creator of a system of metaphysical concepts which later proved sufficiently flexible to provide theological structures for Judaism, Islam, and Christianity. It is not surprising that Dante spoke of Aristotle as "the master of those who know" and Thomas Aquinas invariably referred to him as "the Philosopher."

Aristotle was born in 384 B.C. at Stagira, a small town in Thrace, located on the north coast of the Aegean Sea. His father, Nicomachus, a physician, like most members of the profession claimed descent from Asclepius, god of medicine and son of Apollo. While Aristotle was still a boy, his family moved to Pella, the capital of Macedonia where Nicomachus became the court physician to King Amyntas II and Aristotle became the friend of Amyntas' son Philip. At age seventeen or eighteen Aristotle was sent to Athens to enroll at Plato's Academy, which was already a famous institution. Here he remained for almost twenty years until Plato's death in 347 B.C. After several years of travel, Aristotle was invited in 343–342 B.C. to return to Macedonia as the tutor of Alexander, the son of King Philip of Macedonia. This relationship lasted for two or three years and gave rise to speculations and anecdotes attempting to evaluate the influence Aristotle and Alexander may have had on each other.

By 335 B.C. Aristotle had returned to Athens to establish a school of his own, the Lyceum, under the protection of the Macedonian statesman Antipater. Here he discoursed on philosophy and the sciences as he walked about the lawns and colonnades of the Lyceum, for which fact the school was called *peripatetic* ("peropatein"—to walk about). In the afternoons and evenings he often expounded on less technical topics in a more formal lecture to larger audiences. His written works which have survived lack the literary skill and dramatic quality of Plato's dialogues. Although we know that Aristotle's prose style was praised in antiquity, in these works we find that the prose style is unfinished and choppy, full of redundancies, often unintelligible in brevity, and plagued with interpolations. No one knows how these writings were composed, but it is widely believed that they are notes prepared by Aristotle for his lectures, perhaps supplemented by notes of students put together after Aristotle's death by friends and disciples with a minimum of editing.

When Alexander died in 323 B.C., a strong tide of anti-Macedonian feeling swept over Athens, making Aristotle's position precarious. Not having the temperament of a martyr and saying he did not want "the Athenians to sin twice against Philosophy," he took refuge in the town of Chalchis in Eubola. Here he died a year later of a digestive ailment. His will, which has been preserved, reveals something of his character and personality in its provisions for his family, his generosity to his slaves, and a touching sentiment for his long-dead wife, beside whom he asked to be buried.

Some critics have drawn a sharp contrast between Platonism and Aristotelianism. It is true that Aristotle was Plato's first major critic and that in the course of his philosophic development he departed more and more from the basic positions of Plato. It is also true that there were fundamental differences in temperament between the two philosophers. Aristotle was analytical, realistic, empirical, and devoted to common sense, while Plato was more idealistic, utopian, other-worldly, mathematical, and mystical. Yet these undeniable differences have often been emphasized to the point of concealing their common interests and positions. Both men were typically Greek in their emphasis on reason, their cosmology was thoroughly teleological, and they shared more of the Greek emphasis on moderation than was immediately apparent. Of course Aristotle's early dialogues and other writings were in substantial agreement with Plato; his personal devotion to Plato kept him in the Academy until Plato's death. Even when this early period of Platonic influence ended and Aristotle clearly moved in directions of his own choosing, the influence of Plato on his thought remained large and significant.

Aristotle's Psychology

Aristotle's *De Anima* or *Concerning the Soul* is the oldest systematic treatise on psychology we have in the West. For Aristotle psychology is not the exclusive study of consciousness or mental phenomena. He emphasizes the contrast between purpose (meaning or value) and matter rather than the contrast between mind and matter. The "soul," or "psyche," is the principle of vital life and organic functions (nutrition, growth, and reproduction) and not merely the principle of conscious thought. Thus Aristotle's psychology is a biological science and not a rationalistic or mechanistic one.

In Aristotle's language, soul is "the first actuality (entelechy) of a natural body furnished with organs" (*De Anima*, II, I, 412b). The soul is the form of the body and cannot be separated from it. It is as essential to and characteristic of the activity of a living organism, as vision is to the eye or cutting to the ax. The soul is dependent on the body and cannot exist without it. He rejects Plato's notion that the soul is not tied down to a particular body, that the soul could leave the body of a man and transmigrate to a flute. Aristotle insists that the soul pertains to a particular body, so that it is not possible to view it as disembodied.

The capacities of the soul are not actualized simultaneously in the hierarchy of nature but gradually in three steps or levels. Living bodies appear first with the functions of nutrition, growth, and reproduction, thus constituting the "vegetative" soul, which is the matter or po-tentiality of which the "sensitive" soul is the form and actuality. Animal life rises above vegetable life in its complexity of organization and range of function as in locomotion, desire, and sensation (seeing, hearing, and smelling). Man is a living body with still more complex structures and activities. Beyond all the capacities of animals, which are presupposed and involved, the human soul is distinguished by its marked rational activity. Man is, then, the rational animal.

Sense perception, for Aristotle, is never in direct contact with the object. Basically it is a change initiated in the soul by things perceived, through the intermediary sense organs. The five senses inform the soul of the qualities of things. (For Aristotle, in perception the form of the object, but not the matter, enters the mind, whereas in digestion the matter, not the form, is received.) The common sense, whose organ is the heart, is the meeting place in which the separate reports of the individual senses are organized and unified. Thus we can experience a single unified apple instead of five disparate sensory reports. Aristotle employs common sense to account for generic images, composite im-ages, memories, and associations. He allows for error in connection with common sensation and indirect sensation (as when one sees the mirror and sees that it is smooth, although smoothness is a matter of touch), but not in connection with sensation proper when one sees blue as blue. Do we actually see one thing as longer than another or merely judge it so? Aristotle believes the former. In general, Aristotle has a direct apprehensional theory of perception, without any theory of representationalism. If two persons stand at different distances from an object, which one then sees it correctly? Aristotle provides no satisfactory answer to this problem.

Aristotle's Metaphysics

Aristotle calls his *Metaphysics* First Philosophy, the fundamental principles of which are basic to his detailed account of the world. He defines metaphysics as the science of "being *qua* being," in other words being as such rather than being of this or that specific kind. He is seeking the common denominator or the most generic qualities that anything has in common with every other thing. His concept of "being" or existence differs from that of Plato, for whom "Idea" or "Form," a universal or relation, is (ultimate subject or) substance. For Aristotle only the individual, not a universal or relation, is ultimate subject or substance. Substance is "that which is not asserted of a subject but of which everything else is asserted." If we say, "The barn is red," we mean that the barn is something which "has" the quality of red or which is the substratum in which the quality of redness inheres. For Aristotle a quality like red cannot change. It is simply what it is and cannot become something else; it can only be succeeded or replaced by another quality. If there is such a thing as change, it is because substance is a continuum which makes it possible for us to attribute different qualities (like "young" and "old") at different times to the same subject ("Socrates"). It is true that Aristotle refers to universals, but, unlike Plato, he does not regard them as self-subsistent things with a separate existence of their own in a transcendent world.

Aristotle makes a number of criticisms of Plato's theory of Forms based on his understanding of the theory. He does not accept Plato's claim that the Forms are necessary to make scientific knowledge possible. Science requires knowledge of universals, but this merely reveals that universals are real rather than that they possess a supersensible separate existence. Plato's Forms are merely duplicates of sensible things and cannot in any way explain them. Also, since Plato's Forms are without motion and the objects duplicate the Forms, how can the motion of the objects be explained? Again, if Forms hold the essence of sensible objects, how can they exist separate from objects? Talking about the relation of Forms to particular objects in terms of "imitation" and "participation" provides metaphors rather than explanations. In making such criticisms Aristotle is giving expression to his own confidence in the reality and value of the world of becoming, of nature and its changes. Nature is a harmonious order in which universals are real as immanent in individual substances and not transcendent to them.

For Aristotle any metaphysical analysis of an individual substance must be made in terms of form and matter. Substance is not occult, but has an intelligible form which may be defined. The form of man is being a rational animal. The form of a table is not only a shape, but its logical function and structure. In this respect Aristotle's form is in accord with Plato's Form or Idea. But when Aristotle is dealing with a plant or animal he goes beyond this and includes biological organization. The form then constitutes "that without which not"—that which is characteristic of the species and differentiates it from other kinds. Matter is the substratum in which the form is realized. It functions as the principle of individuation or "twoness"—what you must add to form to get the concrete individual. Matter then explains why there are many different things with the same form, for example ten pennies with the same form. Matter also bears the responsibility for imperfection, for when we discover a flaw in a sculptor's work, we blame matter either in the statue or sculptor and not the form. All matter has form except primary matter, which we never find in our experience and which we can thus only postulate.

The distinction between the form and matter of a substance may be made at any moment of its history. Since he is particularly interested in explaining the change by which substance passes from one state to another, Aristotle introduces the distinction between "potentiality" and "actuality." Potentiality enables us to think of something as it is and as it is not. Thus actuality and potentiality are complementary. The child is potentially what he may become as a man. What is the reality of a potentiality for Aristotle? A man can swim even when he is not actually swimming. If you deny potentiality, you become a disciple of Protagoras, who claims we have nothing but what is given immediately in sensation. Neither the blind man nor I actually see in the dark, but I can see and he cannot. A potentiality then is a habit or capacity. The man who has it is different from the man who lacks it. All potentialities are determined; you do not get figs from thistles. But not all substances have all potentialities. A potentiality is a program or line of action; in this sense actuality is prior to potentiality and potentiality is rooted in actuality. The potentialities of substances in nature could not be actualized without the agency of an external cause wholly actual to set them in motion. This is the claim which Aristotle makes in his argument for God as the Prime Mover.

In a famous passage in *Metaphysics* Aristotle elaborates his doctrine of the four "causes." The term "causes" here may be better understood as "principles," "conditions," or "approaches" in seeking an interpretation of the changes in nature. Of anything in nature Aristotle says we may ask: (1) What is it? (2) What is it made of? (3) What produced it? (4) For what end or good is it made? The answers we receive will be respectively in terms of (1) Form, or formal cause; (2) Matter, or the material cause; (3) Agency or efficient cause; (4) Purpose, or final cause. Thus every substance is a union of form and matter, produced by the activity of some agent to serve an end.

In asserting that every substance is a union of form and matter, Aristotle explicitly rejects Plato's two-world separation of Forms and particular things. Thus form for Aristotle is a name for *what* a thing is and matter is a name for the fact *that* it is. For Aristotle all knowledge consists of detaching from matter the form and getting it into the mind. Eating an apple is different from knowing it botanically. It is the matter of the substance which provides the evidence that the substance exists.

Matter by itself is inert, so a lump of clay cannot become a statue by itself; form by itself never creates anything. To account for change Aristotle introduces his third cause or principle—the efficient cause which is always a concrete individual. The statue comes out of the sculptor, who already has the form and matter of the species. You get an infant from a mother. The efficient cause is a transaction between an active (form) and passive (matter) agent in which the form passes into matter. This is about as far as Aristotle gets in his account of generation. The clay has its own form, but the artist forces his higher form on it. The matter would not take on the higher form if that form were not already potential in it. For Aristotle there is an efficient cause only in the sublunary world of change and generation—not in the celestial world.

Aristotle's fourth cause is the final cause, which should be interpreted as more of a purpose or an end in view than an end in time. For him the final cause of an acorn is an oak tree, even if circumstances block the acorn from achieving its natural end. In this view any existence involves of necessity being good for some specific conscious or latent end. This is immanent teleology in which mechanical causes are secondary to final causes.

Aristotle's metaphysics culminates in his proof of the existence of the Prime Mover in Book XII of *Metaphysics*. As a cosmological argument for God as the First Cause of all change in the world, it is a major contribution to philosophical theology. Aristotle thinks of the world process of realizing potentialities as a system of motions. The motions of particular beings point beyond themselves, and their movers are in turn moved by something else. But this whole system or series of motions must have an ultimate source in a prime mover which is either self-moving or immovable. This Unmoved Mover, or Prime Mover, is the eternal principle of motion, an actuality without potentiality and matter. In somewhat metaphorical language Aristotle speaks of the Unmoved Mover as being peculiarly the object of love and of desire, since the universe turns in emulation of His perfection and every good thing is desired in so far as it is known. Thus, in contrast to Christian theology where God is held to love the planets, Aristotle is suggesting the heavens move because the planets love God, the Prime Mover, who is eternal and perfect. Since Aristotle's God is completely actual, He has no body to limit his activity or to provide unrealized potentiality. This eliminates sensation and desire. Such a perfect being can engage only in the activity of thinking. What is worthy of His thought? Only Himself, so His knowledge must be immediate and complete self-consciousness.

Such a theology is not religious in the usual sense of the term. It is inconsistent with divine providence, for Aristotle's God does not know or care about the universe. Such a god is not an object of worship or mystical union. It performs a metaphysical function for a system which requires an unmoved mover, a completely actual and fully realized form. It makes the world an intelligible order. And in a sense it also determines Aristotle's account of man's end, for if God's happiness lies in thinking, so does man's.

In the Aristotelian body of writings as arranged by an ancient editor, the treatises on logic, collectively known as the *Organon*, come first because they deal with the method of science and provide an analysis of the nature and criteria of knowledge. Aristotle recognizes and uses the experimental method, but he does not subject the process of inductive reasoning to rigorous logical analysis. When he is hailed as the inventor or first systematizer of logic, it is his analysis of formal logic or deductive reasoning which is being praised. In a few paragraphs we can only point to his work rather than to outline it.

Since Aristotle believes logic reflects in its formal structures the metaphysical structures of the world, a proposition can be neither true nor false without referring to some existence. Aristotle follows Plato in asserting that we reach knowledge only when form is apprehended, but he departs from Plato in insisting that we have knowledge only when the form is properly predicated of some substance. The basic unit of knowledge according to Plato is a detached form, whereas for

Aristotle it is a judgment, expressed in a proposition, in the predicate of which the form appears. To sever the intuition of form from the function of form in an integral judgment is to claim that we can have knowledge without its being knowledge of anything.

A survey of logic must at some point assess the structure of language and what can be asserted in it. In the Aristotelian *Organon* this is discussed in a work called "Categories." In discourse we may distinguish substance, quality, quantity, relation, place, date, position, state, action, and passivity. Whenever we think of a definite subject matter, we think of a subject and its predicates, or of some substance and its accidents. Thus we may think of a man, like Socrates, who is a substance with whom the other nine categories or predicates can be connected. We may assert that Socrates has quality (of being a philosopher), quantity (150 pounds), relation (teacher of Plato), place (the Assembly), date (February 7th), position (seated), state (clothed), action (helping), and passivity (being helped). These categories are not artificial creations of the human mind, although in our thinking we use them for classification and for arranging substances into more and less inclusive classes which we designate as *genera* and *species*. The propositions in which genera and species are found will contain certain relations of necessary implication among them. Thus, in order to be logical and productive of knowledge, our thinking must follow the facts and structures of the natural world.

Each science contains different kinds of propositions, including some appropriate first principles and certain other subordinate propositions, which, if uncovered in inductive investigations, will be organized in logical structures derived from first principles. This will be done most often in syllogistic form, which Aristotle feels to be the most perfect form of organization. "A syllogism is discourse in which, certain things being stated, something other than what is stated follows of necessity from their being so" (*Prior Analytics*, 24b19). From two premises having one term in common, a third proposition or conclusion is deduced about the other two terms. If "All A is B" and "All B is C," we can certainly conclude that "All A is C." But the premises "All C is B" and "Some A is B" do not justify a certain conclusion, while the premises "No B is C" and "No B is A" do not yield any conclusion. Aristotle lists all ways in which universal or particular affirmations and universal or particular negations can be combined as premises, and then determines what valid conclusions can be derived from any pair of premises. Thus he establishes which syllogisms were valid and which rules governed valid reasoning.

Aristotle does not regard logic as purely formal, for he holds that thinking parallels existence. The first principles of a science cannot themselves be demonstrated. "The premises of demonstrated knowledge must be true, primary, immediate, better known than, and prior to, the conclusion, which is further related to them as effect to cause" (*Posterior Analytics* 71b20). These true premises are evident to any competent mind familiar with the relevant subject matter. All demonstration depends on prior knowledge. If it were necessary to demonstrate every premise, one would be involved in an infinite regress, and knowledge or science would never begin. If there were no world of substance with which we maintained contact prior to, during, and after our analyses, our thinking would be meaningless and propositions would be incapable of being true.

Aristotle's Ethics

Aristotle's *Nicomachaean Ethics* is one of the great classics of moral philosophy containing penetrating and pioneering philosophical analysis which has had great influence down to our own day. It is also a repository of Greek value judgments and prejudices which once led a French philosopher, E. Bréhier, to characterize Aristotle's morality as "the morality of a middle-class lady in comfortable circumstances who is determined to make the best use of her social advantages." The careful reader of the *Nicomachaean Ethics*, then, must distinguish the universal from the parochial.

Aristotle's ethics is an application of his psychology and is intimately related to his political philosophy. Of course, for the Greeks there was much more unity and continuity between the individual and the community than there is for us, so that ethics and politics tend to be "two sides of one coin." Aristotle's ethics, like his general philosophy, is teleological or purposive. Aristotle is seeking the good of the individual man and not Plato's "absolutistic" good. The good, then, is indigenous and autonomous to the individual. Aristotle pursues this in Socratic fashion. Everything has a function which is its good—a flute player has the function of flute playing. Has not man a similar function? What is good for man is to fulfill his function or destiny. What is his destiny? Man should be happy or have well-being (eudaimonia). This is the highest good—the end of ends. About everything else it is proper to ask "why?" or "what for?"

What is happiness or eudaimonia? Aristotle says some people think happiness is pleasure, wealth, or honor. Since these suggested objects are only a part of man's activities, they can neither be identified with nor excluded from happiness. Happiness must be something which is concerned with the totality of man's activities and with his distinctive "species" character. Thus happiness is the activity of the soul under the control of reason, or the full realization of the program of the organism in a complete life. Happiness is not mere virtue or goodness, for a sleeping man could be virtuous, but only a waking man can be happy. Happiness is active rather than passive.

Does happiness depend on external goods? In contrast to the Stoics, Aristotle says "yes." He thinks that children are necessary for happiness. The human does not fulfill his destiny if he is childless. Likewise one cannot be happy unless he has health and sufficient wealth, is free in a free state, and has friends. Only animals and gods can be happy without friends. Aristotle is not altogether consistent with reference to the role of reason in the happy life, for he changes his mind in his philosophic development. Sometimes he talks as though reason in the form of speculation and philosophy is necessary for happiness, as in the last book of the *Ethics*, where he pits the philosopher's life against the domestic or political life. On the other hand, he does think of "reason" as the rational direction of the whole of life, so that reason functions practically as the arbiter between conflicting desires. Perhaps this is his most mature view.

Aristotle defines virtue as "a state relating to choice, being in a mean relative to us, which is determined by a rule, and as a man of good sense would determine it" (*Ethics*, 1107a). Virtue is a state, a settled disposition of character acquired by persistent practice, for it is required by the equilibrium or health of the organism. The virtuous man must be happy because the mean is good and pleasant and permits the uninterrupted activity of the program of the organism. Since the mean is always viewed as being related to one's circumstances, it would appear to permit an extreme course of action on occasion rather than always demanding what others regard as the middle course. The rule is to be determined by a man of good sense and trained judgment—one who possesses the intellectual virtue of practical wisdom.

Aristotle distinguishes between moral and intellectual virtues, which are related respectively to the irrational and rational parts of the soul. There are irrational or nonrational elements which are not subject to the control of reason. If one possesses the excellence of good looks or a well-proportioned body, he enjoys good fortune or luck rather than virtue. One cannot be blamed for the lack of these gifts of fortune. But there are irrational or nonrational elements or desires which are subject to rational control and may become, through the formation of right habits, moral virtue or excellence. The state of moral excellence is a mean between deficiency and excess. Thus courage is a mean between cowardice and rashness; liberality between stinginess and prodigality. A man may by accident stumble on the mean in a given situation, but he can be said to be morally virtuous only when he continually exhibits the mean through long training and firmly established habits. Here the teacher and legislator have special responsibilities. Aristotle emphasizes acts which flow from deliberately chosen and well-rooted habits revealed through long stretches of time. He reminds us: "One swallow does not a summer make, nor does one day a happy man."

Intellectual virtue has various forms, depending upon the content and range of our reflections. Basically it is correctness of understanding which alone initiates right behavior. It results from teaching rather than practice and habit. It is in the contemplative or speculative life that man, the rational animal, finds his excellence or full development. It is here that he finds the realities made known to us by mathematics, metaphysics, and philosophy of nature. It is the end for which the moral virtues have their being. Man cannot contemplate adequately or wisely if he is subject to evil desires or if his life is disrupted by the unsatisfied claims of his fellows.

Aristotle suggests that Socrates was both right and wrong in his claim that the virtues are one and that the one virtue is knowledge. Each human activity has its peculiar virtue, but none, except reason, can claim to possess knowledge of itself. The moral attitude toward each activity is the same, namely, *knowing* the golden mean in each.

Yet he feels Socrates errs in thinking that right acts must necessarily flow from the correct knowledge of the end to be followed and of the means to its achievement. Socrates did not assess properly *incontinence*, as Aristotle labels it, which is the customary and deliberate defying by desire of the knowledge of good and evil. This defiance is not simply the defeat of clear reason by naked passion. In many cases the fact that we immediately *desire* to do something may outweigh our uncertainty as to whether the contemplated act is advantageous to us in the long run. The hope of improving the incontinent man lies in establishing in him the habit of denying on rational grounds the claim of desires whose morality is questionable.

Our contemporary ethical treatises do not usually discuss the subject of friendship, but Aristotle devotes much space to it, even comparing different types of friendship with state constitutions to show how important he feels friendship to be. The Greeks thought of friendship as one of the things which distinguished their life from that of the barbarians. As we have earlier noted, Aristotle believes that the good life requires one to have friends to consult and lean on in any kind of circumstance. He feels that friendship is needed to cement together all our relations and associations. Friendship requires good will, kindly feeling toward one another, ability to confer benefits, some association, and the possibility of reciprocation. Thus one cannot have very many friends because of the limitations of time and the requirements. The love of others is basically an extension of self-love, for the friend is the alter-ego. For Aristotle self-love becomes a vice only in excess. There are three types of friendship: pleasure, utility, and the good. The friendship of *pleasure* grows out of play and spontaneous companionship such as we find in the play of children. Friendships of *utility* arise from reciprocal helpfulness, as in a business partnership. Friendships of the *good* involve the sharing of important activities for the realization of a common goal, as with two scientists cooperating in the laboratory or the husband and wife in the rearing of a family. Perhaps Aristotle divides these types too sharply for purposes of analysis. What is important for Aristotle is the activity—loving is more important than being loved. Man cannot be friends with God because He cannot love us. If Aristotle's emphasis on activity is sound, then it does not matter whether our love for God is not reciprocated. Some critics have charged that Aristotle's account of friendship is completely lacking in devotion or love. Aristotle's treatment is probably characteristic of himself in being sober, prudential, objective, sensible, unimaginative, and nonmystical.

Aristotle's description of the great-souled or magnanimous man is thought by many to reveal something of Aristotle's ideal for himself, and has often come in for heavy criticism. His ideal should not be identified with the Christian saint, the Stoic sage, or Plato's philosopher-king. It is not an ideal for all men, but an ideal for a class—the upper class. In some respects it reminds one of the British ideal of a gentleman, or Castiglione's Courtier, or even, in some respects, Machiavelli's Prince. The magnanimous man is formal toward his superiors and kind and gracious toward his inferiors. He confers benefits but is ashamed to receive them. With honors that are great and conferred by good men he will be moderately pleased, but honor from casual people and on trifling grounds he completely despises. He is one who owns beautiful and profitless things rather than profitable and useful ones. To him a slow step, a deep voice, and a level utterance are proper.

Aristotle's Political Philosophy

Aristotle's political philosophy both shares common viewpoints with, and diverges sharply from, Plato's perspective. Plato is inclined to be analytic and *a priori* in his thought, while Aristotle is more inductive. Both work within the context of the Greek city-state and approach the state with an ethical and teleological point of view. Both ground their political thought in an analysis of human nature. Although Plato is concerned with the implications of his own position, Aristotle is much more interested in determining the best procedure to follow in practice.

Aristotle begins with the conviction that the state is an association for the good of the community. The state, as the supreme and all-embracing community, must aim at the supreme good. Against the cynics and other anarchistic critics of the state, Aristotle argues that the state is natural and the completion of simpler groups like the family. "If the earlier forms of society are natural, so is the state." Although states first arose to enable men to survive and later, through mutual aid and exchange, to meet a wider variety of needs, they are maintained because they enable men to lead the good life of moral and intellectual activity, including education and the speculative life. Aristotle believes "a social instinct is implanted in man by nature" and "man is a political animal," that is, one whose capacities can only be brought to full development by life in the city-state (*polis*). It is no wonder, then, that Aristotle hails the first founder of the state as man's greatest benefactor. He says that man can be the best or the worst of animals depending on the environment. "When separated from law and justice man is the worst of all."

The Stoics in the Hellenistic-Roman world condemned Aristotle for his belief that some men by nature are slaves—a belief which he justifies by appealing to a hierarchical principle running through the universe. Slaves by nature are those who do not have sufficient reason to participate in the governing of a city-state and would be better advised to obey the commands of their natural masters. Aristotle does not condone slavery by mere right of conquest in war, for superior power is not to be equated with superior excellence. Why certain men are slaves by nature is not a problem which Aristotle is interested in investigating.

Aristotle is sharply critical of a number of aspects of Plato's *Republic*. He particularly attacks Plato's proposal for communizing the property, women, and children of the guardian class—a policy which he ascribes to Plato's overemphasis on unity and rigidity. He believes such communism removes direct responsibility, since "that which is everybody's business is nobody's." He denies that the proposed communization of wives could really destroy the formation of personal affection. "How much better to be a real cousin than to be a son in Plato's fashion?" he asks. Basically Aristotle believes Plato uses excessively the analogy of the army and the household. A state involves differentiation with integration rather than conformity. Thus Aristotle is more inclined to appeal to education, morality, and enlightened self-interest. He tells us, "It is clearly better that property should be private but the use of it common; and the special business of the legislator is to create in men this benevolent disposition" (*Politics*, II, 4–5).

Aristotle seeks to determine the type of political organization which is best for the good state. Should authority be concentrated in a single ruler, an aristocracy, or a constitutional democracy? The rule of the state when directed toward the common welfare in accordance with strict principles of justice and the supremacy of law is compatible with all three forms of organization. When law and justice are destroyed kingship becomes tyranny, aristocracy turns into a plutocratic oligarchy, and constitutional democracy or polity degenerates into unbridled democracy in which the lower classes are favored at the expense of the common welfare. Under ideal conditions monarchy is perhaps best, but under actual conditions and pressures it too often lapses into tyranny. He advances as the most practicable form of government a moderate democracy. He believes that a city ought to be composed, "as far as possible, of equals and similars; and these are generally the middle classes. Wherefore the city which is composed of middle-class citizens is necessarily best constituted." No one should infer from this that Aristotle is an apostle of equalitarian democracy. It is true that he believes that all citizens should take their turn of governing and being governed and that equality consists in the same treatment of similar persons. But Aristotle does not think it undemocratic to exclude from the body of citizens not only slaves, resident aliens, and women, but the mechanics, tradesmen, and husbandmen. From the perspective of the twentieth century, Aristotle seems perverse in regarding a majority of men as by nature slaves and unfit to participate in political life, thereby throwing away one of the main advantages of the small size of the city-state, which makes it possible for all of its inhabitants to share fully in its life. It should be noted that in his numerous comments on equality Aristotle is usually discussing not arithmetic equality, but proportionate equality—to each according to his deserts or virtue. This kind of equality is, for Aristotle, just and necessary for the good life. The absence of a fair deal, proportionate equality, is what splits the city-state into factions and destroys the essential sense of community.

Aristotle's interest in political stability leads him to investigate the causes and prevention of revolutions. His own knowledge of the

Greek city-state disposes him to assign the causes of revolution to two strong motives in men: the desire for equality and the demand to be superior. The disadvantaged want to remove their disabilities and gain equality with their superiors. But this bid for equality is obnoxious to the privileged who seek to overthrow their opponents and retain their exclusive privileges. Thus revolution may be the fruit of either arrogance or greed and envy.

A good state is most likely to protect itself against these revolutionary upheavals by restricting the power of public officials, avoiding the abuses of class legislation, and educating youth in obedience to law and respect for the constitution. "Men think . . . that freedom means the doing what a man likes; . . . But this is all wrong; men should not think it slavery to live according to the rule of the constitution; for it is their salvation" (*Politics*, 1310a).

Aristotle's Theory of the Fine Arts

Although there is a brief passage in the *Politics*, our knowledge of Aristotle's views about art comes mostly from his *Poetics*. Only the first book of this work, that dealing with tragedy, has survived. No other single work has had such a profound influence in the history of literary criticism. It is still read carefully and critically by contemporary students of literature, even though Aristotle's reflections center on the Homeric epic and Attic tragedy and comedy.

Like Plato, Aristotle thinks poetry is an imitation of nature or life and thus conveys information or knowledge. Man is an imitative animal whose reason and senses delight in the act of imitation. But Aristotle differs sharply from Plato in maintaining that art succeeds in revealing what is universal and eternal in the particular. The poet's purpose is not that of an agent of the state seeking to reform us or to indoctrinate us with a moral lesson. To insist that virtue always triumph and vice be defeated is, he feels, the mark of a second-rate audience.

The end or purpose of tragedy is, for Aristotle, to relieve us of the oppressive emotions of pity and fear like a cathartic purging the body of some excessive "humor." The poet stirs our emotions in such a way as to purge and refine them. Aristotle's definition of tragedy is well known. A tragedy is "the imitation of an action that is serious and also, as having magnitude, complete in itself; in language with pleasurable accessories, each kind brought in separately in the parts of the work; in a dramatic, not a narrative form; with incidents arousing pity and fear, wherewith to accomplish its catharsis of such emotions."

There are six chief constituents of a tragedy: plot, character, thought, diction, spectacle, and melody. The first three receive Aristotle's primary attention. Character is important for him, but plot, or action, is the very soul of a tragedy since it is in action that each creature is fulfilled. Indeed, he speaks of the plot as the end, or *telos*, of a tragedy to which character is the means. A tragedy should not show us the ruination of either a thoroughly good or completely evil man. Rather, it is one which involves "a man not preeminently virtuous and just, whose misfortune, however, is brought upon him not by vice or depravity, but by some error of judgment, of the number of those in the enjoyment of great reputation and prosperity."

In the best kind of tragedy, the downfall of the hero must be sudden and unexpected, and accompanied, where possible, by an unanticipated "discovery" or "change from ignorance to knowledge, and thus to either love or hate, in the personages marked for good or evil fortune." The catastrophic outcome must be prepared for in logical fashion by a series of interrelated events which express honestly the psychology of the characters. Pity or fear is most likely to be aroused when the person planning or executing the tragic deed is closely related to the intended victim. In the ideal plot he will prepare for the deed without being aware of the relationship and will learn of it only at the last moment. Often parricide, matricide, and fratricide provided good material for tragedy. The successful tragedian must be a great poet and playwright—a complete master of poetic diction, "at once clear and not mean," and of rhythm and meter. He must have the skill to shape the dialogue and choral songs and dances into a single unified work so that it may provide us with an esthetically pleasing experience. Aristotle concludes the book with a brief discussion of epic poetry. The second book of the *Poetics*, in which Aristotle discussed comedy, is lost.

Aristotle: Suggested Additional Reading

Abernethy, George L. and Thomas A. Langford, eds., *History of Philosophy: Selected Readings*. Belmont, Calif.: Dickenson, 1965, pp. 121–182.*

Allan, D. J., *The Philosophy of Aristotle*. New York: Oxford University Press, 1952.*

Anscombe, G. E. M. and P. T. Geach, *Three Philosophers*. Ithaca, N.Y.: Cornell University Press, 1961.*

Apostle, Hippocrates George, *Aristotle's Philosophy of Mathematics*. Chicago: University of Chicago, 1952.*

Aristotle, *The Basic Works of Aristotle*. Edited by Richard McKeon. New York: Random House, 1941.*

Aristotle, *The Philosophy of Aristotle*. Edited, with introduction and commentary, by Renford Bambrough. New York: New American Library, Mentor, 1963.

Else, Gerald Frank, *Aristotle's Poetics: The Argument*. Cambridge: Harvard University Press, 1957.*

Grene, Marjorie, *A Portrait of Aristotle*. Chicago: University of Chicago Press, Phoenix, 1967.

Guthrie, W. K. C., "Development of Aristotle's Theology," in *Classical Quarterly*, vol. 27 (1933), 162–171.

Guthrie, W. K. C., *Greek Philosophers from Thales to Aristotle*. New York: Harper and Row, Torchbook, 1960.

Hamburger, Max, *Morals and Law: The Growth of Aristotle's Legal Theory*. New Haven, Conn.: Yale University Press, 1951.*

Jaeger, Werner W., *Aristotle: Fundamentals of the History of His Development*. Translated by Richard Robinson. New York: Oxford University Press, 1962.

Kaufmann, Walter, *Philosophical Classics*. Englewood Cliffs, N.J.: Prentice-Hall, 1961, I, 357–532.*

Moracsik, J. M. E., ed., *Aristotle—A Collection of Critical Essays*. Garden City: Doubleday, Anchor, 1967.

Mure, G. R. G., *Aristotle*. New York: Oxford University Press, Galaxy Books, 1962.

Oates, Whitney J., *Aristotle and the Problem of Value*. Princeton, N.J.: Princeton University Press, 1963.*

Randall, J. H., *Aristotle*. New York: Columbia University, paperback, 1962.

Ross, William David, *Aristotle*. New York: Barnes and Noble, 1960.

Taylor, A. E., *Aristotle*. New York: Dover, 1955.

Chapter Five

Epicurus

In a real sense the summit of Greek philosophical achievement had been reached by the time of Aristotle's death in 322 B.C. In the post-Aristotelian period very little of philosophical speculation can be called original or creative in comparison with what preceded it. The Academy and Lyceum, of course, continued their work under the direction of the successors of Plato and Aristotle, who primarily elaborated or commented on the work of their masters, although there is some evidence of the inroads of skepticism in their midst. This post-Aristotelian period is ordinarily called the Hellenic-Roman or Hellenistic period. For purposes of convenience, it may be dated from 322 B.C., the death of Aristotle, to approximately 430 A.D., the death of the great church father Augustine. The first 300 years constitute the ethical period and the last 430 years the religious period.

Alexander the Great had dreamed of a world empire with a world culture, predominantly Hellenic in speech and spirit. Alexander's early death brought on the disintegration of his empire and the vigorous struggle for power among his military commanders. The Macedonian empire became a separate nation. The Asiatic generals moved the center of their operations from Babylon and Persia to Syria, where the Seleucid dynasty made Antioch an important political, economic, and cultural center. The Egyptian territory fell to Ptolemy and his successors, for whom the capital city of Alexandria, at the mouth of the Nile, became a great world market for commerce and ideas. Here the greatest library of the ancient world became a mecca for the intellectuals of many different cultures whose stimulating interaction produced a number of brilliant contributions, especially in mathematics.

In this new Mediterranean world of racial and religious interaction, Greek thought was the cultural yeast. But the Greek cities on the mainland and their former colonies became pawns in a series of military conquests. The Greek city-state, the *polis*, as an effective unit of government, had died, as had the social systems which Plato subjected to critical attack in the *Republic*. As one writer put it, "In the

Greek philosophy of life, the former union of ethics and politics was now obsolete. Statesmanship was no longer an available career, or political reform an issue, or social theory a problem." With the disruption of former political units by military occupation, the challenge to traditional cultural standards, and the displacement of large numbers of persons, many turned readily to the religious cults to satisfy their craving for security and consolation. Philosophy was under pressure to provide not so much theoretical understanding as a practical standard of conduct which would guide men through conflicts, uncertainties, and frustrations to the achievement of a happy, satisfying life. New teachers, principally the Epicureans and Stoics, appeared to speak to the needs of the Hellenistic age. We turn first to the Epicureans.

Epicurus was born in 341 B.C., the son of an Athenian colonist in Samos who apparently was a poor schoolmaster. At age eighteen, about the time of the death of Alexander the Great, Epicurus journeyed to Athens to establish his citizenship and to complete his term of military service. In 322 B.C. Perdiccas, the successor to Alexander, drove the Athenian colonists from Samos. Epicurus rejoined his family, which had fled to Colophon, near Ephesus, in Asia Minor. At some stage which cannot be dated precisely he probably received philosophical instruction from a certain Nausiphanes, a follower of Democritus, in the coastal city of Teos. Although the philosophy he developed owes much to Democritus, Epicurus never acknowledged his indebtedness and constantly referred to Nausiphanes with contemptuous epithets such as "lung-fish" and "imposter." In 311–310 B.C. in Mytilene, he founded a school which he later transferred to Lampsacus. About 307–306 B.C. he brought some of his followers to Athens, where he purchased a small house and a separate walled-in-garden. He taught in the garden, so that his school soon became known as "the philosophers of the garden."

The garden community included relatives, disciples, friends and their children, slaves, and *hetaerae* (intellectual courtesans). This coeducational feature aroused from the school's enemies charges of profligacy and scandal which were probably baseless. Epicurus has been historically the victim of a bad press, so that in our day "epicurean" has come to mean "eat, drink, and be merry, for tomorrow we die." The term stands in sharp, and even ironical, contrast to the austere version of hedonism actually taught by Epicurus. His contemporaries praised Epicurus for his contentedness, tenderness, friendliness, and goodness. He led a simple life, eating no meat and drinking no wine. In a letter he even asked a friend to send him some cheese as a special luxury, thereby indicating that the community was partially dependent on voluntary contributions. Epicurus seems to have been so revered by his devoted followers and his teachings memorized with such dogmatic finality that in contrast to the shifting history of its rival Stoicism no new developments in theory were made by subsequent generations of disciples.

Like the early Stoics, Epicurus was a prolific writer; Diogenes Laertius credits him with 300 volumes on a wide range of topics. As with the early Stoic writings, not one of these volumes has come down to us. He also made two condensations of his entire system of teachings. One was entitled *The Major Epitome*, a popular work for beginners, the other entitled *The Minor Epitome*, a work designed for more advanced students. This latter work, frequently called *Letter to Herodotus*, is an important source of our knowledge of Epicureanism. *The Major Epitome* may have been the work which the Latin poet Lucretius relied upon 200 years later for the composition of his great poem, *De Rerum Natura*. It is a valuable source for both details and the main outline of Epicurean teaching. Another work, *Letter to Pythocles*, is regarded by scholars as not having been written by Epicurus but more likely compiled by a second- or third-generation disciple. A third extant letter is the *Letter to Menoeceus*, dealing with ethics. There is also a collection of forty short statements called the "Principal Doctrines," a sort of practical manual for Epicureans, and a number of fragments which have come to light.

Epicureanism shared certain characteristics with Stoicism. It, too, divided philosophy into three parts: Canonic, Physics (including psychology and theology), and Ethics. It espoused a fundamental materialism in which only bodies are substantially real and capable of functioning as causes. Like its rival, it was a philosophy of salvation based on reason and designed as a practical way of life in opposition to a fading religious faith and a crumbling traditional morality. It sought to give an inner peace which the world could neither confer nor destroy. This peace was *ataraxia*, a state of tranquility which immunized man against the disorganizing and disruptive forces of the world. But there were sharp differences between the two schools which acerbated their rivalry. In varying ways and degrees Stoicism at different stages in its development felt the influences of Heraclitus, Pythagoreanism, Plato, and Aristotle. The only earlier philosophy to which Epicureanism is indebted is the atomism of Democritus and Leucippus which Epicurus proclaimed, with some significant modification, in the fashion of a zealous preacher rather than as a disinterested seeker after truth. Epicurus denied the notion of Divine Providence which the Stoics taught because he was seeking release from fear, especially fear of gods, of divine intervention, and of death. His system, then, is less developed and less comprehensive than the Stoic, for after all it was an individual, rather than a collective, effort.

The first major division of Epicurus' philosophy, the Canonic, is concerned primarily with the canons, criteria, or tests of truth. Epicurus, unlike the Stoics, was not interested in dialectic or logic as such. He did not analyze propositions, the forms of valid arguments, or the art of disputation. He concentrated entirely on the tests or canons of knowledge and the criteria of truth. His system denotes four criteria: (1) sensations or perceptions (*aisthēsis*), (2) concepts (*prolēpsis*), (3) feelings (*pathē*), (4) apprehension of the mind (*epibolētēs dianoiās*). All are forms of immediate physical or sense experience—the ways in which our material souls are physically affected by other material things. Epicurus espoused the essential position of naïve realism held by the man in the street: all our perceptions or sensations are true and irrefutable. In some sense seeing is believing, appearances are realities. It was his firm conviction that if we seriously and systematically doubt sense perception, we make both knowledge and action impossible.

Something is "true" if it actually is as it is said to be, "false" if it is not actually as it is said to be. The true and the real are held to be fundamentally one. A true affirmation consists, then, of nothing but the actually existing characteristics present to the observer. The problem is to distinguish true judgment from the false or to determine whether an image corresponds to an external object.

(1) In dealing with Epicurus' first criterion, sensations, we must note that they are infallible. Blueness is blueness. In a strict sense the question of truth or falsity does not arise. However, a sensation may be clear or unclear, and thus a clear sensation may be compared with an unclear one. Someone can pay closer attention to something which he wishes to see more clearly, or he can move nearer to it. Each thing is made up of atoms and is continually giving off and taking in streams of atoms as long as it continues to exist. The atoms given off are "films" or "peelings" or miniature images (*eidōla*) which keep the shape and characteristics of the object emitting them. These "films" or images float through the air in streams until they encounter a perceiving subject. Those images composed of larger and less subtle atoms make an actual physical impression on the proper sense organ. Those composed of very fine and subtle atoms penetrate our pores directly to the mind (which itself is made up of small round atoms) and consequently cause the images we experience in dreams, illusions, and imaginations. In their passage through air these images may become mixed, resulting

in what we call hallucinations and the images of mermaids and cen-taurs. Thus we have a consistent materialistic explanation for per-ceptual "errors" which are not strictly errors.

(2) The concept, in Epicurus' sensationalistic theory of knowledge, is presented as essentially a memory image. One may accumulate a number of actual images of his pet dog. On occasion when one is not observing the dog one may have remnants of these previous perceptions which give rise to a mental picture or memory image of the dog. In so far as a concept is a memory image, then it is infallible like other images.

(3) In the criterion of feelings (*pathē*), pleasure is the ultimate test of what men should choose. The feelings which are congenial to one are called pleasant; those which are not congenial are called painful or unpleasant. Feelings are simply what they are and cannot be doubted. They provide the raw materials for judgments of value which in their way can be as reliable as judgments of fact.

(4) Another criterion of sense experience is "apprehension of mind" (*epibolētēs dianoiās*). It is something of an intuitive process by which we apprehend very subtle images like those of gods or grasp certain concepts as clear and self-evident truths in contrast to mere opinions. Again we have an infallible form of sense experience.

If the various types of sense experience are all infallible, then how does the problem of error arise? How do we explain mistakes? Epi-curus' answer is that errors can be explained by man's propensity to make judgments (*doxa*) or to express opinions about what infallible sensation reveals to him. In haste or confusion one may express judgments which do not correctly report what sensations actually reveal or are. One may confuse a man with his fraternal twin in judging his identity. The remedy here is to take a closer look. The stick partially submerged in water may appear bent. One Epicurean response is to hold that it is so at the moment of perception for the viewer. Another response is to hold the intervening medium (air) between the observer and the thing he observes responsible for knocking off the corners or otherwise altering the *eidōla* or images. The remedy for this is to get closer to the *eidōla* as they are emitted by the object or, in the case of the submerged stick, to run one's fingers over the entire length of the stick to avoid the distortion induced by the intervening medium of water. If one makes judgments about future events, then these judg-ments must be confirmed by some sense experience. If one's judgment refers to atoms, the void, or gods, which cannot be directly experienced, then it must not contradict experiences. Historically such an inter-pretation of the knowledge process has made sense to many generations of thinkers down to our own day, while for others it has raised more questions than it has answered.

Epicurus' interest in theoretical philosophy or metaphysics stems from some very practical considerations. He teaches that two of the most important sources of fear are religion and the terrors of hell. If man is to be freed from the devastating consequences of these superstitious fears in the interest of achieving the state of tranquility or *ataraxia*, then the nonexistence of divine intervention or providence and of a life beyond the grave must be established by scientific means. This scientific proof Epicurus finds in the atomistic philosophy of Democritus, which he adopts with some significant modifications. Epicurus never develops an interest in science as such, nor does he encourage its free development as an independent source of truth. His interest in science is utilitarian; he adopts it as a foundation for his moral concerns. The atomism of Democritus explains everything by the mechanical motions of atoms, thereby rendering superfluous any appeal to divine intervention. Since it explains the soul as well as the body in terms of atoms, it makes conventional doctrines of immortality appear pointless.

Epicurus is a materialist. Nothing is created out of the nonexistent, and nothing passes into nothingness. The bodies and things which we experience are composed of preexisting material atoms which cannot be observed by unassisted sense perception. Their death or destruction is nothing more than a change or reconstitution of the collection of atoms which constitute them. Thus the ultimate constituents of the universe are atoms and void or empty space through which the atoms move. These atoms are indivisible, unchangeable, and compact and possess the qualities of size, shape, and weight. Epicurus does not consider the secondary qualities of atoms to be real, so he denies that they possess color or taste, qualities which we impute to them. The number of atoms and the void are both held to be infinite, and the variety of atomic shapes indefinitely large.

Although Epicurus is a materialist, he is not a determinist. As we have seen, he believes in the efficacy of mechanical causes and rejects the belief in providence or teleology. But he also teaches the doctrine of human freedom and seeks some explanation of it. What is to be gained if one substitutes for the tyranny of unpredictable divine intervention the overriding necessity which would determine every detail of one's existence? Better to believe in the fables told about the gods than to be trapped in the inexorable determinism of the physicist! Complete determinism is for Epicurus no road to human *ataraxia*. In the interest of moral freedom he is led to make a significant modification in the direction of spontaneity in the atomistic philosophy of Democritus.

Democritus taught that the heavier atoms must fall faster than the lighter ones as they plunged downward in space. Thus there would be collisions which would account for the formation of worlds or planets. Epicurus, following a suggestion from Aristotle, repudiates this and argues that atoms, falling through a void without resistance, will all fall at equal speeds without regard to weight. Thus a heavier atom cannot catch up with a lighter one. Since all the atoms fall straight downwards, they cannot "sideswipe" each other. Epicurus' modification of Democritus consists in allowing for an occasional spontaneous deviation of an atom from the straight downward path. In this fashion occurred the first collision which, together with the entangling movements, led to the formation of innumerable worlds separated by empty space. Although some felt this to be a backward step and some, like Cicero, felt that it invalidated atomism, it is interesting to note that in recent times the writings of Eddington and Heisenberg in physics have revived the discussion of the possibility of indeterminacy in the universe. Epicurus, unwilling to be bound by either religious orthodoxy or a fatalistic physical science, places an arbitrary undetermined chance factor as a separate principle alongside physical determinism.

In his psychology Epicurus is also indebted to Democritus. He maintains that the soul is composed of the smallest and most subtle atoms, but in contrast to the animals the human soul possesses a rational part located in the breast which is responsible for the emotions of fear and joy. At death the atoms of the soul are separated and go their separate ways, thus ending the possibility of the individual's continued perception. Thus no soul remains in existence to experience remorse or retribution.

Epicurus also has a theology which provides an interesting account of the gods on materialistic lines. He views them anthropomorphically, for they likewise are composed of atoms, the finest, and eat and breathe like men. How else could one account for their frequent appearance in the dreams and visions of men and for the widespread belief in their existence? These deities live in the interstellar spaces in carefree happiness and excellence. They are unconcerned with human affairs and exact no retribution. Man may honor them, but he has no occasion to fear them. The man who attains *ataraxia* on this earth will be leading a life worthy of the gods. This is a religious ideal for a small spiritual aristocracy.

We have noted how historically the Epicureans have been charged erroneously with having offered men a version of "eat, drink and be merry, for tomorrow we die" as an ethical philosophy. The accusation more accurately should be directed to the teaching of Aristippus (435–350 B.C.), who was the more typical pleasure seeker. Aristippus was, according to Diogenes Laertius, "capable of adapting himself to place, time and person, and of playing his part most appropriately in any circumstances. . . . He derived pleasure from things that were present and did not toil to procure any enjoyment from things not present." He was a sycophantic guest at the court of King Dionysius of Syracuse, and when reproached for having obsequiously knelt before the king in order to beg some favor he retorted coolly, "that is not my fault but Dionysius', who has ears in his feet." His way of life received formal expression in his hedonistic philosophy, which came to be known as Cyrenaicism after the town of Cyrene where he made his home. He taught that a man should endeavor to secure for himself as large a sum as possible of particular pleasures, that very intense pleasures of the senses are to be preferred even if they involve pain and disgrace, and that one may more likely obtain pleasures if he has the wit and courage to control a situation. This last belief is exemplified in Aristippus' famed remark about his mistress, the lovely courtesan Lais: "I possess her, I am not possessed by her." This slender account of Cyrenaicism suffices to reveal the distance which separates Aristippus from Epicurus. Pleasure is indeed an elastic term if both these teachers are exponents of hedonism.

In what sense, then, are we to consider Epicurus a hedonist? Epicurus is a forthright spokesman for pleasure as the aim and end of life. But he says, "By pleasure we mean the absence of pain in the body and trouble in the soul. It is not a succession of drinking feasts and of revelry, not sexual love, not the enjoyment of fish and other delicacies of a luxurious table that produce a pleasant life; it is sober reasoning, searching out the grounds of every choice and avoidance of and banishing mere opinions, which cause the greatest tumults to take possession of the soul." Yet Epicurus goes out of his way to denounce asceticism and to remind us that the happy life is impossible if we neglect the claims of the body. He states: "The beginning and root of all good is the pleasure of the belly, and even wisdom and culture depend on that." Some of his opponents charged him with the inconsistency of preaching simultaneously self-indulgence and asceticism. However much inconsistency one may discover in his theory, it is evident that his own example and precept were clear and consistent. As to the pleasures of the table, he says: "Plain food brings me no less pleasure than costly diet once the pain of want has been removed, and bread and water give the highest possible pleasure when they are brought to hungry lips." Simple fare, such as found in abundance in nature, satisfies hunger. If plain fare seems to be unpalatable, a little exercise will add more to one's enjoyment of it than the artifices of the cook. Similarly, if one is really tired from work, a hard couch will provide a restful sleep. In these emphases Epicurus is not propounding asceticism as such, but rather suggesting that one ought to eat, drink and clothe oneself from an interest in health instead of from an interest in social status or the exploitation of sensation.

Epicurus' remarks on the pleasures of sex were not encouraging to the libertine or sensualist. "The wise man will not fall in love." "Sexual intercourse has never done anyone good; and he will be lucky if it did not actually do harm." "Love is a strong yearning for sexual pleasure accompanied by goading and restlessness." As was the case with so many other things, love involved just too many pains to be considered a pleasure. Lucretius, who later in Rome celebrated Epicurus' philosophy in a magnificent poem, followed his master in denouncing love but saw no harm in sexual intercourse provided it was divorced from passion. Yet the vigor of his attack on love suggests that he regarded it as a common threat to the achievement of *ataraxia*.

If the good life consists, for Epicurus, in gaining as much pleasure and avoiding as much pain as possible for one's self, one needs to be able to ascertain the amounts of pleasure or pain likely to follow as a result of one's choice. Although he has no precise scale of measurement, he does offer some guidelines for his followers. The pleasures of the mind, including anticipation and memory, are preferable to those of the body. In general, passive pleasures, consisting basically in the absence of pain, are more valuable than the more active pleasures. He tells us: "Freedom from mental disquietude and from pain are pleasures of repose: joy and delight we regard as activities of change." In fact, pleasure seems to a great extent to be the removal of pain or desire and to possess no degrees of more or less. He puts it in this fashion: "The end of all our actions is to be free from pain and apprehension. When once this happens to us, the tempest in the soul becomes a calm, and the organism no longer needs to make progress to anything which it lacks, or to seek anything further to complete the good for soul and body. For we only need pleasure so long as the absence of it increases pain. As soon as we cease to be in pain we have no need of further pleasure. This is why we call pleasure the beginning and end of the happy life. It is recognized by us as our primal and connatural good, and is the original source of all choice and avoidance; we revert to it when we make feeling the universal standard of good. Now it is *because* this is our primal and connatural good that we do not choose to have every pleasure, but sometimes pass by many pleasures when a greater inconvenience follows from them, and prefer many pains to pleasures when a greater pleasure follows from endurance of the pain. Every pleasure then is a good, as it has the specific character of the good (that is, to attract us for its own sake), but not every pain should be always avoided." As regards measurement of pain, Epicurus offers little other than the reminder that intense pains are usually short in duration and that a life relatively free from pain is within the possibility of attainment.

Epicurus believes that the traditional Greek virtues are necessary means to the production of pleasure. The virtues of moderation, simplicity, cheerfulness, and temperance are more likely to produce pleasure and happiness than are unrestrained luxury and ambition. "It is not possible to live pleasantly without living prudently, and honorably, and justly; nor to live prudently, and honorably, and justly, without living pleasantly." But for Epicurus, the most fundamental virtue is prudence which chooses the means for producing pleasure. It is through prudence that we select the more passive pleasures in preference to the more intense ones whether in diet, sex, or friendship. The value of prudence, then, lies in its ability to enable us to reach the pleasure the Epicurean calls to our attention.

Strictly speaking the Epicurean ethic is an egoistic hedonism, a selfish pursuit by the individual of his own pleasure. But the Epicurean community was, in practice, better than its initial theory. The Epicurean acted on the assumption that it was more pleasant to do a kind act than to be the recipient of one. The record reveals that Epicurus was commended for acts of kindness and generosity. The Epicurean placed a high value on friendship and taught that a wise man loves the friend as himself. "The happiest men are they who have arrived at the point of having nothing to fear from those who surround them. Such men live with one another most agreeably, having the firmest grounds of confidence in one another, enjoying the advantages of friendship in all their fullness, and not lamenting, as a pitiable circumstance, the premature death of their friends." "We choose our friends because of the pleasure they afford us, but we are willing to undergo much suffering for them." Thus they recognized, as did Aristotle, that the solitary life is no life for a man who aims to lead a happy life. It should be noted that the importance given to the Epicurean community united by friendship while devoted to the teachings of the founder replaces the older Hellenic devotion to the city-state, which is so central in the political and ethical thought of Plato and Aristotle. This is obvious in their attitudes toward the state. While

Aristotle taught that man is a political animal who finds his fulfillment only in the organized life of the city-state, Epicurus revived the old distinction (of the Sophists) between the "natural" and the "conventional" and urged the conventional view that political societies are merely utilitarian institutions created by the agreement of men to avoid the inconvenience of mutual aggression. The circumstances of the Hellenistic age reinforced Epicurus' normal tendency to urge his followers to withdraw from the entanglements of political and family responsibilities on the grounds that they were destructive of *ataraxia*. Obviously the Epicurean who needed to enter politics to safeguard his personal interests or who had vigorous motivations toward a political career which could not be frustrated without destroying his *ataraxia* could always establish his own justification within the framework of orthodox principles. The Epicureans recognized that they could achieve more pleasure and less pain in a society where law prevailed and rights were acknowledged than in a society controlled by an unpredictable tyrant. Their pessimism about the immediate political prospects together with their normal quietism and devotion to their individual interests and those of their friends made it appear prudent not to risk political involvement. Our own age, in which Epicurean attitudes are more widespread than often admitted, might well temper its tendency to render a hasty judgment of "irresponsible, selfish parasites" on the Epicurean garden community. A more considered judgment might point to elements in the garden community which could be interpreted as ancient Greek anticipations of the monastic orders, the early Christian community, or even contemporary suburbia.

The Epicurean school survived until the fourth century A.D. During the lifetime of Epicurus and his colleagues, Metrodorus, Hermachus, and Colotes, their main competitors and critics were the Platonists and the Peripatetics. During the last two centuries B.C. the Stoics became their chief rivals and opponents. Despite certain similarities and agreements their intellectual relations were often filled with bitterness. During this period the more prominent Epicureans were Appollodorus, Zenon of Sidon, who taught Cicero, and his pupil, Philodemus of Gadara, of whose works some fragments have been recovered. At the death of Cicero in 43 B.C. the period of acrimonious controversy with the Stoics ended, and at the turn of the century we find the process of syncretism well under way. This is most evident in the work of Stoics like Seneca, Musonius Rufus, Epictetus, and Marcus Aurelius. The most prominent Epicurean figure in Rome was of course Lucretius. We do know that the two great figures of Augustan literature, Virgil and Horace, were both influenced by Epicureanism, especially in their early years. Epicureanism suffered a great decline at Rome in the years following the extinction of the Republic, for it was out of keeping with the spirit of the age and with the program of moral and religious revival that Augustus was sponsoring. Of course, before the year 200 A.D., Christianity had emerged as the chief and last rival of Epicureanism. By the end of the fifth century A.D. the school seems to have been absorbed into the Christian community.

Historically Epicureanism has presented itself in ambivalent terms and provoked corresponding reactions. When the reactions have been favorable they have been due to its ethical creed of austere or very restrained hedonism, based on love or friendship and the kindly social virtues that promote peace of mind, tolerance, and high-minded companionship. When the reactions have been hostile, as in the case of Platonists, Stoics, and Christians, the basic causes have been the theology of Epicurus and the baseless slanders maliciously spread about life in the Garden. Epicureanism played down the acquisitive, aggressive, and domineering motives and provided a sanctuary for men seeking to subject such motives to sustained discipline. Thus it was that a philosophy of retirement from a weary world of social and political confusion may be characterized as escapist, negative, and yet therapeutic. In its defensive strategy it was profoundly individualistic, sensing that friendship was therapeutic as well as constitutive of value. It made a real contribution in stressing the readily available reservoir of simple and inexpensive goods which anyone can appropriate for the good life and in emphasizing the need to eliminate or redirect certain desires that are unrealistic or unproductive in the achievement of pleasure. Despite its strong tendency to withdraw from life it still maintained a vital sense of mission to alleviate human unhappiness rooted in neurotic fears. After one has catalogued and weighed all the negative criticisms which may properly be made of Epicureanism it still appears evident that Epicureanism remains relevant to the predicament of some men in every age and of many men in particular ages of confusion, fear, frustration, and defeat.

Epicurus: Suggested Additional Reading

Abernethy, George L. and Thomas A. Langford, eds., *History of Philosophy: Selected Readings*. Belmont, Calif.: Dickenson, 1965, pp. 183–199.*

Bailey, C., *Epicurus: The Extant Remains*, with short critical apparatus, translations, and notes. Oxford: Clarendon Press, 1926.*

DeWitt, N. W., *Epicurus and His Philosophy*. New York: World Publishing Company, Meridian, 1967.

Epicurus, *Letters, Principal Doctrines and Vatican Sayings*. Edited by Russell M. Geer. Indianapolis: Bobbs-Merrill, Liberal Arts Press, 1964.

Festugiere, A. J., *Epicurus and His Gods*. Translated by C. W. Chilton. Harvard University Press, 1956.*

Festugiere, A. J., *Personal Religion Among the Greeks*. Berkeley: University of California, 1954.

Hadzsits, G. D., *Lucretius and Epicureanism*. Boston: Marshall Jones, 1926.*

Hicks, G. D., *Diogenes Laertius: Lives of Eminent Philosophers*. New York: G. P. Putnam's Sons, 1925 (Loeb Classical Library).*

Hicks, R. D., *Stoic and Epicurean*. New York: Scribner, 1910.*

Kaufmann, Walter, *Philosophical Classics*. Englewood Cliffs, N.J.: Prentice-Hall, 1961, I, 533–552.*

Murray, Gilbert, *Five Stages of Greek Religion*. New York: Doubleday, Anchor, 1955.

Oates, W. J., ed., *The Stoic and Epicurean Philosophers*. Complete extant writings of Epicurus, Epictetus, Lucretius, Marcus Aurelius. New York: Random House, 1940.*

Pater, Walter, *Marius the Epicurean*. New York: Macmillan, 1909.*

Strodach, George K., *The Philosophy of Epicurus*. Evanston: Northwestern University Press, 1963.*

Wallace, William, *Epicureanism*. London: Society for the Publication of Christian Knowledge, 1880.*

Zeller, Eduard, *Stoics, Epicureans and Skeptics*. Translated by O. J. Reichel. New York: Russell and Russell, revised edition, 1962.*

Chapter Six

Hellenistic Philosophy:
The Stoics of Greece
and Rome

S toicism was the first really Hellenistic philosophy. In many
ways it was an impressive achievement. As a recognized school
with varying emphases in its tradition, the Stoa had a continuous existence of six centuries, from the beginning of the
Hellenistic age, *c.* 300 B.C., to the declining Roman Empire in 300 A.D.
It made an impact on Roman law and the constitution of the Roman
Empire, as well as on certain aspects of Christianity. The term "stoic"
has entered our common speech and today bears connotations not
altogether unrelated to its historical origin.

In the beginning Stoicism was a response to the radically new world
situation which had come into existence following the extensive
conquests which Alexander the Great made in his eastward sweep.
In the fifth and fourth centuries influences were at work loosening
the tightly knit fabric of the independent, self-contained Greek city-
states. But Alexander's conquests produced a profound change in the
thinking and attitudes of the educated élite. The expansion of geographical and political boundaries destroyed much of the individual's
sense of insulation and security and the feeling of being able to direct
with confidence the religious, moral, and social details of one's daily
life. Walls were down and familiar landmarks were disappearing, so
that many felt rootless and uncertain as little men in a strange and
overwhelming environment. Men today can appreciate the motivations and social stresses which impelled many Hellenistic people to
seek a way of life which would produce peace of mind, confidence,
and stability in the face of large-scale change and the certainty of
death.

Although Stoicism made its first appearance in Athens, it was not
basically Athenian. Stoicism utilized many ideas from various Greek
philosophers, yet its leadership from the very beginning was cosmopolitan and largely non-Hellenic. Its Greek representatives were
drawn chiefly from the colonies rather than from Athens. The Stoic
leadership came from practically every country in the ancient Mediterranean world and spread its influence over a wide area. When the

school declined in Athens it came into great influence and power in imperial Rome.

The Stoics acknowledged that they derived a great deal of their characteristic outlook from a striking group of ascetics called Cynics who, finding the complexities of civilization irksome and artificial, led an unconventional "back to nature" movement. Antisthenes and Diogenes, the most famous of the Cynics, attempted to cut down the necessities of life to the barest minimum and to lead the life of wandering beggars "living upon the alms of people too industrious to be saints." Complete poverty and detachment from all worldly ties produced the kind of tranquility and indifference so highly prized in the famous anecdote relating the encounter of young Alexander the Great with Diogenes, then some seventy years of age. One day, as the old Cynic teacher lay sunning himself in a tub at Corinth, Alexander and his retinue drew rein in front of the tub. The young man announced: "I am Alexander the great King." "And I am Diogenes the dog," replied the old man with typical indifference. "Are you not afraid of me?" asked Alexander. "Why, what are you, something good or something evil?" "Something good, of course." "Well," retorted Diogenes, "who would be so foolish as to fear anything good?" Filled with admiration of this answer, Alexander exclaimed, "Ask of me anything you wish, and I will grant it." "Then be so kind," said Diogenes, "as to get out of my sunlight." Struck by the refreshing honesty in Diogenes' lack of deference, the young ruler observed wistfully, " If I were not Alexander, I would be Diogenes." History does not record that the philosopher returned the compliment.

The sincere Cynic, in contrast to the charlatan, felt a deep sense of mission to destroy false standards by ferocious criticism, to dispel the illusions of mankind, and to teach by dramatic example the way of truth and virtue. In so doing he carried freedom of speech to great lengths and used unconventional behavior as a shock technique. We are told that Diogenes performed the duties of nature and the rites of love in the sight of all. Once he was found begging alms from a statue in order to get practice in being refused. The Cynics' cosmopolitanism, extreme individualism, asceticism, and devotion to a wandering life of popular moral teaching and criticism did point to values which had enduring worth and which the Stoics sought to preserve and advance in more rational ways while assuming individual and social responsibilities.

The founder of Stoicism was Zeno (c. 350 – c. 258 B.C.) of Citium, not to be confused with the earlier Zeno the Eleatic. His native city was a Greek settlement in Cyprus partly settled by Phoenicians. Probably he was of mixed Hellenic and Semitic parentage. According to Diogenes

Laertius ("Life of Zeno"[1]) at the age of twenty-two, while sailing
for Athens with a cargo of Tyrian purple, Zeno was shipwrecked on the
Attic Coast. Arriving in Athens he dried out his clothes and empty
wallet while reading the second book of Xenophon's *Memorabilia*
of Socrates in front of a bookseller's shop. Fascinated by the character
of Socrates, he asked: "Where are such men to be found today?"
At that moment Crates the Cynic philosopher passed by and the bookseller said: "Follow that man." He enrolled in Crates' school and
rejoiced in his discovery of philosophy: "I made a prosperous voyage
when I was shipwrecked." Although he was impressed by the stern
simplicity of his Cynic teacher, Zeno found the philosophy too thin
intellectually and too narrow and unconventional in its social relevance.
For a time he studied under a more moderate Cynic Stilpo the Megarian,
and under Xenocrates and Polemo at the Academy founded by Plato.
After twenty years of preparation he finally opened his own school
where he talked informally to his disciples as he walked to and fro
under the colonnades of the beautiful *stoa poikile* or painted porch with
paintings by Polynotus. In this way the school received its traditional
name Stoic, or the Philosophy of the Porch. Zeno taught a rule of
life based on a rational doctrine about the universe and man's knowledge
of it which drew disciples from many lands. Unfortunately we have to
rely on fragments and secondary sources for the reconstruction of
what Zeno and other early Stoics actually taught. The only complete
works which survive are those by later Stoics—for example, Seneca,
Epictetus, and Marcus Aurelius in the first and second centuries A.D.
The accounts differ as to whether Zeno died at the age of seventy-two
or ninety. But he lived such an exemplary life that the phrase "more
temperate than Zeno" became a proverb in Greece. The Athenians
honored him with a golden chaplet, a tomb built at public expense,
and a monument of brass.

Cleanthes, a former pugilist, next headed the school for approximately thirty years, but he apparently lacked administrative skill and
philosophical ability, and the school declined in vigor. He is best
known as the author of the celebrated "*Hymn to Zeus*"[2] and for
instilling religious fervor into Stoicism. He was succeeded by Chrysip-
pus of Soli or Tarsus in Cilicia (282–209 B.C.), who became a sort of
second founder of Stoicism by formulating the definitive system in an
extensive series of works which has been lost. Subsequently, the
Stoics of a transitional period known as the Middle Stoa became in-

---

[1] "Life of Zeno" reprinted in M. Hadas, *Essential Works of Stoicism* (New York: Bantam, 1961), pp. 1–48.

[2] See Hadas, *op. cit.*, pp. 51–52.

volved in technical controversies with other schools and with Stoics exhibiting skeptical tendencies. The Stoic doctrine was carried abroad by teachers in Asia Minor, particularly to Tarsus in Cilicia (where St. Paul in his early education undoubtedly encountered it), the island of Rhodes, and Alexandria. About the middle of the second century B.C., Panaetius (185–109 B.C.) of Rhodes brought the Stoic teaching to Rome and toned down its harsher elements. The later Stoics— Seneca, Epictetus, and Marcus Aurelius—proved to be the most influential spokesman for the Stoic witness.

The Stoics divided philosophy into three major divisions: Logic (including theory of knowledge and rhetoric), Physics (including theology and psychology), and Ethics. The Stoics made logic an integral part of philosophy. It included within its scope definitions, syllogisms, paradoxes, etymology, grammar, dialectic, and rhetoric. In the scientific study of grammar they made significant advances, and moved beyond many of Aristotle's successors in formal logic. They formulated the theory of hypothetical and disjunctive syllogisms and discovered the logical relation which in contemporary logic is called material implication. The overwhelming dominance of Aristotelian logic prevented the Stoic suggestions from being followed up and developed.

To understand the Stoic theory of knowledge one must remember that the Stoics were and always remained materialists. For them, all reality was material, both mind and matter. They reasoned that only matter can move or be moved. Yet there was a significant distinction between an active force and passive matter. The active force was *logos*, divine reason, the all-pervading principle of the universe. Since only bodies had a real substantial existence, God and the soul were bodies. The Stoic theory of knowledge thus was concerned with describing how one body, the soul (a subtle, fiery part of the pervasive Divine Principle), is affected by other bodies, the things we ordinarily know. The Stoics, in contrast to the followers of Plato, believed that the knowledge of truth is valid only when firmly rooted in sense "impressions." By an "impression" they meant any image, perceptual or otherwise, produced in the mind by an external object—thus an impression made on the soul. The wise man, or Stoic sage, could escape perceptual errors and illusions by withholding his assent from impressions whose significance is unclear or uncertain. An accurate representation of a real object is so vivid that it figuratively grabs one by the hair and compels his assent. Circumstances may compel a wise man to act where his knowledge is inadequate, but he is not to be blamed so long as he does not give his full assent to the impression. This is made clear in an anecdote related about Sphaerus, a disciple of Zeno, to whom King Ptolemy at a banquet served a pomegranate made of wax. When the Stoic put the fruit to his mouth and realized that he was the victim of a practical joke, Ptolemy accused him of having given his assent to a false impression. His Stoic guest protested that he had assented not to the reality of the pomegranate but only to the probability of its being real. Faithful to the Stoic standard of conduct he had acted appropriately in the circumstances, but without giving his full assent.

The crux of the Stoic epistemology lies in the distinction between true, accurate images and those which are erroneous or unclear. In the Hellenistic age there was a great deal of skepticism about the possibility of having any real knowledge of things. As against this skepticism, the Stoics were dogmatists; they vigorously asserted the existence of truth that is available to man, basing their dogmatism on the distinction between true and false images. After the wise man has given his assent to true representations, his mind produces concepts or notions. Most of these become clear enough through the ordinary means of education. Others, called common notions, are produced by the mind spontaneously and are found naturally in every reasonable being. They form the basis, next to true images, of all that we know. Any true theory is reducible to common notions.

All of this Zeno "illustrated with a piece of action. When he stretched out his fingers and showed the palm of his hand, 'Perception,' said he, 'is a thing like this'. Then, when he had a little closed his fingers, 'Assent is like this'. Afterwards, when he had completely closed his hand and held forth his fist, that, he said was comprehension. . . . But, when he brought his left hand against his right, and with it took a firm and tight hold of his fist, he said that knowledge was of that character, and that was what none but a wise man possessed" (Cicero, *Academics*, II, xlvii).

Under the heading of physics were included all of the problems of metaphysics, physics in the modern sense, astronomy, anthropology, psychology, and religion. The Stoics placed everything except Logic and Ethics within the scope of physics. The Stoic interpretation of man and the universe shows the influence of Heraclitus, Pythagoreanism, Platonic dialectic, and Aristotelian metaphysics. But the blending and tension which held together these diverse influences were peculiarly Stoic in their motivations and emphases. It was not a disinterested search primarily for the sake of knowledge and understanding. It was a search for a way of life to provide guidance and devotion and to give expression to natural piety. Consequently, systematic consistency was not held to be the chief value.

As we have already noted the Stoics pictured the world in material terms. Nature is a system of bodies and corporeal processes. They taught that not only all substances, including soul and deity, are corporeal but that all qualities of things also consist of something corporeal, of air currents which are diffused throughout them and provide them with the tension that holds them together. Thus, virtues, emotions, wisdom, walking, and talking, as states of the soul, are also considered to be bodies and living things. In the effort to explain how the soul is spread through the body and the qualities of things throughout things, the Stoics had to reject the notion of the impermeability of bodies. They maintained instead that one body could completely permeate another without becoming identical with it. They criticized the Epicurean failure to recognize qualitative levels of matter and real change in the corporeal world. They insisted on distinguishing between matter and the forces which work on it. Strictly speaking, matter by itself is without qualities. All qualities or things are derived from the rational force which permeates it. They called it, as Heraclitus called it, the *Logos*. But it has many names and aspects. It may be designated as mind, life, steersman, or creative fire. However, it is necessary to regard the *Logos* also as that which furnishes material for the created universe; this material they referred to as *pneuma*, breath. Thus rational, creative energy continually shapes a material aspect of itself. Wind or breath is perpetually ordered by fire, and the term '*Logos*' covers these meanings as it does providence, fate, nature, and universal law.

To form the world, God first transformed a part of the fiery vapor of which he consists into air, and then into water in which He was immanent as the formative force. He then precipitated a portion of the water into earth while another part was transformed into air, which after rarefaction became the elementary fire. In this fashion the body of the world was formed as distinguished from its soul, the Deity. But even this opposition will disappear in the course of time. The Stoics taught the doctrine of universal conflagration which will return all things to a huge mass of fiery vapor from which God will at some preordained time emit it in what is an endless series of world-constructions and world-destructions. Since an eternal necessity determines all events, the same persons, things, and events repeat their existences down to the smallest detail in this succession of worlds. This notion invites comparison with Nietzsche's theory of "eternal recurrence" as developed in the nineteenth century. By identifying God with cosmic fire the Stoics reaffirmed their cosmological monism. God thus is held to be most subtle and the purest of matter. Our own reason is a flaming spark of the divine fire in our bodies.

We have noted that Stoic cosmology involved universal determinism. Consistent with this is the view (which Spinoza was to develop in the seventeenth century) that human freedom consists in doing consciously and with assent what one will in any case do necessarily. But this necessity in man and nature is not interpreted as the blind necessity of mechanics. Rather it is presented as an aspect of Fate and Providence, different aspects of God, something like an immanent teleology in which everything is directed or ordered rationally, wisely and for the best. But the Stoics insist on the freedom of the inner man, who can change his evaluations and attitudes so that he can greet determined events as the expression of God's will. In the twentieth century many men, like the ancient Stoics, seek to hold together, despite tension, universal determinism, teleology, denial of chance, and the affirmation of personal responsibility and freedom. They do not seem to be any more successful than the Stoics in finding an adequate or completely satisfying explanation of the problem of evil. The most conspicuous difference in contemporary accounts would be the larger roles which pessimism and irrationality seem to play.

Since our reason is a flaming spark of the divine fire in our body, the object of a man's life must be to live in complete harmony with this reason which is a part of Divine Reason. In a universe which is completely determined man will be compelled to obey the decrees of Divine Reason or Fate. Since the inner man is free, he will have the choice of obeying willingly or unwillingly.

What is the good life for the Stoic? In theory at least the Stoics seem to have accepted the position that no acts are bad in themselves. Wealth, power, or health are neither good nor bad. Ultimately only virtue is good, only vice is bad. Since rational action and virtue are one and the same thing, we may say that rational behavior is good while irrational behavior is bad. The passions, emotions, and desires are not just inferior activities to be guided and controlled by reason. They are really "irrational reason"—wrong judgments about what is good and bad for us. Hence they are to be completely eradicated. *Pathos* is a collective term used by the Stoics to indicate everything in man that is irrational. The Stoic ideal is *Apatheia* (which corresponds to Epicurus' *ataraxia*), which is not to be understood as apathy in the ordinary sense of the term in our language, but as a form of self-discipline which secures one against *pathos*. *Apatheia* is impassivity in the positive and energetic sense of leading the life of rational self-discipline. I cannot control the external circumstances of my life, but through *Apatheia* I can confront pain, misfortune, and death with freedom from the passions, emotions, and affections which would pervert my reason. For the early Stoics the Stoic sage was a grim, determined, and heroic figure. Consequently, the difference between the life of wisdom and the life of folly is absolute. Perfection or nothing. If you sin in one point, you sin in them all. If you miss the mark, it makes no difference whether you miss by an inch or a mile.

As time went on the Stoics began to distinguish between the wise man or the fool and the man who is on his way to wisdom through a process of learning. There is a corresponding blurring of the rigorous division between what is good or bad and what is simply indifferent. The category of the indifferent or neutral is subdivided into those things which are desirable and can be advanced and those which are undesirable and not to be promoted. Although health is not strictly a good thing and is therefore indifferent, a Stoic might prefer health to sickness and seek to maintain it without feeling that he had compromised his philosophy. Life and death, however, were among the things classified as absolutely indifferent. This led the Stoics to adopt a permissive attitude toward suicide which distinguished the Stoic morality from the Platonic. When the Stoic sage found that the proportion of undesirable external circumstances surrounding his life was permanently in excess of the desirable external circumstances he was free to leave this life by committing suicide without incurring any moral stigma. In dealing with the question of how death was to be faced the wise man could appeal to the familiar distinction in Stoic ethics between the things that lie within our power and the things that do not. We have no control over what our impressions of external circumstances will be; we control only the uses to which we shall put them. If the emperor condemns a man to death, the victim cannot control his impressions of the sentence, of his confinement, torture, and execution. But because of inner freedom he can decide to acknowledge it to be part of God's universal perfection providentially allotted to him, so that he can willingly greet it with fortitude and composure.

"What aid then should we have ready at hand in circumstances such as these? Why, what else but the knowledge of what is mine and what is not mine, of what is permitted me and what is not? I must die: very well, but must I die groaning? Be fettered: shall it be lamenting? Go into exile: does anyone prevent me from going with a smile, cheerful and serene? Betray the secret! No, I will not, for this is something within my own power. Then I will fetter you. What's that you say? Fetter me? You will fetter my leg, but not even Zeus can overcome my power of choice. I will throw you into prison; I will behead that paltry body of yours. Well, when did I ever tell you that mine was the only neck that could not be severed?— Let philosophers study such responses as these, let them write them down daily, and practice them" (*Discourses of Epictetus*, Bk. I, Ch. 1).

Living in accordance with reason means that the Stoic will acknowledge that all circumstances, even disease and death, as integral parts
of universal perfection, are good and thus to be faced with *apatheia*.
Although every part of the universe is rational, man is rational in a
special way, for he has the ability to make use of reason in his own
person—even to elaborate the doctrines of Stoicism. The good life
then depends on the active working of the reason, so we note again
that the emotions must be eradicated lest they choke out the activity
of reason. Even pity is an evil which must be replaced by rational
benevolence in which the Stoic sage does his duties without desire.
Even when doing one's duties proves ineffectual or leads to unintended
consequences the wise man feels no regret. If he has responded to circumstances in accordance with reason it is a matter of indifference to
him what actually ensues. Here again the Cynic heritage of Stoicism
shines through.

Stoicism had another heritage—the heritage of cosmopolitanism.
They referred to themselves as "cosmopolitans," for the Cosmos was
their *polis*, and their environment was coextensive with the world they
knew. It broke through all political, racial, and religious boundaries,
and ignored all distinctions of class and birth. It stressed that all men
were specific vehicles of the same divine rational principle before which
accidental differences or peculiarities are insignificant. As monists they
believed that what we have in common is more important than what
separates us. For them, the universe was the great City of God, a
realm of moral individuals ruled by divine justice. Unlike the Platonists,
the Stoics were not transcendentalists. Their City of God was the
actual material universe omnipresent, but discernible only through
reason. The wise man was a citizen, not of a particular temporal state,
but of the world. Even when the duties of the Stoic emperor Marcus
Aurelius required him to take an active role in the political life of his
age, he still looked upon himself primarily as a citizen of the world.
Thus his basic moral allegiance was given not to Rome, but to all of
mankind without discrimination. As emperor, and because of the
specific circumstances of his career, Aurelius had special duties to
advance the peculiar interests of Rome, but never would his judgment
assent to the unqualified rightness of those particular interests. While
performing all the duties of the station to which God had assigned him,
he was rational enough to acknowledge that the outcome of one's
acts must be left to God. The individual in Stoic ethics is primarily
responsible for his own integrity and the use of his rationality. Only
when man lives in accordance with nature can this responsibility be
properly discharged.

Our general review of Stoic teaching has tended to minimize the many differences among individual thinkers. To somewhat redress this imbalance we now briefly consider three later Stoic writers whose complete written works are extant—Seneca, the wealthy tutor and minister of Nero, Epictetus, the freed slave and cripple, and Emperor Marcus Aurelius.

Seneca (*c.* 3 B.C. to 65 A.D.) was a Spaniard, the son of a rhetorician living in Rome. He followed a political career with some success, becoming first the tutor of, and then a minister under, Nero. Although theoretically indifferent, Seneca amassed a huge fortune—according to some estimates about twelve million dollars. He preached nonattachment in this fashion:

"All these fortuitous things, Marcia, that glitter about us,—children, position, wealth, spacious halls and vestibules, packed with a throng of unadmitted dependents, a high reputation, a well-born or beautiful wife, and all else that depends upon uncertain and fickle chance—these are not our own but borrowed trappings; not one of them is given to us outright. The properties that adorn life's stages have been lent, and must go back to their owners; some of them will be returned on the first day, others on the second, only a few will endure until the end" (Seneca, *To Marcia On Consolation*, 10).

Seneca justified his great wealth on the ground that it happened to come his way, and that he, being a philosopher, could use it with more wisdom than others. Other Stoic philosophers were more firmly committed to *apatheia* than this. As one can easily imagine, Seneca lacked the interests of a reformer and undoubtedly in his political career acquiesced in abuses and even bowed before power sometimes associated with tyranny. As Nero's excesses mounted, Seneca gradually fell out of favor at court until he was accused, possibly with justice, of complicity in an extensive conspiracy to murder Nero in favor of a new emperor. In view of his long service to the regime he was permitted to commit suicide. When informed that he had no time to prepare a will he is reported to have said: "Never mind, I leave you what is of far more value than earthly riches, the example of a virtuous life." He then opened his veins and summoned his secretaries to take down his dying eloquence.

Seneca emphasized the practical side of philosophy; in ethics he wrote exhortations to virtue rather than inquiries into its nature. He resembled the Cynics in his negative attitude toward speculative studies and more systematic doctrine. Whenever he showed an interest in physical theories or philosophy it was always for some utilitarian end.

Seneca preached the official Stoic materialism, but in practice he had a tendency to regard God as transcending matter. At times he spoke of a conflict between soul and body in dualistic and Platonic terms. Sometimes he was accused of softening the harsher aspects of Stoicism because of his involvement in court life, where luxury and even debauchery prevailed. Some have seen hypocrisy and inconsistency in his situation. Others have defended him on the ground that his preaching of detachment came out of a profound realization of the emptiness of wealth, power, position, and degradation. Others have suggested that boredom with luxury led some of the wealthy to find Seneca's presentation of the simple life a welcome change and challenge to self-discipline.

Seneca lived a life of uneasy compromise. His announced desire to prove his virtue did not avail itself of many opportunities under Nero. He tempered the strict moral ideals of earlier Stoics to fit the needs of those who were only partially converted to the Stoic doctrines. He gave practical advice to those who were interested in moral progress rather than martyrdom or nonattachment. He did stress the need of active benevolence in dealing with one's fellows. Yet he did not like his fellowmen in the mass. He reported that there were as many vices as there were men and that society has some of the aspects of a concourse of wild beasts. His advice to Lucilius was to avoid crowds and to mix only with those likely to make him better or to be made better by him. Perhaps his sensitivity, wealth, ingenuity, and refinement did not prepare him too well for the role of Stoic moral teacher. Something of the atmosphere of a decadent society and something of the stance of a court chaplain attach themselves to his role, so that our image of the Stoic sage becomes blurred.

Epictetus (c. 60– c. 138 A.D.) was an entirely different type of man. He was a native of Hieropolis (in Phrygia) who was a slave of Epaphroditus, a member of the bodyguard of Emperor Nero. Later he was set free, became a disciple of the Stoic Musonius Rufus, and finally a teacher of philosophy at Rome, where he taught until Emperor Domitian expelled all of the philosophers in 89 or 93 A.D. He next founded a school in Nicopolis in Epirus where he probably taught until his death. A typical characterization of Epictetus as a young man is related in an anecdote by Origen. Once when his master was angrily twisting his leg, Epictetus warned: "You will break my leg," whereupon the master twisted harder and broke the leg. To this Epictetus calmly replied, "Did I not tell you so?" Apparently from his experience as a slave he learned a combination of independence and submission which stood him in good stead whenever his philosophy was put to the test.

For Epictetus what is fundamental is the traditional Stoic distinction between what is under our control and what is not. We must control our attitudes toward events to the best of our ability; the events themselves are a matter of indifference. When man is freed from attachments and is secure in the rational knowledge of what is his own, he is prepared to meet death, exile, and imprisonment with a cheerful demeanor. The free man then is the man subject to no restraints, and in order to be free from restraints one must be ready to abandon all that can be affected by the actions of others. Epictetus preaches a more rigorous doctrine of nonattachment than Seneca when he writes: "Stop admiring your clothes, and you are not angry with the man who steals them; stop admiring your wife's beauty and you are not angry at her adulterer. Realize that a thief or an adulterer has no place among the things you own, but only among the things that are another's and not under your control." (*Arriah's Discourse of Epictetus*. I, XVIII, 11–12.) Virtue is a condition of the will wherein it is governed by reason, with the result that the virtuous person seeks only those things which are within his power and avoids those which are not. Morally, he is a self-sufficient person.

Although Epictetus was among the philosophers expelled by Domitian, he decided that it was his responsibility not to change the circumstances of society, but to provide what the statesman cannot offer—peace of mind and tranquility of spirit. "See," he says, "Caesar provides us with profound peace; there are no wars any longer, no battles, no large scale brigandage or piracy; at any hour we may travel by land or sail from the rising to the setting of the sun. But can he give us peace from fever or shipwreck, fire, earthquake, lightning? Can he give us peace from love, sorrow, envy? No, from none of these things. It is for philosophical teaching to give men peace from these" (*ibid.*, III, XIII, 9–11). In this view the preservation of peace and security solves the political problem, but there remains the moral problem of achieving a mind at peace with itself and in harmony with nature. This is the real problem of freedom and morality. Thus it is not external goods that make a man free, but the knowledge of the right way of living. Epictetus, or any Stoic of his type, would endure any sort of external evil that befell his lot—persecution, exile, imprisonment, or execution, but like Socrates whom he reveres he would decline to do wrong willingly. Thus the wise man's resistance would be passive. Epictetus' teaching and example underline the point that the Stoics might be martyrs or rational mystics, but they were not made of the stuff we find in revolutionaries or architects of a new social order. They reveal the acquiescence or resignation which is more appropriate to a static or declining society rather than to a progressive or expanding society. It would seem that Domitian was unduly nervous in banishing Epictetus from Rome.

Although he encourages patriotism and participation in public life, Epictetus urges a cosmopolitanism which transcends narrow patriotism and teaches, like the Christians who admired him, that we should love our enemies. "Will you not remember who you are and whom you rule? that they are kinsmen, that they are brethren by nature, that they are the offspring of Zeus?" (*ibid.*, I, XIII, 4). We are not to return evil for evil.

Unlike Seneca and other Stoics, Epictetus addresses his message to the common man rather than to the élite. His insistence on brotherhood and equality marks a considerable advance over Plato and Aristotle. The humanity, dignity, nobility, and relevance of his teaching sparkle and crackle in the *Manual* or *Enchiridion* and the four surviving books we have from the almost stenographic notes of his pupil Arrian. Succeeding generations of men living in troubled times and circumstances have found these teachings helpful both as consolation and inspiration. They make the peace of mind literature in our day appear, by contrast, cheap and synthetic.

Marcus Aurelius (121–180 A.D.), the Stoic emperor, wrote twelve books of meditations or self-examination in Greek entitled "To Himself." These are partly leaves from his diary in the field on military campaigns, written in aphoristic form. They reveal a profound, sensitive, scrupulous, admirable, and introspective man. He has a great admiration for Epictetus whom he follows in eschewing speculative theories for practical moral teaching and in stressing the wisdom of Divine Providence. He is more eclectic than Epictetus and reveals more directly the influence of his reading of Plato, as when he modifies the strict Stoic materialism in the direction of dualism. Yet he does not share the typical Platonic belief in immortality; he enunciates a more typical Stoic tradition in saying: "Since it is possible that thou mayst depart from life this very moment, regulate every act and thought accordingly." He allows only the possibility of the soul's reabsorption into the cosmic Reason.

Despite the burdens and responsibilities which he faithfully discharged as emperor, Marcus Aurelius did not appear to have his heart in his work. He paid his proper respects to his life at court, but his real devotion he gave to Mother Philosophy. "Go to her often and refresh yourself with her, and she will make court seem tolerable to you and you tolerable in it" (*The Thoughts of Marcus Aurelius Antoninus*, VI, 12). He gave his human allegiance not to

Rome but to the great society of the universe which included all rational beings. "I am by nature a reasonable and social creature; my city and fatherland as Antoninus is Rome, as a human being it is the universe" (*ibid.*, VI, 44).

Marcus Aurelius makes it plain that a man violates his soul whenever he "turns away from any human being or is borne against him with intent to injure him" (*ibid.*, II 16, cf. II, I. V, 33). Since he was human, and since Stoicism was not a gospel of love, this must have been a very difficult precept for him to live up to. He tells us the men he encountered were "inquisitive, ungrateful, violent, treacherous, envious, uncharitable." He often dwells on the consolation death will bring in freeing him from the company of such men. "You should not be offended with them but care for them, bear them gently; yet they are not likeminded with you and death will bring a release from such" (*ibid.*, V, 10. II, 1. IX, 3).

Marcus Aurelius, like Epictetus, preaches continually the nothingness and futility of all earthly possessions and goods. There emerges from all this a profound sense of austerity and weariness, as though the goal one was seeking had imperceptibly changed its positive character to something negative.

Marcus Aurelius was the last great Roman Stoic. After his death the philosophy of Stoicism, which had for so long a compelling interest for the Roman mind, rapidly diminished in stature and influence. Perhaps the key to understanding the long influence of Stoicism is the fact that it produced a long line of dedicated teachers whose "living word" or example impressed people as much or more than their written words. When the supply of such teachers ended Stoicism became an historical phenomenon, the memory of which was preserved by rhetoricians and historians.

Stoicism had an enormous practical influence on Roman life, the like of which Platonism and Aristotelianism had never known. The Greek Stoics were mainly men devoted to the intellectual or academic life as such. But the Roman Stoics were for the most part men participating actively in public life and often bearing heavy government responsibilities. Whatever may have been the theoretical shortcomings and inconsistencies of Stoicism, there is no question about its relevance to the practical moral, religious, and social needs of many thoughtful and responsible Romans. It gave them fortitude, consolation, and dignity. Still its main appeal was, despite Epictetus, to the élite rather than to the common man. It demanded more self-control and self-cultivation than most men were interested in attempting to achieve. Stoicism developed no congregations, no basic myth, no cultus, and no rewards other than the satisfaction of having done one's duty. It lacked anything corresponding to Christian revelation and grace. Interestingly, Stoicism had influence, at many points, on Christianity. The Apostle Paul's early life was spent in an area of deep Stoic penetration. Epictetus was read and appreciated by many Christians. The Church Fathers often studied points of agreement found in Stoic teachings and quoted and evaluated them on occasion. These connections were so real and so appreciated that there developed legends concerning a correspondence supposedly carried on between Seneca and St. Paul.

The Stoic contribution to Roman jurisprudence is frequently noted. A number of Roman jurists such as Gaius, Ulpian, and Marcian introduced postulates of the Stoic natural law into their presentation of justice. Ulpian declared for example that "all men, according to natural right, are born free and equal." This echoes the words of Zeno, the first Stoic, who five centuries earlier had asserted: "All men are by nature equal; virtue alone establishes a difference between them." The Stoic jurists hammered out the distinction between natural law (*jus naturale*) and the law of nations (*jus gentium*). At times it was held that the law of nations coincided with natural law; at other times the law of nations was held to be only an approximation of natural law. Slavery was recognized as lawful among the nations but at the same time contrary to natural law. The doctrine of natural right as it came to be known in modern times was a revival of the Stoic doctrine adapted to different conditions. In the seventeenth century these Stoic notions linked with certain other notions were to emerge in a dramatic fashion in the Puritan Revolution in England to provide a seed bed for American political and social thinking which still has relevance in our own day. The relevance of certain Stoic philosophical positions subsequently appeared in the thought of such philosophers as Spinoza, Kant, and Leibniz.

The Stoics of Greece and Rome: Suggested Additional Reading

Abernethy, George L. and Thomas A. Langford, eds., *History of Philosophy: Selected Readings*. Belmont, Calif.: Dickenson, 1965, pp. 195–223.*

Arnold, E. V., *Roman Stoicism*. Cambridge: Cambridge University Press, 1911.*

Aurelius, Marcus, *Meditations* (with Epictetus' *Enchiridion*). Chicago: Henry Regnery, Gateway, 1956.

Aurelius, Marcus, *The Meditations of Marcus Aurelius*. Translated by George Long. New York: Doubleday, Dolphin, 1963.

Bevan, E. R., *Stoics and Skeptics*. Oxford: Clarendon Press, 1913.*

Epictetus, *Enchiridion*. Translated by T. W. Higginson. Indianapolis: Bobbs-Merrill, Liberal Arts Press, 1958.

Hadas, M., ed., *Stoic Philosophy of Seneca*. New York: Norton, 1968.

Hadas, M., ed., *Essential Works of Stoicism*. New York: Bantam, 1961.

Hicks, R. D., *Stoic and Epicurean*. New York: Scribner, 1910.*

Kaufmann, Walter, *Philosophical Classics*. Englewood Cliffs, N.J.: Prentice-Hall, 1961, I, 553–569.*

Mates, Benson, *Stoic Logic*. Berkeley: University of California, 1961.

More, P. E., *Hellenistic Philosophies*. Princeton U. Press, 1923.*

Shapiro, Herman and Edwin M. Curley, *Hellenistic Philosophy*. New York: Modern Library, 1965.*

Wenley, R. M., *Stoicism*. Boston: Marshall Jones, 1923.*

Zeller, Eduard, *Stoics, Epicureans and Skeptics*. Translated by O. J. Reichel. New York: Russell and Russell, revised edition, 1962.*

Chapter Seven

Plotinus

Plotinus (205–270 A.D.), the founder of Neoplatonism, is considered by many to be the greatest of the philosophers between Aristotle and Descartes. Unquestionably he is the last of the great philosophers of antiquity. His life spanned the third century, which was an unhappy, and even disastrous, time for the Roman Empire. Externally it was threatened by the barbarians to the North and by the Persians to the East. Internally the Empire was characterized by civil wars, regular assassination of emperors, increased taxation and economic distress, and the decline of urban life. Culturally there was great confusion with the incursion of strange ideas from the East and the competing claims made by the worshippers of Isis and the Great Mother, Mithraism, the Imperial Cult of the deified Emperor, and Christianity. Stoicism and Epicureanism had already run their courses through five centuries as moral guides for the élite with no power left to combat the attacks of the philosophical sceptics like Sextus Empiricus (c. 250 A.D.). One looks in vain for mention of these problems and movements in the writings of Plotinus. Yet the philosophy of Plotinus was profoundly influenced by the spirit of the times, as evidenced by his turning from the sight of misery and despair in the contemporary world to the contemplation of a timeless universe of goodness and beauty. In this respect he shared the attitude of many thoughtful men, both Christian and pagan, who found their hope in the Other World rather than in the crumbling world of practical affairs. In contrast to Mithraism and the mystery cults, Neoplatonism was concerned with epistemological and metaphysical issues. In reworking Platonism, Plotinus developed a philosophy of religion which was to have an enduring influence on the subsequent development of Western thought. Indeed Plotinus worked out an idealistic and monistic version of certain features of Plato's philosophy which not only provided an alternative to Aristotle's interpretation and a modification of Plato's philosophy, but actually supplanted it for a long time. Thus what we today call Neoplatonism appears to us to be a distinct and important philosophy, although in the eyes of Plotinus his work was only the revival and clarification of Plato's philosophy.

We know very little about the origins of Neoplatonism or about the life of Plotinus, the chief representative of the early history of the movement. Practically all of the available information comes from a *Life of Plotinus* written by his disciple and editor Porphyry, who was closely associated with him during the last six years of his life at Rome. Plotinus himself would never speak of his birthplace or early life, for Porphyry reports that he seemed ashamed of being "in the body" at all. Probably he was born in 205 A.D. in Egypt. It is definitely known that in 232 he came to Alexandria to study philosophy and found no satisfying teacher of philosophy until he met the Neoplatonist Ammonius Saccas, under whom he studied for ten or eleven years. We know little of this mysterious teacher except that he was also the teacher of the famed Church Father Origen of Alexandria and claimed to have "reconciled Plato and Aristotle." Some think that he was a Christian before finally giving his allegiance to Greek philosophy.

At the age of 39 Plotinus left Ammonius Saccas to join the expedition of Emperor Gordian II against the Persians, with the hope of studying firsthand Persian and Indian philosophy. When the youthful Gordian was murdered by his own generals in Mesopotamia in 244 A.D. Plotinus barely escaped with his life to Antioch. Unable to consummate his hopes of studying with Persian and Indian sages, he settled in Rome in 244 and opened a school where he taught for the remainder of his life. He won many hearers and disciples and became known for his very practical kindness. He appears to have been a good friend of the Emperor Gallienus and the Empress Salonina. Porphyry reports (*Life*, Ch. 12) that Plotinus almost persuaded the emperor to establish in Compagnia a city of philosophers, to be called Platonopolis and to be organized according to Plato's *Laws*. In 269 Plotinus' illness, believed to have been a form of leprosy, caused him to retire to a friend's country estate—here he died in 279 at the age of 66. The last nine treatises he wrote in his final two years reveal attitudes toward suffering and death which place him in the company of the noblest spirits of the Platonic, Stoic, and Epicurean traditions.

Although he did not begin to write until he was fifty (in about 254 A.D.), Plotinus wrote many philosophical essays. Most of them he submitted to Porphyry during his last six years of teaching and at his death he left all of them with his trusted Porphyry for editing. Porphyry ignored their chronological order and placed them in six groups of nine *Enneads* or "sets of nine." The first group of nine essays treats of human and ethical problems, while the second and third treat philosophy of nature and the material universe. The fourth examines the nature of the soul, while the fifth studies rational intelligence. The last set deals with the contemplation of the one Perfect Reality or the Good.

This ordering of the *Enneads* reveals Porphyry's desire to present the philosophy of Plotinus as reflecting the nature of man's true spiritual career. Proceeding from the activities of the self and the sensible world, it gradually ascends to the originating principle of the world which is the soul, then to the principle of the Soul which is the Intelligence, and finally to the universal principle of All which is the One or the Good.

Plotinus was not a professional teacher like the earlier Sophists. His lectures were open to the public, and his students came without having to pay fees. His audiences were composed of mature men previously trained in philosophy, usually in some other school. The *Enneads* were not written as a systematic presentation of Plotinus' doctrine. They discuss topics as they arose within the context of lively discussion in the school. Basically a treatise in the *Enneads* consists of (1) the aporia in which the question to be examined is stated, (2) the demonstration which advances dialectically, (3) the persuasion which seeks conviction, and (4) a sort of exaltation, hymn, or meditation which extols the blessedness or peace which comes from having access to the intelligible world. This pattern is employed in a somewhat flexible fashion and aids in conveying the force of Plotinus' thought.

The background for Plotinus' philosophy lies in the teaching of the Platonic school. In the first two centuries A.D. there developed a new interpretation of Plato along with a revival of interest in Aristotelianism and Pythagoreanism. This movement was known as Middle Platonism, and its chief representatives were Plutarch, Albinus, Apuleis, and Maximus of Tyre. Insofar as it can be characterized as a school it also reveals a certain amount of Stoic and Aristotelian influence. It stresses a transcendent Mind or God as the basic reality. It gives expression to "negative theology," the effort to describe what God is not rather than what He is, which anticipates something of the approach of Plotinus. We find in both Neopythagoreanism and Middle Platonism the suggestion that the Platonic Ideas or Forms exist in the Divine Mind as "thoughts of God." Among the Middle Platonists there is sometimes found the belief in a Second Mind or God, lower than the Supreme God, charged with a world-moving function. At still a lower level there is the Soul of the World. Thus there is a hierarchy of spiritual powers. These suggestions are developed with boldness and originality in the more complex thought of Plotinus.

Plotinus did not think of himself as establishing a new system of philosophy called by the modern name of Neoplatonism. He thought of himself as faithfully expounding Plato's philosophy and clarifying difficult points in it. The judgment of historians with the advantage of considerable hindsight is that Plotinus arbitrarily selected only a limited number of Plato's positions which he often took out of context and forced into Plotinus' own system, with the result that there exist profound similarities and differences between the two philosophers. It should be noted that both philosophers divide reality into two worlds: (1) the eternal, spiritual, or intelligible, (2) the temporal, material, or sensible. Plotinus shares the view of Plato that the material world is ordered by divine intelligence and good within its place in reality, and the soul has work to do in it before it "returns home." But Plotinus' doctrine of the final mystical union of the Soul is not found in Plato. Nor should one seek to trace to Plato Plotinus' emphasis on life and the organic view of reality, his doctrine that there are Forms or Ideas of individuals, his placing of Forms or Ideas in the Mind of God, or the doctrine of Divine Infinity. Plotinus drew much from Aristotle's *Metaphysics* and *De Anima* and seems to have been both more accurate and more critical in his use of this material than in what he drew from Plato. Since there are striking parallels between some of Plotinus' comments on God and traditional Christian language, some students have been led to speculate that this may be a carryover from the early Christian training of Plotinus' teacher Ammonius Saccas. Since we have no direct evidence of the teachings of Ammonius Saccas, it is not possible to assess the truth or falsity of such a claim.

The philosophy of Plotinus is also a religion—a way of salvation by which the mind ascends to God. Yet it should be pointed out that the contemporary mystery religions and cults had no ideas or doctrines for Plotinus to employ in developing his thought. It may be that he borrowed the language of light symbolism and the belief in a close relation between divinity and light, but this was a feature common to most of the religions and religious philosophies of the century. Plotinus himself seems to have had little or no direct contact with Christianity, although Porphyry attacked the movement. Although Christians from St. Augustine onwards have often appreciated much in Plotinus' writings, it should be clear that a great deal of the *Enneads* is incompatible with orthodox Christianity. There are of course some similarities between the teachings of the *Enneads* and the teachings of Gnosticism, a strange and vigorous contemporary religious movement. But in the ninth treatise of the second *Ennead* Plotinus criticizes severely the Gnostic quest for a secret sacred knowledge, a *gnosis*, the possession of which would automatically bring salvation to the élite in possession of it and thus make unnecessary the discipline of intelligence and virtue. But as a religion Neoplatonism is to be distinguished from both Christianity and Gnosticism.

Plotinus' philosophy is the effort to give a systematic account of the intelligible structure of living reality, which moves eternally from its transcendent foundation or First Principle, the One or Good, and descends in a continuous series of stages from the Divine Intellect and the Forms or Ideas found there through the Soul with its multiple levels of experience and activity to the last and lowest realities, the forms of bodies. In addition it reveals the means by which the soul of man can, if it will, ascend from any level to a higher one through moral purification and intellectual enlightenment, until finally it achieves that mystical union with One or the Good that alone can bring satisfaction. Thus we see two basic movements in Plotinus: (1) the outgoing or emanation from unity to multiplicity and (2) the return from multiplicity to unity and unification. Plotinus tries to furnish an objective and rational metaphysical account of reality, while at the same time giving an honest report of his own mystical or spiritual experience of the ascent and union with the One. It is tempting to stress one of these aspects of Plotinus' thought at the expense of the other, but it is not possible to separate the mysticism from the metaphysics of Plotinus, although at times there appear to be serious tensions between them.

Plotinus frequently emphasizes the completely transcendent foundation or First Principle with which he begins; the One or Good is prior to and independent of all things, so that it stands beyond the reach of human language and thought. This ultimate deity, which he sometimes calls God or even Father without the traditional Christian connotations, is ineffable and incomprehensible. No terms like essence, being, or life can be predicated of the One, for they would only attempt to limit what is beyond limit. Plotinus sets the One beyond Mind and Being. This does not mean that the One is nonexistent; rather it transcends all the objects of our experience. It transcends the concepts based on these objects. Plotinus is so anxious to maintain the unity of the One that he adopts the strategy of negative theology, in which any determination or predication of the deity is denied lest the ascription of positive attributes imply a duality of substance and accident in the

One. Thus Plotinus is reluctant to ascribe thought or will or even activity to the One. He is willing to refer to the One as *The Good* but not as "good," for that would be an inhering quality. Here one may note how Plotinus differs from Plato. The One or Good, for Plato, was itself a Form and a substance, the all-inclusive Form containing all the other Forms. It lacked the special and complete transcendence or otherness which Plotinus assigns the One. Of course, even when he says the ultimate deity is One and the Good, Plotinus recognizes the inadequacy of such predicates and is aware of the fact that they must be used analogously.

With this interpretation of the One or the Good, the question arises as to how Plotinus can explain the multiplicity of finite things. Obviously the One or ultimate deity cannot create finite things by a free act of will since the attribution of activity to the One would not only be a limitation but would raise doubts about the unchangeability of the One. Neither can the One be limited to finite things. Plotinus falls back on the metaphor of emanations or "pouring forth" or proceeding from the One. He denies explicitly that the One is in any way affected or diminished by the emanation. Although this emanation or "pouring forth" is necessary, it is held to be spontaneous and free from any constraint. Plotinus also compares the One to the sun, which illuminates while remaining undiminished, and to the mirror, which reduplicates an object without any loss of its own being. The One is generous and outgoing in its nature, pouring forth until every possible form of existence is actualized.

The first great emanation from the One is thought or mind (*Nous*). In *Nous* or divine mind exist the Ideas or Forms, not only of classes but of individuals (the totality of being in Plato's sense). *Nous* is identified with the Demiurge of the Platonic *Timeaus*. It is in *Nous* that multiplicity first appears. Yet *Nous* is unity-in-diversity and knows all things together in an eternal present. *Nous* is infinite in power and immeasureable, since it has no extension. Nevertheless, it is infinite in that it is a totality of an actually existing number of forms which are specific and limited realities.

The second emanation, Soul, proceeds from *Nous* and is akin to the World-Soul of Plato's *Timeaus*. This World-Soul is incorporeal and indivisible, acting as an intermediary between the worlds of intellect and sense. It has two levels: (1) a principle of order and direction standing close to *Nous* and without direct contact with the material world and (2) the soul of the phenomenal world or Nature which functions as an immanent principle of life and growth. Nature owes all its reality to its participation in the Ideas or Forms, which are in *Nous*. Since these Forms do not function in the world of sense, Plotinus postulates reflections of the Forms in the World-Soul.

Plotinus stresses both the unity of the World-Soul and the multiplicity and variety of individual souls. Individual souls must be separate and distinct or we would experience everyone else's inner life. Yet all individuals are interrelated and share the general nature of the soul much like each part of a developed tree contains the nature of the seed from which it originated. The soul existed prior to its entrance into a body, which was both a necessity and a fall, and survives the death of the body without any memory of its bodily existence. Although Plotinus writes of the unity of soul in the World-Soul, he argues for personal immortality. But he is not arguing for the everlastingness of the soul, which would be merely endless imprisonment in time; rather he calls for the soul to put off everlastingness and to put on eternity—to awake from dreaming.

Spread below the sphere of the Soul is a physical universe of bodies which move in space and follow one another in time, submitting to inexorable necessities that demand that nothing should occur without sufficient or appropriate effect. Individual souls descend into some of these bodies and influence their growth and behavior. Why should there be a physical universe with individual souls descending into parts of it? The answer simply is that the generation of the physical universe continues the process of emanation which necessitated the generation of *Nous* by the One and of the World-Soul by *Nous*. Since vast unrealized possibilities lie before and beyond it, the World-Soul must overflow or emanate, which it does without pain or disruption. Likewise the descent of the individual soul into a particular body is an emanation which is ultimately an outpouring of the light and power originating from the One.

The physical universe is corporeal and spatial. It is a material rather than a spiritual world. Still the universe taken as a whole is a perfect body—a standard which it cannot exceed without ceasing to be a body. But when we inspect the parts of the universe we find them to be perishable and often in conflict or frustration. Often generation of the individual body by the individual soul is accompanied by labor and pain. Often the soul is enslaved to bodily desires. Thus we have a "fall" through which sin enters the world. Matter, as we have seen, was ultimately an emanation from the One, but in itself it was the lowest stage of the Universe and thus the antithesis to the One. To the extent that matter is illumined by form and enters into the composition of material objects, it is not complete darkness. To the extent that it stands as the antithesis of the One, it is unilluminated, darkness, the privation of light. Matter thus accounts for the evil and imperfection of the material universe. But as we have already noted, the physical universe taken as a whole is good and a necessary emanation. It gives us the best possible image of the world of the spirit that can be secured on the material level in which it is necessary for it to express itself.

For Plotinus though, the process of emanation is not in itself a fall, but rather a fulfillment. But the turning away of the individual soul from its source to preoccupation with the body is a rejection of reality and literally ends in chaos or nonbeing. If it were not for this opportunity to move in the direction of nonbeing or chaos, universal perfection would prevail. Thus the individual soul, preoccupied and encrusted with the body and its desires, is lost unless it comes to itself, reestablishing a proper relation to the source of its being, and ridding itself of the impediments.

The basic purpose of philosophical contemplation and of Plotinus' teaching was, then, to lead men (at least those who were capable of it) back to communion and eventual union with God, or the One and the Good, which as the source of all gave men both being and the inner impulse to return to the source of being. The true road of life is one which leads the individual soul to itself in its unity with *Nous,* and thus to the One. The successful achievement of this spiritual journey requires perfect moral purification and sustained intellectual effort of a very high order. Mystical experience of the One is not a quick and easy substitute for moral and intellectual discipline, but the attainment of the mystical vision by the man who is wise and good enables him to pass beyond his highest intellectual endeavor.

The evil souls are lost, alienated, or exiled from God, either through having been misdirected or having "deserted towards the abyss." But in the soul that makes the right choice and holds firmly to it, the contest between higher and lower impulses is won by intelligence or reason. In this struggle Plotinus recognizes the necessity of the "civic virtues" like prudence, fortitude, temperance, and justice. Since they are concerned mainly with life in the physical universe, they are insufficient. Hence the soul must look beyond and free itself from all enslavement or attachment to matter and external impediments. A program of purification is required to free the soul from all that it has acquired in its descent from a higher world. Plotinus uses the analogy of a creator of a statue: ". . . he cuts away here, he smoothes there, he makes this line lighter, this other purer, until a lovely face has grown upon his work. So do you also. . . ." (*Enneads* I, 6.9). In all his ethical writings and injunctions Plotinus really looks through them and beyond them to a greater fulfillment. "For it is to the Gods, not to the good, that our Likeness must look: to model ourselves upon good men is to produce an image of an image: we have to fix our gaze above the image and attain Likeness to the Supreme Exemplar" (*ibid.* I, 2.7).

The mystic quest involves, for Plotinus, not only detachment from externals, but the turning inward to seek the One that is "within, at the inmost depth" (*ibid.* VI, 8.18). This effort, often called "the flight of the alone to the Alone" (*ibid.* VI, 9.11) reveals how the soul in perfect stillness can be filled with God. This mystical experience does not involve a moral isolation which cuts off the individual soul from contact with other souls. But the effort to find the unity of the One leads to the breaking down of the barriers and separation so characteristic of the soul in its descent.

The detachment from externals and the entrance into deep inner solitude do not automatically guarantee the achievement of the mystic vision. It is a necessary, but not sufficient, preparation. Plotinus reminds us: "We must not run after it, but fit ourselves for the vision and then wait tranquilly for its appearance, as the eye waits on the rising of the sun, which in its own time appears above the horizon— out of the ocean, as the poets say—and gives itself to our sight" (*ibid.* V, 5.8).

The ascent of the soul to the One has, for Plotinus, nothing to do with spatial movement, since the mystical union can occur while the human soul is still in the body. Porphyry reports that Plotinus attained this mystical union four times in six years, but it is Plotinus' conviction that *permanent union* can be achieved only when the soul has departed from the body. Plotinus teaches that we must first ascend to *Nous*, for it is only as *Nous* that union with the One becomes possible for us. In *Nous* we complete and confirm all we have done in the perfecting of our moral and intellectual life to the fulfillment of our consciousness and activity. The final mystic vision is an experience of unity which transcends the characteristic intuitive perception which distinctively unites subject and object in the *Nous*. In the pure unity of this final mystical experience we are no longer aware of being different or separated from the One; there is no longer the distinction between the seen and the seer. The act of vision is itself identical with the object of the vision. But there never is any hint in Plotinus' thought that all things other than the One are fleeting appearances of illusions. In a famous passage, Plotinus uses the analogy of a choir standing before its conductor. "We are always before it: but we do not always look; thus a choir, singing set in due order about the conductor, may turn away from that centre to which all should attend; let it but face aright and it sings with beauty, present effectively. We are ever before the Supreme—but off in utter dissolution; we can no longer be—but we do not always attend: when we look, our term is attained; that is rest; this is the end of singing ill; effectively before Him we lift a choral song full of God" (*ibid.* VI, 9.8).

After the death of Plotinus in 270 A.D. we find Neoplatonism being expounded by a line of teachers down to the closing of the schools in Athens by the Emperor Justinian in 529 A.D. But in the process there was considerable modification of doctrine and emphases in the teaching of Porphyry (233–305), Iamblichus (died *c.* 330), and Proclus (412–485). Iamblichus introduced a great deal of superstition, including divination, soothsaying, astrology, dream interpretation, and demonology, while Proclus, along with more substantial work in theology and metaphysics, expressed considerable interest in developing hymns, prayers, and ceremonies as means of purifying the soul. The more philosophical tendencies of the later Neoplatonists tend to become rather scholastic in nature, while their religious interests become corrupted by the inroads of magic and superstition. Their chief practical concern is the attempt to revive the traditional pagan worship, in which Plotinus had had little interest, and to create a defense of it in the face of Christian hostility. Emperor Julian, who tried to revive the pagan cults in the fourth century, was a follower of Iamblichus. But the more significant influence of Plotinus is to be sought in other directions. St. Augustine became a Christian by way of Plotinus, and his writings often reveal it. It is fair to say that a great deal of Plotinus came into Christian teaching through Augustine and the pseudo-Dionysius. No other intellectual has exerted the influence of Plotinus on the development of both Catholic and Islamic mysticism. With the rediscovery of classical literature in the sixteenth century, Plotinus became an important stimulus for the growth of Protestant mysticism. Even in our own century the writings of Dean Inge reflect the continuance of the influence of Plotinus. The hasty reader of mystical writings should be warned that in the process of development Christian mysticism has transformed the thought of Plotinus so that it is even further removed from its original Platonic inspiration.

Plotinus: Suggested Additional Reading

Abernethy, George L. and Thomas A. Langford, eds., *History of Philosophy: Selected Readings*. Belmont, Calif.: Dickenson, 1965, pp. 224–237.*

Armstrong, Arthur H., *The Architecture and the Intelligible Universe of Plotinus: An Analytical and Historical Study*. Cambridge: Harvard University Press, 1940.*

Bréhier, Emile, *Hellenistic and Roman Age*. Translated by Wade Baskin. Chicago: University of Chicago, Phoenix, 1966.

Bréhier, Emile, *The Philosophy of Plotinus*. Translated by Joseph Thomas. Chicago: University of Chicago, 1958.*

Inge, William R., *The Philosophy of Plotinus*, 2 vols., third edition. London: Longmans, Green, 1952.*

Kaufmann, Walter, *Philosophical Classics*. Englewood Cliffs, N.J.: Prentice-Hall, 1961, I, 576–580.*

Pistorius, Philippus V., *Plotinus and Neoplatonism*. Cambridge, England: Bowes and Bowes, 1952.*

Plotinus, *The Enneads*. Translated by Stephen MacKenna. Revised by B. S. Page, third edition. London: Faber & Faber, 1962.*

Plotinus, *Works*. Edited by A. H. Armstrong. New York: Macmillan, Collier, paperback, 1962.

Plotinus, *The Philosophy of Plotinus*. Edited and translated by Joseph Katz. New York: Appleton-Century-Crofts, 1950.

Plotinus, *Essential Plotinus*. Translated by Elmer O'Brien. New York: New American Library, Mentor, 1964.

Chapter Eight

Augustine

Aurelius Augustine (345–439 A.D.) is the most important Christian theologian and philosopher during the millennium following the close of the biblical writings. Not only was he important as the reservoir and purifier of previous positions, but he became, through his creative reinterpretation of Neoplatonism, the basic influence upon theology and philosophy until the revival of Aristotelianism in the thirteenth century. After this period the impact of his thought was through the theologians of the Franciscan order, as well as among Protestants. In philosophy elements of his tradition were kept alive by such men as Descartes and Leibnitz.

Augustine was born in North Africa. His father, Patricius, was a pagan whom Augustine describes in his *Confessions* as, "A poor freeman of Tagaste" (25). Patricius was an official in North African provincial administration; he was never free from financial burdens, but he was ambitious for his precocious son and extended himself to provide the boy with a good education.

However, Monica, the mother, was the dominant influence in Augustine's life. She was a devout Christian and importunate about her son's relationship to God; she was also instrumental in her husband's conversion during Augustine's seventeenth year. At an early age, Augustine says, he learned about eternal matters and began to pray to God as his "aid and refuge" (*Confessions*, 10). In looking back with some self-deprecation, he says that these early prayers were often petitions that he not be beaten in school. Once during a childhood illness he asked to be baptized, but since baptism was administered only at death, and since he showed signs of recovery, this was withheld. Nonetheless, the request indicated his readiness at the time to affirm the Christian faith.

Like her husband, Monica was ambitious for her son. She was proud of his brilliant mind and gifts in speech. She even opposed an early marriage fearing that a wife might prove "a clog and hindrance" (*Confessions*, 27) to his promise. Yet she was also concerned for his moral character and warned him against promiscuity.

The death of Augustine's father before he had completed his education threatened to end his school life. But a wealthy citizen of Tagaste offered aid and made it possible for him to go to Carthage to study for two years. Augustine describes this period as one when he "desired to be eminent, out of a damnable and vainglorious end, a joy in human vanity" (*Confessions*, 39). In the course of his study he discovered a book which changed all his purposes and inflamed him to seek wisdom. The book was *Hortensius*, a dialogue on philosophy by Marcus Tullius Cicero (whom Augustine refers to in his writings as Tully). Some years later he was to describe this experience as the beginning of his rediscovery of religious faith.

But this was only the beginning of his transformation. For while Augustine was engaged in his study he was also a profligate youth and says, "I walked the streets of Babylon" (*Confessions*, 27). Because of his view of the heinousness of his sin, *Confessions* can be read as a commentary on Psalm 139:8, which is quoted on the second page, "If I go down into Hell, Thou art there." Due to the ambiguity within his own mind and life, he was most concerned with the problem of evil. This problem he felt to be both personal and theoretical, and he set his attention to its solution. Along with his passion for goodness he possessed an equally strong passion for truth: "O truth," he cries, "how inwardly did even then the marrow of my soul pant after Thee" (*Confessions*, 41).

In his search for wisdom and for some resolution to the problem of evil he several times changed his position. Unwilling to stand by a position which he did not find intellectually and emotionally satisfying, he committed himself to following the lead of his studies. Remembering his heritage, he started his search by turning to the scriptures but he found them wanting on two counts. First, they lacked the literary merit which he as a teacher of rhetoric demanded; they were "unworthy to be compared to the stateliness of Tully." Second, he could not accept the scripture's claims for truth because he could not prove them rationally for himself.

Turning from the direct study of the scriptures he was impressed by the teaching of the Manichees which maintained that they represented the original Christian position and promised to prove by pure reason the truths of their faith. The teaching of the Manicheans provided a thoroughgoing materialism and offered a new way to deal with the problem of evil. Fundamentally, they taught that there are two forces which govern the world—one good (the power of light) and the other evil (the power of darkness), a position sometimes called ultimate or cosmic dualism. The two forces which rule the world are also present in each individual, every man having two distinct souls, one good and one evil. By means of this division of the governing powers, the Manicheans claimed that the theoretical problem of evil was answered by attributing the different aspects of this world to different causes, and practically the problem of evil was answered by refusing to obey the evil powers which impinge upon one's life.

For ten years, as a teacher in his home town and then in Carthage, Augustine studied this position assiduously, for it seemed to answer both his moral and intellectual needs; but finally he rejected it because he felt that its conception of God was inadequate and it only answered the question of evil by failing to recognize its permeative influence and by refusing to acknowledge personal responsibility for evil. The Manichees, he became convinced, were unable to provide what they promised either morally or intellectually.

When he turned from Manicheeism he moved to a skeptical position and surrendered most of his previous affirmations, though he admits that he continued to believe in the existence of God and in personal immortality. Nonetheless, doubt was pervasive, and for a while he felt that he could set the problem of evil aside by questioning the possibility of finding any viable answer.

Eventually his pilgrimage led him to Rome and to a study of Neoplatonism. The works of Plotinus had just been translated into Latin by Victorinus, the most celebrated rhetorician of Augustine's day and whose work therefore attracted his attention. In this philosophy, which we have already described in our discussion of Plotinus, he moved to a monistic position and was especially interested in the treatment of evil as nonbeing. He accepted Neoplatonism with enthusiasm and found in this philosophy, as he later recognized, a stepping stone on his return to the Christian faith. Some commentators describe Augustine as moving from this Neoplatonic position to Christianity, but Anders Nygren recognizes the continuity of his later thought with Plotinian emphases and says that Augustine came to Christianity as a Neoplatonist. But a problem remained for him, and he believed for all Platonists, for while he saw the good he still was not able to do the good. And thus a disquietude remained.

Augustine's return to the Christian faith was completed under the guidance of Ambrose, the Bishop of Milan. This man, whom Augustine significantly says was known, "To the whole world as among the best of men" (Confessions, 99), and who therefore exemplified in his life the character Augustine sought, led him at the age of thirty-two to the Christian faith in the year 386, and at Easter 387 he was baptized

along with his fifteen-year-old son, by a mistress, Adeodatus, and with
his friend, Alypius.

In the year 391 Augustine became the helper of the Bishop of Hippo,
Valerius, and four years later when the Bishop died Augustine was
appointed in his place. For thirty-five years he remained in this post
and became the chief defender and interpreter of the church. In 430,
while Hippo was being attacked by the Vandals, Augustine died of
fever.

Augustine's Epistemology

The influences upon Augustine's development of his theory of
knowledge are obvious from the previous discussion. There was
always an influence from the scriptures and the Christian tradition
with its sacraments. In addition there was the influence of the Platonic
tradition, both from the philosophy of Plotinus and from the Christian
Platonists such as Justin Martyr, Irenaeus, and the Alexandrians—
Origen and Clement. While it is later Platonism to which he is especially indebted, it is possible that he refers directly to Plato in his
City of God, Book VIII. From the Platonists, and especially Plotinus,
Augustine gained his assurance of the existence of nonempirical reality,
that is, the conviction that there are Ideas or Forms, so that behind
the sensory world there is an eternal realm, a realm of most real Being.
In addition, he is also convinced that the most direct way of knowing
reality is by the utilization of *a priori* rational concepts.

We shall look at these convictions as they find expression in Augustine's development of his philosophy. But it must be remembered
that while reason has an important place in his thought, it is the relation of the total man to God which dominates his interests. In his
early *Soliloquies*, Augustine expresses the primary concern of his
struggle, "Two things I wish to know, God and the soul." This
treatise is a clear restatement of the Platonic position; it makes the
first task of philosophy an investigation of the distinctively human
qualities, and therefore it is based upon the conviction that there is a
congruity between the structure of man's mind and the intellectual
structure of reality as such. Through the faculty of memory, which he
discusses at length in the *Confessions*, Book X, he argues that "There
[in the memory] are all things preserved distinctly and under general
heads [Ideas]" (X, 13). It is not by images derived from the senses
that knowledge is made possible but through relating the sense impressions with the intuited Forms (X, 18).

Since the purpose of knowledge is to bring true happiness, Augustine is primarily concerned with the question of what can be known for sure, what can assure beatitude. He seeks truth because it can bring happiness, and only absolute truth is sufficient for genuine happiness. He begins, therefore, by arguing that there are degrees of probability about judgments regarding the nature of the real world—for instance when one judges that one object (such as a circle) is better than another. Such a judgment implies that we have a standard by which we make such comparisons. To indicate what this norm is, he turns to Platonism and says that there can be assured knowledge about Forms or Ideas, especially about logical and mathematical entities.

The external world which is perceived by the senses does not have the certainty of immediately intuited Forms. In his *Soliloquies* there is an argument which is later to be developed by Descartes (*Soliloquies*, II, 1 ff). He begins by saying that even if one can doubt the existence of everything received through sense impressions, he cannot doubt himself. For to doubt is to raise questions, and to raise questions is tacitly to affirm one's own existence. In other words, the doubter may doubt everything except the fact that he is doubting, and hereby he does have knowledge of his own existence.

But how is one to move from the fact of his own existence to the affirmation of the existence of reality outside of himself? Augustine says that God is the source of all that is, both the Forms and the external world. Following the Platonic thought forms, he is arguing that man is a part of the created realm which is, literally, *in*formed by the *logos* or reason of God; therefore man can know the external world because both his own mind and the external world have been created by the same Supreme Reason and there is, consequently, a congruence between man's intellect and the formal structure of the material world.

But the question remains, how does man come to see the eternal ideas? Since this realm cannot be reached by going through the objects of sense, how does man come to know it? Augustine insists that our minds are illumined by God himself, so it is the grace of God which provides for man what he could not gain for himself. Illumination in Augustine's thought takes the place of "recollection" in Plato's system. It is possible that Augustine finds adumbration of this position in the Gospel of John, but whatever its source, Augustine finds proof of God's existence in man's direct awareness of necessary and eternal truths and of the source of these truths. Throughout his discussion, however, he stresses that his interest in the existence of God is not academic, but rather he wishes to indicate how the God—whom men are universally called to worship—is known.

The Doctrine of Creation

Following the Old Testament tradition, Augustine affirms that the world is created good. In the Genesis account, God not only calls the world into existence, but He says "that it was good." This means for Augustine that evil can have no substantial being, in so far as a thing *is* it is good; it also means that the world is created according to the Ideas which God has given to the world. In agreement with Plotinus' position he thinks of the Good as an Idea in the mind of God (*Nous*), though unlike Plotinus he conceives of God as a Personal Being; in opposition to Plotinus, he insists that the world is created, called into being "out of nothing," and is not an emanation of the One.

The world is created good, but Augustine describes this as a positive good rather than a perfect good. Only God is perfectly good in the sense of being immutably, incorruptibly good. The world, being transitory and contingent, is also imperfect; it has come from non-being and can lapse back into nonbeing. It has the possibility of conforming to the ultimate good, but its conformity is always partial and therefore involves some degree of imperfection. The good creation may be degraded and turned into evil by rational and free beings (either angels or men), and this results in a privation of being and therefore in a distortion of the good.

Following Plotinus, Augustine calls this privation of the good a lapse into nonbeing, but in his own distinctive manner he says that this privation comes about through man's self-assertion or pride. To lose goodness is to lose being, for all being has its existence precisely because it is the expression of God's good intention. Nonbeing is not itself necessarily evil, but evil is equated with the limitation which nonbeing imposes upon the realm of being, a limitation which strictly speaking means the loss of one's proper status in being.

But what causes the evil? This is a basic problem which hounded Augustine's thought from an early time. In the period of his Christian interpretation he says that the locus of evil is to be found in man's free decision; evil is the result of man's mischoice or his deliberate turning toward the finite world of becoming. It must be clear that in Augustine's discussion it is not reason which is reprobate; rather, the reason is misdirected and therefore misused because of the misdirection of the will. The large concessions which he makes to man's rational ability are a part of his indebtedness to the Platonic tradition. But he will not concede that evil is simply a false understanding.

In Plato, as we saw earlier, evil is attributed to the subrational, or appetitive, nature of man. Evil is due to the fact that though reason is intent upon the good, it can be clouded over by man's irrational mistaking of sensuously perceived nature for ultimate reality. But Augustine claims that it is the rational will that causes the defection, and consequently this evil reorientation of man's life is to be located at the core of his life, in his volitional decision to forsake the supreme good. The choice of evil is not simply a rational mistake, it is due to a volitional perversity. This is, Robert Calhoun has claimed, a new departure in the understanding of man.

In his explication of this point of view Augustine reflects upon Adam's sin (*City of God*, XIV, 13). He argues, "Our first parents fell into open disobedience because already they were secretly corrupted; for the evil act had never been done had not an evil will preceded it. And what is the origin of our evil will but pride?" The evil will, he goes on to argue, is not the result of nature; on the contrary, it is due to man's desire for undue exaltation. "Vice is contrary to nature," but man, because he is made "out of nothing," has an element of nonbeing. By his exercise of an evil will he repudiates his proper place in being and becomes a lesser creature than he was intended to be by virtue of his creation.

Consequences of the Fall

To fasten one's devotion upon some lesser value than the supremely Good issues in man's fall from his state of original goodness to a condition of sin; and such a fall has debilitating consequences. Psychologically man becomes self-centered and is not able to break away from his inordinate self-love, for every desire to forsake the self leads one back into an evaluation of his freedom and thereby refocuses attention upon the self. It is the same principle as when a man says, "Here now, I must forget about my headache," and then checks every few minutes to see if he really has forgotten, which only means that he has not forgotten. Ontologically, there is also an impediment: man cannot recover his lost status because he is not the Creator, and a new status in being requires a new creative act. Therefore, if man is to be freed from his privation of being, it must be by some new gift of being by God.

To use Augustine's own terminology we can say that when men and angels were created they were both able to sin (*posse peccare*) and able not to sin (*posse non peccare*). But when man falls he loses the power not to sin and therefore retains only the possibility of continuing in sin (*posse peccare*). Augustine argues that this does not mean that man has lost his freedom, but that he is only free to follow his will and his will is perverted. To say that a man can do something other than what he is doing is to fail to recognize the unitary structure of personality. The will is the person; as a man wills, so is he.

But not every man is born with the possibility of either sinning or not sinning. That condition was only true of Adam. Augustine insists that man, since Adam, inherits the propensity to sin. Adam's sin and guilt affect all of his descendents, for his sin is seminally passed (that is, by the very physical act of creating new life) from this forefather to all of his progeny.

It is important to recognize the epistemological consequences of the fall. Since it is the will which directs the use of man's reason, when the wilful attention is wrongly placed the reason is used only to understand the lower levels of reality and does not attempt to attain unto God. When the will is focused upon God the mind is released to know God and search out His attributes. In Augustine's view, man must begin in faith (with a rightly ordered will) to go on to understanding.

The Redirection of the Will

If man is caught in the prison of his false will and cannot devise any means of escape from himself, how then is he to find release? The reader must remember that this was the critical problem which Augustine faced all of his life. And now in his return to the Christian faith he finds that such a renewal of status is given by God's grace. It is, first of all, a matter of grace that man was created, and it is by the continuance of God's grace that man is related to ultimate reality and retains his being and the possibility of knowledge. Some interpreters make this universal and prevenient grace primary in interpreting Augustine.

Every expression of grace, Augustine insists, is rooted in the freedom of God. The initiative in man's salvation is taken by God. Augustine's thought may be summarized by saying that prevenient grace is given to all men, it is universal; but to this grace must also be added strength for action; for man's problem is that he cannot do the good he knows. Augustine sometimes calls this new ability "sufficient," "following," or "sustaining" grace. Speaking of these two aspects of grace, he says, "It goes before him when unwilling, that he may will; it follows him when willing, that he may not will in vain" (Enchiridion, 9.32).

To prevenient grace, therefore, must be added other expressions of God's gracious activity, expressions which supplement and bring the prevenient grace to its fruition. Sometimes Augustine speaks of the following or sufficient grace as God's election, which is expressed through the sacraments of the church. The one who receives these sacraments is restored to his original status and once again possesses the ability not to sin (*posse non peccare*). At other times he stresses the role of Jesus Christ as mediator. When he presents this argument he claims that when men are encountered by the Christ of the church's faith they see both their ensnaring egocentricity and God's reconciling power which brings them to a new status in being.

In terms of his theory of knowledge this means that man's will is freed from self-centeredness and so reoriented that it is focused upon God. In this condition man is enabled to see his world properly and think clearly about himself and his context. Thus, it is by sufficient grace that man is brought to his true rational home. Whereas before he could only see with a blurred vision (as, for instance, the Platonists were able to see), now man can see all reality under the aegis of God's will (*Confessions*, XIII, V, 6; *City of God*, X, 32).

Freedom of the Will

Throughout this discussion the question which has clearly been before Augustine is that of the freedom of the will. In his earlier period he wrote a major treatise on *The Freedom of the Will* in which he stresses man's freedom in making value choices and in pursuing these values. But in his last works he stresses much more the election of God.

Several general statements can be made which indicate the main direction of his argument. Augustine is unwilling to think of the "will" as some faculty in man which always remains in a position of perfect equilibrium and which can at any moment move in any direction. Rather, for him, the will is intimately associated with a person's character or with the total structure of his personality. Therefore a person's will is the basic character of the person, it is the expression of his structured self-hood.

In addition, Augustine thinks of all choices as being made within a context of other factors. This might be illustrated by saying that choices are influenced by the home in which he is nurtured, his geographical location, impinging cultural and social factors, and the decisions others have made. If the grace of God is given a paramount place in this environment, then it is possible to understand his comment, "Neither was it the grace of God alone, nor was it he himself alone, but it was the grace of God with him" (*Grace and Free Will*, 11).

Only as a man is genuinely free is there the possibility of speaking of responsibility. But only as a man is recognized to be a unified personality within the larger family of influences is there the possibility of understanding the dynamics of personal choice. It must be noted that, in this understanding, the word "will" is used to indicate decision which results in action, for Augustine maintains that if a person says he "wills" to do a thing which he does not do, then he does not fully "will" that thing at all. But where a person does genuinely "will" it is the grace of God which works both to make the choice possible and to sustain the choice.

The distinction between choice and ability to fulfil or enact what one wills lies at the heart of Augustine's analysis of the human will (*The Spirit and The Letter*, 47; *On Free Will*, Bk. I, XIV, 30). Man's sinful condition does not deprive him of the ability to will, but it does incapacitate him so that he cannot do what he wills (*On Nature and Grace*, 54–55; *On Free Will*, Bk. III, xviii, 52). Since man is genuinely free (or, as Harnack says, is *freed*) when he has the capacity to love God and do His will, then the true freedom of the will comes when man has the power to do what he wills when this is in accord with God's purposes (*On Free Will*, Bk. I, xv, 32).

Augustine and Pelagius

Shortly after the turn of the century (400 A.D.) there appeared in Rome a British monk who had already established himself as a scholar through several books on the doctrine of the Trinity. This man was Pelagius, and he was to challenge Augustine's interpretation of the source of Christian faith. Pelagius was shocked at the low moral tone of the Romans, but when he spoke of his disapproval he was met with pleas of human weakness. Evidently he sought to counter this moral failure by exhibiting the natural capacities of man for ethical living. Augustine's teachings, especially his teaching on man's dependence upon the grace of God, infuriated Pelagius and he replied by calling attention to man's sense of moral obligation, and said, "If I ought, I can." A younger disciple, Coelestius, publicized his views and a controversy developed.

The most noteworthy features of Pelagius' teaching (which we know only at second hand) may be summarized as follows: Adam's sin was not passed to his posterity; rather, the Creator has given to each man an absolute freedom so that every moment, in spite of one's past decisions or experience, the will is equally capable of choosing good or evil. Man is born without a predisposition either way, and whether he follows one road or another is the result of individual decisions autonomously arrived at. Pelagius does want to retain a place for grace, but it is not to have a part in the initial movement of the will. The human will, unassisted, could take the first step, but the fact that man has such a freedom is due to the creative grace of God. Augustine's objection to this position was twofold: first, Pelagius assumed that man has the native power to obey the law (which Augustine, with Paul, denied) and, second, there was no real place for the redemptive grace of God.

The major councils which considered this problem tended to agree with Augustine, but supporters were found for each side in the controversy until finally the Council of Orange (539) approved Augustine's position on sin and grace (although it denied absolute predestination), and it became the official position of the Church.

More than fifteen of Augustine's treatises which were written during this controversy have been saved, and these indicate how consistently Augustine attempted to defend his doctrine of grace and yet affirm man's freedom in ways which were consistent with his earlier statements. But whatever the answers proposed, the question of the nature of the freedom of the will as related to the activity of God is given new impetus and remains to be discussed by many subsequent philosophers and theologians.

Moral Philosophy

In Augustine's discussion of ethics we find him applying his general position to specific problems. The good life, as he defines it, is rooted in the orientation of man's will upon God. Therefore the most fundamental character of the good man is a good will which is directed toward the Highest Being. When man is so directed he is expressing the unique fact of his creation in the image of God, and he is thereby expressing what is characteristic of his proper place in the order of creation. When man is in this relationship he also actualizes the true end of human conduct, namely happiness or beatitude, which is to say he finds his *raison d'etre*. Augustine's position may be summed up by saying that God is the objective good of life, and happiness is the resulting subjective experience when man is properly related to this ultimate good. Virtue, therefore, is defined in his treatise *On The Morals of The Catholic Church* as "the perfect love of God" (*Basic Writings*, 328). He writes, "The greatest commandment, therefore which leads to a happy life, and the first is this: 'Thou shalt love the Lord thy God with all thy heart, and soul, and mind.' For to those who love the Lord all things issue in good" (*Basic Writings*, 328).

While Augustine is dependent upon the Greek tradition and shows no inclination to repudiate what he finds that is good in the pagan traditions, he does reject all attempts to establish man's happiness by

adjustment to the world of becoming, whether this be in the form of
Stoic or Epicurean approaches. Just as the libertine attempts to equate
happiness with enjoyment—only to find that the senses are never
satisfied with the pleasures allowed them—so those who attempt to
adjust to the maelstrom of experience by apathy or sheer courage find
them no more satisfying. Only as the whole man, body and soul, is
fully actualizing his possibilities is there beatitude, and this can come
only when man is rightly related to his highest good, a good which
encompasses all of his potentiality.

But the Platonists would also say this. However, Augustine maintains
that here as elsewhere the failure of this philosophy is that while it
shows man the goal it cannot provide him with a way to reach that
goal (*City of God*, X, 29). So again he falls back upon the grace of God
which arouses, sustains, and increases man's love for Him.

Augustine illustrates his position by investigating the traditional
Greek virtues of temperance, fortitude, justice, and prudence. He is
convinced that the endorsement of these virtues is a reflection of man's
native moral conscience. But when these virtues are pursued for the sake
of self-love, they become only "splendid vices." What he therefore
finds necessary is an interpretation of these qualities which will keep
them focused upon God and the neighbor and thereby undercut the
tendency to interpret them in a self-interested manner. The redefini-
tion he suggests is as follows: "Temperance is love giving itself
entirely to that which is loved; fortitude is love readily bearing all
things for the sake of the loved object; justice is love serving only the
loved object, and therefore ruling rightly; prudence is love distinguishing with sagacity between what hinders it and what helps it. The object
of this love is not anything, but only God" (*Basic Writings*, 331–332).
Each of these reinterpretations are, finally, to be seen in the perspective
that God is the object who is to be loved.

To love God means two things: a proper love for one's self and a
proper love for one's neighbor. Augustine insists "It is impossible
for one who loves God not to love himself" (*Basic Writings*, 342).
To love God with genuineness is to understand one's own place in the
scale of being. Thus man loves himself best when he loves God best,
for through his love of God he sees himself as he was intended to be
—as God's creature.

Moreover, what must be sought in the concern for our neighbor is
what we seek for ourselves, namely that he also, "may love God with
a perfect affection" (*Basic Writings*, 343). Throughout the discussion
God stands as a middle term between man and his neighbor, so that
the love of one's neighbor is a special case of man's love for God.

Augustine is one of the most insistent defenders of the position that the inversion of self love is the standard by which we should love our neighbor. This may be understood as another form of the golden rule, "Do unto others as you would have them do unto you," or of the injunction of Jesus, "Thou shalt love thy neighbor as thyself" (Matthew 22:39).

The City of God

In one of the best known books in Western civilization, *The City of God*, Augustine writes a defense of the Christian faith. This book was written in 410, the time Alaric was sacking Rome. Many Romans argued that the fall of the empire was due to the forsaking of the traditional Roman religion. In this apology, Augustine presents Christianity in the form of Biblical history from Genesis to Revelation. In this presentation he outlines not only his own philosophical and theological principles, but also gives his understanding of the nature of human society. We are, at this juncture, primarily interested in his description of human society as an interpretation of political life.

Once again the dependence of Augustine upon the Platonic tradition is obvious, and Werner Jaeger goes so far as to claim that he took Plato's *Republic* and gave it Christian baptism in his *City of God*. Man is by nature a social being, and like Plato he sees the resulting society as the individual writ large. Society, as individuals, is to be understood by its basic love or wilful commitment. Every society has a character which is expressive of this commitment and which is governed in its life by its commitment.

Fundamentally there are two loves which characterize the direction of societies' attention: one is the love of God [which forms the character of the City of God (*civitas Dei*)] and the other is the love of power [which forms the character of the City of Earth (*civitas terrena*)]. The two cities are mythical symbols of the good and the bad within and among men and angels.

His most succinct description is found in the following quotation: "Accordingly, two cities have been formed by two loves: the earthly by the love of self, even to the contempt of God; the heavenly by the love of God, even to the contempt of self. The former, in a word, glories in itself, the latter in the Lord . . . In the one, the princes and the nations it subdues are ruled by the love of ruling; in the other, the princes and the subjects serve one another in love" (*City of God*, XIV, 28).

The City of God finds its distinctiveness precisely in the fact that it is the community of people who have a common love for God. This city is not to be equated with the Church, but the Church is the closest earthly approximation to it. The City of Earth is distinctive because it is composed of those who have a common love for power, for the obsession to hold political power is an expression of man's pride and is therefore sinful. Rome is the closest approximation to this city, but again there is to be no simple equation of the City of Earth with the Roman Empire. These two loves are in operation in all human life and can be sharply distinguished in theory, but in theory only. In this world they are mixed, but in the eschatological age, at the final time, they will be decisively distinguished. A diagram may help to make the individual person's participation in each of these two cities clear.

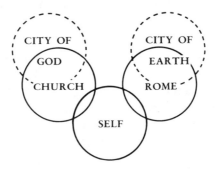

In their present existence men live in the ambiguity of having more than one allegiance; they are participants in more than one community, citizens of more than one city. But each man and each larger community has a main stream or a dominant drive which basically characterizes its life, and each man is basically identified with one reality or the other. At the same time, the admixture of conflicting loves is so thorough that in practice one cannot always distinguish the two cities.

The very fact that the organized communities of men do live by some principal commitment indicates to Augustine that the object toward which they are directed may be changed. This means that the will of the community needs reorientation, just as does the will of the individual. While Augustine is cautious about expressing hope for the transformation of society, he is convinced that in principle Christ can transform the social order, and he accepts as a Christian responsibility the task of attempting to redirect the will of the community.

Finally, this also makes manifest Augustine's philosophy of history. The course of history is not that of cyclical repetition, as the Greeks thought; on the contrary, history is moving toward a goal and has direction and purpose. The historical experience of man is under the guidance of God, and ultimately the sovereign Ruler of the world will assert His power and will reign triumphantly.

Augustine: Selected Additional Reading

Abernethy, George L. and Thomas A. Langford, eds., *History of Philosophy: Selected Readings.* Belmont, Calif.: Dickenson, 1965, pp. 238–260.*

Augustine, *Library of Christian Classics*, vols. VI, VII, VIII. Philadelphia: Westminster, 1953–1957.*

Augustine, *Basic Writings of St. Augustine.* Edited by Whitney J. Oates. New York: Random House, 1948.*

Augustine, *Essential Augustine.* Edited by V. J. Bourke. New York: New American Library, Mentor, 1964.

Augustine, *Selected Writings.* Edited and with an introduction by Roger Hazleton. Cleveland: Meridian Books, 1968.

Battenhouse, Roy, W., *A Companion to the Study of Saint Augustine.* New York: Oxford University Press, 1955.*

Bonner, Gerald, *St. Augustine of Hippo: Life and Controversies.* Philadelphia: Westminster, 1963.*

Bourke, Vernon J., *Augustine's View of Reality.* Villanova, Pa.: Villanova University Press, 1964.*

Cochrane, C. N., *Christianity and Classical Culture.* Fairlawn, N.J.: Oxford University Press, Galaxy, 1957.

Copleston, Frederick C., *A History of Philosophy: Augustine to Scotus*, vol. II. Garden City: Doubleday, Image, 1962.

Gilson, E., *The Christian Philosophy of St. Augustine.* Translated by L. E. Lynch. New York: Random House, Vintage, 1960.

Kaufmann, Walter, *Philosophical Classics.* Englewood Cliffs, N.J.: Prentice-Hall, 1961, I, 581–603.*

Marrou, Henri I., *St. Augustine and His Influence through the Ages.* Translated by P. Hepburne-Scott. New York: Harper and Row, Torchbook, 1957.

Portalie, Eugene, *A Guide to the Thought of Saint Augustine.* Introduction by Vernon J. Bourke; translated by Ralph J. Bastian. Chicago: H. Regnery, 1960.*

Pryzara, Erich, *Augustine Synthesis.* New York: Harper and Row, Torchbook, 1958.

Chapter Nine

Medieval Philosophy: Erigena, Anselm, and Abelard

The term *Scholasticism* is appropriately used to characterize the total philosophical thought of medieval Christian Europe. Thus it embraces the long history of Western philosophical and theological thought from the ninth to the fifteenth century. Much of it was complex, varied, and subtle and was expressed in a rigid logical structure. Basic to the early history of Scholasticism were the writings of St. Augustine and the Church Fathers. As learning was revived in the ninth century, it came to be influenced by Platonic and Neoplatonic thought, as we shall see in the case of Erigena. By the eleventh century the Scholastic thinkers were wrestling with the problem of universals as formulated in the rival views of nominalists and realists. Another major controversial issue in Scholasticism emerged over the place of reason and faith in man's knowledge. The thirteenth century is often referred to as the Golden Age of Scholasticism, which became possible only after such developments as the translation from the Arabic of previously unknown works of Aristotle, the founding of the universities of Paris, Oxford, and Bologna, and the establishment of the mendicant orders, the Franciscans and Dominicans. All of this led to lively controversies both before and after Thomas Aquinas' brilliant attempt to synthesize Aristotelian rationalism and Christian thought. The Aristotelian rationalism of this Dominican thinker was opposed by such Franciscans as Duns Scotus, St. Bonaventure, and William of Ockham, who emphasized the necessity of faith and the inadequacy of reason in the solution of theological questions. After William of Ockham there were no more great Scholastic thinkers. The next great philosophers did not appear until the Renaissance.

We begin our examination of early Scholasticism by surveying the work of John Scotus Erigena.

John Scotus Erigena

John Scotus was the single original philosopher in the six centuries of the period from Boethius to St. Anselm. He was an astonishing figure as a Neoplatonist, a famed Greek scholar, a pantheist, and a Pelagian. We know relatively little about his personal life. He was born probably around 810 in Ireland and at some point studied in an Irish monastery, where he presumably acquired his knowledge of Greek. "Erigena" means "belonging to the people of Erin," while "Scotus" does not necessarily imply Scotland, since ninth century Ireland was referred to as *Scotia Maior* and the Irish as *Scoti*.

Sometime in the forties John Scotus journeyed to France, where by 850 he had been appointed to the chair of Alcuin as head of the Palace School. He was admired by Charles the Bald for his erudition and his ready wit. Once in a bibulous moment, King Charles glanced across the table and asked: "What separates a Scot from a sot?" John Scotus is reported to have replied without hesitation: "Only this table." It is not clear that John Scotus was ever ordained to the priesthood, but he was persuaded by Hincmar, Bishop of Rheims, to write a treatise, *Divine Predestination*, in refutation of the Monk Gottschalk's teaching of double predestination. John's Pelagian doctrine pleased neither side to the dispute and subsequently the doctrine was condemned by two councils. This experience turned him toward philosophy. At the request of Charles the Bald in 858 he began the translation of the works of Pseudo-Dionysius from Greek into Latin, which he followed by the translation of other Greek works. These translated works were all deeply affected by Neoplatonism, which stressed the basic unity of the world—a view which was to exert an enduring influence on John Scotus.

The philosophical work for which John Scotus received lasting fame is *On the Division of Nature*, which he wrote possibly between 862 and 866. It consists of five books and appears in the then-popular dialogue form of a conversation between Master and Disciple, which introduces many digressions in the effort to clarify specific points. It is, however, really a philosophical theology and a system of metaphysics.

At the beginning of the *Division of Nature* John Scotus indicates that he means by "Nature" the sum of reality, or the totality of "things that are" and "things that are not." Immediately the question arises, "How can things that are not be part of the totality of all that is?" This question assumes that the "things that are not" are tantamount to nothing, while John Scotus assumes there are different modes of nonbeing. Some things may surpass sense and understanding because they are superior to perception and understanding or fall so short of reality as to be incomprehensible; also, potential being is not actual being.

The whole of Nature can be seen to have four aspects: (1) what creates and is not created, (2) what creates and is created, (3) what is created but does not create, (4) what neither creates nor is created. These four divisions may be reduced to a basic division between the Creator and the created. The first and fourth apply to God, while the second and third apply to creation. The first division is the first principle or first cause of all things, while the fourth is God as the final end or purpose of all things, immanent and not transcendent, for all that emanates from God seeks to return to Him. The second is the divine (*Platonic*) Ideas, or principles of being, and the third is the created universe itself. The second and third divisions not only appear in the course of our thought but also are discovered in the very nature of created things.

In John's doctrine, God remains above or beyond all the categories of being, for any attempt to describe Him as a being or as being itself will only delimit him. John employs the affirmative, negative, and symbolic or superlative theology of Pseudo-Dionysius to develop this doctrine. When we ordinarily assert that God is good or has being, we are asserting something that is misleading or false unless we supplement it by corresponding negative assertions such as God is not good or He is not being. These denials are, in turn, misleading unless we understand them as suggesting that God is more than being or goodness and thus cannot be limited to them. It would appear, then, that statements in affirmative theology must always be supplemented by statements in negative theology. Following Pseudo-Dionysius, John believes this can be done more easily in superlative theology by single assertions like God is super-God, God is supergood, God is super-essence, rather than by using pairs of statements like God is good and God is not good. These superlative terms place Him beyond all finite categories and words. No finite mind can know what God is, but only that He is. John leans on the concept of *learned ignorance* found in Pseudo-Dionysius when he espouses the view that God is best known by our knowledge that He is forever unknown. In addition, God remains unknown to Himself, for He is beyond all fixed modes of thought. If He were to define Himself, His knowledge would determine Him and thus limit Him. His own ignorance is a recognition of his infinity which cannot be encompassed by either the human mind or the Divine Mind.

We come now to the question of how John understands the relation of God to the world. One way of describing this relation is to say that the whole of creation is a process of divine revelation with each particular being a finite and limited aspect of God's nature. Since all that exists is in God, God can be held to be created in the things He creates.

To say that God creates *ex nihilo* means that He created the world from His Superessential being, which is properly called "nothing" because it is superior to anything we know in finite existence.

The mode of creation is merely God's vision of the whole universe, for to Him it is the same thing to see and to make. In other words, God can see only Himself, for nothing exists outside of Himself. The simple act of God's seeing Himself is what we mean by creation of the universe. The traditional doctrine of divine Ideas, as formulated by St. Augustine, holds that the Ideas inhere in God eternally as an indivisible aspect of Himself. John holds instead that the Ideas are posterior to God. They are created and have their principle in God, while in turn they become creators supplying the principle, or pattern, for everything else. Thus Ideas cannot be synonymous with God if they are created subsequent to Him.

The word or Logos (the second Person of the Trinity) is the intermediary of creation from the One to the many. The Logos contains the "primordial causes," or Ideas (goodness, being, life, truth, wisdom, intelligence, reason, virtue, justice, health, greatness, omnipotence, eternity, and peace), which are transmitted through the Holy Spirit into actual things, divided into their genera, species, and individuals. Although in our sense experience we regard them as a plurality in their effects, considered in themselves in the Logos they are one. In this sense John holds that all things have existed eternally in their immaterial archetypes; the generation of the Son (the second Person of the Trinity) was the creation of the world. Obviously this view is closer to that of eternal manifestation of God through Platonic Ideas than to the orthodox teaching of God's direct creation of the world in time.

The third division of nature, created and not creative, longs to return to the "beyond being" source from which it came. Since everything participates in God's nature as expressed in creation, deriving from Him as a first principle and drawn toward Him as an end, the whole of nature is to be viewed as a movement powered by the love of God. Here we have again the direct influence of Pseudo-Dionysius on John.

The fourth division of nature is God conceived as that which neither creates nor is created—the desired goal toward which creation moves. Here we have the final reaffirmation of reality which is one, universal, and infinite through the absorption and transcendence of all finite multiplicity and individuality. Here the distinctions between me and thee are left behind. John's account of the "return home" reflects Latin Christianity more than Neoplatonism. It may be briefly summarized. Since the fall, with the consequent impairment of his nature, man has shared the condition of animals with similar sorrows, instincts, and death. Nevertheless, man's soul is brought back into contact with the Logos through the Incarnation.

In Christ God became man in order to redeem the effects of the primordial causes which He possesses eternally in his divinity, and to return them into their causes, so that they might be saved in them, together with the causes themselves. John stresses that contemplation by the soul is inadequate for the saving knowledge of truth. This must come from divine illumination, which must be added to man's natural faculties. This concept of divine grace is what enables man to return to God. Thus we note that John is using the Neoplatonic structure of the universe to provide a framework for the Christian incarnation and redemption. The general resurrection is viewed as a resurrection not only of man but of every creature, so that the natures of all creatures will return into the primordial. All things visible are saved by returning into their invisible causes. All men participate equally in human nature and thus share equally in the restoration of that life to its original quality of eternal life. But the elect upon whom God bestows donations of grace beyond their merit will be deified by a superintellectual knowledge and love of God. To his critics John seemed glaringly unorthodox in proclaiming the doctrine of universal salvation and in abandoning the traditional doctrine of the punishment of the damned. Perhaps the term "universal salvation" was not accurate, for the universal restoration or absorption of all finite beings into the undifferentiated, infinite perfection was not what orthodox theologians and believers had in mind when they talked about salvation.

Some of John's basic problems came from his use of Neoplatonic philosophy to maintain an orthodox interest in both the transcendence and immanence of God. But his development of this interest was one-sided and involved him in the charges of heresy. Although he was not a simple pantheist, he did blur the distinction between the Creator and the created. The Neoplatonic and Augustinian aspects of his system stand out clearly: the eternal Ideas in the Logos, the inapplicability of finite categories to God, the soul as the image of God, knowledge through Ideas. When these are added to the notion of God as beyond being, the Logos as the source of all being, creation as theophany or manifestation of God and the ultimate return of all things to God, we can appreciate how fully he utilized Plotinus' descent from the One to the many and the ascent from the many to the One.

There were serious difficulties in John's metaphysics. His interpretation of God as beyond being tends to make religion a private affair and his general metaphysical position moves toward subjectivism and mysticism. The Church could see that John's use of Neoplatonism and the Pseudo-Dionysius was heretical. But the prestige of St. Augustine and the Pseudo-Dionysius was so great that Neoplatonic elements could not be completely rejected by medieval thinkers. It was not until the rediscovery of Aristotle's writings that it appeared possible to formulate an alternative philosophical framework for Christian metaphysics. It has sometimes been suggested that John Scotus was the last ancient philosopher, for there is continuity in the work of Plato, Plotinus, Augustine, and John Scotus in their search for truth. If this is a fair judgment, we may then regard Anselm in the eleventh century as the first of the medieval philosophers who sought, not so much for truth which the Church claimed it possessed, but to understand that truth and to explain how it could be known. Then we are into the building of the foundations of Scholasticism.

Anselm

In his general orientation St. Anselm is Augustinian, but in his desire to provide a rational foundation for his beliefs and to do justice to the role of dialectic he points to the developments that mark the rise of Scholasticism. He was born in 1033 in Aosta in the southeast corner of ancient Burgundy near the Lombard border. Attracted by the revival of learning in France he came to study, first as a secular student and in 1060 as a Benedictine monk, under the Lombard Lanfranc at the monastery at Bec. He followed Lanfranc as prior at Bec in 1063 and became abbot fifteen years later. He was named the successor to Lanfranc as Archbishop of Canterbury in 1093 by William II, William the Conqueror's son and successor. He participated vigorously in the controversy over the rights of Church and State in the appointment of ecclesiastic officials during the reigns of William II and Henry I, and died in 1109.

The structure of scholastic thought was built upon the assumption that faith and reason are distinct, and that a proper relationship must be established between them. Although there is a considerable range of interpretation of this relationship, no scholastic thinker ignores it. Anselm points out that Scripture and the Church impose dogmas on the faith, such as the existence of God and the Incarnation. The believer accepts them only on the basis of authority, and reason contributes nothing to his understanding. But Anselm takes as his motto Augustine's formula *fides quarens intellectum*—faith seeking an intelligible understanding of itself. He has the confidence that, if one makes careful logical analyses, he can demonstrate the doctrines of the

Church, including the Trinity and the necessity of the Incarnation. Here Anselm walks a middle road between pure faith, which excludes any normal use of reason, and mysticism, which seeks the beatific vision in this life. Despite the demands of a busy life with heavy ecclesiastical responsibilities, Anselm wrote a number of treatises. In 1070 he wrote a meditation, *Monologium*, in which he sought a proof for the existence and triune nature of God. Since he subsequently became dissatisfied with the adequacy and self-evidence of these proofs, he wrote in 1078 a *Proslogium* in which he developed his famous formulation of the ontological argument for the existence of God. This was challenged by Gaunilo, a fellow Benedictine monk, in a reply entitled *In Behalf of the Fool*. To this Anselm made a careful reply. A third major work, *Cur Deus Homo*, which Anselm completed in 1098, dealt with the Incarnation and Redemption.

Anselm "believed in order that he might understand" (*credo ut intelligam*), a view which was to characterize the whole approach of Scholasticism, and which supported St. Augustine's basic assumption that belief was the prerequisite of knowing. There is a double motivation in Anselm's work in that he wishes to (1) present doctrines in a logical manner that will make clear their inherent necessity and (2) stress that he could not carry through the argument unless he were initially a believer. Consequently, his system is marked by the application of dialectic to every aspect of dogma. In his writings he develops the argument to be independent of even Biblical texts and the authority of the Church Fathers. He wants his arguments to carry by the force and clarity of reasoning, so he pays close attention to objections and doubts. It should be pointed out that Anselm concerns himself with theological issues such as the existence of God, the Trinity, the Incarnation, original sin, and how these doctrines are to be established. He does not set out to provide a metaphysical explanation of nature and being or even a comprehensive examination of faith itself. Such projects had to wait upon the rediscovery of Aristotle's works in the twelfth century. Anselm insists that his approach was not developed to convert unbelievers or backsliders who do not recognize Biblical authority. Instead he wants believers to have the joy that comes from understanding the faith as evidently true. Reason can clarify what was already given in revelation and furnish supplementary evidences of its truth, but it cannot provide the truth. In a sense it is a highly developed and unique meditation upon faith and presupposes it.

In the *Monologium*, meditations and reflections on God, Anselm employs an Augustinian pattern in developing three arguments for the existence of God.

(1) The first argument is that the presence of degrees of better or worse, greater or less, implies that there is a supremely good or supremely great. Only God can be supremely or absolutely good or great. God is not simply a continuation of the scale of comparative goodness, but actually the ground of all other being.

(2) Everything which exists, exists either through something or nothing. Nothing can exist through nothing. Therefore everything exists through itself or another, which is either one or many. If the ground of being is plural, we have three possibilities: (a) things exist in virtue of something other than themselves, (b) they are self-existent, or (c) they are mutually interdependent. If we adopt (a), we have what is the effect of the first result—a single ultimate ground. If we accept (b), we suppose that each is self-existent or exists through the possession of a single power of self-existence, which is then the one ultimate ground. If we choose (c), we assert that each exists through the others, and that no one of them is self-existent except by the power of the others. But Anselm rejects this latter possibility as absurd, as in effect saying that (a), which is the indispensable ground of (c), nevertheless depends on (c). Therefore only one alternative remains for Anselm. There is one thing through which all things in existence are grounded. It alone exists through itself, and thus is the greatest of all things which exist.

(3) Anselm has a third argument which combines the previous two. We recognize degrees of better and worse which must be referable to an ultimate ground, either unitary or plural. If it is unitary, it is supremely good and great. If plural, the question arises whether these goodnesses are dependent on some more ultimate goodness. At this point he repeats essentially his second argument that anything exhibiting degrees of goodness implies the being of an ultimate ground not dependent on anything other than itself.

In the foregoing arguments we see the use of maxims from ancient philosophy, adapted to fit the requirements of a basically Augustinian metaphysics. The Platonic assumption that a plurality of resembling things requires an attribute(s) in terms of which such resemblance is possible is joined to the causal assumption that whatever exists in the finite world must have a cause. This fusion of the Platonic doctrine of the Forms with the principle of causality is required by Anselm's Christian belief that the source of the attributes of things cannot be distinct from the source of their existence. Reality lies outside things, but one may look to things themselves as evidence of God's existence. In all this he is making explicit what Augustine held more or less implicitly. But Anselm does not stop here. In his *Proslogium* he seeks a single proof which is more immediate and rooted in inner experience. Here he develops the ontological proof for the existence of God—a proof for which he is celebrated in the history of philosophy as the inventor, although there are preliminary suggestions of it in Augustine, Boethius, and Seneca.

The ontological proof differs from the three in the *Monologium* in starting from faith rather than reason. Its validity for Anselm rests on the knowledge which came through God's illumination and grace. "That which I first believed thanks to your gift, I now understand through your illumination" (*Proslogium*, Ch. iv).

The heart of Anselm's argument is put by him in a compact paragraph. When believers say "God," they conceive "that than which nothing greater can be conceived." Yet the Psalmist admits: "The fool hath said in his heart, there is no God" (Ps. 14:1). But even the fool has an idea of God. This idea of God must exist in reality, for otherwise it could not exist in our minds. If it existed only in our minds, then we could conceive of a greater being—one which existed both in our minds and in reality. If we say "God" or "that than which nothing greater can be conceived," and at the same time assert He exists only in the mind, we are contradicting ourselves since we can conceive a greater who exists both in mind and reality. Anselm is insisting that God exists so truly that we cannot conceive him not to exist without falling into contradiction. Since God is supremely good and great, as well as self-existent, we cannot conceive of Him as a content of our thought. That which exists in thought involves the presence of something in thought.

It has been pointed out that there are two arguments in Anselm's presentation. The first tries to prove that God cannot fail to exist, and the second is concerned with demonstrating that God cannot be thought not to exist. The second argument depends on the first. If the second argument holds, it cannot demonstrate the first, since the fact that I cannot conceive God's nonexistence, does not show there is a Being whose existence is such that its nonexistence cannot be conceived. The force of Anselm's argument rests on the fact that he regards God's nature and His existence to be the same and that he stresses God is greater than can be conceived rather than simply as the greatest being conceivable.

Gaunilo, his fellow Benedictine monk, in a reply *In Behalf of the Fool*, offers reasons for denying that Anselm's proof is cogent. (1) If the proof were cogent, there would be no fools to deny God's existence. Since there are fools, Anselm's reasoning is not self-evident. (2) There are other beings than God, including myself, whose nonexistence I cannot deny without landing into self-contradiction. This does not prove that they or I am God. (3) If Anselm's proof were valid, one could conceive of a perfect island existing and it would therefore have to exist.

Anselm's reply is unyielding but friendly, and he ordered that henceforth Gaunilo's objections and his replies be published with the *Proslogium*—a practice not often copied in the history of philosophy by other philosophers. To the first criticism he replies that the fool may use the word "God" in a statement without understanding its meaning. The purpose of the ontological proof is to help him understand the meaning. In answering the second objection, Anselm states that a man or a winged horse may or may not exist. Its existence is not undeniable. But God is on a different level from every other being. The question is whether the existence of God is such that its very existence is implied in the act of denying it. In response to the third criticism, Anselm states that he does not call God *something greater than all things*, but *than that which a greater cannot be thought*, and this phrase can be understood even if what it denotes cannot be understood. The case of the island is beside the point, for an island is not that than which a greater cannot be thought. God is unique in being of such a nature that He cannot be thought nonexistent.

Is the ontological argument sound? Down through the centuries philosophers have debated it from opposing vantage points. Most medieval philosophers accepted it, although St. Thomas rejected it. Descartes and Spinoza accepted it in slightly different forms. Leibniz was favorable to it. Kant rejected it with an influential criticism, while the British empiricists largely ignored it. Hegel, while critical of Anselm's version of it, attempted to reformulate it. In our own day there has been a revival of lively discussion, pro and con, of Anselm's ontological argument. If the amount of critical analysis, refutation, and defense devoted through the centuries to a philosopher's writing is any indication to his stature, Anselm is clearly a distinguished philosopher even though his primary concerns were largely theological. His methods of dialectical reasoning and the stress he placed on the role of reason made such a large impact on the development of Scholasticism that we can regard him as the first great Scholastic thinker.

Abelard

Peter Abelard, the most striking personality among the twelfth century thinkers, was born in the year 1079 near Nantes, France. This scion of a Parisian noble family gave up his opportunity of becoming a great soldier for the prospect of becoming a great philosopher or theologian. He studied first under Roscellinus of Compiegne, who as a nominalist held that universals are mere words and that there are no common substances or properties. Subsequently he studied under William of Champeaux, a realist who held that universals exist prior to and independently of things that embody them. Employing Roscellinus' arguments against William, he succeeded in forcing his teacher to change his position. Next he studied theology under Anselm of Laon (not to be confused with the Archbishop), whom he found incompetent, and with typical confidence in his own powers undertook to replace him. Returning to Paris, he taught at the Cathedral School and fell in love with Heloise, the niece of the Canon of Notre Dame, to whom he managed to be assigned as tutor. The ensuing events in this affair are well known: the birth of their baby, their marriage, Heloise's withdrawal to a convent, the castration of Abelard by her uncle's henchmen, and Abelard's retirement to the Abbey of St. Denys. He began to write theological treatises and soon returned to teaching, first at Nogent-sur-Seine, then from 1136 to 1140 at Le Paraclet.

The method of Abelard's teaching and his intellectual arrogance displayed toward his teachers and opponents were calculated to produce censure by theologians. His *On the Divine Unity and the Trinity* was condemned by a council at Soissons in 1121. About 1140–1141 he was summoned to a council at Sens because of his *Introduction to Theology*. St. Bernard contrived Abelard's condemnation even before he had the opportunity to provide a defense. Abelard withdrew and set out for Rome to make a personal appeal to the Pope. On his journey he was well received at Cluny, where the Abbot, Peter the Venerable, managed subsequently to arrange a truce between Abelard and St. Bernard. In 1142 he died a broken man at Châlons-sur-Saône, a religious house affiliated with the Cluniac Order.

Abelard is important because of his unusual acumen in defining philosophic method and in his reformulation of the complex problem of the nature and status of universals. His most famous book, written in 1121–1122, is *Sic et Non*, "Yes and No," in which the conflicting opinions of the Church Fathers on 158 theological questions are set out in parallel fashion. His purpose, he says, is not to bring the faith of the Church into doubt; rather it is didactic—to stimulate young men to seek truth by exercising their minds and improving their skills in eliminating ambiguities and overcoming differences. He champions reason, but not a reason to subvert the Christian faith and extend doubt. He once wrote: "I do not wish to be so philosophical that I resist Paul, or so Aristotelian that I am separated from Christ."

Like Anselm, Abelard believes it to be a defect if we do not make the effort to understand that which we believe on the basis of proper authority. A teacher who proposes to inculcate faith in others is undermining his own work if he does not understand what he seeks to share with others. Although his dialectic serves chiefly to elucidate dogma, defend the faith against its opponents, and support authority by reason, it is in his logical treatises that Abelard makes his most significant contribution to philosophy. Even if he did not invent the method of Scholasticism or first formulate the logical doctrines developed in his writings, he is original and penetrating in his work on the controversy over universals.

Abelard's treatment of the nature and status of universals is found in his *Glosses on Porphyry*, which is his commentary on Boethius' commentary on Porphyry's *Introduction* to Aristotle's logic. In what became typical Scholastic fashion, he approaches the text sentence by sentence in a completely analytical, unhistorical, and vigorous manner with other purposes in mind than the mere exposition of the text. Abelard asks the three questions which Porphyry raised in his *Isagoge*, but did not answer. (1) Is the universal real, or merely a verbal expression? (2) If it subsists, is it corporeal or incorporeal? (3) Does the universal exist separately or is it placed in sensible things? To these Abelard adds a fourth question: If the individual were destroyed, would the universal remain? Is the species "horse" dependent upon the existence of individual horses?

Boethius, the sixth century Christian scholar, regarded the individual as the embodiment of the universal. The individual represents the universal as particularized by matter and individual accidents of shape, color, and quantity. "Socrates" and "Aristotle" were the material embodiments of the species *man* which in itself is immaterial and can only be discerned in thought. In twelfth century language, this position is that of realism. It apprehends the existence of the universal as a thing (res). Opposed to this position of realism is Roscellinus, who views only the individual as real and the universal as a mere word (vox) or mere breaths of air blown from the mouth.

Abelard rejects both these alternatives. The first view of realism held by Boethius and, initially, by William of Champeaux is rejected because it makes one and the same substance have mutually inconsistent qualities. Since *animal* is present in both "Socrates" and also in an ass, the substance *animal* will be at the same time both rational and irrational. Likewise the common universal is simultaneously one in many individuals and thus in a contradictory fashion one and many. William of Champeaux shifts to another position—the theory of indifference, in which he argues that individuals of a kind are discrete from one another, not only because their accidents are different but also because their natures or essences are not the same. Still, two men can be called the same *indifferently*. Since they are both men they are indifferently men or do not differ in so far as they are men. In criticizing this theory of indifference, Abelard retorts that it says that if Socrates and Plato were united by an absence of difference, they shared a common existence; negatively it means no more than that they did not differ from a stone.

In opposition to Roscellinus' nominalistic rejection of universals, Abelard appeals to the evidence of reality. If logic were reducible to grammar, the only standard would be the correct use of words. Yet it is true that grammatically correct statements like "A boy is a pony" can be meaningless or literally false. For Abelard, the way out of such difficulties is to be found not in denying universals, but in abandoning the interpretation of them as things (res). The mistake of the realists is in treating genera and species as things. "It is monstrous to predicate the thing of a thing." Abelard goes back to the Aristotelian definition of the universal as "that which can be predicated of several things, like man." On the other hand, "the individual is that which cannot be predicated of more than one thing, as with Callias." You cannot predicate a particular fact of anything else. The nominalist who claims that the universal is particular holds a logically untenable position. This criticism also applies to the conceptualist view that holds a particular thought to be the universal. You cannot maintain that mind is characterized by that thought. Thus the universal is not a word as such, but a word which can be predicated of things. Here Abelard moves away from Roscellinus.

Having rejected the views which he regards as erroneous or inconsistent, Abelard is able to construct his own position. His problem is to show that the same word could be used to describe a group of individuals. The word for *man* in Latin (*homo*) and in Greek (*anthropos*) is different, but each has the same reference. We are concerned here not with the word as such, but with a meaningful word with symbolic reference that points in two directions: (1) to the thing which the word means and (2) to the thought which apprehends the thing. We do not predicate *anthropos* of ourselves, but the *meaning* of which *anthropos* is a symbol. That meaning is not merely a symbol of the group taken collectively. It is attributed to the group. The thought is particular and the thing is particular, but the meaning can be and is universal, whether it be asserted of the thing or the thought.

The meaning is not an existing thing about the particulars to which it refers. There is no universal particular thing. We can use universals as meaningful symbols without ascertaining their metaphysical status. The uniqueness of Abelard's position is to be found in the fact that he insists knowledge of the universal comes through intellectual activity. One's mind is engaged in working upon the things encountered in sense experience and has the intellectual power to abstract logical terms which are related both to things and concepts. The primary ground of the universal is objective in the common *status* of the things actually denoted. In summarizing Abelard's answers to the four questions with which he initiates his discussion of universals, it may be noted: (1) The universal as a word does not exist in itself but designates something described as a state; (2) universals are not corporeal, except to the extent that a spoken word is a sound; (3) universals exist in sensible things and yet represent concepts which can only be understood through abstraction from sensible things; (4) although universals are always derived from individuals, they are not things and thus are logically independent of them when abstracted.

Abelard in his discussion of this problem keeps it on the logical and psychological levels rather than attempting to discuss it on the metaphysical level. This does not mean that Abelard did not have his own metaphysical views. Plotinus, Neoplatonists, and Augustine believed that the ideas in the intellectual realm of eternity are not species, but individual ideas, so that every particular in this realm has a counterpart in the ideal realm. Abelard shared this view. Thus we are not accidental individuations of a species; for each of us, for each particular, there is a counterpart in the mind of God.

Abelard left no school of philosophy, but he left a great impact on his time. His contributions to logic and theory of knowledge are impressive when viewed against the fact that Aristotle's major works were not available to him. His analyses of universals and abstraction and his refinement of dialectical method make him a substantial contributor to the development of Scholasticism.

St. Anselm, Erigena, and Abelard:
Selected Additional Reading

Abernethy, George L. and Thomas A. Langford, eds., *History of Philosophy: Selected Readings*. Belmont, Calif.: Dickenson, 1965, pp. 261–266.*

Anselm, *St. Anselm's Basic Writings*. Translated by Sidney N. Deane. LaSalle, Ill.: Open Court, 1958.

Barth, Karl, *Anselm: Fides Quarens Intellectum*. New York: World Publishing Company, Meridian, 1962.

Bett, H., *Johannes Scotus Erigena: A Study in Medieval Philosophy*. London: Cambridge University Press, 1932.*

Burch, George B., *Early Medieval Philosophy*. New York: Columbia University Press, 1951.*

Clayton, Joseph, *Saint Anselm: A Critical Biography*. Milwaukee: Bruce Publishing Company, 1933.*

Fairweather, E. R., ed., *A Scholastic Miscellany: Anselm to Ockham*. Philadelphia: Westminster, 1956, pp. 261–265.*

Hartshorne, Charles, *Anselm's Discovery*. La Salle, Ill.: Open Court, 1967.

Kaufmann, Walter, *Philosophical Classics*. Englewood Cliffs, N.J.: Prentice-Hall, 1961, I, 603–604.*

Leff, Gordon, *Medieval Thought from St. Augustine to Ockham*. Baltimore: Penguin, 1958.

McIntyre, John, *St. Anselm and His Critics*. Edinburgh: Oliver and Boyd, 1954.*

Sikes, J. G., *Peter Abelard*. London: Cambridge University Press, 1932.*

Plantinga, Alvin, ed., *Ontological Argument: From Anselm to Contemporary Philosophers*. Garden City: Doubleday, Anchor, 1965.

Weinberg, J. R., *A Short History of Medieval Philosophy*. Princeton, N.J.: Princeton University Paperback, 1967.

Chapter Ten

Medieval Philosophy:
Thomas Aquinas

A transition in theological interpretation occurred in the thirteenth century. While Franciscans defended the traditional Augustinian theology, Dominican theologians became innovators in an effort to provide an Aristotelian framework for classical Christianity. Although the struggle was complex, the view put forward by the Dominicans eventually prevailed. We turn now to the chief architect of this new theological style, Thomas Aquinas.

Thomas Aquinas (1224?–1274) was born into the prominent family of the Count of Aquino near Naples; he was educated at Monte Cassino and entered a house of the Dominican Order in his home town. Eventually he was sent to Cologne to study under Albert the Great and then accompanied Albert to the university in Paris where he completed his education and remained to become a teacher. In 1261 he was called to Italy, probably Bologna, then appointed to the "University of the Papal Court," a school that traveled with the Pope. In 1265 he became head of the Dominican school in Rome and while there wrote his great defense of the Christian faith, *Summa Contra Gentiles*, which was addressed to Arab intellectuals in Spain. Once again he was recalled to Paris, in 1269, but returned to the Dominican convent in Naples in 1272, where he wrote his greatest theological work, *Summa Theologica*. Two years later, he was invited by the Pope to be one of his two theological advisors, the other being Bonaventure, for his conversations with leaders of the Eastern Orthodox Church. On the way to this convocation, he died. Although his work was immediately recognized for its importance, his status in the Church was assured when in 1879 he was designated the official philosopher and theologian of the Roman Catholic Church by Pope Leo XIII.

The thirteenth century was notable philosophically for the impact which the rediscovery of Aristotle's philosophical works made upon Christian, Jewish, and Islamic thought. Thomas Aquinas came to intellectual maturity in this time of new budding and himself participated in its fruition. Not only did he write commentaries on Aristotle's works, but, more significantly, he used Aristotle as the philosophical base for his own theological construction.

Aquinas was always a theologian in intention, but he was concerned that a theological system be built upon a sound philosophical foundation. At no point in his exposition do we find him denying the essential teaching of the Christian tradition as this was inherited from Augustine and the other Fathers, but he did intend to reinterpret the foundation and the framework of theological statements. Consequently, since he was convinced of Aristotle's superiority over Plato, he felt free to reformulate the Christian doctrines in the light of Aristotelian philosophy.

Nevertheless, Thomas was never slavish in his following of Aristotle. In fact, the uses which he made of Aristotle are so distinctive in their character that the claim may be made that Thomism did not grow out of Aristotelianism "by way of evolution, but of revolution," as Etienne Gilson has said.[1] Thomas creatively utilized Aristotle for his own purposes, and these were primarily theological.

Two facts need to be pointed out in the beginning. First, in contrast to Augustine and the entire Platonic tradition, Thomas, as a Christian believer, does not take the theologian's immediate awareness of reality to be the proper beginning point for philosophy. Thus Thomas works with an entirely different epistemology from that of the Platonic tradition. No longer can he accept the validity of immediate, intuitive apprehension of ultimate reality as a viable philosophical foundation. Rather, he seeks to establish an objective exposition and interpretation of the theoretical foundation of Christian doctrine which will be as objectively teachable as that of any other science.

In order to achieve his goal, Thomas insists that a careful and radical distinction must be drawn between faith and reason. The foundation of his argument is a firm conviction of the essential harmony of all truth; thus, while both approaches exist with their own separate validity, they are not, in the end, incompatible. The truth which faith accepts is the truth which has been revealed by God as this is taught by the Church. The truth which reason knows is the truth which man, by the responsible (and sometime strenuous) use of his rationality, is able to decipher about the world. In the last analysis these two truths will overlap to a degree, but only to a degree, for there are truths of revelation which the natural reason of man cannot reach.

---

[1] *History of Christian Philosophy in the Middle Ages* (New York: Random House, 1955), p. 365.

Human Intelligence

To understand the way in which Thomas approaches his philosophical work, it is necessary to begin with his understanding of the nature of man. Being, as he understands it—that is, as predicated analogously—constitutes a great chain which extends from God, as "highest Being," down to the most elemental piece of matter. Man has his distinctive place in this chain; therefore, to understand what man is capable of "knowing," we must be clear about his status in this scheme of creation. In the diminution of being from God downwards, man stands between angels and animals. Angels are described as pure form and therefore are incorporeal or immaterial beings. In a thoroughly Aristotelian sense, Aquinas insists that the forms are of universals, or, contrariwise, there are no forms of individuals. If angels are pure form, then each is a species unto himself; and the type of knowledge angels may possess is peculiar to their status in being.

Another step downward in the hierarchy of being is man. Because he has a soul, man still belongs to the series of immaterial beings, while at the same time the fact that man is also body qualifies the means by which he comes to know and the content of what he is capable of knowing. As soul and body, man is a mixture of form and matter, for the soul is the form of the body. In men, the potentiality inherent in their materiality is actualized in such a way as to form individualized, distinctive men: Joe or Bill or Mary. The differences in men are to be ascribed to the indeterminate nature of their materiality, which is susceptible to a variety of determinations by the same Form. Each man, therefore, in his own distinctive manner, is a composition of essence and existence.

For Aquinas, possession of an active intellect is that which gives man his peculiar dignity. It is the highest faculty of the soul. It is a capacity for grasping eternal truth, an inner light or divine illumination present to men. The active intellect works within the system of eternal forms that constitutes the intelligible structure of the universe. Being human, however, means that man's understanding functions within his composite character of form and matter, actuality and potentiality. Since his mind is largely an unrealized capacity for knowledge, that is, a passive intelligence, man's vision is only partial and any enrichment must be laboriously achieved by utilization of the active intellect. The passive potential provides the context in which the intellect works, the active component is that by which intellect works.

The point of this discussion from the standpoint of understanding Thomas' theory of knowledge is to be found in the fact that for him each manner of being has its own form of knowing which is appropriate to its nature. Thus, for man to "know" he must employ both his body and his soul. The soul has the power of sensing, but it cannot exercise this power without the body. Even more, since the soul inhabits the body, the soul is dependent upon the transmission by the bodily senses for the incitement of its ability to comprehend the external world. Since, in contrast to Augustine, Thomas holds that there is no direct knowledge of God or immediate apprehension of the intelligible forms, the soul must depend upon sense experience for its cognitive data.

Perhaps some comparison of Thomas' epistemology with that of Augustine is helpful. Let us look at one much debated issue, namely, the question of whether the will or the intellect is primary in man's thought and action. Thomas follows Aristotle in placing the intellect at the apex of the psyche of man. He does, of course, acknowledge the influence of the will in human decision making, but basically he regards the will as being determined by the knowledge of the good—in grasping the good the intellect guides the will. Thus, faith may presuppose natural knowledge and perfect it; and reason may precede faith and establish a valid foundation upon which faith can build.

Augustine, and those who followed him, consistently maintained that there is a unity of personality of such a character that one cannot easily distinguish between the various aspects of the human psyche. Nevertheless, Augustine did argue that the will is the fundamental power of the soul and, consequently, the will guides or determines the utilization of the intellectual powers. For Augustine, therefore, the use of reason is dependent upon the volition, while for Thomas reason is autonomous and is capable of functioning so as to guide the will. For Augustine, faith (volitional, affectional commitment) precedes and guides reason, while for Thomas faith is not contradictory to reason, and when properly understood may be shown to be dependent upon reason, although it can also move beyond the reach of reason.

The mind of man is a receptacle upon which the external objects make their impression through the senses. As a combination of matter and form, man is one among a large number of material bodies, each of which is likewise a combination of matter and form. As we have said, it is the material element which individualizes each of these bodies. Nevertheless, and this is the crucial point, knowledge comes by the activity of discerning the universal element which individual bodies contain. This is to say, knowledge is knowledge of the forms, and matter can be "known" in the strict sense only as it is formed.

Knowledge is gained, therefore, when the substantial form is received and recognized by the rational soul or mind.

The process by which the form in the material object is transmitted to the mind is through the "sensitive soul," which comprises the five senses as well as the powers of memory and discrimination. This sensible species is "examined and shaped by the active intellect so that it is recognized as an expression of a universal form. To put this a little more simply: sensible objects act upon the senses and impress (imprint) themselves upon the human intellect. The active intellect takes these impressions and finds in these objects their universal form.

The Existence of God

For Aquinas this movement of understanding is reversed when one wants to establish cosmological theism. Consequently man must begin with his active intellect, move back through the sense impressions to the external objects and finally to the singular cause (Prime or First Cause) which "informed," literally, all of the created beings (the sensible species). We can now turn, therefore, to the question of God's existence, which Thomas holds may be established through the power of natural reason.

The five arguments for the existence of God are presented by Thomas in the *Summa Theologica*. The first argument is taken from the observation of motion. Whatever is in motion is put in motion by something else; which is to say all motion has a cause, and the cause must be something other than the being which is in motion. Motion, he goes on to argue, is a reduction from potentiality to actuality, and nothing can be reduced from potentiality to actuality except by that which is in the state of actuality. That which is moved, therefore, must be moved by another, and that by still another. Hence, the series must either be infinite or there is a finite point at which it stops at a primary cause or first mover which is self-moved. Thomas believes there is such a primary cause and this is what everyone understands to be God.

The second argument is taken from the nature of efficient cause. There is, Thomas maintains, a hierarchy of causes so that every cause is subordinate to the cause above it. Nothing can be its own efficient cause, for in order to produce itself, it would have to be prior, as cause, to itself as effect. In efficient cause, as in motion, it is not possible to go on to infinity, for to take away the cause is to take away the effect which we perceive; therefore it is necessary to admit a first efficient cause, which everyone designates by the name of God. It should be noted that this argument is not taken by many Thomistic scholars to refer to regress of causes in a linear or a temporal sense, but rather in an ontological sense. Thus, the argument is intended to show that if the primary cause or unmoved mover is not predicated there will be no causation. But, as a matter of sense experience, we witness motion and causation, and because of this we can trace these expressions of being back to their ultimate ground and thereby argue for the necessity of a first cause.

The third argument, and one to which most Thomistic scholars tend to give precedence in terms of its importance, is based upon the transitoriness of being, namely the fact that everything comes into being and perishes. As we observe things we are aware of a continual generation and perishing; their existence is not necessary. If existence is not necessary, then there must be a cause to explain it; this is to say, if there are things which exist there must be some being the existence of which is necessary, which needs no cause to exist since it exists of itself. Aquinas argues, once again, that it is impossible to go to infinity to account for cause. Thus, we can postulate the existence of some being having its own necessity. And this all men speak of as God.

The fourth argument is taken from the gradation which is found in sensible objects, or in the different degrees of perfection which different sensible objects possess. Among beings there are distinctions in goodness, truth, nobility, and so forth. But to refer to things as being "more" or "less" good, for instance, is to refer these things to some absolute norm, to that which is maximum (otherwise there could be no comparative statements). Now the maximum in any genus, Thomas argues, is the cause of all in that genus. Therefore there must be something which is to all beings the cause of their being, whether it have the quality of goodness or any other perfection; and this cause men speak of as God.

The fifth and final argument is taken from the governance of the world, and is usually designated the teleological argument. This is to claim that all natural bodies, even those which lack knowledge, act for an end. The way in which they actually achieve this end is a fair indication that they do not arrive at it by chance and that such achievement must be intentional and willed. Since such natural bodies are without knowledge, someone has to plan for them and to direct them. This primary, intelligent Being who is the cause of the purpose in the natural world is called God.

As a summary of his argument, the principal case which Aquinas makes may be put as follows. The mind is first acquainted with material objects, as these are transmitted through the senses. In considering these objects it comes to see them as dependent upon some cause beyond themselves. Being unwilling to admit an infinite causal sequence, he arrives at a first cause, or a cause which exists of itself. This primary cause men call God. Thus, Thomas argues that all rational men can know God by investigating the conditions of existence.

The Nature of God

But what is the nature of this "something," this cause, this ultimate reality? Thomas is convinced that by the exercise of natural reason some knowledge of God's attributes can be established, though there must remain a degree of agnosticism since what can be known can be indicated only negatively. The philosopher can, by rational deduction, know that this final cause of God is immutable (not mutable), infinite (not finite), simple (not composite), eternal (not temporal), incorporeal (not corporeal), and so forth. While this knowledge is not unimportant, it is abstract and lacks positive content. To know God more exactly than this one must rely upon God's self-disclosure of his nature, which he has given in the scriptures and through the Church. By means of revelation man can come to the additional knowledge of the Trinity, incarnation, original sin, sacraments, eschatology, resurrection, future life (with reward and punishment)—indeed all of the content of the Church's dogma.

But we are here concerned with Thomas' philosophy, and we need to return to his discussion of the nature of God as being. Beginning with the Exodus account in the Old Testament where God names Himself for Moses, "I AM WHO I AM," Thomas defines being as the *act* pointed out by the verb "to be." In human experience, to be is to exist; thus he understands God to be that being whose entire nature is the act of existence. The only proper manner of speaking of God or referring to Him is in the simple words "He is," for God "is" absolutely. In the strictest sense, it must be claimed that God is ineffable or unknowable to us, for while we can establish *that* God is, we cannot know *what* He is. This is so because there is no *what* in God, for God's essence is His existence and we cannot decipher what it is to be a being whose only essence is "to be." To make this clear, we may compare our knowledge of God to our knowledge of other things. In our usual experience, a "being" is "*something* that is," or "*something* that exists." But, since in God there is no *something* to which existence can be attributed, we are using the verb "is" in a unique way and a way which we cannot, strictly speaking, know.

In spite of this limitation, Thomas does go on to claim that it is possible for man to know God indirectly by way of analogy. This is to say, man can know God to a degree, though not perfectly, through the consideration of the created order. The two most basic things which can be known are that God is completely different from his creatures and that He is at least what he must be in order to be their cause. This type of knowledge is called "analogical" and by it there is established some relation or proportion between our knowledge of the created world and our knowledge of God. Hence when we speak of God as the first cause, we are not directly describing him but we are saying that there is some resemblance between our knowledge of cause and effect in the natural world and the manner in which God causally affects the world. It is on the basis of this assumption that Aquinas proceeds to the arguments for the existence of God and deduces what may be legitimately known about this existence through its analogy with the created world. The exact character of the resemblance between man's knowledge of the natural world and man's knowledge of God remained as a question to be resolved by the scholastic successors of Thomas.

Ethics

For Aquinas, the standard which governs moral thought and action is set by man's status in the hierarchy of being. Not only can man know what is proper to his condition as "man," as was discussed in his theory of knowledge, but now it must also be said that man can do only that which is possible for "man." It is God's intention that man should reach the end for which he was made: perfect happiness or the vision of God. Consequently, man is endowed with the ability to achieve this end.

Every man, Thomas claims, is imbued with the capacity to distinguish right from wrong (*synteresis*) which, when properly nurtured by reason, enables man to apply universal moral principles to practical situations. This means that in one's personal life his drives and impulses (which Aquinas, following Aristotle, calls his appetitive faculties) must be guided into patterns of behavior which are in conformity with the universal principles. On the social level, this means that the natural law must be properly interpreted and implemented. Let us look at each of these two dimensions of the moral life in order.

Virtue, Thomas says, is "a settled disposition of doing good." With this definition, it is possible to lift up the two elements which are essential for moral action: namely, there must be a "settled disposition" or habitual inclination toward the good, and there must be the concrete expression of this intention by actually performing the good. On this basis, it is possible to say that for Thomas the good life is a life of good deeds, that is, action which is directed by the reason to its proper end. In the personal life of man, this means that this goodness will be characterized by the practice of the four classical virtues: temperance, fortitude (courage), justice, and prudence (wisdom).

The first three of these virtues which Thomas designates the "moral virtues" give rise to right actions, which is to say, if one acts according to temperance, fortitude, or justice he is doing the thing he should. But one should do the right thing for the right reason. Hence, the moral virtues must be implemented by the "intellectual virtue" of prudence. Prudence gives rise to truly virtuous action because now the right action is governed by correct understanding. The moral and intellectual virtues Aquinas combines under the designation of "cardinal virtues"; and all of the cardinal virtues should be present in the life of the good man.

But beyond the cardinal virtues which are possible for all men and to be expected of all men, there are the theological or distinctively Christian virtues of faith, hope, and charity. These virtues, Aquinas held, were not to be acquired by any amount of human effort. Rather, their origin is to be found in the infusion of character by God's grace, an act which is accomplished by the sacraments. The grace which infuses faith, hope, and love into Christian character may go further and infuse moral virtues as well, so that once again that which the natural man may work out by the careful exercise of his reason is also revealed by God, plus the fact that more than the natural man can discover is also revealed. There is an exact parallel between Thomas' understanding of the relation of reason and revelation in the knowledge of God and in the moral life.

In social life, the norm of virtue is the law. According to Aquinas, law is an external principle by which God directs men to their end and thereby aids them in the realization of their good. Since it is reason which directs man to his proper end, law is a product of reason. So God imposes laws upon his creatures which are in accordance with His intellect, and which man may discover by the exercise of his intellect. It should be clear that for Aquinas God is the ultimate source of all law, and to discover this law is to discover the will of God for the community of men.

Aquinas mentions four types of law: eternal law, natural law, human law, and divine law. The eternal law exists in the mind of God; this is the reason of God and constitutes the blueprint of the whole order of creation—in theological language this eternal law is called the "providence" of God. This law, because it is the reason of God, can never be known directly or completely by man; there are, however, indirect analogies.

The natural law is that part of the eternal law which is understood by man. This is an expression of man's capacity to distinguish right from wrong (*synteresis*), and thus the natural law may be said to be imprinted upon man's reason in the form of universal principles. The principles of natural law are, therefore, self-evident to reason. The first "precept" of this natural law is that "good is to be done and promoted, and evil is to be avoided" (*Summa Theologica*, question 94, article 2). From this basic distinction all other precepts are to be derived. What are these derivative precepts? The answer is that effort to preserve life, which man shares with all animals, is understood also as a requirement to preserve human life; also one can find such general principles as the demand for equity between persons, the right of possession of private property for the common good, and regulations regarding sexual intercourse and the education of children. The presupposition which lies behind all of the precepts is the Aristotelian ethical theory that man's good consists in the realization of the potentialities of his nature by activity under the control of reason. This natural law is open to all men, is valid for Christians and non-Christians alike, and consequently provides the foundation for political sanction and action.

The human law is that part of the natural law, or the precise determinations of the natural law, which become positive, written laws for human society. Human laws are diverse, and the reason for this is that the common principles of the natural law cannot be applied to all men in the same way because of the great variety of human conditions. But every particular human law should be in keeping with the general natural law; if it departs from this norm it is a perversion. But if it is in keeping with the natural law, then the human law is a positive good for the ordering of society. The good person obeys these laws because he recognizes their worth (prudence once again is important), but these laws must be enforced upon the evil for the good of the social order.

The human law is just and authentically reflects the natural law when it is directed to the common good, when it does not exceed the authority of the legislator (which is to say, the legislator recognizes that his own legal rights are subject to natural law), and when it places an equitable burden on the subjects. Consequently, human laws may be changed and, as a matter of fact, do need to be changed when, for instance, there is an advance of reason or when there are changed contextual conditions.

Finally, Aquinas discusses the divine law. This law might also be called God's grace, for it is that aspect of the will of God which has been revealed directly to man. Once again, there is a parallel to the cardinal virtues and to the relation of reason to revelation. The "Old Law," which consisted of God's revelation of his will to man before Christ, though universally perceived, may be reduced to the Ten Commandments. All of the moral precepts of the "Old Law" belong to the natural law since they are in accord with reason.

But to this "Old Law" must be added the "New Law," which comes by a new infusion of God's grace. Jesus Christ is this "New Law," which becomes a part of man's life as brought to him by the Holy Spirit. Thus the new law issues in the imitation of Christ. Such a radical new way of life does not deny the validity of that which is gained by natural knowledge, but it does heighten the importance of the old law and extend it so that the prohibitions against murder and adultery, for example, now also apply to "interior acts" of anger and lust. The most significant form of this new law is the gift of the most excellent of all virtues—love. For by the infusion of this new grace man is given the capacity to attain to God; he is enabled to love God for God's sake alone. While the divine law governs all Christian living, its counsels of perfection are radically followed by the few who are willing to give themselves wholly to its accomplishment.

Throughout the discussion of the thought of Thomas Aquinas, his theological as well as his philosophical interests are evident. In this he both reflects his time and propels the dominant concerns of his time into the continuing philosophical discussion.

St. Thomas Aquinas: Selected Additional Reading

Abernethy, George L. and Thomas A. Langford, eds., *History of Philosophy: Selected Readings*. Belmont, Calif.: Dickenson, 1965, pp. 266–292.*

Aquinas, *Summa Theologica*. Literally translated by fathers of the English Dominican Province. New York: Benziger Bros., 1947–1948.*

Aquinas, *Nature and Grace: Selections from the Summa Theologica*. Edited and translated by A. M. Fairweather. Philadelphia: Westminster, 1959.*

Aquinas, *Basic Writings of Saint Thomas Aquinas*. Edited by Anton C. Pegis. New York: Random House, 1945.*

Aquinas, *On the Truth of the Catholic Faith: Summa Contra Gentiles*. Translated by C. J. O'Neil. 4 vols. New York: Doubleday, Image, 1962.

Aquinas, *Philosophical Texts*. Edited by C. Gilby. New York: Oxford University Press, Galaxy Books, 1960.

Aquinas, *The Pocket Aquinas*. Edited and translated by V. J. Bourke. New York: Simon and Schuster, Washington Square Press, 1960.

Bourke, V. J., *Aquinas' Search for Wisdom*. Milwaukee: Bruce, 1965.*

Brennan, Robert E., ed. *Essays in Thomism*. New York: Sheed and Ward, 1942.*

Copleston, Frederick C., *Aquinas*. Baltimore: Penguin, 1967.

Garrigou-Legrange, Reginald, *Reality: A Synthesis of Thomistic Thought*. Translated by Patrick Cummins. St. Louis: Herder, 1950.*

Gilson, E., *The Philosophy of St. Thomas Aquinas*. Translated by Edward Bullough. Cambridge, England: W. Heffer and Sons, 1929.*

Gilson, E., *The Spirit of Thomism*. New York: Harper and Row, Torchbook, 1966.

Kaufmann, Walter, *Philosophical Classics*. Englewood Cliffs, N.J.: Prentice-Hall, 1961, I, 604–629.*

Maritain, Jacques, *St. Thomas Aquinas*. Translated by J. F. Scanlon. London: Sheed and Ward, 1938.*

Pieper, Josef, *Guide to Thomas Aquinas*. New York: New American Library, Mentor, 1964.

de Wulf, Maurice, *System of Thomas Aquinas*. New York: Dover, 1959.

Chapter Eleven

Medieval Philosophy: Roger Bacon, Duns Scotus, and William of Ockham

Roger Bacon

It was once thought that the Middle Ages somehow constituted a single intellectual outlook to which every thinker from St. Augustine to St. Thomas Aquinas gave allegiance. It is of course true that thought in the Middle Ages operated within a range of interests and assumptions which differentiated the period from the Classical Period of Greece and Rome and from the thought of the post-Renaissance age. But there was actually a very considerable amount of diversity in attitudes, interests, phases, and movements among medieval philosophers and theologians. Some revealed themselves as fairly independent thinkers, who, in some degree, anticipated "waves of the future." Roger Bacon, a contemporary of St. Thomas, was one of these colorful and independent thinkers who "upset the establishment." Unfortunately our knowledge of Roger Bacon's life is incomplete and even sketchy. Consequently, some have interpreted him as a "modern man" ahead of his time, while others have viewed him as an irascible and arrogant charlatan. The truth probably lies some place between these two extremes.

The exact date of Roger Bacon's birth is not known, but it is assumed that he was born around 1214 at Ilchester in Somerset, England. He seems to have come from a noble family which suffered financial reverses and exile for loyalty to King Henry III in his struggles against the barons (1258–1265).

Bacon enrolled at Oxford, where he came under the influence of Robert Grosseteste, who kindled his interest in philology and science and left him with a permanent distaste for incorrect translation of Aristotle. Grosseteste, probably influenced by Arabic science, repudiated the Greek teaching that circular motion was the original form of all natural motion. He held instead the original motion to have been rectilinear, and circular motion to have been derivative. This speculation supported the interest in the study of motions in their own right—an interest which Bacon furthered. In general, Bacon stressed the value and utility of experimental science and mathematics, the need for the study of ancient languages to provide a purer text of the Bible, and the need to eliminate obscurantism in philosophy.

From Oxford Bacon went to Paris where he possibly studied under Albertus Magnus and Alexander of Hales. He felt that the men of Paris were inferior to his teachers at Oxford. After acquiring the degree of Master of Arts at Paris, sometime around 1250, Bacon returned to Oxford where he subsequently joined the Franciscan Order. St. Bonaventure, the General of the Franciscan Order, forbade Bacon to lecture at Oxford and in 1257 ordered him to Paris, where for a number of years he was under strict surveillance and was prohibited from publishing his ideas. But in 1266 Pope Clement IV, who had earlier served as Papal Legate in England and had heard of Bacon's teaching, asked for copies of Bacon's treatises. However, the manuscripts were not in final form. Within eighteen months he finished his three large treatises: the *Opus Majus*, the *Opus Minus*, and the *Opus Tertium*. The three lucidly written books were designed to appeal to Clement's practical interests and to convince him of the utility of scientific studies. It is uncertain whether the books actually reached the Pope, for Clement died in 1268. But before his death he had arranged for Bacon's return to Oxford in 1267. In 1272 Bacon wrote a bitter treatise, *Compendium Studii Philosophiae*, filled with invective. He attacked the corruption of the clergy and the Pope and lashed out at the inadequacies and pretensions of Scholasticism. In 1278 Jerome of Ascoli, the General of the Franciscan Order, condemned him to prison for his writings, which were suspected of containing theological novelties, the teaching of black arts, attacks on Dominicans and members of his own Order, and the defense of Arabian scholars. He remained in prison until 1292 when a new General of the Franciscan Order set him free. He died shortly thereafter.

Bacon's chief work, *Opus Majus*, is an interesting mixture of materials from many fields, including comparative philology, optics, alchemy, and astrology. Among other things it contains proposals for constructing huge magnifying glasses to set afire the Saracen fleets at sea. But the unifying thread in the entire treatise is the ultimate utility of science shown in the service of the Church and the knowledge of God. For Bacon, eternal wisdom guides the Church, governs the Commonwealth of the Faithful, produces the conversion of infidels, and restrains evil men. There are four causes of the ignorance of this wisdom: First, following frail and unsuited authority; second, the influence and bad effects of custom; third, the opinions of the uninformed mass of men; fourth, the concealment of one's ignorance in the display of apparent wisdom. Of these evils the fourth is the worst;

and Bacon characteristically directs his scorn at some of the leading thinkers of his day. All of this anticipates Francis Bacon's discussion of the Four Idols in a later century.

It should be stressed that Friar Bacon's own aim was theological. He opposed the dogmatism of godly men, not their godliness. For him, theology is the supreme science which must be explained by philosophy and Canon Law. All truth comes from Christ, and thus it is that the truths which have been unearthed by philosophers come from the divine light. "Hence it follows of necessity that we Christians ought to employ philosophy in divine things, and in matters pertaining to philosophy to assume many things belonging to theology, so that it is apparent that there is one wisdom shining in both" (*Opus Majus*, I, 65). This emphasis on divine illumination hearkens back to Augustine and the Neoplatonists and suggests a deep medieval deposit in Bacon's thought.

Mathematics was highly prized by Bacon. In fact, he described it as "the gate and key of the natural sciences, the alphabet of philosophy." He argued that the fundamental concepts in the physical sciences could be expressed by mathematical concepts. He believed mathematics to be the most certain of the sciences, for it employs demonstrations which proceed from the definitions of essences rather than from the fact. Yet for all his confidence in, and appreciation of, mathematics Bacon was not able to achieve any great results from his use of mathematics; indeed he emphasized that the queen of the natural sciences was experimental science. The experimental method has three primary merits: it can test the factual validity of scientific conclusions obtained by reason; it provides knowledge of facts and laws which cannot be obtained by other means; it explores new areas of investigation and thus extends the scientific domain. It would be misleading to suggest that Bacon made the careful distinctions between mere observation and experiment that one would find in a contemporary research scientist; nor did he have the same interest in exact verification. Moreover, his zealous interest in alchemy and astrology would of course distinguish him from modern scientists, who would be even further removed from Bacon's belief that the sciences obtain their value from the extent to which they throw light on the meaning of Scripture and assist us in the quest for salvation.

The last portion of *Opus Majus* turns to the subject of moral philosophy, or insight into godly living. Bacon delineates man's basic duties to God, to others, and to himself. Man's beatitude is the highest good of which man is capable. Morality and revelation both are necessary to its realization. His emphasis here shows the influence of

Aristotle, of Seneca and his Stoicism, and, in a different direction, of monasticism.

Bacon was in various respects strongly medieval, while at the same time he was forward looking and guilty of vigorous and cantankerous criticism of those committed to medieval values. The phrase, "the Baconian reform of science," might be equally applied to Roger Bacon in the thirteenth century and Francis Bacon in the seventeenth century. The Friar demonstrated that his day was not ripe for his ideas or for his methods of promoting them. But his work was significant both for revealing what was to come and how Augustinianism could remain as a continuing cultural influence.

Duns Scotus

John Duns Scotus, the "Subtle Doctor," was perhaps a more typical medieval thinker in the Scholastic tradition than Roger Bacon, but there are aspects of his views which indicated symptoms of Scholastic decline and collapse. Our knowledge of his life is meagre. It is believed that he was born about 1265 at Maxton, in Roxborough County, Scotland. As a young man he joined the Franciscan Order and was ordained a priest. He studied at Oxford and at the University of Paris, possibly from 1293 to 1296. He returned to Oxford, where he taught until 1301. In 1302 he went back to Paris to study and lecture. Becoming involved in a dispute between the Papal Party and Philip the Fair of France, he found it necessary to leave the country. In 1304 he returned to Paris to resume his theological studies, which culminated in his being awarded the degree of Doctor of Theology in 1305. Two years later he was sent to Cologne to teach, but his death in 1308 prematurely ended a brilliant career which had already brought him great fame. He was known for dialectical skill and critical acumen in analyzing the doctrines of his predecessors, especially those of St. Thomas Aquinas. He drew large numbers to his lectures. It was ironic that a later shift in intellectual values led people to use the name of the "Subtle Doctor" of Scholasticism to coin the word "dunce."

The systematic philosophizing of Albert the Great and St. Thomas Aquinas had shifted Scholastic thought from an Augustinian-Platonic orientation to an Aristotelian one. It was not surprising that this largely Dominican effort met with some resistance among Franciscans, who had Aristotelian training but wished to retain more of the Augustinian emphases. It is not clear whether one ought to interpret Duns Scotus as basically an Aristotelian tempered with Augustinian interests or an Augustinian tinctured with Aristotelianism. In some matters in which he opposed Aquinas, he revealed an independent mind and went beyond the Augustinians. His own philosophy was not systematized and must be extracted from numerous critical and polemical discussions of specific issues, which partly explains why so many divergent interpretations of Duns Scotus have appeared.

Duns Scotus, like St. Thomas Aquinas, made a distinction between theology and philosophy and believed that there can be no conflict between the truths of faith and the truths of reason. He had a certain distrust of philosophical reasoning, though he used it to support his views and to criticize those of his opponents. He limited much more sharply the area and significance of natural theology than did St. Thomas Aquinas. Although proofs for the existence of God have to rest on an inference from effects to their causes, Duns Scotus argued that this type of proof cannot be absolutely conclusive or possess the validity St. Thomas assigned to it. In particular, he rejected St. Thomas' argument from motion on the grounds that the cause of motion need not be the cause of being, so that the argument at best could only prove the existence of Aristotle's unmoved mover and not that of the Christian God. In general, Duns Scotus felt that claims about the nature of God, providence, the divine prescience and predestination, and the immortality of the soul do not lend themselves to rational demonstration. We are much less able to prove through reason the doctrines of faith than St. Thomas believed. Theology is basically a matter of revelation, while knowledge through reason is knowledge of the natural world. Reason is not competent to prove the existence or nature of that which is prior to reason. In God, will is prior to reason. Reason is simply the awareness and understanding of what God's will has produced. Thus no human being can give a rational account of God's nature; we must depend on revelation. Duns Scotus believes that will is primary in man also and that God seeks basically to move the wills of men rather than to inform their minds. Man's salvation depends, not on understanding and knowledge, but on conforming his will to that of God. Thus Duns Scotus' emphasis on faith differs markedly from that of St. Thomas.

Further differences between positions taken in epistemology by Duns Scotus and St. Thomas Aquinas may be seen in the status they accord to universals. Although his position may be designated as moderate realism, the emphasis of Duns Scotus differs from that of St. Thomas. Aristotle was ambiguous in that he failed to make clear whether the mind makes or discovers the distinctions of form, matter, particular, and genus. Duns Scotus wished to validate these distinctions as objective. For him, the universe comes into being as a system of Forms already enacted as particular instances. Thus it is of the nature of the Form itself to be particularized. To be human implies being *a* human. Individuation, then, is necessary to the complete expression of the universal. One cannot be human in the universal sense unless he has the particular form of a Joe Smith or a Tom Brown. All essences and species are both universal and individual. As concepts in our minds or in that of God they are universal. In the things to which we apply concepts, they are groups of individuals. Although his insistence on universal forms reflects Platonic realism, his insistence that actually existing things are individual things does prepare the soil for William of Ockham's nominalism.

This Scotist emphasis on individual things may have been partially influenced by Roger Bacon's insistence on the need to study directly the facts of particular nature. In any event, the "Subtle Doctor" attacked the problem of individuality. We know Plato and Aristotle as men, philosophers, and rational animals, but what makes Plato a real individual distinct from Aristotle? We know the difference between a horse and a dog, but what are the differences which distinguish one pup from another in the litter? Aristotle and St. Thomas held that the differences between individual men are not to be found in the essential formal principle, but in variations in the matter possessed by men. Duns Scotus admits that "Plato" possesses not only "whatness" (*quidditas*) which gives him the form of human, but also "thisness" (*haecceitas*) which individuates him from every other man. What makes him "Plato" is that which is different from what characterizes every other man—"thisness" is "not-that." Individuality is neither form nor matter. We cannot define it or develop a knowledge of it—we can only name it *haecceitas* and point to it. It is simply the ultimate reality of a given form.

Duns Scotus holds that the soul is only formally distinct from its various powers which are, in turn, distinct from one another. Soul and body exemplifying matter and form respectively make a substantial unity in man. Yet the soul remains a unity of form and matter, and the body itself, as a particular body of a particular soul, has its form. Duns Scotus defends, then, a belief in the plurality of substantial forms in man while holding that the soul is a subsistent form which can exist independently of the body. In his own words: "Thus every composition is divided into two essential parts: on one part, its own act, that is to say, the ultimate form by virtue of which it is what it is; on the other part, the potentiality proper to the act, which includes the first matter with all the preceding forms. In this sense, I agree that this total being (*esse*) takes its complete existence from a single form which confers on everything that which it is; but it does not follow from there that everything contains simply one form, or that several forms are not included in the totality, not as specifically constituting the composition but as included in the total of the composition" (*Opus* Ox., I, IV,16,3). Thus he states the formal distinction.

The most obvious Augustinian emphasis in Duns Scotus appears in his conception of the relations between the intellect and the will. As a member of an Order whose original inspiration came from the life of St. Francis offered as a response to the love of God as revealed in the Incarnation and Passion of Christ, it is not surprising to find Scotus viewing man as a will directing the intellect to obey its commitments. This is in contrast to the Thomist view of the will as a blind faculty which is determined by the good as soon as the mind has seen and recognized the good for what it is. Scotus comes close to ethical indeterminism in teaching that the whole cause of the will's willing rests with the will. Intellect has other causes than itself, but will has no other cause than itself. Thus he believes that St. Thomas is mistaken in maintaining that we necessarily will what we see to be good. Our will is always contingent so that we could have chosen otherwise and thus have had a real Pelagian choice.

Duns Scotus is, in effect, seeking a return to God of the powers taken from Him by the philosophers. Thomism views God's creation of the world as the necessary expression of his perfect rationality—that He could create no other. In opposition Duns Scotus asserts that no determining reason can be assigned for God's creativity. All we can say is that He has willed it and must have willed it eternally. He is absolutely free to will it or not to will it. This we must accept as Christian dogma.

There are of course ethical and even social-political implications in a doctrine of the primacy of will over reason. Although Scotus was not interested in exploring these, his successors spelled them out. If the world is the creation of God's absolute and arbitrary will and the laws of nature are edicts, what status are we to assign to the moral law? Are the cardinal virtues good merely because God arbitrarily prefers them? Could he equally prefer their opposites? Duns Scotus did not devote much attention to ethics, for he was a speculative and not a practical theologian. It is difficult to see how he could have developed a systematic moral theory consistent with his theological teaching and with traditional Christian moral teaching. In practice Scotus emphasized that the Divine Legislator, not the Law, is eternal, so acts in themselves are strictly indifferent. He relied on traditional evaluations of moral worth on the assumption that they reflected God's direct commands made in His absolute and arbitrary freedom. Subsequent thinkers were to wrestle with the problems that face an ethics based on will and power.

Duns Scotus was an acute thinker and showed how refined analysis could become even within the limits of orthodoxy. Students today have come to appreciate in a new way the subtlety and relevance of his work. In the effort to correct and improve upon the synthesis of St. Thomas his intentions were positive, orthodox, and systematic. Yet in narrowing the range of natural theology and exalting revelation over an increasing use of reason as a secular instrument, he upset the delicate balance between faith and reason. By his emphasis on faith and will, Scotus was suggesting to men that knowledge and proof were not available in theology. This tended to encourage men seeking knowledge to pursue it in the sciences. The suggestion that reason is primarily a secular instrument tended in the later "Age of Reason" to relegate religion to a less significant role in human affairs. These were consequences Duns Scotus did not have in view, and he would have deplored them if he had been able to anticipate them.

William of Ockham

If Duns Scotus showed how far analysis could go within the framework of orthodoxy, William of Ockham revealed the results of developing fully the deviations from Thomism that appear in Scotism. He was undoubtedly the last of the great medieval thinkers who shaped the course of European thought. The circumstances of this British schoolman's life are not fully known. Estimates of his birth date range from 1270 to 1300. He died on April 10 in either 1349 or 1350. Like Duns Scotus and Roger Bacon, he was a Franciscan who studied at Oxford and later at Paris. It is not certain whether he attended the lectures of Duns Scotus or only read his works and argued with his disciples. In 1324 he was ordered to the Papal Court at Avignon to answer charges of unorthodoxy. During the nearly three years he waited for the decision which finally condemned fifty-one propositions from his writings, he occupied himself with studies and with preparing defenses of the Franciscan Order in its dispute with Pope John XXII over Apostolic Poverty. When arrest seemed imminent in 1328, Ockham and Michael Cesena, the general of the Franciscan Order, fled to Pisa to join the emperor, Louis of Bavaria, who was involved in a controversy with the Pope over the succession to the Imperial crown. According to tradition, Ockham greeted the emperor by saying, "Do you defend me with your sword; I will defend you with my pen." The Pope of course excommunicated them. Ockham took up residence in Munich, where he produced a series of treatises on papal power and civil sovereignty in which he charged the Pope with heresy. When Pope John XXII died in 1334, Ockham continued his polemical writing against the Avignon Popes until 1347, when Louis of Bavaria died and his cause with him.

Ockham's chief contributions to subsequent philosophical develop-ment are to be found in epistemology, logic, and metaphysics. He began his work as a scholastic theologian. The primary problem of scholastic theologians from the beginning of the thirteenth century had been that of harmonizing Aristotle's philosophy with orthodox Christian doctrine. St. Thomas Aquinas had effected a reconciliation between natural philosophy and Christian theology which required only a minimal reinterpretation of Aristotelian positions. The Franciscan theologians moved in a different direction by stressing Platonic teach-ings, much as had been done by the Greek Neoplatonists and the Mus-lim philosopher Avicenna. All of the thirteenth-century philosophers stood in the philosophical tradition of realism which stressed the doc-trine that universal concepts or terms have an intelligible reality which is independent of the mind and ontologically prior to particular things or contingent events. Ockham shares many specific teachings with one or another of his predecessors, but what distinguishes him from them is his complete rejection of every form of realism, whether Platonic, Scotist, or Thomist. For Ockham all that is known is individual and singular, and the process of knowledge is intuitional. He says: "No universal is existent in any way whatsoever outside the mind of the knower" (*I Sentences*, d.2 q.8). The universal is something purely intramental. A particular object like a horse or a chair evokes a mental "sign" to which we give a name or term which may designate many particular things. Universals then are tools with which we think. Except in logic, universals are not objects of thought. Logic is the science of signs; it studies the various ways in which we may combine signs and is not concerned with the question of truth or falsity or the problem of how signs arise in the mind. Ockham is careful to point out that a sign may be used to stand for an individual existent or for another sign or term.

Since he argues that universals have no existence outside the mind and are not inherent in things, Ockham thinks it absurd to hypostatize ideas, or to make things from abstractions. Thus he sets it down as a rule that men should not employ such superfluous explanations. This principle of parsimony, which he did not invent, came to be known as Ockham's Razor or described as "Entities should not be multiplied beyond necessity." Among his own formulations of this rule are: "What can be done with fewer assumptions is done in vain with more." "Plurality is not to be assumed without necessity." Today we often state this methodological rule in a slightly different way: "As between two hypotheses, both of which will account for a given fact, prefer the simpler." Ockham enjoins us to avoid accounting for facts with explanations which are not required by direct experience, logical reasoning, or the articles of faith.

Ockham carries even further than Scotus the process of narrowing the domain of natural theology. He denies that God's existence, unity, or infinity could be known intuitionally by man through use of his own finite powers. Since intuition is the only form of knowledge, we cannot know God at all. In theology faith is supreme and reason irrelevant. It seems to Ockham that this follows from the doctrine of God's omnipotence. God is able to do anything He wishes that is free from contradiction. Thus everything in the created world is contingent. St. Thomas argued from the contingency of the world to the existence of a God which is necessary. It is this view which Ockham rejects, for contingency strictly means that things are only facts which cannot be inferred one from the other by a principle of sufficient reason or causality which is neither self-evident nor demonstrable. If you reject the principle of causality or sufficient reason, then the whole basis of St. Thomas' natural theology disappears. For Ockham, then, whatever theology we accept is the result of faith and not natural reason. He pushes the consequences of God's omnipotence. We have no way of knowing when an observed effect is natural or not, or whether an intuition on any particular occasion is, or is not, given directly to our minds, even when no object to account for the intuition is present in nature. Ockham says: "Even if a thing has been destroyed the intuitive knowledge of it may be given to us (by God) and so intuitive knowledge is not of itself and necessarily the knowledge of something that exists; it may well be of something that does not exist." It is clear that he can also use this argument to deny the existence of universals when we have mental experience of their meanings.

As we have already suggested, Ockham does not believe that either God's being or His ways of acting can be analyzed. In Ockham's radically simple view, God's will is not grounded in reason and therefore must be disclosed rather than demonstrated. Thus theology is put beyond the reach of reason and everything of importance in religion becomes a matter of faith. We know by revelation that God was incarnate in Jesus; but as far as reason could establish anything, God might have been incarnate in an animal or a mountain or not incarnate at all.

The emphasis on the omnipotence of God is accompanied by an emphasis on the absolute freedom of God. Following the example of Scotus, Ockham stresses the primacy of the will over intellect and the central role of freedom in both God and man. Since God's nature and mighty acts are beyond the knowledge of human reason, ethics is completely dependent upon revelation, the only means by which God's will is available to us. Ockham's voluntarism issues in fiat morality. It is the divine will which arbitrarily imposes the moral law which man is under obligation to obey. God does not will something because it is antecedently good; it is good because he wills it. God has forbidden adultery and murder and they are thus wrong. If God were to command a man to practice adultery, murder, or hatred toward Him, it would be meritorious. God did not do this, so Ockham is not seeking to subvert traditional moral teaching. Instead he is seeking to exalt divine freedom and omnipotence by spelling it out. But a completely authoritarian moral theory that depends entirely on revelation undoubtedly fails to do justice to the moral experience or capabilities of men.

Ockham carries the voluntarism of Duns Scotus to extreme positions. His subtle criticisms of Aristotelianism and Thomism contributed to the disintegration of the foundations of Scholasticism and thereby undermined what many had taken to be certainties. We find in him the germs of subsequent philosophical developments such as voluntarism, pragmatism, and logical positivism. By insisting on the possibility of studying logic and human knowledge freed from metaphysics and theology, Ockham's work stimulated scientific research. He encouraged the anti-Aristotelians like John Buridan, Nicholas of Oresme, and Albert of Saxony and, in some respects, anticipated some of the views of Descartes and Newton. In all of this he was a man of warm human sympathies and Franciscan piety. He did not question the authority of the Church in spiritual matters, or the supremacy of theology. He would not have been sympathetic with all the consequences to which his work eventually led. He was the last great Scholastic thinker looking forward from Christian-medieval culture to the dimly perceived dawn of the forces producing modern philosophy.

Roger Bacon, Duns Scotus, and Ockham:
Suggested Additional Reading

Abernethy, George L. and Thomas A. Langford, eds., *History of Philosophy: Selected Readings*. Belmont, Calif.: Dickenson, 1965, pp. 292–304.*

Bettoni, Efrem, *Duns Scotus: The Basic Principles of His Philosophy*. Edited and translated by Bernardine Bonausea. Washington, D.C.: Catholic University, 1961.*

Copleston, Frederick C., *Medieval Philosophy*. New York: Harper and Row, Torchbook, 1961.

Duns Scotus, *A Treatise on God as the First Principle*. Translated by Allan Wolter. Chicago: Franciscan Herald Press, 1965.*

Duns Scotus, *Philosophical Writings*. Edited and translated by Allan Wolter. Edinburgh: Nelson, 1962.*

Easton, Stewart C., *Roger Bacon and His Search for a Universal Science*. New York: Columbia University Press, 1952.*

Harris, C. R. S., *Duns Scotus*. Oxford: Clarendon Press, 1927.*

Leff, Gordon, *Medieval Thought from St. Augustine to Ockham*. Baltimore: Penguin, 1958.

Moody, Ernest A., *The Logic of William of Ockham*. New York: Sheed and Ward, 1935.*

Ockham, *Ockham: Philosophical Writings*. Edited by P. Boehner. Indianapolis: Bobbs-Merrill, Liberal Arts Press, 1964.

O'Connor, D. J., *A Critical History of Western Philosophy*. Glencoe, Ill.: Free Press, 1964.*

Tornay, Stephen C., *Ockham: Studies and Selections*. La Salle, Ill.: Open Court, 1938.*

Weinberg, J. R., *A Short History of Medieval Philosophy*. Princeton, N.J.: Princeton University Paperback, 1967.

de Wulf, Maurice, *Introduction to Scholastic Philosophy*. Translated by P. Coffey. New York: Dover, 1956.

Chapter Twelve

Hobbes

On Good Friday, the fifth of April 1588, when the rumors of the approaching Spanish Armada spread terror throughout the English countryside, the philosopher Thomas Hobbes was born prematurely. Many years afterwards in his autobiography he observed that Hobbes and Fear were twins. His father was vicar of Westport, an adjunct of Malmesbury in Gloucestershire. Aubrey (in his "Life of Hobbes") describes this parent as an ignorant vicar who "could only read the prayers of the Church and the homilies, and disesteemed Learning, . . . as not knowing the Sweetness of it." [1] He also possessed a choleric temper. One Sunday on leaving church he was provoked by another cleric into a quarrel during which he struck him with his cane. As a consequence he had to flee the parish for London. He left his family in the care of his rich brother, a glover and alderman in Malmesbury, who thereafter directed and paid for Thomas' schooling. At the age of six he was learning Greek and Latin. At age fourteen he was sent to Magdalen Hall, Oxford, where he spent five years acquiring his bachelor's degree. He apparently was an indifferent student, preferring to spend his time perusing books of travel and maps in booksellers' shops. Later in life he reported his contempt for the Aristotelian logic and scholastic physics he was taught at the university.

On leaving Oxford in 1608 Hobbes had the good fortune to be employed as a tutor to the young son of Sir William Cavendish, first Earl of Devonshire. Off and on he served approximately fifty years in the household of the first three Earls of Devonshire. In this sheltered environment he had the use of an ample library, met many influential and stimulating people, and had the advantages of foreign travel. For so brilliant a philosopher Hobbes was slow in developing his interests and viewpoint. His three visits to the continent, before he became a voluntary exile to Paris, had a profound effect upon his intellectual development. On his first trip he discovered the low estate into which

---

[1] "Life of Hobbes" from J. Aubrey, *Brief Lives*, edited by O. Dick, p. 147; quoted in Richard Peters, *Hobbes* (Baltimore: Penguin, 1946), p. 13.

Aristotelianism had fallen on the continent. He returned from Italy with his knowledge of Latin and Greek greatly strengthened and with a determination to become a classical scholar. It was at this time (during the years 1621–1626) that he served as a sort of secretary to the Lord Chancellor Francis Bacon, who dictated notes to him on walks. Hobbes helped Bacon translate several of his essays into Latin. Although there were many similarities between certain of their interests and views, it is difficult to come to any definite conclusion as to the nature and amount of the influence Bacon may have had on Hobbes since the latter never acknowledged any.

The first Earl of Devonshire died in 1626, and the second in 1628. As a temporary economy, the Countess of Devonshire dispensed with Hobbes' services. Thereupon Hobbes accompanied the son of Sir Gervase Clinton to Paris, Orleans, and possibly Venice. It was at this time that his intellectual development received some important stimulation. His friend, Aubrey, tells us, "He was forty years old before he looked on geometry, which happened accidentally. Being in a gentleman's library, Euclid's Elements lay open and 'twas the 47 El. libri I. He reads the proposition. 'By G--.' sayd he 'this is impossible.' So he reads the demonstration of it, which referred him back to such a proposition—that to another—and at last he was demonstratively convinced of that trueth. This made him in love with geometry." [2] He came to the conclusion that all reasoning is mathematical or deductive in character. Later he wrote often on mathematical topics, sometimes showing ability, but often involving himself in controversies with others possessed of more mathematical competence who were able to worst him in many an argument. For a long time he foolishly and stubbornly maintained that he had succeeded in squaring the circle.

At the end of his prose autobiography he reports that in a (undated) gathering of learned men someone raised a question about the nature of sensation. Hobbes was astonished that no one present understood the nature of sensations. He afterwards brooded over the problem until he subsequently came to the conclusion that if all things were at rest, or all moved equally, the ability to discriminate would disappear and sensation with it. Thus he maintained that all causes must be traced back to variations in movement. Since he felt philosophy should be concerned with the relations between causes and effects, he kept returning to geometry and physics.

Hobbes reentered employment with the Devonshires in 1630 and accompanied the next Earl to the continent from 1634 to 1636. During

[2] J. Aubrey, *op. cit.*, I, 332; quoted in W. K. Wright, *History of Modern Philosophy* (New York: Macmillan, 1941), pp. 53–54.

his stay in Paris he moved in the lively intellectual circle around the Abbé Mersenne, the mathematician, who patronized Descartes, Gassendi, and other leading figures. In 1636 he paid a personal visit to Galileo in Florence, Italy. Returning to England in 1637, the year Descartes produced his *Discourse on Method*, he decided at the age of fifty to develop his own philosophical system in three great divisions: Of Body; Of Man; Of Citizenship.

When Charles I was compelled to summon the short Parliament in 1640, Hobbes wrote a political tract, the *Elements of Law*, which was circulated in manuscript form among his friends. It did not analyze "body" but it did discuss man and citizenship, maintaining that sovereignty is one and indivisible, carrying with it the right to levy taxes and declare war. With characteristic timidity and fear that his political views might embroil him in difficulties, Hobbes fled to Paris— "the first of all that fled." Here he remained until 1651, disputing with Descartes and Gassendi and working on his greatest book, *Leviathan*, which the fall of the Stuarts in 1645 apparently stimulated him to write. For a time during his exile Hobbes was one of the tutors of the future Charles II.

Leviathan was published in 1650–1651. Hobbes' political views expressed in it seemed to please no one. They angered the royal exiles in Paris, because of their apparent justification of Cromwell's successful usurpation, and irritated the French and the fugitive English clergy. Again fearing for his safety, Hobbes returned to London, where he made submission to Cromwell and abstained from political activity.

On the news that the Stuarts had been restored to the throne in 1660, Hobbes found it advisable to go from one of the country homes of the Cavendish family, where he had been sojourning, to their London residence. Hobbes was soon received at court and became the warm friend of Charles II. Although he was now an old man, he still had many years of activity ahead of him. He walked every day and sang every night for exercise. We are told that he played an occasional game of tennis even at the advanced age of 75. At eighty-four he wrote a lively autobiography in Latin couplets and in the next two years he translated the whole of the *Iliad* and the *Odyssey* to occupy his time. At ninety he was still writing. There were also other striking characteristics. He was more than six feet tall, red-haired, generous to those in need, witty, contentious, and much in demand as a conversationalist. Aubrey reports him as saying that he had been drunk about a hundred times in his lifetime, although he seems to have been an abstainer in the last thirty years of his life. By the standards of his age, Hobbes was a temperate man. But it is admitted that he had an illegitimate daughter for whom he made provision. Although he was frequently attacked for being an atheist, among the few books most frequently found on his table was his Greek New Testament. On December 4, 1679, he died after an illness of two months and a paralytic stroke of a week's duration. The executor of his will reported to Aubrey that he died "rather for want of the fuel of life than by the power of disease." [3]

The Body

Hobbes presents the first, and probably the greatest, philosophical materialism of modern times. He is the first modern philosopher to attempt a philosophical synthesis from the viewpoint of the new science. Like all reformers, he is impatient with the past; he has no time for Greek philosophy. Scholastic logic and physics and all that goes with them are not only impediments to the acquisition of knowledge but strengthen the Catholic Church and encourage political sedition. Specifically he rejects the teleology of Aristotelianism—especially as it was incorporated in the synthesis of St. Thomas Aquinas. He denies that there can be a science of God or a doctrine of angels, and he repudiates the spiritualistic notion of soul as it appears in the philosophy of Descartes. Like Bacon, he espouses the practical purposes of knowledge; knowledge is power which can be used to increase man's control over science, his own activities, and nature. He accepts the new developing thought of Copernicus, Galileo, Harvey, and the other founders of modern science. In his philosophy of materialism he boldly deduces the consequences of the mechanical theory. Greatly enamored of mathematics, Hobbes believes that the axiomatic method of geometry applies to all thought and so employs it in his own efforts to construct a unified world view. His nonmathematical language made his works more readily accessible in England. Although he shares the rationalism of Galileo and Descartes, he is, somewhat in the fashion of Francis Bacon, an empiricist in his theory of the origin of knowledge. The presence of rationalism and empiricism side by side creates some tension and inconsistency in his system.

What, for Hobbes, is philosophy? He defines it as a "knowledge of effects from their causes and of causes from their effects." Knowledge of effects from causes is analytic or deductive, and thus certain; knowledge of causes from effects is synthetic and inductive and hence can provide us at best only with probability. Both methods have their appropriate uses, but philosophical knowledge, or knowledge of the causes of things, can be had only by analysis. Philosophy should deal

[3] J. Aubrey, *op. cit.*, I, 383.

with the motions of bodies; thus a substance in which there can be no change (God) cannot be a proper object of study for philosophy. For knowledge of God we must turn away from philosophy to revealed religion, which we should accept on the authority of the ruler of the state. Likewise, history is excluded from philosophy, since it is usually based on authority and the experience of past events rather than on ratiocination. This is not to deny that history has its uses, even that of stimulating the study of philosophy. But for Hobbes, philosophy must deal with bodies in motion, that is, with a universe in which everything that occurs can be reduced to the behavior of material particles obeying simple mechanical laws. Under this account of the nature of reality the task which confronts philosophy is the construction of consistent social, political, and ethical or psychological theories. And to this task Hobbes gives time, energy, and a pungent style of writing.

Hobbes' espousal of materialism was not new, but the simplicity and rigorous consistency of his system were. "First philosophy," for him, is a science of the fundamental axioms or definitions of all science. It defines and elaborates the concepts of space, time, body, cause, effect, relation, quantity, and similar concepts. Reality consists of body, defined as "that which having no dependence upon our thought, is coextended with some parts of space" (*De Corpore*, I, 102). All body is either at rest or in motion. "Whatsoever is at rest, will always be at rest, unless there be some other body besides it, which, by endeavoring to get into its place by motion, suffers it no longer to remain at rest" (*De Corpore*, I, 115). "Whatsoever is moved, will always be moved on in the same way and with the same velocity, except it be hindered by some other contiguous and moved body" (*De Corpore*, I, 125). Hobbes here is indebted to a portion of Galileo's statement of the principle of inertia. To grasp Hobbes' conception of reality we must put aside our ordinary, man-in-the-street tendency to think of "bodies" as heavily laden with all sorts of sense experience. Such perceptible bodies are only aggregates of appearances produced in us by the motions of real bodies—extramental things—which are unlike anything we experience. Extension and motion are the only qualities which exist absolutely in expressing directly the fundamental mathematical-mechanical reality. All secondary qualities such as color, taste, and touch are subjective. Hobbes is here maintaining the distinction, made by Galileo and reiterated by Descartes, between primary qualities existing objectively and secondary qualities subjectively dependent upon a perceiving mind.

Hobbes rejects final causes and any *a priori* concept of cause and effect. He believes that we can deduce causal laws from the changes of

motion in the physical world. Whatever happens has, looking back-
wards, a "necessary cause" and, looking forwards, a necessary effect.
Causation then, is a continuous process in which one set of motions is
always being transformed into another set. If motion ceased, we would
in this view have no adequate understanding of cause and effect
relationships. But fortunately, Hobbes asserts, the motion of the physical world cannot be destroyed and causal law can continue to be
applied to scientific knowledge. Since Hobbes rejects the idea of the
void, he maintains that the spaces between the smallest particles of
solid matter are filled with an insensible ether, through which the
motions of one body are transmitted to another. Motion is everywhere
present and continuous, as is matter.

Man

Man is a body with certain organs. Other bodies coming into contact
with an organ of sense exert pressure either immediately, as in touch
and taste, or mediately, as in seeing, hearing, and smelling. This
pressure sets in activity motions leading to the brain or heart; in return
there is a response or "endeavour" (as Hobbes calls it). These responses may be colors, sounds, odors, or sensations of heat, cold, or
touch. Thus we may say that the motion of an external object-stimulus
has been transmitted to the internal movements of the brain. Some of
these "endeavours," responses, or images may remain after the stimulus
disappears or ceases its pressuring. The "imagination" is the term
given to this faculty for retaining images. All our knowledge and thought
then are responses our bodies make to other bodies. Our knowledge is a
construction of the internal movements of our bodies, which generate
the phantasms constituting the "imaginary" or mental world. There
is no reason why a sensation or internal movement should resemble
the external stimulus-object or movement. In Hobbes' metaphysical
system matter has only the qualities physics says it has—extension and
motion. Simply stated, Hobbes' position is that if the blueness we
attribute to a garment were actually a part of the garment, we could not
experience it separately in either sensation or thought. All secondary
qualities—colors, tastes, sounds, temperatures, and the like—are
feelings or phantasms produced in our brains in response to the pressures
of external objects. Hobbes is not altogether clear as to the nature of the
secondary qualities. As a consistent materialist, he should always
interpret them as simply physical motions in the brain. Yet when he
calls them "phantasms" and "fancies" he seems to suggest that they
are not really motions. If they are byproducts or epiphenomena of

physical motions, it would appear that his basic materialism is being altered to allow for the existence of something which is neither motion nor matter.

Hobbes appeals to the principle of inertia in maintaining that each impression of itself would remain indefinitely were it not for the competition of other motions. Since we are continually bombarded with new impressions, it results that the greater the time interval elapsing since a first impression, the more will it have "decayed," or been overshadowed by subsequent impressions. These decaying sensations comprise the "imagination," and "Memory" is the term for our recognition that our recall is growing feebler or dimmer. Portions of decayed sensation may be combined in the imagination in ways that differ from the order or the original impressions. Thus we may explain the content of dreams which are basically motions occurring during sleep. What we call "thoughts" are the pattern of decaying sensation organized according to the rules of logic, which do not appear to be derived from the laws of motion. For Hobbes, the conception of color and shape derives from visual sensations. The general terms, or universals, should also be residues of decaying sensations. But how a group of motions which excite us to impressions which result in sensations of red, blue, and green could change into *color*, which is not a specific color, is something that Hobbes never makes clear.

Hobbes talks about trains of thought or mental discourse as if they moved according to what were in later British philosophy and psychology the laws of the association of ideas. (See *Leviathan*, Ch. III; and *Human Nature*, Ch. IV, sec. 2.) These may be undirected, without conscious purpose and irregular, as in ordinary conversation. Even so, one may note causal connections as in the example given by Hobbes in which a conversation on the betrayal of Charles I in the Civil War led one man to ask the value of a Roman penny. "For the thought of the war introduced the thought of the delivery of the king to his enemies; the thought of that brought in the thought of the delivering up of Christ; and that again the thought of the thirty pence, which was the price of that treason; and thence followed that malicious question; and all this in a moment of time—for thought is quick" (*Leviathan*, Part I, Ch. I). At other times Hobbes talks of mental discourses as being controlled by human desires and ends. A man seeks to restore something he has misplaced so he recalls places and times in which he used it. Or he imagines what it will take to produce some desired effect. "The 'present' only has a being in nature; things 'past' have a being in the memory only, but things 'to come' have no being at all, the 'future' being but a fiction of the mind, applying the sequel of actions past to the actions which are present, which with most certainty is done by him that has most experience, but not with certainty enough. . . . The best prophet naturally is the best guesser, and the best guesser he that is most versed and studied in the matters he guesses at, for he hath most 'signs' to guess by" (*ibid.*).

Certain questions emerge from Hobbes' views. If all trains of thought are internal mechanical motions as he claims, and if mental discourse can be guided by human desires and future purposes as he sometimes admits, then how is one to interpret the status of a future purpose or objective? How is a "fiction of the mind" presumably produced by mechanical movements to be distinguished from other effects of mechanical movements which are not "fictions"? If all our trains of thought are caused by internal mechanical movements, how can men ever err? If our thoughts are given logical patterning by our subjective experiences, how can we have public truth except by chance?

Hobbes considers processes of feeling and willing to be motions in the body. Men and animals share two kinds of motion: (1) *vital* or as he puts it "the course of the blood, the pulse, breath, the concoction, nutrition, excretion, etc., to which motions there needs no help of imagination," and (2) *voluntary* such as "to 'go,' 'speak,' or 'move' any of our limbs in such manner as is fancied in our minds" (*Leviathan*, Part I, Ch. VI). Thus the first internal beginnings of any voluntary motion are imagination. Before the initiation of it becomes visible to public observation it may be called endeavor (*conatus*, conation). It is this notion of conation which plays later an important role in Spinoza's philosophy. We call this endeavor *desire* or *appetite* when it is directed towards whatever causes it, *aversion* when it is turned from some object. More commonly men are said to love those things they desire and to hate those for which they have aversion. The chief difference lies in the fact that when we speak of desire and aversion we mean the absence of an object, while in speaking of love and hate we usually assume the object as present. To these basic notions may be traced the distinctions between pleasure and displeasure, good and evil. In his psychology of endeavor, Hobbes calls the last appetite or aversion immediately preceding the overt motor response of the body in a process of deliberation the *will*. Thus the action depends on the final inclination of the will. The will, including each inclination appearing in the process of deliberation, is just as dependent on a sufficient cause as anything else. To call an agent free means he has reached the end of the process of deliberation, and can do if he will, forbear if he will. A man is free to act, but not free to will other than as he wills.

Hobbes argues that ultimately the evaluation of objects or actions as good or evil is rooted in desires and aversions. Nothing is good in and of itself. Men label as "good" the objects which they desire, while placing the stigma of "evil" on the objects of their aversions. Thus values are transitory and subjective. One's desire for an object may in time turn to indifference and even aversion. The same object may elicit love, hate, and indifference from three different individuals on the same occasion. In this view absolute good and absolute evil are merely fictions of the human mind. Hobbes warns us against attempting to impose these concepts upon the metaphysical structure of the universe.

Hobbes uses colorful terms to describe the state of nature existing prior to the formation of a political state. It is a state of nature in which man's condition is "solitary, poor, nasty, brutish, and short." Everyone seeks his own self-preservation and the gratification of his own desires. Man is not pictured by Hobbes as Rousseau's noble savage or as Aristotle's political animal but as a ferocious animal (*homo homini lupus*). There is consequently no morality as we know it. All men are constantly attacking other men or anxiously awaiting the attack of others in the perpetual war of all against all (*bellum omnium contra omnes*). Under such circumstances the notions of right and wrong, justice and injustice, are irrelevant. Anything goes, for there is no common power and no law. Poverty and fear rule such a state of nature, since no man can hope for long to gather sufficient strength to preserve himself against his enemies for any length of time. If one objects that Hobbes has overdrawn this grim picture of human nature, Hobbes would reply that the state of international relations among nations, the conditions existing among certain primitive peoples, and our own practice of locking our doors at night and storing our valuables in locked boxes all seem to suggest the approximate applicability of certain of his descriptions to contemporary men.

At the same time Hobbes believes paradoxically that men naturally and reasonably seek a state of peace and security. The first precept of reason or natural law is that men should seek peace by every means at their disposal. This leads to a second: "that a man be willing to, when others are so too, as far-forth as for peace and defense of himself he shall think it necessary, to lay down this (natural) right to all things, and be contented with so much liberty against other men as he would allow other men against him." Obviously no man can be expected to transfer any of his rights, and the right of self-defense in particular, without some right or good being transferred in turn to him. This mutual renunciation or exchange of rights is *contract*. Hobbes was one of the first modern thinkers to defend the view that the state originated in a *social contract*. The third natural law is that men perform the obligations made in their contracts. To distinguish justice from injustice it is necessary to have a coercive power to compel men equally to keep their contracts. There is no question of injustice until such a commonwealth is instituted. The ten other natural laws are: the obligation to good will; mutual accommodation; pardoning the offense of the repentant; infliction of punishments only for the correction of offenders or deterrence of others, and not from vengeance; avoidance of contempt or hatred of others; acknowledgment of all men as one's equals; abstinence from reserving any rights for oneself that one is not content should equally be reserved by others; a just or proportionate distribution of goods held in common; safe conduct; and settlement of disputes by judicial process. "These laws of nature are immutable and eternal; for injustice, ingratitude, arrogance, pride, iniquity, acception of persons, and the rest, can never be made lawful. For it can never be that war shall preserve life and peace destroy it." These laws are called laws of nature because they are for Hobbes dictates of reason; they are called moral laws because they are involved in man's relations with his fellows. They are also divine laws in respect to the author of them. The laws of nature are always binding in a man's conscience, but they are binding in overt behavior only when men have some guarantee that the laws will be observed reciprocally by their fellows. Although reason is able at all times to ascertain the moral desirability of peace, honesty, and mutual kindness, unaided reason cannot create the circumstances in which men can reasonably undertake reasonable actions. But the moment a sovereign power is established with the means to compel all men equally to keep their contracts, the laws of nature are binding on both the conscience and behavior of all men.

In his political philosophy Hobbes stresses repeatedly the need for conferring absolute sovereignty upon government. The social contract is a contract entered into by the people with each other and not with the sovereign. The grant of absolute sovereignty by the people is final, absolute, and indivisible. The absolute sovereign or Leviathan has the authority to make laws, appoint the judiciary, wage war and conclude peace treaties, determine punishments and establish the state religion. The people are the subjects of the sovereign and owe him obedience, although the sovereign owes the people nothing other than to act as sovereign. His will is the law and thus the basis of all obligation. Although his own preferences are for monarchy, Hobbes recognizes in theory that democracy or aristocracy might possess sovereign power and rule absolutely. He believes that the hazards of division and dissension leading to anarchy were greater in democracy or aristocracy. He never tires of emphasizing that an inefficient government is better than a state of nature, and thus citizens of a state are not morally justified in overthrowing even an evil state. Only God can judge the iniquities of a ruler. Men are better advised to await the Last Judgment rather than to take things into their own hands. Since the formation of the commonwealth is rooted in egoistic interests, "the obligation of subjects to the sovereign is understood to last as long, and no longer, than the power lasteth by which he is able to protect them." If the sovereign is conquered by an invader, then his subjects become the subjects of the new conqueror. It was this recognition of *de facto* sovereignty which led to charges by Hobbes' fellow royalists that he had sold out to Cromwell.

Hobbes wishes the Leviathan to have absolute power in every department of life. Because of the bitterness and confusion generated by conflicts between the claims of church and state in his day, Hobbes places particular stress on the sovereign's control over ecclesiastical institutions and religious doctrines. He devotes a large portion of *Leviathan* to severe criticism of the temporal claims of the Catholic Church and of the arrogance of Protestant divines and sectaries. Since for Hobbes the basic difference between religions rests upon subjective preferences and invites the activities of deluded reformers or scheming cynics who hope to manipulate the feelings of the masses for self-appointed ends, it is much better in the long run for the sovereign to decide what kind of religion it is in his interest to establish. In this view clergymen are agents of the sovereign and responsible to him for obedience. Religion is viewed then as a system of law and not of truth; the sovereign communicates the law. Since we cannot know the attributes of God but are limited to expressions of our adoration, and since the essence of Christianity consists of the simple belief that Jesus is the Christ, Hobbes feels that he has not interfered with the individual's private or subjective religious feelings when he has rejected the pleas for deviant actions based on claims of individual conscience, or when the sovereign has established the official or public form of worship. It is instructive to compare the difference between medieval and modern conceptions of the role of religion by contrasting the views of St. Thomas with those of Hobbes as to the functions performed by religion and as to its ontological status in these two systems of thought.

Significance of Hobbes

It is difficult to assess the significance of Hobbes, for his work evoked an unusually large number of bitter and vindictive attacks which tended to caricature his personal views and to scare off those who might have been interested in defending him or in extending popular understanding of his work. Some of Hobbes' views were so extreme or thoroughgoing that they were instructive in a negative sense. They showed clearly what a philosopher must avoid to solve certain problems and what he must compromise to obtain the support of others who are seeking various combinations of values. Hobbes' views, for example, on the origin and authority of church and state pleased no one in the seventeenth century. The Puritans of course believed in the right of the people to choose and change the form of state and church government as they saw fit. The Stuarts and their followers, of course, maintained the belief in the divine origin of church and state. The Glorious Revolution of 1688 showed that it is possible to muddle through between the extremes of anarchy and absolutism with beliefs in the feasibility of changing the Constitution, in holding the rulers morally accountable to their subjects, and in granting subjects certain individual liberties or rights.

There were certain basic difficulties in Hobbes' political views. Fundamentally he presented his "laws of nature" not in the medieval or traditional sense but as "utilitarian maxims" ("a theorem concerning what conduceth to men's conservation and defense"), which a group of rationalistic egoists would follow in pursuing their long-range interests. Thus they are presented in factual or descriptive terms rather than with a traditional moral connotation. Yet Hobbes' rationalism invites the charge that he views men as being more rationalistic than they are, and that he is in turn urging the adoption of his own program of moral values to replace more traditional ones. There is the further difficulty that in elaborating his picture of the state of nature as something from which one would want to escape at all cost, he presents men as so irrational and selfish that it becomes impossible to see how men would have sufficient rationality to formulate a social contract. If this "miracle" did occur and if men were as rationally egoistic as Hobbes claims they are, it remains a great puzzle why they would give the sovereign a blank check instead of reserving some rights to protect their own interests and prevent a possible drift into abject slavery. We come then to a fundamental issue: whether men or laws ought to prevail. When this question is answered the further questions remain as to which men or which laws. Hobbes never really resolves the conflict between a descriptive and normative account of politics. Sometimes he adopts a purely descriptive approach toward the facts of political power; at other times he employs "good," "reason," and "contract" as moral standards in evaluating or judging the political behavior of men. Obviously he cannot have it both ways. If Hobbes insists on employing moral criteria, he must assume the problem of showing they can have meaning in a world in which only matter in motion is real.

From the vantage point of the centuries of subsequent work in philosophy and the sciences it is easy for some to criticize Hobbes' work in metaphysics as crude, ignorant, inconsistent, and full of strange gaps. However, one must remember that he was a pioneer, not a natural scientist. When he borrowed from the sciences of his day he uncritically accepted their assumptions and used details which he understood only imperfectly. Although he gave us only rough sketches of a systematic philosophy based on the view that all reality is matter in motion, he did illumine problems and bring forcefully to the attention of contemporary and subsequent thinkers many issues which they would otherwise have only briefly noted. He wrestled with problems in logic and epistemology, optics, mechanics, physics, physiology, psychology, ethics, politics, and jurisprudence. Some of our contemporary analytic philosophers are inclined to think his most important contribution was his theory of speech, in which he sought to unite a mechanical theory of the causes of speech with a nominalistic account of the meaning of general terms. In anticipation of modern psychologists he insisted that speech was essential to reasoning and it was reasoning in the form of establishing definitions and working out the consequences or implications of general names which really differentiated men from the animals.

Leibniz, after meditating on some of Hobbes' doctrines in *De Corpore*, is said to have exclaimed, "What a man!" Perhaps this is an appropriate reaction to the totality of Hobbes' life and achievement.

Thomas Hobbes: Suggested Additional Reading

Abernethy, George L. and Thomas A. Langford, eds., *History of Philosophy: Selected Readings*. Belmont, Calif.: Dickenson, 1965, pp. 337–358.*

Bowle, J., *Hobbes and His Critics: A Study of Seventeenth Century Constitutionalism*. New York: Oxford University Press, 1952.*

Brown, Keith C., ed., *Hobbes: Studies by Leo Strauss and Others*. Cambridge: Harvard University Press, 1965.*

Goldsmith, M. M., *Hobbes' Science of Politics*. New York: Columbia University Press, 1966.*

Hobbes, *The English Works of Thomas Hobbes*. Edited by William Moles-
worth. 11 vols. Oxford: Oxford University Press, 1961.*

Hobbes, *Leviathan*. Introduction by John Plamenatz. New York: World
Publishing Company, Meridian, 1963.

Hobbes, *De Cive, or the Citizen*. Edited by Sterling P. Lamprecht. New
York: Appleton-Century-Crofts, 1949.

Kaufmann, Walter, *Philosophic Classics*. Englewood Cliffs, N.J.: Prentice-
Hall, 1961, II, 92–124.*

Laird, John, *Hobbes*. London: Ernest Benn, 1934.*

Macpherson, C. W., *The Political Theory of Possessive Individualism:
Hobbes to Locke*. Oxford: Clarendon Press, 1962.*

Mintz, Samuel I., *The Hunting of Leviathan*. Cambridge: Cambridge
University Press, 1962.*

Peters, Richard, *Hobbes*. Baltimore: Penguin, 1956.

Stephen, Leslie, *Hobbes*. Ann Arbor, Michigan: Ann Arbor Paperbacks,
1961.

Warrender, H., *The Political Philosophy of Hobbes*. Oxford: Clarendon
Press, 1957.*

Chapter Thirteen

Descartes

René Descartes (1596–1650) is usually called the founder of modern philosophy, and with good reason. He was the first modern thinker possessed of great and original philosophic talent to be profoundly influenced by the new astronomy and physics. He was an original mathematician whose contributions to coordinate geometry paved the way for many subsequent achievements. His formulation of philosophic method had a pervasive influence on the whole development of modern thought.

Descartes was born March 31, 1596, in Touraine to a family long established as country nobility in central France. His father was a councilor of the provincial parliament of Brittany; his mother died of consumption soon after René's birth. It soon became evident that the young Descartes' frail body housed a brilliant mind. His father wisely sent him to be educated from his eighth to sixteenth years at the Jesuit college of La Flèche (near Tours), where his teachers assigned him a private room and permitted him to lie in bed mornings while his precocious mind mastered all their assignments. The Jesuit curriculum at La Flèche included the traditional classics and scholastic philosophy, but he was also introduced to the new developments in science and apparently received a firmer grounding in mathematics than he would have at many universities in his day. When the satellites of Jupiter were identified by Galileo's telescope at the University of Padua, a sonnet celebrating the discovery was written and read to the student body at La Flèche. Although he later subjected the traditional scholastic learning to severe criticism, Descartes continued to regard the Jesuits of La Flèche and their educational program with respect and affection. Father Mersenne, one of his older acquaintances at La Flèche, became his close friend and the advocate of his ideas.

After leaving La Flèche, Descartes, with an ample allowance and a valet, was sent by his father to Paris, where he soon found the round of fencing, card playing, and social life boring. He turned his attention to studies and he withdrew to a secluded retreat in Faubourg Saint

Germain where he worked on geometry, and then for a short time
studied law and medicine at the University of Poitiers. At age 20 he
decided to read "in the book of the world," seeking a knowledge useful
for life. For this reason he enlisted (1617) as a voluntary gentleman
without pay in the Dutch army of Prince Maurice of Nassau, a noted
military engineer. Since Holland was at peace at this time, Descartes
was able to devote two years to mathematical studies and to the writing
of various papers, including a treatise on music, *Compendium musicae*,
which was published after his death. The coming of the Thirty Years'
War led him to enlist (1619) in the army of Maximillian of Bavaria.
Stationed at Neuberg on the Danube he had, on November 10, 1619,
a remarkable mystical experience, described in his *Discourse on Method*;
through three consecutive dreams he became convinced that Physics
should be reduced to geometry and all the sciences interrelated "as by
a chain," and that his mission in life was to seek truth by reason.
Descartes was so deeply moved by this experience that he vowed to
make a pilgrimage to the Lady of Loretto in Italy to express his thanks
for it—a vow which he fulfilled in 1623. All his life Descartes treasured
the memory of the mystical experience of this single evening, which
occurred at an auspicious time. It was approximately the same time at
which Galileo composed the famed dialogues in which he explained the
Copernican astronomical system in the language of the layman, a
task for which the Inquisition ultimately punished him. It was only a
little later, in 1629, that Thomas Hobbes had the crucial experience of
capitulating to geometry following a chance reading of the work of
Euclid. This is a significant era, for these three men brought about a
revolution in science by spelling out the impact of mathematical method
for a host of others to read and utilize.

In 1625 Descartes settled in Paris, where he repeatedly found that his
friends could be very annoying in their morning visitations, which
thwarted his desire to meditate in bed until noon. In 1628 he joined the
French army, which was besieging the Huguenots in their stronghold
of La Rochelle. Holland at this time had a reputation as a country
where freedom of speculation remained a real possibility. Hobbes
had his books published in Holland, and for varying periods of time
Bayle, Locke, and Spinoza carried on their work there. Descartes
also found refuge there for two decades (1629–1649), except for brief
business trips to France and England. His *Treatise of the World* was
ready for the printer when he learned of the condemnation and imprisonment of Galileo in 1633. Since his work shared Galileo's heretical
conclusions with reference to the earth's rotation and the infinity of
the universe, he directed Father Mersenne to discontinue his plans

to publish the book. As a consequence only fragments of the work were published after his death. All his life Descartes remained a devout Catholic and continued to affirm his practical loyalty to the church, even when his personal conclusions were at variance with it. Despite his prudence, both Protestant and Catholic theologians were antagonistic to his position, and his works were put on the Index in 1663. His most important philosophical works were *Discourse on Method* (1637), *Meditations on First Philosophy* (1641), *The Principles of Philosophy* (1644), and *The Passions of the Soul* (1649). An earlier work, *Rules for the Direction of the Mind*, was written by 1628 but not published until 1701. In addition, he left a mass of correspondence which helps to elucidate his thoughts, and of special interest is his correspondence with Princess Elizabeth of Bohemia and Queen Christina of Sweden. In September 1649, as a result of a pressing invitation from Queen Christina, he boarded her warship for Sweden. The rigors of the Swedish winter plus the busy Queen's desire to receive philosophical instruction at five in the morning proved too much for a philosopher long accustomed to arising at noon. Descartes came down with a fever at the end of January and died February 11, 1650.

Descartes was known as a kind, gentle, moderate, and even timid man who always maintained the appearance of a gentlemanly amateur working short hours and reading little. He seemed to accomplish the most by engaging in intense concentration for short periods of time. He did not care for social life and felt that the cause of philosophy would not be advanced by oral exchanges. He did welcome criticisms from his correspondents, to whom he made careful replies after due reflection. He is known to have been generous and kind to his servants, who were devoted to him, but he never married because he insisted upon a quiet life without interruptions for his work. Nevertheless, he had a natural daughter who died at the age of five to his great sorrow. Descartes combined a deep sense of concentration and mission with a sense of moderation and proportion. He died piously in the Catholic faith believing that the road to heaven was open both to the learned and the ignorant. He avoided the discussion of theological issues and concentrated on issues which he believed could be solved by reason without reliance on revelation. Thus we find a dualism which runs through his interests, philosophy, and character.

Method

In both *Discourses* and *Meditations* Descartes presents his philosophizing in the form of an intellectual autobiography emphasizing his own personal development and his optimistic expectation that a new era of enlightenment is soon to dawn. He pictures himself as being plunged at first into hopeless doubt and anxiety, from which he was finally rescued by certain indubitable insights which provided the foundation for his new philosophy. His fundamental aim is to obtain philosophical truth by the use of reason. He states: "I wish to give myself entirely to the search after truth." "I always had an excessive desire to learn to distinguish the true from the false, in order to see clearly in my actions and to walk with confidence in this life." He believes in the universality of rational ability. "The power of forming a good judgment and of distinguishing the true from the false, which is properly speaking what is called Good Sense or Reason, is by nature equal in all men." This assumption that reason is adequate and equal in all men was to bear fruit in the social and political institutions of the American and French Revolutions in the latter part of the eighteenth century.

Although both Hobbes and Descartes agree that reason is exemplified in the scientific method and that a philosophical method should be modeled on mathematics, they are in profound disagreement as to what gives mathematics its certainty. Descartes believes that mathematical knowledge is synthetical and that our clear and distinct intuitions give us trustworthy insights into the objective and rational order of reality. For Hobbes mathematics is analytical and primarily a manipulation of signs which makes it possible for one to clarify his meanings in order to determine which ones he will accept or reject. This basic difference in outlook and interpretation continues to divide mathematicians, scientists, and philosophers down to our own day.

It is Descartes' contention that philosophy should develop a method by means of which it could derive conclusions as certain as those in arithmetic and geometry. If one could develop a kind of universal mathematics, then he could apply it to the various problems of philosophy. Descartes attempts what contemporary mathematical logicians have recently achieved—finding a method defining the basic concepts that underlie all the specific forms of mathematical thinking.

In geometry we begin with some self-evident and independent truth like "a straight line is the shortest distance between two points," and then place in proper sequence the various theorems of Euclid which depend on this self-evident truth. In similar fashion, in philosophy we must seek some basic or indubitable metaphysical truth upon which may be erected the dependent truths to provide an absolutely true interpretation of objective rational reality and not just a consistent system of values which we happen to prefer.

Until he discovers this basic indubitable metaphysical truth, Descartes proposes to doubt everything—his own experience, the teachings of Scholasticism, traditions, the dogmas of Christianity. Thus he intends to use skepticism not as a cynical pose or a self-defeating instrument, but as a new method of establishing what is indubitable, self-evident, true, and independent, in contradistinction to that which can be doubted or shown to be false or dependent. In Part Two of *Discourse on Method* he summarizes in simple fashion four rules which he believes must be followed if one is to do clear and certain thinking. "The first of these was to accept nothing as true which I did not clearly recognize to be so; that is to say, carefully to avoid precipitation and prejudice in judgments, and to accept in them nothing more than was presented to my mind so clearly and distinctly that I could have no occasion to doubt it." The second is to break up difficulties or problems into as many parts as possible or necessary in order to solve them; the third, to begin with the simplest elements, passing by regular steps or degrees to the knowledge of the more complex; and the fourth, to make enumerations so complete and reviews so searching that he can be sure of having omitted nothing essential to the proof.

These rules indicate the kind of rationalistic procedure one would employ in solving an original problem in geometry. Descartes gives us a terse summary of the twenty-one rules (*Rules for the Direction of the Mind*) which he wrote earlier and circulated privately in manuscript form among his friends.

How is one to distinguish between what is known for a certainty and what is believed upon more or less adequate grounds? For Descartes the criterion is "clearness and distinctness of intellectual apprehension"; thus a proposition must be clear as a whole and distinct in its several details and relations. Obviously, this criterion rules out sense-perception, which is often vague, ambiguous, and confused. Memory and imagination are so dependent upon sense-perception that they cannot meet this criterion for knowledge either. The mind apprehends directly and intuitively the axioms of geometry as clear and distinct propositions. Descartes is a rationalist rather than an empiricist; he relies on intuition and not sensation as the basic source of knowledge. For him deduction is an ordered chain of intuitions. In geometry each step in a series of theorems is apprehended intuitively as true and seen to stand in a discernible relation to another, which is related to still another. The mind cannot hold before it at one time all the details in a long demonstration or series of intuitions; but it can remember that each step in the chain of deduction has been immediately or intuitively apprehended with clearness and distinctness in all its details and placed in a logical order so that nothing essential has been omitted or taken for granted. Obviously no chain of deduction is stronger than its weakest link. How can we be sure that our chain of deduction is valid? Descartes' fourth rule, enjoining complete enumerations and searching reviews, is not concerned merely with the repetition of the steps, but with ultimately reducing the chain of deduction to a complex intuition from which all uncertainty has disappeared. Only then can we be sure of validity.

Descartes finds the source of all clear and distinct ideas (whether "simple ideas" or "absolute ideas") in innate or *a priori* ideas implanted in us by "nature" or God. Although this doctrine reminds us in some ways of Plato's belief that such ideas have a validity superior to sense-perception, there is no conjecturing about a reminiscence derived from a previous existence. Innate ideas are not actually present at birth, but individuals are born with a facility for acquiring them. Descartes seems to include the axioms of mathematics, the laws of logic, his idea of self, his idea of God, and certain philosophical axioms among the innate ideas. His insistence upon innate ideas stems from the fact that he wishes to champion the claims of the intellect or reason to embrace truth, in opposition to the claims of the passions, the senses, or even the imagination. If our ideas were produced mechanically in response to pressures, we would lose any objective standard of truth or knowledge. Our judgments of sensory data should be made in the light of principles that are innate. In this way innate ideas developed in our minds free us from slavery to the physical and social pressures which constantly impinge upon us. They bring to our minds a "pure intellection," from which issues rational judgments that give us insight into necessary truths.

Error, in Descartes' view, arises from the will. If we restrict our judgments to what is intuitively or deductively clear and distinct, we shall never commit an error. If we give free rein to confused ideas or to our emotions and prejudices, we permit our wills to frustrate reason and make judgments for which we have only inadequate evidence. This is the nature of error.

Cogito Ergo Sum

We have already noted that Descartes' initial skepticism, or use of skepticism as a method, is motivated by the desire to discover that which is absolutely certain—that which cannot be doubted without assuming its existence. It is a method of separating the true from the false. The doubt may be called theoretical in that Descartes does not intend to apply it to matters of conduct where we are frequently required to act on merely probable opinions. He is engaged in an effort to rethink philosophy systematically from its foundations.

To begin with, Descartes doubts the senses. "I have sometimes experienced that these senses were deceptive, and it is wiser not to trust entirely to anything by which we have once been deceived." He recalls that on occasion he has dreamed in the night of sitting in his dressing gown by the fire when actually he was in bed. It would seem that the propositions of mathematics are immune to doubt, for awake or asleep he has always found that two and three equal five, while a square never has more than four sides. Yet Descartes is able to entertain the hypothesis that some powerful evil genius has been deceiving him into accepting these mathematical propositions as inevitably true when they may not be. Of course Descartes does not assert that this is a probable hypothesis. But in his search for absolute certainty he is willing to doubt anything that can be doubted, so he finds it theoretically possible then to doubt sense-perception, memory, waking thoughts, the existence of the external world, and even the truth of mathematics. But there remains one thing about which no evil genius, however powerful or deceitful, can deceive him. "But there is some deceiver or other, very powerful and very cunning, who ever employs his ingenuity in deceiving me. Then without doubt I exist also if he deceives me, and let him deceive me as much as he will, he can never cause me to be nothing so long as I think that I am something. So that after having reflected well and carefully examined all things, we must come to the definite conclusion that this proposition: I am, I exist, is necessarily true each time that I pronounce it, or that I mentally conceive it." "I think, therefore I am" (*Cogito ergo sum* or *Je pense, donc je suis*) becomes the cornerstone of Descartes' theory of knowledge and metaphysics.

Cogito ergo sum, he maintained, is not a syllogism, but a simple movement of thought, known immediately without inference, a direct intuition. Here then is an idea so clear and distinct, so self-evident, that in denying it, one affirms it. This passes the test for completely certain knowledge. Here Descartes is in essence repeating an argument used before him by St. Augustine and Campanella. But in the case of St. Augustine the argument was incidental to theological considerations and not basic to his philosophy. Descartes' use of it is significant because he emphasizes the importance of self-awareness and establishes his whole philosophy upon it. In much of philosophy subsequent to Descartes there is a strong tendency towards subjectivism, a tendency which becomes especially marked in continental idealism and British empiricism. Descartes' task is to reestablish philosophy on this basis; he moves from the self to God and from God to the physical world. The self or I which has been proven to exist is derived from the fact of thinking. The self, then, is something which doubts, understands, affirms, denies, wills, conceives, and imagines or entertains hypotheses. Its essence consists in thinking; it is a substance whose chief attribute is thought. Descartes goes on to say that the rational self requires no place or material sphere for its existence. Thus the mind is completely distinct from the body and can be known more certainly than the body. It is the only existent thing that can be known directly; therefore, whatever else may come to be known must be known by deduction from this basic intuitive knowledge.

God

For the thinker to be convinced of his own existence beyond a shadow of a doubt is one thing. For him to be convinced equally of the existence of other objects is something else. It is, consequently, necessary for Descartes to establish some one thing outside of his mind which will guarantee the existence of other things and the possibility of our having certain knowledge of them. Before he can perform these functions in the development of the Cartesian system, Descartes must initially show that God exists. Although he employs a rather complex analysis, his arguments may be summarized briefly as being basically three in number.

First, in examining the content of his thoughts Descartes discovers that he has an idea of God, "a being omniscient, all-powerful, and absolutely perfect." How could he, a finite being, have constructed by his own power out of his own resources such an idea? There is no source in the finite world to which such an idea of an infinite being could be referred. To Descartes it is evident by the natural light of reason that these ideas come from somewhere, that every effect has a cause and (in scholastic fashion) that "there must be at least as much reality or perfection in the cause as there is in the effect." Descartes presupposes that "less perfect ideas depend upon more perfect for their existence." God must therefore exist external to and independent of the mind which thus far had been certain only of its own existence and finitude. If the idea of God, a being eternal, infinite, immutable, without blemish or imperfection, is immediately intuited, it stands to reason that God cannot be a deceiver since "the light of nature teaches us that fraud and deception necessarily proceed from some defect."

The second argument is similar and stems from a consideration of the same idea. The thinking mind exists just so long as it thinks. If one says that his existence at a given moment guarantees the persistence of it at the next moment, he must face the fact of a last moment—death—when persistence from past experience is not warranted. What is true at the last moment is true of every moment of contingent experience. Therefore, one must postulate an adequate ground for the conserving through time of one's own being. To make sense of finite continuance the adequate ground must be an eternal Being whose existence is not precarious.

The third of Descartes' arguments for the existence of God is a restatement of the ontological argument of St. Anselm in the eleventh century, who was in turn anticipated earlier by St. Augustine. Descartes offers it as a proof, without dependence on intuitions and as rigorous as that of any geometer offering a demonstration of a proposition that is necessarily true.

In *Discourse on Method* Descartes gives a brief statement of the argument after making some comments on the demonstrations of geometers. He states:

I also noticed that there was nothing at all in them to assure me of the existence of their object. For, to take an example, I saw very well that, if we suppose a triangle to be given, the three angles must certainly be equal to two right angles; but for all that I saw no reason to be assured that there was any such triangle in existence, while, on the contrary, on reverting to the examination of the idea which I have of a Perfect Being, I found that in this case existence was implied in it in the same manner in which the equality of its three angles to two right angles is implied in the idea of a triangle or in the idea of a sphere, that all the points on its surface are equidistant from its centre, or even more evidently still. Consequently, it is at least as certain that God, who is a Being so perfect, is, or exists, as any demonstration of geometry can possibly be (*Discourse*, IV).

In other words, the very conception of an infinite and absolutely perfect Being logically implies the existence of such a Being. On the other hand, I can conceive of a triangle without being required to ascribe existence to it because existence is not an essential perfection of the idea of a triangle. But an infinite and perfect Being that did not exist could not be infinite and perfect, since it would lack one essential quality of infinitude and perfection, namely existence. Thus I cannot conceive God except as existing, although it "is in my power to imagine a horse with or without wings." Descartes' version of the ontological argument rests then on the two assumptions that (1) existence is a

necessary attribute of an absolutely perfect Being and (2) in at least
this special case existence can be ascertained by a purely analytical
examination of clear and distinct concepts without the appeal to any
empirical evidence. If these assumptions are denied (as they were by
Gassendi in his published objections to the *Meditations*), then the
argument does not establish its conclusion. But for Descartes the
ontological argument is the backbone of his rationalistic metaphysics
because it furnishes the warrant for his method, as well as a demonstrative proof of the existence of God, which Descartes must establish
before he can have any guarantee of the existence or reality of anything
else.

The Three Substances

Having established the basis of his metaphysics, Descartes turns his
attention to the problems of the nature of the physical world and the
relations of mind and body in man. How can we know that there are
actually existing bodies outside of us? We of course have feelings of
pain and pleasure, appetites, and sensation which we customarily
refer to physical causes. Since we do not produce these feelings and
sensations ourselves, they must be produced either by God or by
things outside ourselves. Since our sense perceptions are often confused and deceive us, we cannot prove the existence of external objects
by such evidence. If our sense perceptions of external objects are caused
by God, we are deceived, for we have no knowledge of God as their
cause. God, however, is not a deceiver, as Descartes believes he has
already shown, but a truthful being. Thus our sensations must be
caused by real bodies.

Descartes employs an illustration, now famous, of a piece of wax
direct from the beehive, which is fairly hard, cold, easily handled,
gives off a sound if properly struck by the finger, and retains something
of the sweetness of the honey which it possesses and the odor of the
flowers from which it was gathered. What happens when the piece of
wax is placed close to a fire? What remains of the taste is exhaled, the
smell evaporates, the color changes, the figure disappears, the size
becomes larger, it becomes fluid and hot, and no sound is now given
off when one tries to strike it. Nothing remains of the original sense
perceptions we had of the piece of wax. Yet in some sense the same
wax confronts us. Precisely in what sense? Something extended,
flexible, and movable still confronts us. Here then is a reality to be
understood by thought rather than by the senses.

The real nature of such an external or bodily object consists of what John Locke was later to call its substance and primary qualities. The basic attribute of material substance in Descartes' view is its mathematical properties, which he neatly sums up in the term *extension*, which is identical with the term *body*. Extension is length, breadth, and thickness; thus extension and space are identical. Every body or external object is a limited spatial magnitude. There is no empty space—whenever there is space, there is body or extension. Descartes denies the existence of atoms because space is infinitely divisible. There can be no ultimate material particles of space. The smallest particles of bodies with which we may be working at a given moment are still further divisible. Thus there are not what we would call atoms, molecules, or subatomic particles. We cannot limit extension, for the corporeal world is really infinite. All the processes of our external world are modifications or modes of extension. We may divide extension endlessly; we may separate and unite the parts and derive many different forms of matter.

Descartes defines *substance* in the *Principles of Philosophy* as "an existent thing which requires nothing but itself in order to exist." In reality, there is only one such being, God, who answers this description fully, as a Being that is absolutely self-sustaining. But there are also two relative substances, *mind* and *matter*, which need only the concurrence of God, for each is complete and self-sustaining. Mind and matter are fundamentally different from each other. We know them only through their attributes (essential characteristics or properties necessarily inhering in substance). Mind has the principal attribute of thought, while matter or body has that of extension. The attribute can manifest itself in various ways, *modes*, or modifications. Substance and attribute can be understood without modes or changes, but modes cannot be conceived without substance and attribute. Thus we cannot conceive figure without extension, but we can conceive extension without figure. The substance cannot alter its attributes, but it can alter its modes. An external object or body will always be extended, but its shape or form need not remain the same. God is unchanging, so there are no modes in God. Here, then, are the three substances—God, mind, and matter.

How does Descartes conceive the three substances to be related to one another? He states that God is the creator of mind and matter in a dual sense. God initially brought the two relative substances into existence and, further, He continues to preserve their existence. Obviously they depend on Him, but God does not depend on them.

God's relationship to matter is somewhat different from His relation to mind. God has given matter a certain amount of motion which remains constant. Bodies cannot initiate movement or stop it. Since God is immutable in His perfection, it is necessary to postulate that the same quantity of movement originally given to the universe is continuously maintained in it. In some respects Descartes seems to anticipate the later doctrines of the conservation of mass and energy. God is, for Descartes, the efficient cause of matter. Since our minds are finite, we can never know the final ends for which God made the world. Our knowledge is inadequate and we must guard against transferring the ideals and interests of our limited experience to the inscrutable nature and actions of God. We cannot, therefore, deal with final purposes and ends in physics and biology. Science can develop only if it confines itself to enlarging the understanding of efficient causes. This it can do best by studying the physical world on its own terms, rather than in theological terms, and in applying mathematical laws to physical phenomena.

God's relationship with mind is different. God is the goal, the end, the final purpose toward which our limited minds move. We are aware of our imperfect and finite character, and yet we seek perfection which we can find only in God. The existence of God guarantees the possibility of human knowledge. God's relation to the mind is a teleological one, while He is at the same time the efficient cause of the material universe.

Descartes develops a sharp dualism between mind and body. The attribute of mind is thought, and of body, extension. The two substances are absolutely distinct. Mind cannot be extended and body has no power to think. Mind is basically free and active, while bodies or objects are determined by physical laws. In his interpretations of inorganic matter, of plants and animals other than man, and of the human body itself, Descartes is a thoroughgoing mechanist. The human body is a machine. So Descartes carries the mechanical explanation into physics, astronomy, biology, and physiology. There is then the complete rejection of Aristotle's vitalism and the scholastic version of it in the medieval schoolmen.

Descartes, however, balks at regarding human beings as mere automata responding without consciousness and thought. He is no materialist when it comes to interpreting man. But in man thinking substance is obviously conjoined with extended substances. This of course raises a perplexing problem which Descartes does not adequately solve. Although subjected to much criticism, Descartes was probably the first philosopher to see clearly the problem of the relation between mind and body in modern terms and to enunciate the classical doctrine of interactionism. The basic question is: If the human mind or soul and the body are totally different (relative) substances, how can there be any conceivable real relationship between the two? How can the mind, lacking matter and motion, either influence or be influenced by the motions going on within the human body? Will not some motion or energy be lost each time the mind receives a sensation or sets in motion material particles in the brain eventuating in bodily motions?

Descartes is aware of these difficulties and exercises considerable ingenuity in order to overcome them. He asserts that "thought can be troubled by the organs without being the product of them." In other words, feelings, sensations, and appetites are disturbances in the mind or soul arising from its union with the body. In this view a physical state does not become a mental state, or produce or cause a mental state, or vice versa. The mind or soul merely directs the currents of motion flowing through the body without increasing or decreasing their volume. It is as though one were to switch electrical currents from one circuit to another without increasing or decreasing the current. In the last book he published, *The Passions of the Soul*, Descartes suggests there is likely only one point where the body and the mind might come into contact. This is the centrally located pineal gland deep between the two hemispheres of the brain. Here then is a simple, single center where the mind can intervene to perform its "switching" function. It is obvious, of course, that this strategy does not enable Descartes to overcome the difficulties. The mind cannot alter the direction of the flow of motion in the body without employing physical energy any more than it can increase or decrease the quantity. This is precisely what his clearcut distinction between the attributes of mind and body makes impossible. There are, however, passages where Descartes refers to the soul thinking a particular thought on the occasion of what is going on in the body, or of bodily movements being the occasions of thoughts. The word "occasion" suggests that there is no direct causal relation between mental and bodily events. This notion was taken up and expanded by Geulincx and Malebranche, members of the Cartesian school, who were dubbed "Occasionalists" because of their interest in using this idea to avoid some of the difficulties in Descartes' interactionism. Although Descartes never solves the problem of the interaction of mind and body, he deserves great credit for bringing out clearly the nature of the problem and some of the difficulties involved in purported solutions. His work was a source of intellectual stimulation to Spinoza and Leibniz who developed their systems as alternative approaches to many of the problems Descartes raised.

Ethics

Descartes never works out a fully developed ethics to complete his system. Yet he writes suggestively on ethical themes and on occasion explores topics relevant to ethics. Some of his views are worth noting. Descartes is convinced that by controlling one's desires with inner fortitude and making one's self independent of the world, a man can really live a philosophical life. He feels that we should not be diverted from this goal by sensuous desires. He considers the intellectual love of God to be the greatest of the moral virtues. He remains, however, a rationalist and a scientist rather than a mystic.

Descartes' analysis of the passions has some implications for moral philosophy and involves the theory of interaction. He maintains the position that passion is stimulated or caused in the soul by the body. But he emphasizes that we must distinguish the emotion of fear from our clear perception of the fear and its nature. In his classification of passions and emotions, Descartes names six primary passions of the soul—love, hate, wonder, desire, joy, and sorrow—from which all other passions are derived. In deliberation and choice we face conflicting tendencies set in motion by the animal spirits and the will. In order to make moral choice effective, Descartes, in Stoic fashion, emphasizes that we must recognize what lies within our control; we then have the further problem of choosing those actions which are good rather than those which are bad. True happiness or beatitude will come from the pursuit of virtue and wisdom, which depend upon ourselves. Descartes does give more recognition to the role of external goods like riches and health than do the Stoics. But he is characteristically Stoic in his stress on the self-sufficiency of the virtuous man, the necessity of enduring patiently those things enjoined by Providence which we cannot alter, and the distinction between those things which lie within our power and those that do not. He is least Scholastic when he emphasizes that there is in this life a tranquility of soul which man can obtain by his own efforts. His rationalist bias is often so strongly expressed that he seems very close to the Socratic position that knowledge is virtue. In general, Descartes' ethics reveals something of the basic unresolved ambiguity in his philosophy. Our will shows the free activity of our minds, but not its freedom to directly control the activities of the body. To think and will rationally is to achieve some of the characteristics of God's mind. Herein lies our true perfection and destiny. Over against this lies the strictly mechanical nature of all the bodily processes which the mind and will ought to direct, but from which it is separated by an impossible gulf. The basic split in human nature which the dualistic cosmology of Descartes introduced has perplexed and stimulated subsequent philosophers to develop alternative solutions.

The Significance of Descartes

There is no question that Descartes is the most significant of all French philosophers. The close connection between philosophy and science in his work has been evident in the subsequent history of French philosophy. His emphasis on clear and distinct ideas, expressed in simple language, sets a standard which was so widely influential that it has become traditional to refer to the clarity of French philosophical writing in general. It even had influence on French literary criticism, and Descartes' theory of the passions had repercussions in French literature and painting.

But to establish the claim that Descartes was the father of modern philosophy we must consider other evidence. Descartes' formulation of basic issues in philosophy was so clear and so pertinent that his work determined the development of philosophy for more than a century and subsequently continued to influence philosophical discussion. Perhaps his most important contribution to philosophy was his development of the method of critical doubt which pointed up the great difference in attitude between modern thought and Scholastic thought. Descartes' selection of thoughts rather than external objects as the basic empirical realities had a profound influence on the development of idealism and empiricism. Even though many subsequent philosophers did not share Descartes' views on how one might move from inner psychological certitude to a knowledge of God and the physical world, they often adopted a basically subjectivistic position from which they developed their theories of knowledge. Whether or not Descartes' starting point is viewed as a mistake, his example was prophetic.

Descartes rejected the Aristotelian-Scholastic conception of mind and produced a view of mind which was an important stepping stone to modern theories. He deserves considerable credit for being the first to formulate clearly the mind-body problem and to propose the theory of interaction as a solution for it. They are still topics for contemporary philosophical discussion. He shared with Hobbes the credit for bringing the mechanistic theory before a wide public. His appreciation of physics and of the role of mathematical reasoning in knowledge were important in furthering the development of the new revolution in science during the seventeenth century.

Although there is, as we have noted, an unresolved dualism between what he took from contemporary science and what he preserved from his religious inheritance, Descartes was a more fruitful philosopher than he might have been had he been more logically consistent. As Bertrand Russell has observed, a more consistent Descartes might have been the founder of a new Scholasticism instead of being the source of divergent philosophical schools.

Descartes: Selected Additional Reading

Abernethy, George L. and Thomas A. Langford, eds., *History of Philosophy: Selected Readings*. Belmont, Calif.: Dickenson, 1965, pp. 317–336.*

Beck, Leslie, J., *The Method of Descartes*. Oxford: Clarendon Press, 1965.*

Collins, James D., *Continental Rationalists: Descartes, Spinoza, Leibniz*. Milwaukee, Wis.: Bruce, 1967.

Descartes, *Philosophical Works of Descartes*. Edited by E. S. Haldane and G. R. Ross. New York: Dover Publications, 1955.

Descartes, *Discourse on Method, Optics, Geometry and Meteorology*. Translated by Paul J. Olscamp. Indianapolis: Bobbs-Merrill, Liberal Arts Press, 1965.

Descartes, *Discourse on Method and Other Works*. Translated by E. S. Haldane and G. R. T. Ross; abridged, edited and with an introduction by Joseph Epstein. New York: Washington Square Press, 1965.

Descartes, *Philosophical Essays: Discourse on Method: Meditations: Rules for the Direction of the Mind*. Translated by Laurence J. Lafluer. Indianapolis: Bobbs-Merrill, Liberal Arts Press, 1964.

Doney, W., *Descartes: A Collection of Critical Essays*. Garden City: Doubleday, Anchor, 1968.

Gibson, Alexander B., *The Philosophy of Descartes*. London: Methuen, 1932.*

Kaufmann, Walter, *Philosophical Classics*. Englewood Cliffs, N.J.: Prentice-Hall, 1961, II, 26–91.*

Keeling, S. V., *Descartes*. New York: Random House paperback, 1968.

Maritain, J., *The Dream of Descartes*. New York: Philosophical Library, 1944.*

Mellone, S. H., *The Dawn of Modern Thought: Descartes, Spinoza, Leibniz.* London: Oxford University Press, 1930.*

Sesonke, Alexander and Noel Fleming, *Meta-Meditations: Studies In Descartes.* Belmont, Calif.: Wadsworth paperback, 1965.

Smith, Norman Kemp, *New Studies in the Philosophy of Descartes.* London: Macmillan, 1952.*

Chapter Fourteen

Spinoza

Although not fully appreciated until the end of the eighteenth century, Baruch (Benedict) Spinoza was probably the most significant philosopher of the Renaissance. He was born in Amsterdam in 1632, and was a member of a Jewish family that had fled the Inquisition in Portugal or Spain to seek religious freedom in Holland about the end of the sixteenth century. Spinoza attended the Rabbinical School, where he studied the Bible and Talmud in Hebrew and read the medieval commentators like Maimonides and Avicebron, who had inherited the thought of Arabic Aristotelianism and Neoplatonism. A brilliant student, he enrolled in a Latin class taught by Dr. Van den Enden, a former Jesuit and alleged atheist, in order to read the writings of Descartes and the new works in mathematics and the natural sciences. The rabbis were alarmed by their brilliant student's loss of interest in rabbinical studies and by his unorthodox and skeptical ideas. They unsuccessfully employed persuasion and pressure to discourage him, in order to avoid giving offense to conservative elements in the Christian community by harboring a potential atheist. In 1656 the Synagogue expelled the twenty-four-year-old student with bitter curses of excommunication. Thereupon he withdrew from the Jewish community and the city of Amsterdam to take refuge in the country with some Remonstrants who had been excommunicated by the Protestant Synod of Dort.

Spinoza was able to support himself in his austere existence by grinding lenses for optical instruments. Thus he was able to give most of his time to the pursuit of philosophy. In each of the villages in the vicinity of Amsterdam, Leyden, and the Hague, and in the Hague itself, where he subsequently lived, he won friends among the intellectuals and carried on a wide correspondence with such thinkers as Oldenburg and Boyle of the Royal Society of London, the physicist Huygens, the philologist Voss, and the philosopher Leibniz.

In 1663 Spinoza published a summary and commentary on the second part of Descartes' *Principles*. In 1670 he anonymously published *Tractatus Theologico-Politicus* without the benefit of a Dutch translation in order to forestall persecution. It provoked strong opposition from the Calvinist divines and the Catholic Church, and enhanced his reputation in intellectual circles. Spinoza felt it prudent not to publish other manuscripts during his lifetime. In 1673 the Elector Palatine, Karl Ludwig, offered him a professorship at the University of Heidelberg, which he declined in order to give his full time to philosophical reflections without limiting his freedom by the nominal religious assurances required by the position. He continued to live his frugal and simple life until he contracted consumption and died at forty-five. The world was then unaware that it had lost its greatest living philosopher.

Spinoza's Theory of Knowledge

Out of the despair of his own personal situation Spinoza concludes that no secure, lasting satisfaction can be found in riches, fame, or the pleasures of the senses, or from the love of anything that is perishable. The only real and lasting good can be experienced in love of what is eternal and infinite, that is, God conceived as the substantial underlying reality of all the unchanging processes of nature. Above everything else he seeks to find "knowledge of the union existing between the mind and the whole of nature."

In his unfinished essay, *On the Improvement of the Understanding*, and in a Note to Proposition XL in the second part of *Ethics*, Spinoza examines in a critical fashion the various sources of men's ideas and judgment of things. He distinguishes three kinds of knowledge: *opinion, reason*, and *intuition*. Under *opinion* he places information by hearsay and tradition, the fragmentary and confused operations of ordinary sense experiences, and the often inexact memories of past experiences. As a rationalist, Spinoza feels such opinions are too unreliable to provide a foundation for a system of truths.

Spinoza has complete confidence in *reason* and *intuition*. Reason is possible because all things have certain common features or traits. We share certain ideas with other men because our minds and bodies and theirs have some of the same features. Our initial "common notions" include our conception of extension, motion, rest, solidity, size, figure, cause, line, and all the fundamental ideas of mathematics and mechanics, which all men clearly and distinctly perceive. From such adequate ideas we may infer other adequate ideas by vigorous deduction in the geometrical method which Spinoza celebrates.

Spinoza looks beyond reason and deduction to *intuition*, which provides a more immediate and concrete mastery of the order and complex interrelations of the nature of things than is provided by the step by step inferences of deductive reason, in which even adequate ideas are only relatively adequate. This conception of intuitive reason is akin to Plato's conception of reason in the figure of the divided line. The aspiration for intuitive knowledge is basic to the integrated vision of truth, which remains an ideal by which we measure our achievement of knowledge. Descartes claims to make frequent use of intuitions, but Spinoza observes wryly "The things which I have been able to know by this kind of knowledge are as yet very few."

Spinoza not only adopts the geometrical method in his rationalistic and systematic metaphysics, but actually employs it as the form of exposition for his *Ethics*, which reads like a treatise in geometry. Whatever may be the disadvantages of this as a literary form, it does provide a compact, precise, and impersonal presentation of his philosophy. The argument, however, is so condensed, and at times so obscure, that the serious student of the *Ethics* must read it with the help of a standard commentary.

Substance or Nature of God

Spinoza's *Ethics* is set forth in five books or parts. Part I is entitled "Concerning God" and gives Spinoza's metaphysical doctrine of Nature, Substance, or ultimate reality. Part II deals with the "Nature and Origin of the Mind" and presents his theory of knowledge and his solution of the mind-body problem. Part III deals with passions or emotions and gives his psychological views, which are most relevant to his ethical position. The last two parts present, in sharp contrast, "Human Bondage, or the Strength of the Emotions" and "The Power of the Understanding, or Human Freedom." The work is an ethic, then, concerned with the good life which man seeks to achieve in order to find fulfillment. But this ethic is rooted in what is offered as an irrefutable ontology based on a set of axioms and definitions.

Three important definitions serve as the organizing principles of Spinoza's system. They are the following:

By substance I mean that which is in itself and is conceived through itself, that is, that of which the conception does not require a conception of anything else upon which it depends.

By attribute I mean that which the intellect perceives to constitute the essence of substance.

By mode I understand the modification of substance, or that which is in something else through which it is conceived.

Spinoza's definition of substance is virtually that of Descartes, for whom substance was "an existent thing which requires nothing but itself to exist." Substance, when rigorously analyzed and understood, cannot be conceived as finite, dual, and limited. Two substances cannot exist, since if they did each would be limited by the other and thus they would not really be infinite, but would instead be modes. Substance is eternal, since if it were not it would be preceded by and dependent upon something else and would not be self-sufficient. Substance necessarily exists because it cannot be produced by anything other than itself. God or Nature or Substance is not, for Spinoza, that which is infinite merely in a certain class. That which is infinite only in its kind or class does not possess all attributes. Thus it would be subject to negation, but Substance or God is subject to no limitation or negation of any kind. Whatever necessarily exists is either the one substance or modes of the one substance.

For Spinoza, the terms *Substance, Nature, God* all denote the same reality. All things must be viewed in their relation to God or Nature as aspects of the infinite Substance. The infinite Substance must be understood as having an infinitude of attributes, although we know only two of these attributes—thought and extension. Each of these attributes is "infinite after its own kind" but not "absolutely infinite" like God. Extension is infinite in the sense that it is limited only by extension and not by thought. Thought is infinite in its own kind and cannot be limited by extension. Both are attributes of God and basically in their common substance are identical. Both are ways of interpreting Nature or all-that-is on one side as a mathematical and mechanical system occupying space and on the other as a mental-thinking system of mathematical and logical perfection. It is easy to see why orthodox Jews and Christians in Spinoza's day called him an atheist. He leaves no room for a personal deity who rules providentially over nature and responds to the prayers of believers. Yet Spinoza retains the term, "God" to designate the qualities of being eternal, infinite, necessary and perfect in power and order, which he feels are descriptive of ultimate reality.

As we have seen, Nature is all-there-is and thus is infinite. It has no beginning and no end and thus is eternal. Its productive power has been revealed and will be revealed in the boundless variety of things and events, for it possesses an infinite number of attributes, each of which manifests its infinite and eternal essence. So there "follows an infinite number of things in infinite ways" (*Ethics*, Part I, prop. 16). Nature, in one sense, never changes and, in another, is ever changing. It is like the ocean which ever remains while the waves endlessly come and go. Spinoza distinguishes these two senses by the terms *natura naturans* and *natura naturata*. The self-acting cause of all existence, substance and its attributes, which necessarily and actively brings all things to be he calls *natura naturans*. The particular existent things, states and conditions, modes of substance, are what he designates as *natura naturata*.

Spinoza does not succeed in making clear to his readers how *natura naturata*, the world of changing particulars, is derived from *natura naturans*, the eternal unchanging substance. No matter how carefully we draw our inferences from the basic nature of Substance, we cannot deduce the necessary coming into existence of a single finite mode. Hegel once remarked that Spinoza's God resembled the lion's den in Aesop's fable; one can observe all the animal tracks leading into the den, but none coming out are visible. Before this criticism is pressed too vigorously against Spinoza, we might do well to recognize that no philosopher, in making such claims, has succeeded in explaining how, rather than merely asserting the fact that, the many arises from the one or that transient time is differentiated from changeless eternity. Spinoza's efforts to elucidate the relations between attributes and modes are obscure and the subject of many controversial interpretations which may prove bewildering to the beginning student.

Spinoza's Psychology: His Doctrine of the Passions

In Part III of *Ethics* Spinoza undertakes to develop a naturalistic account of human emotions and human conduct. He announces his intention to treat man as a part of Nature and to consider "human actions and desires exactly as if I were dealing with lines, planes, and bodies" (*Ethics*, Part III, Preface). In Spinoza's view each man is a mode of the universe, a temporal, transient modification of God. From one perspective each man is a mind or particular combination of ideas in the infinite range of divine thought. This combination is associated with a particular body, which is a moving segment of the infinite extension of God. While ideas and bodies are distinguishable, Spinoza denies they are separate and interacting objects. Rather he insists that the occasion of one's ideas parallels the order of bodily events. We have correlation, but not the causal interaction which Descartes offered as an explanation for the relation between ideas and bodily events. Spinoza proposes as his explanation the theory of psychophysical parallelism: body and mind are both parallel aspects of the same thing, the substantial reality of which is God.

Spinoza applies the same rigor in developing his theory of determinism in human nature and activities. He excludes the possibility of free will, final causes, spontaneity, and alternatives. In a completely determined universe nothing could be otherwise than it is. Nature, or all-that-is, consists of attributes, each expressing essences. This is what is. The type of necessity which operates all through the universe is like the logical necessity in defining a plane triangle as having the sum of its three interior angles equal to two right angles. All that exists in the universe is necessary; everything that does not exist is impossible. Man's situation in this completely determined universe is that of a focal point of modes, which in their arrangement comprise the attributes of thought on the one hand and extension on the other. The fundamental reality of man is God—God manifesting himself locally and temporally in specific ways as thought or extension. It is not that mind is a separate being accompanying the body; it is one perspective of the all-pervading Nature, of which the body is another perspective. Thus these two perspectives have no independent being or causal efficacy, but are two parallel versions of the same reality. But what they do possess, according to Spinoza, is *conatus*—the urgency or tendency of each to persist in its own way. "The endeavor wherewith a thing endeavors to persist in its being is nothing else than the actual essence of that thing" (*Ethics*, Part III, prop. 7). Spinoza is not offering simply a psychological generalization about self-preservation in men, but a principle that applies to every finite thing in the universe. *Conatus* regarded in the mental perspective we may call "will," while in referring to mind and body conjointly we may call it "appetite." When "appetite" becomes conscious we call it "desire." Our judgments of approval or disapproval do not determine our desires but proceed from them. When we desire something, we judge it to be good. Similarly we call something "evil" because we feel an aversion to it. When we understand our emotions we know how our judgments of approval or disapproval are determined.

In Spinoza's analysis, the transition to a higher or lower state of vitality or perfection is reflected in consciousness. The transition to a higher state is called "pleasure" (*laetitia*), while the transition to the lower state is called "pain" (*tristitia*). Spinoza is not a hedonist in the simple sense of the term "pleasure." Perhaps it is more accurate to think of him in other terminology as something of a self-realizationist, for "pleasure" (*laetitia*) is the joy or elevation of happiness which accompanies a man's growth in the more mature achievement of his rational powers, whereas pain (*tristitia*) is the awareness of failure and the lessening of one's powers. Spinoza lists forty-eight notions which express the basic affection (*affectus*), "desire." His definitions of regret, joy, cowardice, ambition, avarice, hope, fear, pity, indignation, and many other emotions reveal his keen insight into the nature of passions and actions.

The nature of any passion reveals our reaction toward any object of our attention. We act on the idea that dominates our mind even if it is misleading or inadequate. For Spinoza, the best approach to the good life is to gain more adequate ideas rather than to extinguish emotions entirely and live in Stoic apathy. His goal is to become, as far as possible, the controlling center of his affairs instead of being the helpless victim of the forces from the external world that play upon him. If a man changes his ideas about anything, he will feel differently toward it. His passion will be replaced by a different emotion. With a touch of sadness and realism, Spinoza recognizes, "It cannot happen that man should not be a part of nature and that he should suffer no changes except those which can be understood exclusively through his own nature or of which he is himself the adequate cause" (*Ethics*, Part IV, prop. 4).

Human Bondage and Human Freedom

Parts IV and V of *Ethics* move toward the culminating argument of the book. In dealing with bondage and freedom Spinoza is wrestling with the ancient Stoic distinction between what does and does not lie within the power of man. As a thoroughgoing determinist, Spinoza's rejection of teleology and indeterminism is clear and consistent. Nature or Substance is self-caused, and every event in it occurs with mathematical necessity. Ultimately things are what they are and cannot be otherwise. The terms "good" and "evil" do not apply to Nature as a whole or to things considered in themselves. "Good" and "evil" are terms which we use in connection with our interests and concerns. We call "evil" that which frustrates and disappoints us and "good" that which is advantageous for us. We tend to project these subjective responses to persons and things in the external world. I may hate a person because he once frustrated me, although now he may be seeking to do something advantageous for me. When such an affection becomes dominant, it subjects us to confused ideas about ourselves and the world. The bondage of the soul is found in the domination of the passions, which prevents us from moving toward the clarity which makes possible our genuine fulfillment.

We can free ourselves from bondage to the passions and confused ideas by thinking distinctly and clearly—the same criterion the Cartesians emphasize. Above all, we must recognize our passions and inadequate ideas for what they are. If we think rationally, we shall accept without emotional distress the inevitability of events. If we understand that death is the inevitable outcome of an incurable disease, we do not become emotionally upset by a friend's death. If we understand that an older person's crotchety behavior is a function of his arteriosclerosis, we no longer become angry with him. Such understanding will liberate us, not only from the feeling itself, but from the domination that feeling has over us. If we can bring ourselves to contemplate every event *sub quadam aeternitas specie* (as it were under the aspect of eternity), to realize that every event is a necessary event to be referred to the idea of God or the system of Nature as an established order, we find that the passions Nature produces in us cease to be passions.

Human freedom, then, is the acceptance of the universe as it is through rational understanding. This is what Spinoza meant by the "intellectual love of God." The idea of God is the most adequate of all ideas. In the intellectual love of God one finds real peace of mind, freedom from the passions, the ability to return good for evil, release from envy and body lusts. This was the philosophy which enabled Spinoza to become reconciled to his own excommunication from the synagogue and to finally accept the irrationality of the mob which killed his friends the DeWitt brothers, who were seeking to preserve the liberties of all in Holland. This spiritual achievement Spinoza calls "man's blessedness"—the noblest form of human life. Blessedness is something which is possible for man despite the fact that he always remains a finite being and fails to win a full measure of virtue or freedom. Through understanding he may appraise his own finitude in the presence of the infinite with all its complexity. Spinoza asserts: "There is nothing in nature which is contrary to the intellectual love of God or is able to destroy it" (*Ethics*, Part V, prop. 37). This he holds to be true in the midst of war, persecution, poverty, pain, or any other form of finitude. This exalted vision may come to a few men who understand that God cannot possibly play favorites, for "favor" and "disfavor," "good" and "evil," are meaningless terms in relation to God. It is sobering to recall the final sentence of *Ethics*: "All things excellent are as difficult as they are rare." Yet, as his political philosophy shows, Spinoza does not reveal how the boundary between acquiescence and activity should be drawn.

Spinoza's Social and Political Philosophy

Spinoza studied carefully Hobbes' *De Cive* and *Leviathan* and was to a considerable extent influenced by them in the development of his doctrines of egoism and naturalism. Although, like Hobbes, he justifies sovereign power as the price one must pay for order in society, he is much more progressive and optimistic in his determination to maintain intellectual and political freedom within the framework of a utilitarian state. Spinoza finds mutual cooperation as natural to man as pride and fear. He views man not as an autonomous individual, but more in the Aristotelian sense of a social animal. Thus he is more successful than Hobbes in incorporating his social philosophy into his metaphysical system. Spinoza's two works *Tractatus Theologico-Politicus* and *Political Treatise* constitute a closely reasoned effort to fit his political analysis into an ethical philosophy, to discover the principles which emerge from an impartial analysis of human nature.

The *Tractatus Theologico-Politicus* is basically a defense of freedom of thought. Its title page states: "Freedom of thought and speech not only may, without prejudice to piety and the public peace, be granted; but also may not, without danger to piety and the public peace, be withheld." Spinoza concludes: "That state is freest whose laws are founded on sound reason, so that every member of it may, if he will, be free; that is, live with full consent under the entire guidance of reason." The first half of the *Tractatus* deals with the Old Testament, the authenticity of its books, and the nature of miracles. His treatment is classic and anticipates much of Higher Criticism as developed by German scholars two centuries later. He writes reverently and critically for men of understanding and asks others not to read his book. He seeks to ascertain in what situation an Old Testament book was written, what the author's purpose was, for what particular people it was prepared. He rejects the Mosaic authorship of the Pentateuch. He stresses that "Scripture does not aim at imparting scientific knowledge," but is written to inspire men to live better lives and thus is adapted to the understanding of the masses. It is deliberately allegorical and symbolic, but contains nothing contrary to reason. Religion and science have separate domains. The Bible does not accommodate reason and vice versa. The certainty on which all religious conviction rests is moral certainty, not scientific or rational proof. Religion should be judged in terms of its moral attitudes as expressed, for example, in the duty of loving one's neighbor as one's self and of repentance for sins.

Spinoza explains miracles as natural events. Science reveals the dependable, law-abiding character of the universe, which clearly points to a rational deity. The Providence of God is to be understood as "nothing but Nature's order following necessarily from her eternal law." To say that God performs a miracle and violates the laws of nature is to assert that God absurdly acts against his own nature. In Spinoza's view, the Bible properly emphasizes the activity of God directly rather than through natural causes, but does not necessarily oppose it to natural causes. As we have seen in Spinoza's metaphysical system, God is the eternal order of which both the physical universe and man are partial expressions.

Spinoza refutes the view current in his day that the state has a divine origin, like the Jewish theocracy in the Old Testament, and that it derives its authority from the will of God and thus may legitimately control every phase of human conduct and expression. He argues that Hebrew political institutions reported in the Old Testament were designed only for a particular people in a given historical situation and provide no universal model for human societies.

Like Hobbes, Spinoza roots his social contract in self-preservation and security. "A compact is only made valid by its utility, without which it becomes null and void." The authority of the sovereign extends only so far as he can enforce his will, and this he will not be able to do unless he consults the best interests of his subjects. He defends democracy as being "of all forms of government the most natural, and the most consonant with individual liberty." The purpose of the state is the fulfillment of man's power and reason, the true excellence and life of the mind on the widest scale possible. Thus the state exists for man and not man for the state; it is a means to achieve the security which is necessary for civilization.

Spinoza's utilitarian view of law and political obligation also finds expression in his attitudes toward foreign policy and international relations. Treaties between states remain in force only so long as it is in the interest of each party to adhere to them. No ruler ought to honor his promises when they conflict with the interests of his nation. This has been called Machiavellianism by some critics, but at least it is not a device for making despotism effective; instead it is offered as a flexible policy which supports the largest amount of security and rational activity of the citizenry.

Spinoza lived in a time when religious bigotry, sectarian strife, and religious wars were all evident. He felt keenly the need for tolerance to permit the development of scientific, social, and spiritual progress. Since he was opposed to the efforts of preachers and synods in Holland to emulate the role of Old Testament prophets and issue divine commands to the government, he argued that the secular authorities of the state should have the ultimate power in all legal matters, including the "outward observances of piety and the external rites of religion." The social contract does not limit the inward worship of God and personal piety. The freedom of speculation and publication is not only the right of scholars, but is necessary if men are to make progress in the pursuit of knowledge. These views anticipate in part the subsequent arguments of John Locke for religious tolerance and John Stuart Mill's classic essay *On Liberty*. Spinoza observes: "And yet I must confess that from such freedom certain inconveniences may at times arise. But who has ever so wisely set up anything that no ills could arise from it? He who wishes to rule everything by laws will call forth imperfections rather than diminish them. What cannot be forbidden must needs be allowed, even if it at times leads to harm."

Spinoza's Influence

For a century after his death Spinoza was the victim of an extraordinary amount of abuse from both theologians and philosophers. His theories were called hideous, sophistic, atheistic, and subversive of true morality and religion. In the course of time the tide turned. More romantic and organic thinkers like Lessing, Jacobi, Novalis (who called Spinoza "a God-intoxicated man"), Heine, Goethe, Schelling, Hegel, and Coleridge spoke of him with varying degrees of warmth and appreciation for his emphasis on immanence and totality. In more recent times writers have regarded him as a speculative forerunner of a completely scientific and naturalistic view of the world. Thus different generations of thinkers select from his work what is of value to their purposes.

Many streams of influence converged on Spinoza and appeared in his work. Among the most prominent were rationalism, naturalism, determinism, and mysticism. Although he was highly critical of Cartesian rationalism, Spinoza developed much more explicitly and fully the implications of Cartesianism, especially the assumption that mathematical knowledge provides an insight into the meaning and truth of an objectively existing reality, rather than merely the postulation of hypothetical conceptual entities. He also developed in a more subtle way some of the moral attitudes and determinism of Stoicism. His acquaintance with Maimonides and other medieval Jewish theologians and his knowledge of the mystic lore of the Kabbala undoubtedly influenced him more than he realized.

Today most thinkers would reject Spinoza's assumptions, as well as his geometrical method. Although his naturalism and interest in mathematics are appreciated, there is among contemporary thinkers much more interest in empiricism and the scientific investigation of nature. Most would argue that his moral vision of the good life is too exalted and austere. His critics would ask whether the good of understanding is not only one good and not *the* good. They might accuse him of denying conventional morality and restoring his own morality on the same basis of private vision, exhortation, and subjective preference. In a pragmatic age his critics might convict him of overemphasizing the control of the emotions and ignoring the manipulation and reconstruction of the external world. The fact that Spinoza's vision and rigor continue to intrigue men in every generation, and the fact that he continues to provoke criticism, suggest that he may nevertheless possess more enduring truth and relevance than his critics care to admit.

Spinoza: Suggested Additional Reading

Abernethy, George L. and Thomas A. Langford, eds., *History of Philosophy: Selected Readings*. Belmont, Calif.: Dickenson, 1965, pp. 359–385.*

Feuer, Lewis S., *Spinoza and the Rise of Liberalism*. Boston: Beacon Press, Paperback, 1965.

Hallett, Harold Foster, *Benedict de Spinoza: The Elements of His Philosophy*. London: University of London, 1957.*

Hampshire, Stuart, *Spinoza*. Baltimore: Penguin, 1952.

Joachim, H. H., *A Study of the Ethics of Spinoza*. Oxford: Clarendon, 1901.*

Kaufman, Walter, *Philosophic Classics*. Englewood Cliffs, N.J.: Prentice-Hall, 1961, II, 125–186.*

Parkinson, G. H. R., *Spinoza's Theory of Knowledge*. Oxford: Clarendon Press, 1954.*

Roth, Leon, *Spinoza*. London: Allen and Unwin, 1954.*

Saw, Ruth, *The Vindication of Metaphysics: A Study in the Philosophy of Spinoza*. London: Macmillan, 1951.*

Spinoza, *Political Works*. Edited and translated by A. G. Wernham. Oxford: Clarendon, 1958.*

Spinoza, *The Chief Works of Benedict de Spinoza*. Translated by R. H. M. Elwes. 2 vols. New York: Dover, 1962.

Spinoza, *Ethics*. Edited by James Gutman; translated by W. H. White. New York: Hafner, 1953.

Wolfson, Harry A., *Philosophy of Spinoza*. New York: World Publishing Company, Meridian, 1960.

Chapter Fifteen
Leibniz

Gottfried Wilhelm Leibniz (1646–1716) was born in Germany, just as the Thirty Years' War was nearing its end, four years after the death of Galileo and four years before that of Descartes. In many respects he was the last of the great Renaissance philosophers, although he had some ideas that belong to the Enlightenment and even to later thought. He was the son of the professor of moral philosophy at the University of Leipzig, who died when the boy was six years old. He was educated in the scholastic tradition, but after age ten he was allowed free rein in his father's fine library. The precocious youngster became very proficient in the Greek and Latin classics. At age fourteen he began his studies in law and philosophy at the University of Leipzig. By the age of twenty he had completed all the requirements for the degree of doctor of laws, but the university refused to confer it because of Leibniz's youth. However, the University at Altdorf not only awarded him the degree, but offered him a professorship, which he declined in favor of a less confining life.

Leibniz became an able diplomat and administrator. In 1667 he entered the service of the Archbishop of Mainz, who sent him to Paris on a mission to Louis XIV, whom Leibniz failed to see. But during a four-year stay he became acquainted with Arnauld, the French Jansenist philosopher and theologian, Malebranche, the philosopher, Huygens, the Dutch physicist, and Tschirnhaus, a German count who corresponded with Spinoza. On one occasion he was privileged to visit Spinoza at the Hague and to read some of his manuscripts. On another occasion he visited London, where he met the British chemist Boyle, and Oldenburg, the Secretary of the Royal Society. Leibniz was elected to the Royal Society after demonstrating his calculating machine. On the death of the archbishop of Mainz, Leibniz entered the service of the Duke of Brunswick at Hanover, where he held the post of ducal librarian for the next forty years. In addition he carried diplomatic responsibilities, and during his legal, geneological, historical, scientific, and philosophical studies he conducted a tremendous correspondence with intellectuals in England and on the continent.

Since Leibniz was an able diplomat and one committed to the work of reconciling opposing sides in specific controversies, it is not surprising to find these qualities appearing in his writings. Much of his philosophy appears in letters, journal articles, and brief summaries prepared for laymen. The most famous of these summaries are the *Monadology*, the *Principles of Nature and Grace*, and the *Discourse on Metaphysics*. Of his longer books, the *Theodicy* contains his philosophy of religion, and the *New Essays On Human Understanding* develops his revision of the doctrine of innate ideas to meet the criticisms of John Locke. He made many contributions to symbolic logic, but these lay unappreciated in manuscripts at Hanover until twentieth-century logicians came to study them. In his day he was perhaps most famous for his discovery of integral and differential calculus, which he made independently of Newton and which he brought to the attention of many mathematicians.

His writings reveal a prodigious worker of great originality with varied activities and interests. He fairly bubbled with new ideas—a universal language, the compilation of a Chinese dictionary, a refined calculating machine, and many other projects. He defended the doctrine of the Trinity and sought a theological base on which Catholics and Protestants could be reconciled. In metaphysics he sought a framework in which every philosophical position would have its place. He was patient, tolerant, sympathetic, genial, and always willing to lend an ear to new ideas. Despite his fame and originality, he died in 1716 singularly unappreciated and misunderstood. Fortunately in the twentieth century his ideas are being appreciated and given some of the critical assessment they deserve.

We have seen in another chapter how Hobbes developed a philosophy of materialism based on a mechanistic interpretation of the world. We noted how Descartes had made mechanism supreme in the inorganic world and among plants and animals other than man. At the same time he reduced mechanism to extension, a substance which, he allowed, could interact with thought. The Occasionalists abolished this kind of interaction and made God the miraculous efficient cause of each event. To avoid the difficult problems involved in interaction Spinoza paid the heavy price of eliminating teleology from the world and destroying our ordinary sense of freedom in the effort to show how the fundamental unity of all things could be preserved in the doctrine that thought and extension were only two attributes of the one substance God.

After careful study Leibniz concludes that none of these thinkers have done justice either to the mind-body problem or to the relations between one individual and another. He rejects, in particular, the notion of mechanical causation and the belief that matter can be reduced to extension and thought to consciousness. He maintains that matter possesses inertia in and of itself, and that mind likewise possesses an inertia or a tendency to remain itself even when unconscious. Hence matter is extension plus force; mind is consciousness plus force.

Force is, then, the lowest common denominator of our experience— that which we know best in our experience. It is the substance of which mind and matter are attributes. Force, not motion, always remains constant. Force is ultimate reality. It remains after or beyond extension. Thus Leibniz believes that it must be conceived as unextended, indivisible, simple, and basic.

Force is not monistic like Spinoza's substance. Leibniz believes in a multiplicity of Forces. Each body resists the encroachment of other bodies so that two bodies cannot occupy the same space at the same time. Each point of space may be thought of as a center of force. Each mind resists the encroachment of other minds so that no mind can be identified with any other. Thus each is a distinct center of force, and there are as many Forces as there are individuals. This view is pluralistic, since Leibniz regards all centers of force as substances, each distinct from the others. In terms of the calculus, the number of any units treated as ultimate cannot be less than infinity. Therefore, the number of distinct individual Forces constituting Reality must be infinite.

Leibniz named these substances or centers of force *monads*. This was a term used in the previous century by Giordano Bruno. Monads may be compared with physical points or mathematical points, but unlike physical points they possess no extension, and unlike mathematical points they are objective realities. Since monads have no extended parts and cannot be decomposed, they are indestructible and immortal —subject to the fact that God, the monad of monads, has created them and can, if He so wills, destroy them.

The monads are, as it were, hermetically sealed. No external cause can produce changes in them. Since each monad is provided with spontaneous activity and remains independent of external influence, it differs qualitatively from all other monads, and differs from them eternally. This is a consequence of Leibniz's doctrine of the identity of indiscernibles. If two objects were completely alike in all respects, they would be indistinguishable and thus identical. The differences between monads are mental and stem from the nature or individuality of the self-contained monad, which is without windows through which anything can enter or exit. Yet each monad in some sense reflects the universe from its own standpoint.

In accordance with the principle of continuity, there is a gradation in the perfection of monads. The lowest on the scale are the bare or naked monads of the inorganic world, whose perceptions are confused and lacking in memory or reasoning. Such "swooning" monads exist in a condition of stupor. At a higher level are to be found the monads possessing simple feeling and memory akin to that expressed in the consciousness of animals. Beyond this level are the monads in which reflection, self-consciousness, and reasoning are added to feeling and memory. Here we have the souls of men. The supreme monad of monads is God, who as pure spirit exists in isolation since he has no body composed of other monads. He is the source or primitive unity from which all other monads have come. He is infinite, eternal, absolutely wise and good, and omnipotent, except that he has to choose between possibilities that are mutually incompatible. Leibniz says: "Each monad is a mirror of the universe, from its point of view, and accompanied by a multitude of other monads composing its organic body, of which it is the ruling monad" (*Monadologie*, No. 70). In plants, animals, and human beings there is a central or ruling monad, the soul, which rules the subordinate, less perfect monads that constitute its body. Since he has maintained that each monad is held *incommunicado* from every other monad, Leibniz has to hold that the obedience of the governed monads arises spontaneously out of their own natures and not as the result of external influence. How, then, does the soul appear to suffer in sensation the influence of the body? How does the impression of the external world and of other selves arise? To deal with such problems Leibniz has to invoke his doctrine of preestablished harmony.

God, he tells us, has arranged matters so that each of the created monads implies the others and remains a perpetual mirror of them. When a change or development occurs within one monad, corresponding changes will take place in all the other monads giving rise spontaneously to the experience of apparently observing something occurring in the external world. All the monads mirror the same world with varying degrees of clarity and distinctness of perception. God created all the monads with identical contents differing only in the qualitative aspects of perception. The perceptions within the soul monad of an animal are clearer than those in the monads of its body, but they are essentially in harmony. To illustrate his theory, Leibniz used the analogies of the two choirs and the two clocks. If there are two choirs singing from identical scores, we know what we should hear from the second choir even if we are only listening to the first choir and one choir does not influence the other. If two clocks keep time perfectly, it would mean (on Leibniz's theory) that a clock maker had made the parts of each so perfectly they register time perfectly without mechanical connection between them or external correction. Neither clock influences the other, but each "mirrors" the change in the other. Leibniz believed that the universe is a metaphysical system of parts in perfect harmonious adaptation. The full state of the universe could be seen in the clear and distinct experience of any monad. God alone has the perfect clarity to have this knowledge all at once. Thus all the other monads fit into the hierarchy of varying degrees of perception. The doctrine of preestablished harmony provides an explanation of the relation between thinking and extended substance without recourse to Descartes' interaction in the pineal gland or the infinite number of miracles required by Malebranche's occasionalism.

In the *Monadology*, Leibniz devotes much space to the arguments for the existence of God, for the monads depend on God for their creation and coordination. He begins with a statement of the ontological argument. There are possible or contingent truths which may or may not actually occur, but there must be some necessary and actual ground that makes these truths possible. He defines God as the most perfect Being, the subject of all perfections, and a perfection is defined as a "simple quality which is positive and absolute, and expresses without any limits whatever it does express." Since there are no limitations and negations outside the idea of such a God of perfection to prevent its actual existence, and since we need the assumption of His existence as a necessary ground for contingent and possible truths, he concludes that God actually exists—what is possible must exist.

Leibniz's version of the cosmological argument for God's existence states that every particular thing in the world is *contingent*; logically it is perfectly possible for the world and all that is in it not to exist. There must be a sufficient reason for every particular matter of fact. Therefore the universe as a whole must have a sufficient reason which lies outside the universe itself. This sufficient reason is God.

The third argument develops Leibniz's concept of eternal truths. Matters of fact rest upon eternal truths, which must exist to provide a satisfactory explanation of the particular events in the universe. All statements that deal only with essence, rather than with existence or matters of fact, are either always true or never true. "Eternal truths" are statements that are always true. Truths are part of the contents of minds, and an eternal truth must be part of the contents of an eternal mind. This eternal mind is God. It is assumed here that these eternal truths cannot be produced by a human mind.

The fourth argument depends on his doctrine of preestablished harmony, which implies the acceptance of his metaphysical view that the monads are windowless and yet each mirrors the universe in perfect synchronization. The perfect harmony or agreement of so many substances without interaction or communication of any sort implies a common cause or force—God as creator. Since most people have found it difficult to give up causal interaction, this argument has never enjoyed wide support even among theists who have tended to view Leibniz's arguments with some sympathy.

Basically Leibniz was an optimist, although he lived in a time when his country was seeking to recover from the desolation of the Thirty Years' War. He maintained the doctrine of many possible worlds—possible because they did not contradict the laws of logic. If God is an omniscient monad who knows all the eternal and contingent truths and can contemplate an infinite number of possible worlds, why then did God create or choose this particular world with all its evils? Why did not God choose to create a possible world with less evil or no evil? In its simplest form, Leibniz's reply is that God is good and that his creation is the best of the possible worlds in that it possesses the greatest excess of good over evil. Not all the possibilities of existence are *compossible* or capable of existing simultaneously. Some important goods are logically involved with specific evils. A world created without evil would not be so good as the world we now have with all its evils. God is omnipotent in that He can create whatever is possible, but He can only choose between alternatives that are mutually exclusive and not *compossible*. Our world is one in which "is obtained as great variety as possible, along with the greatest possible order," and thus "as much perfection as possible."

Leibniz distinguishes three types of evil: metaphysical, physical, and moral. Metaphysical evil is the lesser degree of perfection which is necessarily imposed upon every created monad as the price for not being God. Everything other than God is imperfect. Physical and moral evils are simply the ways in which monads must represent to themselves the imperfect level of their perception when they lack the clarity of God. The facts of limitation, finitude, sin, and suffering are the consequences of there being anything in existence other than God. As an optimist, Leibniz argues that the contrast of evil throws into sharper relief the nature of good. Physical sufferings may serve as a penalty for sin and a means of perfecting the good. What would life be like if there were no obstacles to spur our achievements? If Judas had not betrayed Christ, the great miracles and acts of God in the redemption would not have taken place. Much of what man calls evil reveals his limited egocentric predicament which blinds him to the ultimate harmony and perfection which characterize God's knowledge of the good. Like Spinoza, Leibniz as a good rationalist insisted that much of moral evil could be dispelled by clearer and more adequate thinking. Throughout the entire *Theodicy* in which these views are developed, Leibniz's emphasis is more on edification than on analysis.

Leibniz's theory of knowledge derives from his basic metaphysical assumptions. He shares the ideal of rationalists that real knowledge is an integrated system of universal and necessary truths based on principles, and not derived from contingent experiences. The universe then is a mathematical-logical structure which only reason can understand. Since Leibniz asserts that monads are windowless and immune from external influence, he must reject the view of Locke that the human mind is a blank tablet upon which external experience writes. Both sensation and reason arise within the monad itself. Knowledge then is a process of gradual unfolding of that which was already there. Knowledge of eternal truths, like the principles of mathematics, must be derived from innate ideas of which we may be unaware until circumstances and thought bring them within the span of our attention. Locke had argued against innate or *a priori* knowledge on the ground that if we had it we would always be aware of it. In rebuttal, Leibniz argues that there are "minute" perceptions of which the mind is not conscious. In this respect innate ideas may very well exist. In criticism of Locke's empirical view of knowledge, Leibniz stresses that propositions derived from experience lack necessity and universality. Moreover, mathematics, metaphysics, ethics, jurisprudence, and logic furnish propositions that are universal and necessary—propositions which rest on principles furnished by the mind itself. "The senses can arouse, justify, and verify such truths but not demonstrate their eternal and inevitable certitude" (*New Essays on Human Understanding*, Bk. I, ch. I, sec. 5).

Leibniz distinguishes between eternal truths or truths of reason and contingent truths or truths of fact. The criterion of truth for an eternal truth is the law of contradiction, whereas the law of sufficient reason is the criterion of truth for a contingent truth. An eternal truth is a necessary truth in the sense that to deny it is to be involved in a contradiction. All the parts and properties of a circle are logically implied in its definition, and no circle could ever be drawn in contradiction to them.

Except for the existence of God, eternal truths cannot establish anything with respect to the existence of things. They are analytic propositions which furnish us only with hypothetical judgments, such as, if a triangle exists, it will have three sides. If it had four sides, it would contradict the definition of a triangle and be impossible. But whether triangles actually exist at a given time is something one cannot infer from an eternal truth.

Contingent truths, Leibniz admits, are known only through experience. Unlike necessary truths, their opposites can be regarded as possible without contradiction. If one asserts "John Jones exists," another may assert "John Jones does not exist" without being involved in a logical contradiction. If there is a sufficient reason for the existence of John Jones, then it will be false to assert that he does not exist. In Leibniz's view there is always a sufficient reason for every act and experience in the life of every monad. The problem of knowledge is to discover the sufficient reason for the existence of everything. He views this as an investigation in both logic and reality for which reason is competent.

It is difficult to assess the significance of the work of Leibniz. It is especially so if one adopts the hypothesis of Bertrand Russell that there are two philosophies in Leibniz—one written for expediency and one out of private inner conviction. The difficulty is made acute by the fact that so much of importance appears in Leibniz's letters in a form that did not lend itself to full or steady development. But the rediscovery of his Hanover manuscripts leaves no doubt that he was the greatest logician between Aristotle and the nineteenth century. We have noted that, independently of Newton, he was the inventor of the infinitesimal calculus. He was a supreme example of a rationalist philosopher who used logic as a key to metaphysics. He was especially clear and precise in drawing inferences from the nature of language to the nature of the real world. Although subsequently empiricism was to put this type of philosophy into eclipse, Leibniz's rationalism was influential in Germany despite the emasculated version of it made popular by his disciple Christian Wolff.

Although philosophers have not been willing to adopt his monadology, they have found his emphasis on force suggestive. His teaching that space and time are relative anticipated Einstein. Whitehead's theory of "actual entities" and Russell's theory of "perspectives" remind one of Leibniz. Although Leibniz had little understanding of biological evolution, his emphasis on continuity had some impact on later students in biology. His emphases on synthesis and teleology influenced various thinkers even though others ignored them. The familiar confidence of the Enlightenment in increasing progress and human perfectability also owes something to Leibniz.

Gottfried W. Leibniz: Suggested Additional Readings

Abernethy, George L. and Thomas A. Langford, eds., *History of Philosophy: Selected Readings*. Belmont, Calif.: Dickenson, 1965, pp. 409–429.*

Carr, Herbert W., *Leibniz*. New York: Dover, 1960.

Copleston, Frederick C., *A History of Philosophy*, vol. IV. New York: Doubleday, Image, 1962.

Joseph, H. W. B., *Lectures on the Philosophy of Leibniz*. Oxford: Clarendon Press, 1949.*

Kaufmann, Walter, *Philosophic Classics*. Englewood Cliffs, N.J.: Prentice-Hall, 1961, II, 239–274.*

Leibniz, *Philosophical Papers and Letters*. Edited by L. E. Loemker. 2 vols. Chicago: University of Chicago Press, 1966.*

Leibniz, *Philosophical Writings*. Edited and translated by Mary Morris. London: J. M. Dent and Sons, 1951.*

Leibniz, *Discourse on Metaphysics*. Translated by George Montgomery. La Salle, Ill.: Open Court, 1924.

Leibniz, *Monadology and Other Philosophical Essays*. Translated by Paul and Anne Schrecher. Indianapolis: Bobbs-Merrill, Liberal Arts Press, 1965.

Martin, Gottfried, *Leibniz: Logic and Metaphysics*. Translated by K. J. Northcott and P. G. Lucas. New York: Barnes and Noble, 1964.

Merz, John T., *Leibniz*. New York: Hacker, 1948.*

Russell, Bertrand, *A Critical Exposition of the Philosophy of Leibniz*. London: Allen and Unwin, 1951.*

Saw, Ruth L., *Leibniz*. Baltimore: Penguin, 1954.

Yost, Robert M., *Leibniz and Philosophical Analysis*. Berkeley: University of California Press, 1954.*

Chapter Sixteen

Locke

John Locke was born on August 29, 1632, the same year as Spinoza and during the reign of Charles I, at Wrington in Somerset (near Bristol). His father was a country lawyer of modest means who served as a clerk to local magistrates. His mother, who was nearly a decade older than his father, came from a family of tanners. Despite her death in his childhood, Locke late in life still had some recollection of her as "a very pious woman and affectionate mother." He was raised by his father with great care and strictness, and was gradually admitted to full comradeship. Locke always thought of his father with such deep respect and admiration that he advised his friends to raise their sons in a similar fashion. As a boy Locke knew the austere discipline of a Puritan home and the virtues it was intended to inculcate: piety, sobriety, industry, self-reliance, integrity, conscientiousness, and the love of liberty. Although his later experiences broadened his outlook and made him more sophisticated, in many respects he never really left home.

The English Civil War broke out about the time Locke was ten years of age. His father was commissioned a captain in the Parliamentary cavalry by Alexander Popham, a wealthy magistrate with the rank of Colonel. Some years later when Westminster School, the best boarding school in the country, came under Parliamentary control, the Colonel arranged for the admission of the Captain's son. Here Locke came under the influence of a royalist headmaster (Richard Busby), who gave him such a vigorous training in the classics that many years later (1693) he complained in his *Thoughts on Education* about the school's preoccupation with languages and about its severe discipline. In 1652 Locke obtained a scholarship at Christ Church, Oxford, where after four years he obtained his B.A. degree, and two years later received the M.A. This is the period during which John Owen, an Independent divine, served as Dean of Christ Church and Vice-Chancellor of the University and worked diligently to restore the prestige of Oxford. But the shift from Royalist to Puritan control of the University seemed to have had no appreciable effect on the curriculum,

which remained traditional with heavy emphasis on medieval scholasticism. Although he later complained about the sterility of the
scholastic approach in which he had been trained at Oxford, he never
realized the extent to which some of his premises and terms were
derived from Scholasticism. His own interest in philosophy seems to
have been directly stimulated by his private reading of Descartes, whose
clarity greatly impressed him. There is some evidence to suggest that
during his studies at Oxford, Locke, despite his Puritan upbringing
and the Puritan direction of Oxford, actually went through a period
of defending rightwing monarchial views and attacking religious
toleration.

In 1659 he was elected to a Senior Studentship at Christ Church,
a position ordinarily tenable for life. He subsequently became a
lecturer in Greek, reader in rhetoric, and censor of moral philosophy.
His father died in 1661 and left him his small estate, which gave him a
greater degree of independence. He decided upon preparation for
medicine but had some difficulty before finally acquiring his degree.
He practiced only in an amateur and occasional way, never becoming a
full-fledged professional physician. In November 1665 he accompanied
Sir Walter Vane as his secretary on a diplomatic mission to the Elector
of Brandenburg. Upon his return he declined a secretaryship under the
new ambassador to Spain and went back to his medical studies. In the
summer of 1666 Locke began his lifelong friendship with Anthony
Ashley Cooper, then Lord Ashley, later to become the first Earl of
Shaftesbury (Dryden's Achitophel) and the greatest political figure
under Charles II. Locke became Shaftesbury's medical adviser and,
according to Shaftesbury himself, saved his life when it was threatened
by a suppurating cyst of the liver. After this he became a confidante and
political secretary to Shaftesbury, helping him draft a constitution for
the new colony of Carolina, and acting as tutor to Shaftesbury's son.
In his fourth year in Shaftesbury's home Locke wrote the first drafts
of his great work, *Essay Concerning Human Understanding*. In 1672
Shaftesbury was made Lord Chancellor, and Locke was appointed
Secretary to the Board of Trade, a position he held for three years. In
1675 Locke's asthma worsened, and he deemed it advisable to seek
relief in a period of residence abroad, which stretched into a period
of four years during which he met many French physicians and intellectuals and did sustained work on the *Essay* and other philosophical
manuscripts. He returned finally to England and reentered the service
of his patron, although the nature and extent of his activities in this
period are not fully known. In July 1681 Shaftesbury was arrested on
a charge of high treason, but was acquitted in a jury trial. In the

1

following year Shaftesbury thought it prudent to go into hiding because of his activities in behalf of the Duke of Monmouth. He soon fled to Holland where he died at Amsterdam in January 1683. Feeling somewhat anxious about his personal position at Oxford, Locke sought the tolerance and safety of Holland in the fall of 1683. Because of his long association with Shaftesbury the King demanded (1684) Locke's expulsion from his Studentship at Christ Church and made an unsuccessful effort to extradite him from Holland, where for a time he lived under the alias of Dr. van der Linden. Locke's friends secured for him an offer of royal pardon, which he declined on the grounds that he had committed no crime and therefore a pardon was superfluous.

Locke used his five-year stay in Holland to do intensive work on his famous *Essay Concerning Human Understanding* and to write the Latin version of his first *Letter on Toleration*. Undoubtedly he also worked on other manuscripts which were published later.

The Revolution of 1688 made it possible for Locke to return to England with the fleet that brought Queen Mary II in 1689. He resisted efforts to tempt him into diplomatic service but accepted a post as Commissioner of Appeals which carried a small stipend and involved only nominal duties. This enabled him to give most of his time to philosophical studies. In 1689 he published anonymously the Latin version of *A Letter Concerning Toleration*, which he restated and clarified in a second letter in 1690 and in a third in 1693. In 1690 he published *Two Treatises on Civil Government* and *Essay Concerning Human Understanding*. He also published short works on education and economics, in addition to a somewhat unorthodox defense of the reasonableness of Christianity.

In 1691 he took up residence, for the last thirteen years of his life, at the country home of Sir Francis Masham, whose wife, the daughter of the Cambridge Platonist Ralph Cudworth, made him feel a part of the family while he gardened, studied, wrote, and kept up with his circle of learned friends. Even in his retirement he retained his political interests and in 1696 accepted an appointment as Commissioner of Trade and Plantations, but resigned it in 1700 because of his declining health. In 1704, at the age of seventy-two, he died while listening to Lady Masham read from the Psalms. Thus ended a long life devoted to reasonableness, moderation, patience, caution, and freedom.

Theory of Knowledge

Locke's philosophical development was slow and steady as he dealt with successive difficulties and changes in his own interests. His chief work, *Essay Concerning Human Understanding*, reveals this, for it was begun in 1671 and not published until 1690. It was subsequently revised for later editions and was undergoing still another revision when Locke died in 1704.

Locke's announced purpose in writing his *Essay* is "to inquire into the original, certainty, and extent of human knowledge, together with the grounds and degrees of belief, opinion, and assent." To prepare the way for the exposition of his own theory of knowledge, Locke in the first book of the *Essay Concerning Human Understanding* attacks the doctrine of innate ideas held by some Cartesians and the Cambridge Platonists. Such innate and universal ideas were held to include the laws of identity and contradiction in logic, the principle of justice, the idea of God, and conscience. Locke argues that children, idiots, and savages live without formulating or being aware of such innate ideas. He refuses to allow the defender of innate ideas to retreat to the position that man possesses an inborn disposition to acquire them as soon as he attains experience and rational competence, for this would make automatically every idea an "innate idea." Only the lazy and the dogmatists, he claims, will take refuge in innate ideas.

Having disposed of innate ideas, Locke moves on in the second book of the *Essay* to give an essentially psychological explanation of the way in which men acquire ideas through experience. For him, the infant's mind at birth is a wax tablet, an empty cabinet, or "white paper, devoid of all characters." The contents of the mind, then, can come only from experience. Experience is to be understood not only as involving the reception of impressions through various senses but also "the operations of our mind within us, as it is employed about the ideas it has got." Thus our ideas come from sensation and reflection.

Locke believes *simple ideas*, which he does not try to define or systematize, are the atoms or elements out of which our knowledge is composed. Simple ideas of sensation, received from only one sense, are colors, sounds, tastes, odors, and touch. He cites as examples of simple ideas from more than one sense space, figure, motion, and rest. Also, we have simple ideas of reflection—our ideas of perceiving, doubting, thinking, believing, knowing, and willing when we become aware of and observe these mental processes. There are, in addition, simple ideas which we receive from both sensation and reflection, such as existence, unity, succession, pleasure, and pain. It is Locke's view that the human mind cannot create or destroy a single simple idea. The mind is passive in so far as it receives such ideas from external stimulation in sensory experience and from observation of our mental processes in cases of reflection. Thus the mind, in Locke's empiricism, requires stimulation from the outside and is limited to the analysis and interpretation of what the external world provides.

Locke states that our simple ideas of sensation resemble or represent the qualities of objects existing in the external world, specifically in the primary qualities of solidity, extension, figure, number, motion, and rest. Involved in this is Locke's commitment to a metaphysical view of the structure and operation of nature, which involves the relation of his mind to his own body and other bodies. He assumes the existence of "external objects" or physical bodies in which primary qualities inhere whether we perceive them or not. These bodies possess the power to produce certain motions or impressions in our bodies which induce in our minds the simple ideas which truly resemble them. These physical bodies, because of certain insensible qualities, have the peculiar power to produce in us ideas of secondary qualities—colors, sounds, tastes, and temperatures—which are "no more the likeness of something existing without us, than the names that stand for them are the likeness of our ideas." Locke does not argue or offer any extended exposition of his epistemological distinction between primary and secondary qualities. Apparently he is indebted for it to Galileo, Newton, and Boyle, by whose scientific work he is greatly impressed. But it was this side of Locke's thinking which Bishop Berkeley in a later development of empiricism was to find so odious and mistaken.

Complex ideas, Locke writes, are built from simple ideas. The mind does this by collecting, combining, inferring, contrasting, and abstracting simple ideas. Here he is suggestive rather than precise or systematic. Among the complex ideas he discusses are extension, duration, infinity, God, substance, causality, liberty, necessity, matter, and spirit. Locke loosely classifies complex ideas into modes, ideas of substance, and ideas of relation.

Modes are combinations of simple ideas, either (a) variations of the simple idea (simple modes), as when a dozen is constituted by the repetition of the number one, or (b) combinations of various kinds of simple ideas (mixed modes), as when such complex ideas as gratitude, beauty, or obligation are developed. Modes are not, like substances, independently existing objects.

Ideas of substance involve Locke in some difficulties. He points out that in our experience we find certain groups of ideas going together and we tend to think of them as held together by some support or substratum. But material and spiritual substances can be distinguished only by the different kinds of ideas they produce in us. What the substratum is we can never know. When we try to generalize our ideas of particular substances in the effort to arrive at a general notion of substance, we find ourselves in the predicament of the Indian, cited by Locke, who believed that the world rests on an elephant, and the elephant on a tortoise, and the broadbacked tortoise on "something, he knew not what." It is just a way of avoiding an infinite regress. It is an *ad hoc* idea which we are compelled to use even though we cannot define it satisfactorily. Locke's critics were not to take too kindly to this pragmatic approach.

Ideas of relation arise for Locke because man is free to look behind an idea and compare it with others. Language makes it possible to compare one individual with another in a great variety of ways. Locke singles out for brief discussion the relations of cause and effect, identity and diversity, space and time, and human acts to standards of moral judgment. When we perceive one event regularly followed by another, we call the first cause and the latter effect. We find a certain identity between a child and the old man he has become, between our memories of what we did yesterday and a year ago. Such common-sense treatments of causality and identity were later subjected to sharp criticism by Hume. But in the history of psychology Locke's discussion of the association of ideas is classic.

Locke offers in the third book of his *Essay* an analysis of the use and abuse of words together with an empirical and nominalistic interpretation of language. For him universals are not independent or transcendental entities from whose definitions further knowledge may be deduced. The genera and species of logic and the classes and subclasses of classification systems have been devised for human convenience and utility through the process of abstraction. They do not necessarily report what is the case in nature. Following the British empirical tradition stemming from William of Ockham, Locke denies the immutability of species in logic. For him, everything in the sublunary world is subject to change. It is only our words that appear to be fixed and immutable.

Since words are imperfect signs of the ideas they represent, especially in the case of mixed modes and ideas of substance, Locke would have us reduce and refer them to the simple particulars from which they originate in order to get as close as possible to immediate experience. If we take sufficient pains to define clearly and use definitions with consistency, we can employ even mixed modes with profit. When we depart from common usage, we have a responsibility to point this out for all to see.

In the fourth and last book of the *Essay*, Locke sums up his views on the nature and extent of human knowledge. "Knowledge," Locke declares, "then seems to me to be nothing but the perception of connexion and agreement, or disagreement and repugnancy, of any of our ideas." This agreement or disagreement may be of four kinds: (1) identity or diversity, as red is not white; (2) the immediate discernment of relations between ideas, as "two triangles upon equal bases between two parallels are equal"; (3) the coexistence or noncoexistence of ideas in the same object, especially in substances (In the case of gold we find "that fixedness, or a power to remain in the fire unconsumed, is an idea that always accompanies and is joined with that particular sort of yellowness, weight, fusibility, malleableness, and solubility in *acqua regia*, which made our complex idea, signified by the word gold."); (4) the disclosure of real existence or what in the external world corresponds to an idea, as in the assertion "God is." Within these four kinds of agreement or disagreement Locke avers we find all the knowledge we can acquire.

Locke further distinguishes several varieties or degrees of knowledge: intuitive, demonstrative, and sensitive. Intuition is the highest degree of knowledge; it is so certain that the possessor of it has no need of proof. By this we know that white is not black and a circle is not a triangle. But intuition does not permit us to leap beyond the agreement or disagreement of ideas in the mind to a knowledge of things outside the mind. The only piece of knowledge of real existence which Locke admits, in the fashion of Descartes, is the knowledge each man has of his own existence. Demonstrative knowledge proceeds mediately and reaches conclusions from inferences and proofs in which each step is intuitive. It is of course limited by our inability to find logical connections between ideas. Again we are dealing with the agreement or disagreement of ideas and not with the agreement or disagreement of ideas with the external world.

The third degree or variety of knowledge, sensitive knowledge, derives from simple ideas of sensation. Often, Locke asserts, it might be better called faith or opinion than knowledge, for it is sensation of something which does not provide us any way in which to map the relation between primary and secondary qualities or, indeed, any way of knowing the essences of substances whose unknown substrata are the causes of both primary and secondary qualities. Thus, sensitive knowledge enables men to handle things in terms of their nominal essences rather than their real essences. Nominal essences are useful human constructs of associated ideas whose future appearances we can predict with some degree of probability. He offers principles for the selection of hypotheses and methods of estimating probabilities, but in general he does not share Bacon's optimism about the prospects of experimental science.

After studying Locke's theory of knowledge Bishop Berkeley objected that if we can never contemplate the reality which our ideas represent to us, is there any empirical ground for the conviction the external world exists? If knowledge is only of the agreement or disagreement of ideas, how can we ever determine which ideas, if any, agree with the external world? Do Locke's ideas become an "iron curtain" between the observer and the external world? The objections to Locke's representative realism, as well as the efforts to reformulate his theory, have continued to be lively issues of epistemological debate in our own century.

Political Philosophy

The political philosophy of John Locke first gives the impression of being incidental or causal. It appears in *Two Treatises on Civil Government*, published in 1690 with the expressed purpose "to establish the throne of our great restorer, our present King William; to make good his title in the consent of the people; which being the only one of lawful governments, he has more fully than any other prince in Christendom; and to justify to the world the people of England, whose love of their just and natural rights, with their resolution to preserve them, saved the nation when it was on the brink of slavery and ruin." Actually it is much more than a tract for the times and reaches behind the English Civil Wars to make contact with the traditional medieval view of Richard Hooker's *Laws of Ecclesiastical Polity* that government is a delegated power responsible to the entire community. To this he relates the vigorous and developing individualism of the seventeenth century. His justification of property and his emphasis on a thriving economic life are based on the viewpoint first sketched by Fortescue in the fifteenth century. Thus he expresses the sober and cautious common sense of an age weary of the conflicting extremists and doctrinaires of the English Civil Wars and anxious to avail itself of the prosperity looming so large on the horizon. The British colonial expansion, the appearance of a modern banking system, the ascent of a Protestant to the Dutch throne, the triumph of the commercial land-owning class, and the slow stabilization of party politics and government all necessitated some sort of political theory which would protect private property holders against royal interference and provide a foundation for political order other than the rule of monarchy by Divine Right. All this Locke did in a persuasive statement which had wide acceptance and furnished the matrix out of which developed the political philosophy of eighteenth-century England, Europe, and America.

The ostensible occasion for Locke's *Two Treatises on Civil Government* is his refutation of the monarchical theories of Sir Robert Filmer, who expressed the official Tory point of view in his *Patriarcha*. Although it was politically advantageous for Locke to attack Filmer's arguments that the patriarchs in Genesis were monarchs and that kings are the heirs of Adam, with absolute power akin to that of parents over children, there is nothing original or of permanent historical significance in the consideration that Locke advances to refute Filmer in the first of the two Treatises. In the second and more significant *Treatise* Locke discusses primarily two basic problems: the rights of property, and the origin, extent, and limits of civil government.

In a position reminiscent of Hobbes, Locke asserts that the creation of the civil society or state is the result of a social contract. Hobbes was explicit and consistent in maintaining that the state of nature was "a war of each against all," since he began the *Leviathan* with a pessimistic theory of human nature. Locke is a different sort of person from Hobbes—more inclined to trust in peace, reason, and benevolence than force—so he begins with a different theory of human nature. Consequently he denies that the state of nature is a state of license. If the state of nature is peaceful, it is because it is governed by a law which can be known by reason. Thus men know that one ought not harm the life, health, liberty, or possessions of another.

All men in the state of nature are endowed with certain rights, among which the most important are rights to life, liberty, and property. These rights are inalienable and all men possess them equally. In the state of nature men have "perfect freedom to order their actions and dispose of their possessions and persons as they think fit, within the bounds of the law of nature, without asking leave, or depending upon the will of any other man" (*Treatise of Civil Government*, sec. 4).

How does one get his natural rights respected? The law of nature is a moral law showing how men ought to behave, as contrasted with a scientific law describing how men actually behave. Thus everyone becomes the executor of the law of nature. There are of course important philosophical and social implications in this doctrine. There is a social bond which is chronologically and logically prior to the creation of the state; thus social obligation precedes political obligation. It should be noted that Locke hardly ever uses the term "state"—instead he prefers "commonwealth." Occasionally he contrasts "republic" with "monarchy." When he mentions "society," with or without adjectives like "political" or "civil," he means what today we mean by "state." He does not have a term which corresponds to our meaning of "society." To return to our question, Locke is realistic about the enforcement of natural rights in conceding that many natural rights would not be enforced. Since he has a more optimistic view of human nature than either Hobbes or Machiavelli, Locke explains that he takes men out of nature to form a "state" because the "state" is an instrument through which the good of man can be channeled.

The contract or compact is the simple device by which you get men out of a state of nature into a community with a government. In it men surrender some of their rights to a public body expressly established to fulfill specified functions. Unlike Hobbes' contract, Locke's provides for the surrender of only some, not all, rights and for the investing of officials with only the specific powers necessary for the performance of their functions. The notion that the people reserve certain rights for themselves distinguishes sharply Locke's contract from those of Hobbes and Rousseau.

What is the ethical justification of the power wielded by government? The answer which Locke gives is important historically as a factor in eighteenth-century democratic ideas. It is given as a theory of consent which justifies the power residing in government and its employment. No government can claim a moral obligation to obedience on the part of its citizens if it has been set up by conquest or naked force. Even a legitimately established government may be rightfully overthrown if it invades the personal rights which the citizens have reserved for themselves. He underlines this limited right to revolution not simply because he was justifying the "Glorious Revolution" of 1688–1689, but because such a prudent warning would tend to restrain rulers within their constitutional limits.

The theory of government by the consent of the governed raises all sorts of thorny problems with which Locke does not deal. Of course when one is talking about the unanimity of decision no problem arises. Locke tends to stress unanimity when discussing the original social contract. To get out of the state of nature you have to imagine the original contract as being adopted unanimously. Subsequently Locke drags in the doctrine of tacit consent. If at legal age one asserts his rights, Locke insists that he has tacitly consented to the provisions of the original contract. If he refuses to accept or ratify it, he is free to emigrate. Some at that time were emigrating to the colonies in America. Locke is still left with the difficult task of explaining satisfactorily the problem of majority–minority relations in his theory of consent. When members of a minority vote against a majority policy or candidate, in what sense can they be said to be consenting to the victory of the majority? What justifies the majority? For Locke, it is the greater force of the community which must move in one direction. This is virtually a Newtonian conception. It also represents a failure to reconcile a Hobbesian power theory with moral theory. The question remains whether a theory of the greater force might not be used to justify an oligarchical minority. These problems of course still arise in contemporary democratic theory and practice.

A commonwealth can exist only when three conditions are met. There must be a known and determined body of statute laws. There must be a known and impartial judge before disputes can be decided in the light of the statute laws. There must also be a known executive with sufficient power to enforce the laws and judicial decisions. Locke divides, for analysis, the powers of government into legislative, executive, and federative (the control of foreign relations). But this is not Montesquieu's separation of powers with a theory of checks and balances. Locke insists on the supremacy of legislative power—parliamentary supremacy. Locke is summarizing for the Whigs in 1690 the principles on which they acted in the "Glorious Revolution," which capped fifty years of turbulent British political history. Parliamentary supremacy was acknowledged in both politics and law. In the view of law there are no limits to what Parliament can do, although there are practical and moral limits. Although legislative power is supreme in government for Locke, it is still limited by the original contract in its relations to citizens, who possess reserved rights.

Locke believes that every man has the right to self-preservation and freedom. But the natural right which most concerns Locke is the right of property. Since man has the right and duty of self-preservation, he has a right to whatever is required to achieve this end. Locke asserts: "God gave the world to men in common but since he gave it for their benefit and the greatest conveniences of life they were capable to draw from it, it cannot be supposed he meant it should always remain common and uncultivated" (*Second Treatise of Government*, Ch. V, sec. 33).

What constitutes or justifies private ownership of property? For Locke, a man has an absolute claim to his own person. In the state of nature his labor is his own and whatever he removes from its original condition by mixing his labor with it. All of Locke's illustrations reflect an agrarian society in which there is sufficient land to go around. Locke's labor theory of value has roots that go back to Aquinas and fruit that comes to full bloom in the writings of Ricardo and Karl Marx. Locke would be horrified and dismayed by the uses which socialistic writers made of his theory, for he himself expresses the interests of his patrons, the Whig landowners. Locke emphasizes the differences between perishable foods and imperishable metals (which are the source of money and economic inequality). Much of what he says about economics is unsophisticated and unsystematic, but there is no question that he is a pioneer in the development of the science of political economy with his treatise on the consequences of the lowering of interest and raising the value of money. Locke's attitude toward the lower classes is Puritan, especially his belief that poverty is evidence not of misfortune but of a moral deficiency.

Ethical Doctrines

In all his writings Locke makes the basic assumption that the ordinary man has sufficient knowledge to live a good and righteous life if he chooses to do so. But this knowledge, of course, is not exact knowledge. Can one establish a necessary, eternally true system of morals? Locke's *Essay* affirms that such a science or system of morals is possible, although Locke never provides any such system for his readers. He is concerned with other matters and maintains that the Christian Scriptures reveal a system of ethics completely adequate for our practical purposes. However, he may have been inhibited in constructing an ethical system by the fact that his mind was attracted by both hedonism and rationalism. He has difficulty deciding whether our moral judgments rest on our feelings of pleasure and pain or whether reason by itself can ultimately determine what is really good. Probably Locke is more indebted for his hedonism to the Christian hedonism of the French Gassendists seeking to revive Democritus and Epicurus than to Hobbes' version of hedonism. Locke states: "That we call *good* which is apt to cause or increase pleasure, or diminish pain in us; or else procure or preserve us the possession of any other good, or absence of any evil" (*Essay Concerning Human Understanding*, Bk. II, Ch. XX, sec. 2). Such a view then allows him to call "good acts" not only those pleasant in themselves but those also which have consequences which finally turned out to be pleasant. "Pleasure" may be used synonymously with "satisfaction," "delight," or "happiness." Pleasures may be either of the mind or the body or both. In an early paper dealing with rules for his own conduct, Locke mentions five lasting pleasures— health, good reputation, knowledge, "doing good," and eternal bliss. He writes chiefly of an individual's pleasure, although he does recognize the community's pleasure or pain. But an act is always good just as far as it produces happiness or pleasure, whether individual or social. Since evaluations are always individualistic in their formulation and since one often lacks a full knowledge of all the consequences of an act, all our moral judgments are merely probable. Hence the elements of necessity and universality required for a science are lacking.

It should be noted that Locke distinguishes between moral and natural good. Eating when we are hungry is naturally but not morally good. Putting a finger in the fire is naturally (painfully) evil without being morally evil. In order to obtain obedience to His laws God has joined pleasure to them, so that whenever one obeys them he enjoys these pleasures. The pleasure in the case of moral goodness is not the natural consequence of the act but is divinely ordained. "*Moral good and evil*, then, is only the conformity or disagreement of our voluntary actions to some law, whereby good or evil is drawn on us, from the will and power of the law-maker" (*Essay Concerning Human Understanding*, Bk. II, Ch. XXVIII, sec. 5). To discover God's immutable laws is to have knowledge of what will further man's happiness for all time. Thus we do have an objective good or standard independent of subjective human evaluations. Yet if God's choice is arbitrary and His will free, we are not entirely rid of a contingent and irrational element in morality.

On the other hand, if God acts rationally instead of arbitrarily in choosing laws which reason perceives to be intrinsically good, then Locke's version of hedonism may make contact with his basic rationalism. God has, according to Locke, joined inseparably individual virtue and public happiness, and so it is in everyone's interest to act accordingly. God has so arranged the universe that, motivated by the desire for pleasure, man will develop empirically a code of morals. God has also given man reason to enter into God's thoughts and to recognize the truths of morality by rational demonstration—even though those who use their reason this way are few. God has, in addition, revealed in the Scriptures the principles of morality. Thus experience, reason, and revelation all join to establish morality on strong foundations. Locke never pursued these suggestions far enough to give us an ethical system or to indicate how he would have handled certain puzzling problems arising from the overlapping of his hedonism and rationalism.

In Locke's view man is responsible to God and his fellow men in matters of conduct. His mind has the ability either to entertain any idea and the consequences of any act, or to decline to do so. "So far as anyone can, by the direction or choice of his mind preferring the existence of any action to the nonexistence of that action and vice versa, make it to exist or not to exist, so far he is free" (*Essay Concerning Human Understanding*, Bk. II, Ch. XXI, sec. 21). This is freedom from external compulsion. But are we free to will or to choose? In the first edition of the essay, Locke takes the position that we are not free to will, that we are determined as to what we do will. In the second edition he modifies his position by declaring that we are determined by "the most pressing uneasiness"; we lack something and this determines our will. Although it is ordinarily true that we are determined by the greatest uneasiness, it is still possible for the mind to "suspend the execution and satisfaction of any of its desires" (*Essay Concerning Human Understanding*, Bk. II, Ch. XXI, sec. 48). No matter what the strength of our desire or uneasiness, one may still suspend action and demonstrate that he is free from both external and internal compulsion. This is a possibility of great interest to the moralist.

Religion

Throughout his entire career Locke maintained a lively interest in religion. But in his last years religion became a dominating interest. Earlier in life he had to decide whether to cast his lot with the Anglicans or the Dissenters. He chose to remain in the Church of England because he feared narrow sectarianism and disliked what he regarded as the irresponsible and fanatical utterances of many nonconformists. He did share with dissenters some views on church government and the priesthood of all believers.

Locke disagrees with Hobbes' view that the sovereign should determine the religion of his subjects. His sharp distinction between the duties of the state and those of the church is reminiscent of the medieval figure of the Two Swords. The church is a "voluntary society of men, joining themselves together of their own accord, in order to the public worshipping of God, in such a manner as they judge acceptable to Him, and effectual to the salvation of their souls." Locke is equally opposed to the absolute authority of monarchs and of popes, bishops, and presbyters. Considering this attitude, the economic advantages that toleration brought to Holland, and the need for spiritual health and national strength, it is not particularly surprising to find Locke arguing for toleration in religion.

Locke's arguments are simple. First, a church is a voluntary society of men in which its members have surrendered none of their natural rights, so the church has no power to use force. The state, in turn, has no right to use force in religious matters since the religious and political spheres are distinct. Neither God nor man has entrusted the soul of the citizen to the civil magistrate. If churches and individuals receive the privileges of freedom of worship, they will in turn owe the obligation of making no claims to control the beliefs and practices of those who have not joined their religious communities.

Secondly, human knowledge is so limited and the probabilites of error so great in matters of speculation that it is unlikely that anyone can be certain that all his religious opinions are correct and all those of others false and heretical. When men sincerely differ in a sincere search for the truth, there is no justification for intolerance and persecution on the part of one man as against others. If ever there is a time for intolerance, it will be when all the truth is known—a situation far in the future.

Thirdly, intolerance is not only evil but it is ineffective. A ruler of a state may be able through persecution or threat of persecution to secure a formal or outward conformity, "but that he principally intends by those means to compose a truly Christian church is altogether incredible." "It will be very difficult to persuade men of sense that he who with dry eyes and satisfaction of mind can deliver his brother to the executioner to be burnt alive, does sincerely and heartily concern himself to save that brother from the flames of hell in the world to come" (*A Letter Concerning Toleration*).

Although Locke was a particularly influential advocate of toleration, he did not believe in unlimited toleration. First, he would not allow the spread of "opinions contrary to the human society or to those moral rules which are necessary for the preservation of civil society." The belief in and the practice of human sacrifice would be a case in point. This general limitation is vague and obviously leaves the door open for illiberal abuses. Secondly, he would in some unspecified way restrict the activities of people who believe that "faith is not to be kept with heretics" and that "kings excommunicated forfeit their kingdoms." Although he does not mention them by name, Locke is obviously referring to Roman Catholics whom many feared would not remain loyal to their oaths of allegiance to William and Mary (as excommunicated heretics) and would undertake subversive activities in behalf of the restoration of the Stuarts. Locke's third exclusion is atheists, which follows logically from his belief that all morality rests on God's existence and laws. A denial of God's moral covenants increases the likelihood that one will not meet his obligations and will do harm to his fellows. It should be noted that Locke warns against charging men with atheism simply because their views are not in harmony with those of the established church. Locke would grant toleration to Jews, Mohammedans, and all those who accept the common principles of morality and can be trusted to be loyal subjects of the new government of England. However much we may be tempted to be critical of Locke's exclusions, his views on toleration notably helped to generate public support for a policy of religious toleration more liberal than that existing in any European country during the Enlightenment.

Although brought up as a Puritan, Locke gradually adopted a liberal position in theology as a result of influences stemming from Latitudinarians, Cambridge Platonists, and Remonstrants in Holland. This position he sketches in his book, *The Reasonableness of Christianity*, which grew out of his critical study of the Gospels and in some respects foreshadowed the approach of higher criticism in Germany. Locke believes that the theologians with their hair-splitting creeds, mysteries, and dogmas have confused Christianity for the layman. He insists that Christianity basically is a simple, natural, and reasonable creed. Christ offered immortality to mankind contingent upon three conditions being met by the believer: belief in Him as Messiah, repentance, and the forgiveness of others. Any ordinary man can understand these three conditions. They are all that he needs for salvation. In time a further study of the Bible will lead the believer to accept other related truths that are contained in it. But most people are lazy and dominated by superstitions. "Lustrations and processions are much easier than a clean conscience and a steady course of virtue, and an expiatory sacrifice that atoned for the want of it, is much more convenient than a strict and holy life."

In the *Essay Concerning Human Understanding* Locke asserts that the existence of God and the principles of morality can be demonstrated by human reason. He does not deny divine revelation. Instead he insists that revelations from God in the Scriptures do give us knowledge. They may be beyond reason but they are never "contrary to reason." They are attested by miracles. He accepts the doctrines of the immortality of the soul and the resurrection of the body on this ground. He continues in his fashion the medieval distinction between what reason itself can discover about God and what can be known about God by means of revelation. But, for Locke, revelation must always be tested by reason, though this does not mean, as it did for later deists, that we can believe only what our reason gives us. There are of course serious problems in determining what is or is not in accord with reason. Locke does not really explore these.

To many contemporary readers Locke will now appear as a rather cautious, though liberal, defender of Christianity, although his positions were regarded as very advanced in his day. Sometimes Locke has mistakenly been viewed as the founder of deism. The distinction belongs to Lord Herbert of Cherbury (1581–1648), whom Locke attacked for setting forth his positive positions as innate ideas. It is true that

Locke shared a number of doctrines with deists, that he directly influenced Toland and Collins, and that he indirectly prepared a more
favorable intellectual climate for the reception of deistic ideas. But
Locke is not a deist. He argues that since we are finite creatures, reason
is not sufficient to provide us with all we need for living the religious
life. Supernatural revelation thus supplements reason. Locke believes
in the virgin birth and the Resurrection. He accepts the miracles reported in the Scriptures. Thus he is to be distinguished from the deists,
who believed that reason without revelation is sufficient.

Philosophy of Education

Locke's *Some Thoughts Concerning Education* went through several
editions during his lifetime and has become an educational classic.
While in exile in Holland he wrote a number of long letters to Edward
Clarke giving him advice on how best to educate his son. Later, in
1693, he revised these letters and published them as a book. In assessing
the book one should remember that Locke is giving advice on how best
to educate the son of a squire who is to become a squire himself and
who shows no particular promise as a scholar or as one destined for
greatness in any field. Locke starts with a belief in the individual
method in education and in the aim of producing a sound mind in a
sound body. He provides in furtherance of this aim detailed advice on
diet, clothing, and exercise for children which was well received in his
time and some of which would be acceptable even today.

In certain passages he writes with an obvious interest in what we
today would call psychological theories. He writes that the child is not
born with fully developed ideas, and so his parents and teachers can
mould his habits and ideas. Again he insists that careful observation
be made of a child's interests and capacities. It is the responsibility of
the educator to see that these develop in a natural manner, without
artificial discipline and slavish imitation, so that the integrity and
independence of the child may be respected. He takes a dim view of
harsh discipline and corporal punishment. The good teacher does much
of his teaching by suggestion and example.

Character, Locke emphasizes, is more important than learning or
information. Virtue, wisdom, breeding, and learning are the main
objectives in education and are the marks of a sound mind. Virtue is
of prime importance. As one might expect in view of Locke's Puritan
upbringing, it is important to instill in a child love and reverence for
God, and to teach him to pray. Truth-telling should be emphasized.
Wisdom and sagacity in the conduct of affairs come as the fruition of

mature experience, but even a child can be taught to face facts. The basic principle in good breeding is "not to think meanly of ourselves, and not to think meanly of others." Learning should be made interesting to the growing child by mixing it with games and plays as well as in the making of toys. The enjoyment of reading and the learning of a foreign language by the conversational method should begin early in the life of a child.

Locke does not think highly of sending children away to boarding schools or entrusting them to maids. In general, a child is much better off in the care of his parents moving in the company of virtuous, well-mannered, and wise men and women. It is foolish "to hazard one's son's innocence and virtue for a little Greek and Latin." If a maid has more virtue than her mistress, then of course the child should be left to the maid. So Locke definitely prefers that a gentleman's son should be educated at home under parental supervision with a tutor from the outside to carry an important share of the pedagogical task—as he himself had done in the Shaftesbury home.

It is instructive to note the subjects which Locke would teach; his views are very advanced for his day. For example, he feels that English should be studied as thoroughly as Latin. Although instruction in a modern foreign language, like French, might be useful, he reacts negatively to the custom of drilling students in ancient languages— Greek, Hebrew, and Arabic—and in rhetoric and logic. For these he would substitute geography, history, and anatomy, subjects which make small demand on one's reasoning power, but which require some memorization. Simultaneously a start should be made with more abstract subjects like arithmetic, geometry, and astronomy. Somewhat later the youth should acquire a little knowledge of civil law and ethics. To cap his education, the youth should be introduced to various hypotheses and theories in natural philosophy, both physical and metaphysical. He considers the sciences as more adequate, meaningful, and promising than the ancient Platonic and Aristotelian systems of philosophy. He sharply attacks the study of logic on the grounds that truth cannot be discovered through *a priori* rules, but requires mature understanding and the ability to evaluate different problems.

Locke recommends some relaxation in arts and crafts for the serious student, provided he does not take them too seriously. Although the reading and writing of poetry gives pleasure, it should not be encouraged in a young man, for no prudent father can wish to see his son become a poet. "For it is very seldom that any one discovers mines of gold or silver in Parnassus. 'Tis a pleasant air, but a barren soil." Toward music he is more friendly although it does throw a young man into "such odd company." "Men of parts and business" do not commend it. Some recreation is necessary but sports appear to be a waste of time. A young man might more prudently invest his spare time and serve his need for exercise by learning a trade like gardening or carpentry. His views on foreign travel merit some consideration. Travel after the age of sixteen to learn a foreign language is much too late. Foreign travel before twenty-one to meet distinguished men and to study the social or political conditions of foreign countries is much too early.

Locke offers us a class ideal of education with an interesting blend of Puritan, utilitarian, individualistic, and functional ideas. His book, *Some Thoughts Concerning Education*, still lives not only because he wrote in a pleasant and refreshing manner, but because elements of his "blend" are still tantalizing in regard to their relevance for sectors of contemporary liberal education. It is also interesting to note the extent to which his once heretical views became a part of traditional British educational theory and practice.

John Locke: Suggested Additional Reading

Aaron, Richard I., *John Locke*. New York: Oxford University Press, 1955.

Abernethy, George L. and Thomas A. Langford, eds., *History of Philosophy: Selected Readings*. Belmont, Calif.: Dickenson, 1965, pp. 386–408.*

Armstrong, D. B. and C. B. Martin, editors, *Locke and Berkeley: A Collection of Critical Essays*. Garden City: Doubleday, Anchor, 1968.

Cranston, Maurice, *John Locke, A Biography*. London: Macmillan, 1957.*

Collins, James D., *British Empiricists: Locke, Berkeley, Hume*. Milwaukee: Bruce, 1967.

Gibson, James, *Locke's Theory of Knowledge and Its Historical Relations*. Cambridge: Cambridge University Press, 1931.*

Gough, John W., *John Locke's Political Philosophy*. Oxford: Clarendon Press, 1950.*

Kaufmann, Walter, *Philosophic Classics*. Englewood Cliffs, N.J.: Prentice-Hall, 1961, II, 187–228.*

Lamprecht, Sterling P., *The Moral and Political Philosophy of John Locke*. New York: Russell and Russell, 1962.*

Locke, *An Essay Concerning Human Understanding*. Edited by Alexander C. Fraser. New York: Dover, 1959.

Locke, *Treatise on Civil Government* and *A Letter Concerning Toleration*. Edited by Charles L. Sherman. New York: Appleton-Century-Crofts, paper, 1937.

Locke, *John Locke on Politics, Religion and Education*. Edited by Maurice Cranston. New York: Macmillan, Collier Paperback, 1965.

Locke, *Essay Concerning Human Understanding*. Edited by A. D. Woozley. New York: World Publishing Company, Meridian, 1964.

Morris, Charles R., *Locke, Berkeley, Hume*. Oxford: Clarendon Press, 1937.*

O'Conner, Daniel J., *John Locke*. Baltimore: Penguin, 1952.

Chapter Seventeen

Berkeley

George Berkeley (1685–1753) was born in the county of Kilkenny in southern Ireland to a family of English descent. At age fifteen he entered Trinity College, Dublin, to study mathematics, languages, logic, and philosophy. In 1704 he took his A.B. degree, and in 1707 became a fellow of the college. To meet statutory requirements he was ordained deacon in 1709 and priest in 1710 in the Church of England. Visiting London in 1713, he met and charmed a number of distinguished literary men— Swift, Steele, Addison, and Pope. He also made two visits of some length to Italy and France. In 1724 he gave up his fellowship at Trinity College to become Dean of Londonderry in northern Ireland.

Motivated by intense religious convictions, Berkeley persuaded Parliament to vote a grant of £20,000 for the founding of a college in Bermuda for the training of ministers for the colonists and for the education of Indians. In 1728, with Irish impracticality, he sailed with his new bride for Newport, Rhode Island, to await the promised grant. But after three years it was clear that the grant would never be paid and that it would be prudent for Berkeley to return home. He gave his personal library to struggling Yale College and returned home a brokenhearted man. He accepted appointment as Bishop of Cloyne in southern Ireland where he gave himself to scholarly study and to working to improve the wretched conditions of the poor peasantry, both Protestant and Catholic. In 1752 he moved to Oxford and on January 14, 1753, he died. He was buried in Christ Church, Oxford, the cathedral of the Diocese of Oxford.

Berkeley's published writings fall into two groups. The first includes those works on which his philosophical reputation rests: *An Essay Towards a New Theory of Vision* (1709), *A Treatise Concerning the Principles of Human Knowledge* (1710, 1734), and *Three Dialogues Between Hylas and Philonous* (1713). The second group includes *Alicphron, or The Minute Philosopher* (1732), which contains seven dialogues directed against such freethinkers as Bernard Mandeville and the third Earl of Shaftesbury, and *Siris: A Chain of Philosophical*

Reflexions and Inquiries Concerning the Virtues of Tar-Water and Divers Other Subjects (1744), in which Berkeley united a defense of his increasingly Neoplatonic views with a lengthy dissertation on the values of tar water as a cure-all for most of man's ills. Our concern is with some of the characteristic positions he developed in his first group of writings.

Berkeley's Philosophy

Berkeley sees that Locke's epistemology is confused and inconsistent. It does not really permit Locke to maintain the distinction between the inner and outer world. If we are limited to a knowledge of our ideas, as Locke believed, how can we ever know that our ideas correspond to the real world? Indeed, how can we ever know that there is a world beyond our ideas? As an empiricist, Berkeley feels that the difficulty can be avoided by dispensing with Locke's notion of an unexperienced material reality behind or beyond our ideas.

In approaching his task Berkeley first undertakes to clear away what he regards as false presuppositions. Just as Locke rejected innate ideas, Berkeley rejects abstract ideas. Locke thought we could abstract common characteristics from the particulars we experienced and give them names such as "extension," "color," and "man." Berkeley points out that these are simply general names and nothing more. In reality nothing corresponds to them. This is the view called nominalism—abstract ideas or universals are mere names.

It is not possible for us to experience bare "extension," which is neither line, surface, nor solid. We cannot have such an idea. It is not possible to form an idea of a triangle which is "neither oblique nor rectangle, neither equilateral, equicrural, nor scalenon, but *all* and *none* of these at once." Likewise we cannot have an abstract idea of "color" which is neither red, blue, orange, nor any other determinate color. When we perceive a barn, it always has specific characteristics, such as a long red barn with a sagging roof. We can think only in terms of something concrete and imaginal, something expressed in terms of sensation. This view is called sensationalism. Thus Berkeley is both a nominalist and a sensationalist.

Berkeley neatly sums up his own philosophical position in these words:

I do not pretend to be a setter-up of new notions. My endeavors tend only to unite, and place in a clearer light, that truth which was before shared between the vulgar and the philosophers:—the former being of opinion, that *those things they immediately perceive are the real things*; and the latter, that *the things immediately perceived are ideas, which exist only in the mind*. Which two notions put together, do, in effect, constitute the substance of what I advance. (This statement was put into the mouth of Philonous by Berkeley on the last page of his third dialogue between Hylas and Philonous.)

Berkeley's first claim is that the things men immediately perceive are the real things. In vivid language he writes: "It is indeed an opinion strangely prevailing amongst men, that houses, mountains, rivers, and in a word all sensible objects, have an existence, natural or real, distinct from their being perceived by the understanding . . . For what are the forementioned objects but the things we perceive by sense? and is it not plainly repugnant that any one of these, or any combination of them, should exist unperceived?" Berkeley is not denying the existence of bodies which we all immediately perceive. He is denying the material substance of other philosophers—a substance supposed to be beyond human experience and devoid of all the sensible qualities which we immediately perceive bodies to have. "The choir of heaven and the furniture of earth, in a word all those bodies which compose the mighty frame of the world" are immediately perceived by the man in the street as well as by the erudite philosopher. As an empiricist Berkeley is rejecting Descartes' rational intuitions and Locke's distinction between "real essences," which lie beyond knowledge, and "nominal essences," which provide no knowledge of the real nature of things.

Berkeley's second claim is that everything that exists is either perceived as an idea or else is a mind that perceives ideas. Since anything we immediately perceive is an idea, it cannot have any being apart from the mind. Its *esse* is *percipi* except when "to be is to perceive" (*esse est percipere*). All you are aware of when you immediately perceive a flower or an animal is a certain combination of sense qualities in addition to your own awareness as something wholly distinct from your perceptions. Perception then becomes the criterion of reality. To say ideas "exist in the mind" is not to assert that they are in one's head, but that ideas are in relation to a perceiving mind. The perceived world is the only real world, since it is the only one actually experienced.

The most basic argument for Berkeley's position is that it is impossible for us to conceive of anything existing independently of our own thinking. No one can think of anything without having an idea of it, no one can think of anything which is in its nature unthinkable. The very effort to think of something apart from, or independent of, experience makes it a part of our conscious experience. It is a contradiction to assert that we can conceive of unexperienced entities.

Berkeley rejects Locke's distinction between primary and secondary

qualities. Locke had accepted the fact that sensible (secondary) qualities of an object, such as color, taste, or sound, do not exist apart from
perception. But Berkeley points out that the same arguments used to
prove that colors, tastes, and temperatures exist only in the mind can
be brought against the primary qualities of extension, figure, and
motion; our ideas of them change with their distance from us. It
is impossible for us to conceive of an object which occupies space
and still has no color, but this is what is entailed in the position that
primary qualities exist independently while the ideas of secondary
qualities do not. If the secondary qualities are dependent on the mind
and if primary qualities cannot be conceived to exist without secondary
qualities, then any object constituted only by primary and secondary
qualities must be mental—that is, an idea or collection of ideas.

Berkeley insists that "all our ideas, sensations, or the things which
we perceive, by whatsoever names they may be distinguished, are
visibly inactive; there is nothing of power or agency in them. So that
one idea or object of thought *cannot produce* or make *any alteration
in another.*" Thus all the ideas we assign to the outer world are entirely
passive; they can neither do nor cause anything. This doctrine is
central in Berkeley's philosophy. Consequently, Berkeley finds it
impossible to accept the primary qualities of extension, figure, and
motion as the causes of our sensation.

It must be admitted that "we perceive a continual succession of
ideas, some are anew excited, others are changed or totally disappear."
It is necessary that there be a cause on which these ideas depend.
Since ideas are passive and since no material substance exists, the cause
can only be "an incorporeal active substance or spirit." "A spirit is
one simple, undivided, active being; as it perceives ideas it is called the
understanding, and as it produces or otherwise operates about them
it is called the will." Like Locke, Berkeley accepts the belief in spiritual
substance or the self. In the first edition of *Principles* he asserts that
"there can be no *idea* formed of a soul or spirit," and that each of us
has "an immediate knowledge" of himself as "a thinking, active
principle that perceives, knows, wills, and operates about ideas."
In the second edition of the *Principles* (1734) he makes much more use
of the term *notion.* Thus he says we have a notion of spirit, but no
idea of spirit. We know what we mean when we talk about mind, soul,
or spirit although we cannot present it to ourselves as an idea. After
all, ideas are passive, while the mind can be active in dealing with ideas.
However difficult it may be to clarify further the distinction between
notions and ideas, Berkeley clearly emphasizes his mentalism—the
doctrine that whatever exists is either a mind or an idea in some mind.

Nothing else is real. Historically this doctrine is what has come to be called idealism or, more specifically, subjective idealism in contrast to the older idealism of Plato and Plotinus in which Ideas have reality apart from minds.

Although we are aware of our own minds by the fact that we can imagine some ideas as we will, and construct flights of fantasy, we do discover that some ideas usually regarded as objects of the external world are involuntary and continually reappear in our experience. Since our minds have not produced them and passive ideas lack the power to produce themselves, Berkeley concludes that they must have been produced by some other will or spirit, namely God.

The third chief claim that Berkeley's philosophy makes is that the mind of God continually sustains the various ideas which constitute the regular framework of the universe. This was important to Berkeley, for he envisions his philosophy as cutting the ground out from under skepticism, atheism, and irreligion, and providing a new and unassailable foundation for Christianity.

The "houses, rivers, mountains, trees, stones" and all that which we ordinarily regard as regularly and continually constituting the vast world of nature are, in Berkeley's terminology, involuntary ideas. This system of ideas is entertained by God's infinite mind even when our finite minds are not perceiving such ideas. Thus the reality and objectivity of the world is guaranteed philosophically by the omnipotence and omniscience of God's mind. To the extent that we observe real bodies and follow scientific procedures faithfully, we are perceiving God's ideas after Him and are enabled to plan with some confidence our activities in everyday life. In so far as we entertain ideas that exist only in our own minds we are voluntarily engaging in imagination or error. The involuntary ideas can be distinguished from the voluntary by their greater vividness, order, coherence, and steadiness.

From Berkeley's point of view, God "is known as certainly and immediately as any other mind or spirit whatsoever, distinct from ourselves." Each of us experiences a self or spirit in himself. To explain our involuntary ideas as caused by the will of another spirit is to explain the unknown by the known. To explain them as caused by a material substance incapable of being perceived and thus unknowable by the mind is to explain the unknown by the still more unknown.

In summary, we can say that Berkeley's theory of knowledge is a form of realism in so far as it accepts the existence of bodies and rejects the disparagement of sense perception. His version of idealism is the metaphysical position that reality consists entirely of minds and the ideas in minds. His theism is the arch which holds together these two basic doctrines and which provides the practical motivation for his work.

Berkeley's idealism has come in for many vigorous attacks by critics who often failed to understand his philosophy or were unfair to him. Dr. Samuel Johnson was representative of some of them. He facetiously suggested that whoever kicks a stone will know that a stone is more than a mere idea. All one can say in response to this type of criticism is that in kicking the stone Dr. Johnson missed the point of Berkeley's arguments.

Many of the objections raised by critics are anticipated and carefully dealt with by Berkeley, for he is an acute thinker. It may be instructive to consider how he handles possible objections. To the objection that in his philosophy "All that is real and substantial in nature is banished from the world," Berkeley replies that all these things remain as real as ever. He does not question the existence of things we perceive by sight or touch. They are involuntary ideas given to us by God. All he rejects, Berkeley insists, is the notion of an unperceived material substance to explain the ideas we perceive.

To the objection that there is a considerable difference between "real fire and the idea of fire, between dreaming or imagining one's self burnt, and actually being so," Berkeley gives a similar answer. Both real pain and imagined pain exist only in the mind. Real pain and real fire are involuntary ideas given to us by God and are followed by involuntary effects, while imagined pain and imagined fire are voluntary ideas subject only to the control of our own minds and wills. God's experience, or the world of nature, has a structure. Although we could have ideas if we were not conscious, our involuntary ideas are determined by the structure of the divine experience in which we participate. It is sometimes objected that in Berkeley's philosophy "things are every moment annihilated and created anew." This calls for essentially the same reply. The objects of the world of nature, which are ideas in Berkeley's use of the term, exist continuously in the mind of God, whether we perceive them or not. Thus the world of nature has as much objective reality as in any other philosophy. But for Berkeley the ideas are to be explained by spiritual substances or minds rather than by material substance or matter.

It has sometimes been suggested that if figure and extension had existence only in a mind, then the mind itself would be figured and extended. Berkeley's answer to this objection is simple. Figure and extension are only ideas in the mind and not qualities of the mind itself. As in Locke and the physicists, colors such as red and blue are asserted to exist only in the mind, without implying that the mind itself is red and blue.

Some critics have argued that the adoption of Berkeley's philosophy would involve the wholesale repudiation of modern science. It is difficult to see the force of this criticism, for both Berkeley and a scientist committed to materialism could follow the same procedures and obtain the same results in a physics laboratory. Their differences would arise only in the metaphysical interpretation of the significance of their work. As a matter of fact, Berkeley has given a consistent interpretation of what is essentially the world of modern physics in which nature is viewed as the expression of force or energy. Berkeley's interpretation appealed to students of physics like Eddington and Whitehead, particularly as a criticism of Newtonian absolutes.

Although Berkeley moved in later years in the direction of Platonism and Neoplatonism, his earlier work laid the foundation for a new kind of empiricism which formed a bridge between Locke and Hume. His work anticipated certain developments in Kantianism and Hegelianism and helped to usher in the modern revolt against the concept of an unknowable reality, which has subsequently become an important feature of positivism, pragmatism, and phenomenalism.

George Berkeley: Suggested Additional Reading

Abernethy, George L. and Thomas A. Langford, eds., *History of Philosophy: Selected Readings*. Belmont, Calif.: Dickenson, 1965, pp. 430–457.*

Berkeley, *The Words of George Berkeley, Bishop of Cloyne*. Edited by A. A. Luce and T. E. Jessop. 9 vols. London and Edinburgh: Thomas Nelson and Sons, 1948–1957.*

Berkeley, *Principles of Human Knowledge*. Introduction by G. J. Warnock. New York: World Publishing Company, Meridian, 1963.

Berkeley, *Berkeley's Philosophical Writings*. Edited by David M. Armstrong. New York: Macmillan, Collier, 1964.

Berkeley, *Works on Vision*. Edited with a commentary by Colin M. Turbayne. Indianapolis: Bobbs-Merrill, Liberal Arts Press, 1963.

Copleston, Frederick C., *A History of Philosophy*. Vol. V, Part II. New York: Doubleday, Image Book, 1964.

Hicks, G. Dawes, *Berkeley*. London: E. Benn, 1932.*

Hone, Joseph M., *Bishop Berkeley: His Life, Writings and Philosophy*. London: Faber and Faber, 1931.*

Kaufmann, Walter. *Philosophic Classics*. Englewood Cliffs, N.J.: Prentice-Hall, 1961, II, 275–306.*

Luce, Arthur A., *The Dialectic of Immaterialism*. London: Hodder and Stoughton, 1963.*

Ritchie, A. D., *George Berkeley, a Reappraisal*. New York: Barnes and Noble, 1967.

Sillem, E. A., *George Berkeley and the Proofs of the Existence of God*. New York and London: Longmans, Green, 1957.*

Steinkraus, Warren E., ed., *New Studies in Berkeley's Philosophy*. New York: Harcourt, Brace and World, 1966.

Warnock, G. J., *Berkeley*. Baltimore: Penguin, 1953.

Wild, John, *George Berkeley: A Study of His Life and Philosophy*. Cambridge: Harvard University Press, 1936, 1962.*

Chapter Eighteen

David Hume

D avid Hume (1711–1776) is generally recognized as one of the most important philosophers and perhaps the greatest of the British philosophers. The logical rigor, candor, and thoroughness of his thought give him a place of the highest order in the Western philosophical tradition. The care with which Hume presented an uncompromising empiricism led to a number of important contributions, and his work is still seriously studied and discussed by contemporary philosophers.

Hume was born in Edinburgh and received his education in his home city. Trained as a lawyer at his family's insistence, he reports that he felt "an insurmountable aversion to everything but the pursuits of philosophy and general learning." Consequently, after a short time in which he lived in Bristol attempting to participate in a business, he went to France and remained there from 1734–1737. It was while in France that he wrote his first and most important philosophical work, *A Treatise of Human Nature* (in three volumes). This book failed to evoke the response he had hoped for, but with resilience, "being of a cheerful and sanguine temper," as he wrote, he returned to his home. During this time he served as secretary to a general and then to Lord Hertford, but his interest in philosophy continued and in 1741–1742 he published *Essays, Moral and Political* and followed this by rewriting his Treatise, which was published finally in 1751 under the title *An Enquiry Concerning Human Understanding*. In the same year he published *An Enquiry Concerning the Principles of Morals*.

In 1752 Hume became the librarian of the Faculty of Advocates in Edinburgh and started work on his *History of England under the House of Tudor* (1759) and the second volume, *History of England from the Invasion of Julius Caesar to the Accession of Henry VII* (1761). The one philosophical work he published during this period was entitled *Four Dissertations* and contained a section on the natural history of religion.

Hume accompanied Lord Hertford, the British ambassador, to Paris in 1763 and became secretary of the embassy. He was enthusi-

astically received in the literary and philosophical society and was
entertained by the Dauphin at Versailles, where he listened to eulogies
about himself presented by three boys, all of whom were to be future
kings of France. Rousseau also became a close friend, but, due to
Rousseau's personality, a famous quarrel ensued and the two were
sundered, then later reconciled as friends. In 1775 his health started
failing and being aware that the disease was fatal he wrote his autobiography, *My Own Life*. The following year he died.

In 1779 his *Dialogues Concerning Natural Religion* was published by
his direction. His life had been eventful, and his death, as it was
described by his friend Adam Smith, was as impressive as his life.
Though never holding a strictly academic position, Hume's produc-
tivity and the quality of his thought provided a legacy which enriched
the continuing philosophical tradition.

Hume's Empiricism

Hume's major effort, as he himself describes it, is to introduce the
experimental method of reasoning into moral subjects; and it may be
claimed that what he primarily attempts is the extension of the methods
of the Newtonian science, insofar as possible, to human nature. This
project is undertaken in his original *Treatise*, the first book of which is
the most important in terms of revealing the uniqueness of his position.

Hume begins by attempting to derive his philosophy from direct
experience, and, in this, he follows the path charted by Locke.
But such a point of initiation rules out all assumed doctrines of substance; consequently he goes immediately beyond both Locke and
Berkeley since, he argues, we can know from sense experience neither
the essence of the mind nor of bodies. All knowledge is to be deduced
from the process of conscious awareness.

Nothing seems more unbounded, he claims, than man's mind.
Although man's body is temporally and spatially confined, his thoughts
can roam instantly into the furthest reaches of the universe. Moreover,
the imagination is capable of conjuring up the most unnatural and
incongruous appearances, such as flying horses and golden mountains.
The mind is also able to relate ideas, such as those in mathematics.
In spite of these capacities, however, Hume claims that the mind, as it
functions in relation to the external world, is really confined within
very narrow limits. And in the final analysis, the contents of the mind
can be reduced to the materials given us by sense experience.

In the flow of conscious experience, Hume maintains, we can
distinguish two sorts of things: impressions and ideas. He uses the

word "perceptions" to cover the mind's contents in general, and these perceptions he divides into impressions and ideas. Impressions are the immediate data of experience such as sensations, in which are included not merely our sense perceptions but also feelings like love, hate, desire, and will. He describes ideas as the copies or faint images of impressions in thinking and reasoning. The distinction between impressions and ideas is a matter of vividness, or is determined by the degree of force and liveliness with which they strike the mind.

The exploration of the process of experience which Hume thinks is the appropriate intellectual activity is the tracing of every idea to the impression or impressions from which it is derived. Thus Hume argues, "I venture to affirm that the rule here holds without any exception, and that every simple idea has a simple impression which resembles it, and every simple impression a correspondent idea" (*Treatise*, Bk. I, Part I, Sec. I). Experience, on this basis, can be reduced to atomic constituents, namely, impressions of sense data.

Further, Hume divided impressions and ideas into two classes each, so as to make his analysis more exact. Impressions may be those of sensation or reflection; ideas may be classified as memory or imagination. Impressions of sensation are the strongest and most direct reception of sense data, while the impressions of reflection are to be found in the consequent employment of the impressions of sensation. So if one has an impression of sensation of fire and burning, this can give rise to an impression of reflection by which these two are joined and fire is therefore avoided.

In addition to distinguishing between impressions and ideas, Hume argues that there can be no ideas without impressions. An idea, on this basis, is simply a copy of an impression. Every idea, however, reflects a corresponding impression, for no one has seen a flying horse even though he may have an idea of such a creature. Such ideas, which do not reflect impressions, are attributed to the mind's "faculty of compounding, transposing, or diminishing the materials afforded us by the sense and experience." Hence, when we think of a flying horse, our imagination joins two ideas, wings and horse, which we originally acquired as impressions through our senses.

As impressions are received they may take the form of ideas of memory or imagination. The ideas which are retained in the memory are more vivid than those retained in the imagination, which according to Hume are "faint and languid" perceptions that lack steadiness and uniformity. The memory preserves not only simple ideas but also their order and positions, thus helping to retain a composite impression of the sense data. Imagination can freely combine ideas, but it normally

functions by the general principles of association. The qualities to
which the "natural" association gives rise are three: resemblances,
contiguity in time and place, and cause and effect. Such association is
an acquired habit of thought and is not to be found in the sense impressions themselves. The imagination connects, separates, and
recombines, and by this process of association of ideas, complex
ideas are formed. The treatment of these complex ideas in terms of
their relations brings us to the crucial point in Hume's theory of knowledge.

Hume poses the issues: *"What is the nature of all our reasonings
concerning matter of fact?"* The proper answer seems to be that they
are founded on the relation of cause and effect. When again it is asked,
*What is the foundation of all our reasonings and conclusions concerning
that relation?* it may be replied in one word: experience. But if we still
carry on our sifting humor, and ask, *What is the foundation of all
conclusions from experience?* this implies a new question, which may be
of more difficult solution and explication. . . .

". . . I say then, that, even after we have experience of the operations
of cause and effect, our conclusions from that experience are *not*
founded on reasoning, or any process of the understanding" (*Enquiry*,
IV, II).

Through an analysis of the way the reflective mind combines ideas,
Hume presents his answer to these questions. Thus he proceeds by
distinguishing seven "philosophical relations," in addition to the
previously mentioned three "natural relations": resemblance, identity,
space and time, quantity or number, degrees of quality, contrariety
in existence and nonexistence, and causality. In terms of its importance,
the quality of causation is fundamental; therefore we shall give attention to his discussion of this relation. No object, he argues, implies the
existence of any other, if we consider these objects as isolated sense
data. Therefore we cannot derive the idea of necessary connection from
observation of regular sequences. The idea, then, must be derived
from some subjective source or some impression of reflection.

Causation, considered as a philosophical relation, can be reduced to
such space-time relations as contiguity, temporal succession, and
constant conjunction. But here there is no necessary connection between these ideas, and there is no basis for attributing this relation to the
objects themselves. Considered as a natural relation, there is an inseparable connection between ideas, but again this can be explained as a
subjectively compelling association of ideas, even though the idea of
one determines the mind to the idea of the other. Such necessity as is

found exists in the mind and not in the objects. The conclusion which follows from this investigation is that our reasoning concerning causes and effects is only a matter of custom, for they are not a part of the objective world. In place of the uniformity in nature which we describe as causal necessity, Hume would acknowledge only a strong custom of the mind to associate ideas which have been constantly conjoined in experience. Nonetheless, we do reason upon this connection and draw inferences from it. The important point is that the status of this reasoning and its inferences must be clearly understood.

Following this same line of argumentation, Hume also rejects all doctrines of substance. The idea of substance cannot be derived from sense impressions; if, therefore, we have an idea of substance, it must be derived from the combination of simple ideas by the imagination. In the last analysis, this combining can be resolved into our passions and emotions. Consequently, the alleged substance of the perceived object is a "fiction" of our own making, for it cannot be derived from perceptions. To put the case sharply, our experience does not give us any information which makes it possible for us to go beyond such a description of particular qualities and speak of substance. Therefore we cannot confirm that there are either material (Locke) or mental (Berkeley) substances. To say that we cannot speak of substances means, as its most significant consequence, that we cannot properly speak of our "minds" as substances. According to Hume, the mind may be likened to a theater, where perceptions successively make their appearance; pass, repass, glide away, and mingle together in an infinite variety of postures and relationships.

What then can be said of personal identity? Hume gives his answer: The self is not one impression but a collection of individual perceptions. "For my part, when I enter most intimately into what I call *myself*, I always stumble on some particular perception or other, of heat or cold, light or shade, love or hatred, pain or pleasure. I never catch *myself* at any time without a perception, and never can observe anything but the perception."

Hume's empiricism led to the conclusion that there is no rational justification for saying that bodies or things have an independent existence external to us. Our ordinary experience may very well suggest that things do exist outside of us. But if we take seriously the notion that our ideas are copies of impressions, the conclusion must be that all we know is impressions. However, as we have seen above, these impressions may be arranged by certain configurations of association.

Human Passions

In the second book of the *Treatise* Hume discusses human passions, a subject which is of great importance since he held these passions responsible for many of man's ideas and customs. He begins his discussion by dividing human passions into two major categories. First there are direct passions or primary feelings which arise immediately from pleasure and pain; secondly there are indirect passions or reflective impressions founded upon these sensations. By passion, Hume does not mean emotional outbursts, but rather all emotions and affective states. Direct passions are such affective states as desire, aversion, grief, joy, hope, fear, despair, and security. Upon these are built, by means of the laws of association, the secondary or indirect passions such as pride, humility, ambition, vanity, love, hatred, pity, malice, and generosity. The relation between direct and indirect passions is very subtle in Hume's discussion; there is, he says, a double relation between the two. His effort is to combine an association of impressions with an association of ideas so that the cause of a passion produces a sensation, and this sensation has a "natural" reference to the self as object or to the idea of the self. For example, when a man is vain about himself we can distinguish between the cause (or quality) of this pride and the self to which it is related, but the association of the cause and the object are both components of the one experience.

This interrelationship may be stated in a somewhat different manner. Pleasant and painful passions tend to excite all of the other passions which are of the same affective tone, and thereby they call into play associated feelings. So when these passions are concerned with other persons, pleasure tends to induce love for others, or, contrariwise, pain tends to induce antagonism. On this basis Hume constructs his interpretation of such passions as family affection, esteem of the rich and powerful, benevolence and compassion, envy, malice, contempt, and "amorous passions."

What sort of passion involves one in philosophical pursuits? Hume concludes that truth is pursued primarily for the pleasure which the hunt gives. Such pleasure is increased if, as a matter of fact, some prize or game is won. Philosophy, according to this interpretation, combines the satisfactions of the hunt or gamble with that of bagging or winning something of value. Under this general designation, he also includes such academic activity as the study of mathematics and morals as well as philosophy. But Hume insists it must also be clear that in philosophy the prize to be won has a certain extrinsic value, for the understanding of events enhances the prospect of increasing pleasure and reducing pain.

Moral Philosophy

Although the most important aspect of Hume's philosophy was his work in epistemology, he was also significant as a moral thinker. He had described his original *Treatise* as an introduction of the experimental method of reasoning into moral subjects, and he regarded his revision of the third section of the *Treatise*, *Enquiry Concerning the Principles of Morals*, as the best of all his writing.

Traditional moral philosophy, he is convinced, needs some new and simple principle of human nature to provide insight into experience and conduct. Such a fundamental principle, he maintains, is to be found in his theory of the association of ideas. He defines this association of ideas as the method by which we easily move from one idea to another when these ideas resemble and are contiguous to one another. He feels assured that he can apply the same approach to ethics as he applied to human understanding.

Once again, Hume takes his point of initiation to be the data received by the senses; thus he rejects both the theological and the metaphysical criteria for ethics as well as the attempt to grasp the essence of virtue and vice by logical analysis. The first two criteria are rejected because they cannot be found in immediate experience; the latter approach is rejected because no matter how we may analyze or account for particular acts, our judgment about these acts lack a moral quality so long as we limit ourselves to an intellectual statement. In judging any action as good or bad in a moral sense, a person only indicates that he feels a sentiment of approval or blame. Just as in the case of causation, such moral ideas may be subjectively compelling, but they are not establishable as a part of objective reality.

But precisely how does one understand this notion of the "sentiments of approval and blame"? What evokes these sentiments? Hume does not want to support egoistic theories of ethics, though at times he is willing to admit the strength of their contention. He is convinced that men are by and large altruistic and he claims that it was rare to meet a man in whom kind affections, taken together, do not overbalance all the selfish affections. But this was not a general attitude or a universal love for mankind. Rather, this positive feeling seems to be dependent upon personal qualities, and of the services and relations which others may do or have toward oneself. In his reedited *Enquiry* he becomes even more positive in his assessment of human nature than he was in the *Treatise,* and he strongly condemns those who see man as essentially evil and thereby refuse to see the positive and generally intended good to be found in friendship, public spirit, and fidelity.

At no point does Hume attempt to explain the origin of these sentiments, but he is convinced that they are genuine and common in human interrelatedness. Consequently, the feeling which determines moral judgment is one of kindly humanity, benevolent interest in the well-being of others, and sympathy. Indeed he goes so far as to claim that is it possible to find a kind of disinterested benevolence in men which means that action is possible apart from self-interest.

In his account of justice and benevolence, Hume traces the movement from self-regard to social-mindedness. Submission to justice often runs counter to our basic inclinations, he points out; therefore it must be motivated by strong sentiments. Our regard for justice arises from the conflict between private interests and the social good. At such points we acquiesce to justice because we recognize that our well-being is secured by the fair adjustment of rights and privileges. By a further association of ideas we are willing to give our approval to the one principle of justice generally, even when our own rights are not involved, because we now recognize it as a necessary way to construct a social community. In like manner, injustice may ignite our adverse sentiment, even when it does not directly affect us. Thus our acceptance of justice, at first an expression of self-interest and self-protection, can be extended into a general benevolence. Self-interest, the original motive for establishing justice, may be transposed into a sympathy with public interest which then constitutes the source of the moral approbation which attends that virtue.

Philosophy of Religion

Hume continues his philosophical investigations by extending his methodology for ascertaining truth to three important religious issues. While he does not formally begin each discussion with an effort to trace the ideas back to the impressions upon which they depend, this is clearly the method he assumes, and his examination proceeds upon this assumption.

In a famous discussion of belief in miracles, Hume maintains that it is impossible to find adequate empirical evidence for arriving at the conclusion that a miracle or an exception to the laws of nature has occurred. As in the case of the idea of causation, to assert a belief in miracles is to shape the received data by associations of ideas which cannot be shown to be dependent upon that data. Thus, when the exception to normally experienced regularity occurs, rather than talk about the exception as a miracle we should call into question our so-called "laws of nature," which have been constructed out of that experience, and we should doubt the adequacy of the exceptional construction. Consequently, the experience of the unusual would add further information along with the regular incidence of events, and, as a result, what was taken to be a "law of nature" has been reduced to a probability statement. Miracles, then, cannot be experienced directly. Nonetheless, sometimes there are reports by other persons telling of occurrences which are exceptions to the natural regularities. Hume carefully explores the question: Under what conditions is it reasonable to accept such reports?

Once again we must attempt to apply an empirical test, which in this case means that the immediate sense experience which we normally have must be measured against the reports of the exceptional. The final adjudication of this problem Hume finds solved by the application of a general criterion: "No testimony is sufficient to establish a miracle, unless the testimony be of such a kind that its falsehood would be more miraculous than the fact which it endeavours to establish" (*Enquiry*, Sec. X, Part I). He argues that when this rule is applied, the claims of miracle are shown to be so untrustworthy as to make them of no rational importance.

Hume next explores the question: Is there valid evidence to support belief in God? The theological argument which he has to confront directly is the cosmological argument which claims that God is the First Cause of the universe. Two general types of argumentation are employed in his discussion of this problem. First he asks whether the conception of First Cause is not logically and empirically unjustifiable; and, second, if there is such a cause, what kind of a being would a cause of the total experienced universe be?

In regard to the first question, Hume argues that a First Cause is both superfluous and meaningless. It is superfluous because, for instance, in a chain of twenty events, if we account for the cause of each of these events in detail, we have provided all of the causal explanation needed. Each event in the chain is causally accounted for and that is what is demanded. Thus, to ask what is the cause of the whole series is superfluous. In addition, the idea of a First Cause is also meaningless. Previously he has argued that the idea of a category of causality has meaning only where there are a number of experiences in which we find regularity in the temporal occurrence of contiguous events. When, therefore, an event is experienced other than as a term in such a regularly repeated conjunction, there is no basis for calling it a cause or an effect. The most we can say is that it exists. The universe is precisely of this order. There is only one universe, and this cosmos may be observed, but there is no repetition which can give rise to any causal interpretation.

But suppose that we assume that it is legitimate to think of the cosmos as an effect of some First Cause, what attributes could be ascribed to the Cause? Even before discussing this question directly, he makes the point that a fair assessment of the evidence indicates that any analogy capable of being used as a clue is exceedingly weak. So weak is it, in fact, that if we cannot maintain a complete suspension of judgment, we do at least have to recognize that any positive conclusion has only a slight probability of being true.

Several difficulties are mentioned as he investigates the question of the attributes of the First Cause. First, there is no assurance that there is any analogy between individual instances of cause and effect and the cause of the whole cosmos. The consequence of this is to deny that any attributes which are ascribed to individual causes may be attributed to this unique Cause. Secondly, it is not at all clear that the universe is similar to a machine, the analogy most commonly used, and that therefore there must be a causative mind as in the case of other machines. If the universe were more like an animal or a plant, then the First Cause would be conceived as some type of generative principle or blind vitality and not necessarily as intelligence. But even if it were intelligence, we much recognize that in this world intelligence is not a self-explanatory thing; it has its own causal conditions by means of which it is explained. Hence, even the intelligence which created the cosmos, in this analogy, itself demands some explanation. Finally, if the intelligence which created the cosmos is omniscient, as is claimed, then it must be so different from the intelligence we experience that no adequate analogy can possibly be found.

The conclusion Hume seems to be pressing toward, especially in his *Dialogues Concerning Natural Religion*, is that while the evidence can be taken to indicate that there is some principle which orders the universe, we cannot speak meaningfully of this Prime Cause. The main thrust of his argument may be stated tersely: "Allowing, therefore, the gods to be the authors of the existence or order of the universe; it follows that they possess that precise degree of power, intelligence, and benevolence, which appears in their workmanship; but nothing farther can be proved, except we call in the assistance of exaggeration and flattery to supply the defects of argument and reasoning" (*Enquiry*, 144). The result of this line of reasoning is drawn with clarity: while we may ascribe great power to such a First Cause, on the basis of its effects, we cannot ascribe infinite power to it. Further, in regard to moral qualities, such as justice, benevolence, or mercy, we must conclude that the evidence can only support a neutrality of opinion.

Finally, Hume investigates the problem of immortality. Once again, the conclusion is that the belief is unverifiable and that it is a matter of opinion, hope, or unfounded dogma, but it is not a conclusion which may be deduced from sense experience. In spite of the professed pious expectations of religious believers, Hume is convinced that in this case also there is inadequate evidence to support the belief, and one must adopt an agnostic attitude toward it.

In several passages Hume indicates that he questions the applicability of his methodology to religion, for such belief may rest upon a type of faith which, though it cannot be rationally justified, nevertheless has a validity of its own. But in spite of these demurers, he more consistently holds that religious belief in miracles, the existence of God, and immortality cannot be proven, and a suspension of judgment about them is the wisest and most rational course to follow.

Subsequent developments have attested to the importance of Hume's philosophical work. He is now generally regarded as one of the most significant British philosophers, and certainly the leading British thinker of his period. Such an evaluation was not generally made in his own time; consequently, if the impact which he made upon Kant is excepted, his importance has only more recently been appreciated. Modern empiricists have found in him a source whose insights continue to be worthy of study, and, through them, he continues to contribute to philosophical enquiry.

David Hume: Suggested Additional Reading

Abernethy, George L. and Thomas A. Langford, eds., *History of Philosophy: Selected Readings*. Belmont, Calif.: Dickenson, 1965, pp. 458–490.*

Basson, A. H., *David Hume*. Baltimore: Penguin, 1958.

Chappel, V. C., *Hume*. New York: Doubleday, Anchor, 1966.

Flew, Antony G. N., *Hume's Philosophy of Belief*. New York: Humanities Press, 1961.*

Greig, J. Y. T., *David Hume*. London: J. Cape, 1931.*

Hume, *A Treatise on Human Nature*. Edited by D. G. C. MacNabb. New York: World Publishing Company, Meridian, 1962.

Hume, *Essential Works of David Hume*. Edited by Ralph Cohen. New York: Bantam Books, 1965.

Hume, *Inquiry Concerning Human Understanding*. Edited by C. W. Hendel. Indianapolis: Bobbs-Merrill, Liberal Arts Press, 1957.

Hume, *Hume's Moral and Political Philosophy*. Edited by H. D. Aiken. New York: Hafner, 1959.

Hume, *Inquiry Concerning the Principles of Morals*. Edited by C. W. Hendel. Indianapolis: Bobbs-Merrill, Liberal Arts Press, 1957.

Kaufmann, Walter, *Philosophic Classics*. Englewood Cliffs, N.J.: Prentice-Hall, 1961, II, 307–414.*

MacNabb, D. G. C., *David Hume: His Theory of Knowledge and Morality*. London: Hutchison's University Library, 1951.*

Mossner, E. C., *The Life of David Hume*. Austin: University of Texas Press, 1954.*

Passmore, J. A., *Hume's Intentions*. Cambridge: Cambridge University Press, 1953.*

Price, H. H., *Hume's Theory of the External World*. Oxford: Clarendon Press, 1940.*

Smith, Norman Kemp, *Philosophy of David Hume*. New York: St. Martins, 1941.

Chapter Nineteen

Immanuel Kant

Born in the east Prussian town of Köenigsberg, Immanuel Kant (1724–1804) received his education in that city and remained there to teach and live until his death. In an unusual sense it is true to say that while Kant never went to the world, before he died his fame became such that the world—at least the philosophical world—came to Kant.

Kant's parents were members of a strict sect of Lutheran Pietists, and he was raised in this religious tradition. He originally enrolled in the university at Köenigsberg in the theological curriculum, but eventually transferred to the philosophy faculty and finished his career as a student with a brilliant record. After graduation he supported himself for some years as a private tutor in the homes of the gentry living in or near his home city. But in 1755 he returned to the university as a *privat dozent* (instructor) in philosophy. His academic rise was slow—he was not appointed to a professorship until 1770—but he had secured his foundations well, and his careful work reached its fruition when, in 1781, he published the *Critique of Pure Reason*.

With the publication of this book on the theory of knowledge, Kant was immediately considered an important thinker, and students from many countries came to hear him and talk with him. Later, when his *Critique of Practical Reason* was published in 1788 and his *Critique of Judgment* followed in 1790, his place was assured.

It is customary to divide Kant's philosophical development into three periods. The first period was characterized by his indebtedness to Leibniz and Christian Wolff, both preeminent rationalists. During this time he was convinced that it was possible to arrive at ultimate truths through rational construction apart from empirical tests. While he was later to abandon this approach, he never lost his respect for mathematics, which employs this type of deductive thought.

Around 1765 he came under the influence of the British empiricists, especially David Hume. Reading Hume's *Essays* and *Enquiries* in German translation, he was, as he said, awakened "from his dogmatic slumbers." This revolution in his thought led him to conclude that all knowledge must begin with experience, while at the same time the external reality which is the source of our sense awareness cannot be directly known by reason. He resolved this problem by arguing that the mind has native capacities by which it is able to form or shape its sense perceptions. While Hume forced Kant to rethink the foundations of knowledge, Hume's work was so radical that it implied that all knowledge of the natural world is only a probable generalization, grounded in observation to be sure, but in the last analysis based on the association of ideas, which was of a purely subjective character. Since Kant was convinced of the absolute certainty of mathematics and the principles of physics, the problem he faced was this: How can this absolute certainty be reconciled with the fact that all of our knowledge begins in sense data which seem to be discrete and atomic?

In his third, "critical" period, beginning around 1770, the time of his appointment to a full professorship, he works out a synthesis of rationalism and empiricism. It is his thought of this period which shall concern us in our discussion of Kant's position.

The Critique of Pure Reason

As was the case with Locke and Hume, the primary question for Kant is how it is possible for us to know the external world. Therefore the problem of epistemology takes first place in his philosophical work. Kant formulates his work in terms of logic; he begins with the absolutely certain knowledge which man possesses in mathematics and physics. On this foundation he constructs a new theory of the human mind and how it functions. Logically, he contends, it is possible to distinguish two types of judgment: analytic and synthetic.

In an analytic judgment the predicate is implied in the subject and the judgment is simply the explicit statement of the contents of the subject. Thus the judgment, "All bodies are extended" requires only the analysis of the subject, "body," which includes the quality of "extended being." Since it is possible to make this judgment independent of any particular empirical observation, it has universal validity. All analytic judgments, therefore, are *a priori*, that is, they are independent of empirical experience and are therefore universally and necessarily true.

Synthetic judgments are of two types. First, synthetic judgments may be generalizations based upon past experience and are, consequently, *a posteriori*. Here the predicate is not necessarily implied in the subject although it is connected to the subject in the judgment. The judgment that "all crows are black" or "all swans are white" is *a posteriori*, for these are reports from experience. Such a judgment does not preclude the possibility that an exception to these cases might be found, but because of the consistent evidence of experience the probability of truth of these statements is very high.

The second type of synthetic judgment is much more difficult to deal with, namely the *a priori* judgment. To take one of Hume's problems, Kant maintains that the judgment "Every change has a cause" is a synthetic *a priori* one; and so, also, are such mathematical judgments as "7 + 5 = 12." Judgments such as these are not dependent upon experience, for we know *a priori* that no future human experience will ever contradict them. Consequently, even though these judgments contain additional information about the subject, they are universal, necessary, and absolutely certain.

In this analysis Kant raises his most crucial question: How are synthetic *a priori* judgments possible? Can we really have universally valid synthetic knowledge prior to experience? In the first major section of the *Critique of Pure Reason*, entitled *the Transcendental Aesthetic*, Kant attempts to explore these questions and establish the status of synthetic *a priori* judgments.

Transcendental Aesthetic

Kant uses the term "aesthetic" in its classical Greek sense, meaning "to perceive," and it therefore involves a theory of sense experience. The term "transcendental" is more complex, for in Kant's usage it is closely related to the word transcendent. By a transcendent idea he means an idea referring to that which is completely beyond the limits of any possible experience. A transcendental idea goes beyond particular experiences, but at the same time expresses the universal and necessary character of experience. In other words, a transcendental idea is a fundamental form or law of experience; experience must take place according to these particular forms. At the inception of his study, then, Kant makes a critical study of perception in order to ascertain what are its *a priori* elements or its universal and necessary (transcendental) forms.

Kant begins by agreeing with Hume's belief that we cannot know the external world in a direct manner. Reality as it is in itself, the *ding an sich*, is transcendent to us and therefore remains an enigma. But there are objects of experience (phenomena) which impinge upon our minds. Hence, our experience is experience of "something," even though we can know this "something" only through sense perception as molded by our sensibilities and understanding. To state the situation tersely, we cannot know the external world as it is in

itself, but there are phenomena which press upon us and are shaped
by our minds. Consequently we can only perceive as "we" perceive;
the way in which we see the world is determined by those characteristics which are native to human perception and understanding.

In order to clarify terms and indicate the process by which one
perceives and then understands the external world, it may be of
help to use a diagram.[1]

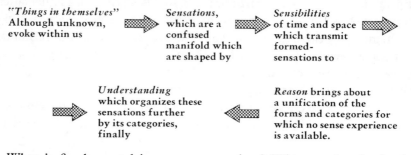

"*Things in themselves*"
Although unknown,
evoke within us

Sensations,
which are a
confused
manifold which
are shaped by

Sensibilities
of time and space
which transmit
formed-
sensations to

Understanding
which organizes these
sensations further
by its categories,
finally

Reason brings about
a unification of the
forms and categories for
which no sense experience
is available.

What is fundamental in sense perception? What are its absolutely
universal and necessary forms? Kant says that in all sense perception
we become aware of the data of sensation as being in space and time.
Consequently, all sensations are organized by the "sensibility." But
space and time are not derived from empirical observation or by
abstraction from sense perception; neither are they general concepts,
or realities apart from perception. Rather, space and time are the mental
filters through which all our experience passes, and any perception of
objects will be perception in terms of space and time.

Kant argues that space and time have *empirical reality*, meaning they
hold for all possible human experience and in this sense are real. In
addition, space and time have *transcendental ideality*, that is, they are
only ideal or subjective and do not apply to "things in themselves."

Transcendental Analytic

The order of perception which is formed by space and time makes
knowledge of a scientific character possible, but this is not to be
identified with scientific thought. To examine how scientific knowledge
is obtained, Kant develops his "Transcendental Logic." In the first
division of his logic, entitled "Transcendental Analytic," Kant replies
to Hume, maintaining that through a process of "understanding"
the field of experience is set into a context of abstract thought for
arrangement and interpretation. These judgments are purely formal,
devoid of content, but the analysis of the Table of Judgments and the

---

[1] Adapted from W. K. Wright, *A History of Modern Philosophy* (New York: Macmillan,
1941), p. 264.

Table of Schematized Categories reveals the way in which we make abstract judgments. The second division of his logic is denominated "Transcendental Dialectic" and examines the confusions common to human reason when it ventures to attain universal knowledge beyond the range of possible experience.

The fundamental problem dealt with in "Transcendental Analytic" is the possibility of a synthetic *a priori*. How are such judgments possible? For example, how can we establish cause and effect relationships? The first answer Kant provides is that the outline of the structure of the phenomenal world is grasped by intuition. Such an intuition is not limited to a particular sense, but space and time provide the background for such an experience. However, even though there may be an intuitive awareness of the structure of the phenomenal world, a more detailed structure is apprehended by the understanding. The sensibility is receptive, but the understanding is active; it shapes and utilizes that which the sensibility receives. The intelligent mind makes a meaningful apprehension of nature possible. Thus Kant claims that while synthetic *a priori* judgments have a purely mental origin, they are, nonetheless, employed in experience; and without these judgments intelligible experience would be impossible. Without this functioning of the mind there could be no knowledge at all, no connected world of experience, for experience is possible only as we are able to utilize such judgments and categories. Consequently, such judgments are *a priori*, and they are the means by which we render our perceptions intelligible. On this basis, knowledge is understood to be the application of pure concepts of the understanding, or categories, to the phenomena furnished us by the senses and perceived as spatial and temporal by the sensibility.

Discrete experiences such as the perception of fire and of heat come to us unrelated, but the mind relates these two perceptions so as to establish a cause and effect relationship, at least in the understanding. Since the mind applies its laws to nature, it follows that we can know *a priori* the universal forms of nature; we know that the perceived world will always, universally and necessarily, be connected in a cause and effect manner. At the same time, the sensibly received phenomena are essential, for the categories have no meaning except as they organize perceptions. Finally, this position means that we cannot know *a priori* the content of experience, such as what particular sensations as colors, sounds, or weight, will be given; but we can assume that any sensations will be organized according to the necessary rules of the mind. Thus, the understanding is indispensable to coherent perception of things and events. Furthermore, substance and causation constitute the outstanding features of the content so apprehended, and they are described as *categories* of understanding. By means of these categories, we are able to grasp both the present of things and events and the way in which these are related to one another.

Kant presented in some schematic detail the Table of Judgments and the Table of Categories. His delineation follows.

TABLE OF JUDGMENTS

Quantity	Quality
Universal	Affirmative
Particular	Negative
Singular	Infinite

Relation	Modality
Categorical	Problematical
Hypothetical	Assertorical
Disjunctive	Apodictic

TABLE OF SCHEMATIZED CATEGORIES

Quantity	Quality
Unity	Reality
Plurality	Negation
Totality	Limitation

Relation	Modality
Substance	Possibility and Impossibility
Causation	Existence and Nonexistence
Reciprocity	Necessity and Contingency

This table represents the way in which the process of abstract thought is carried on by the understanding apart from the sensibility. But before the judgments can be applied to experience, they must be transformed into *categories*, and the categories must be schematized. To put this another way, how can categories, which are intellectual, be applied to perceptions, which are sensible phenomena? There must be something to mediate between the pure concepts and the sense perceptions, and Kant calls this the *transcendental schema*; the utilization of such a schema he designates the *schematism of the understanding*.

As an illustration of such a schema Kant uses the time form. All of our ideas are subject to the time form, for time is the universal rule or "schema" by means of which the categories must be organized. For instance, unschematized experiences "A" appearing in time prior to "B" provide the possibility of schematizing this experience in terms of cause and effect. Such relations between two perceptions Hume could not account for psychologically, but Kant insists that a connection does exist, as physics declares, and he finds the necessary connection in the categories of the understanding.

Kant argues that unless we are aware of a phenomenal world in which substances and events are interrelated in orderly sequence, we cannot be aware of the knowing self as a unity of experience. And unless we can be aware of the self as such a unity, we cannot be aware of an objective order of phenomena. This is to say, unless we are able to recognize the continuity of our present experience with our past experience, we can speak neither of the personal identity of our minds nor of the historical identity of things in the world. As far as our knowledge is concerned, these two identities are inseparable.

The synthesis which the understanding achieves between space and time, the categories and the sensory perceptions, is not an individual or personal mental act. Rather, it is an act which is inherent in all human knowing, and is, therefore, an act upon which all experience depends. (In this sense it is objective and is universal and necessary for every human experience.) Anything which does not correspond to these requirements of the understanding cannot be a part of the phenomenal world.

Transcendental Dialectic

Going beyond his discussion of the sensibility and the understanding, Kant next considers the employment of *pure reason* in fields where there is no sensuous experience. When one attempts to apply thought to these areas he is immediately involved in what Kant calls the "dialectic" of contradictory arguments. There is a strange type of necessity about this dimension of intellectual pursuit. Namely, we are impelled to such dialectical thinking because of the tendency of our minds to find unity or to establish comprehensiveness, and even to gain acquaintance with things in themselves. Yet, at the same time, we can never gain "knowledge" by such speculation and it is a misuse of such "Ideas" to attempt spuriously to apply them to objects of experience.

Kant insists that it is impossible to use the categories to form such comprehensive Ideas of the reason, such as when we refer to the soul, the world, or God to characterize things in themselves. Nevertheless, such Ideas do have a value which he calls "regulating." Consequently, such Ideas reveal that there is a transcendent reality which is beyond experience, and that the world which natural science describes is not the ultimate reality. Positively, it can be claimed, Ideas direct the understanding to a certain goal which gives both unity and breadth to thought. Thus the Transcendental Dialectic indicates the limits of knowledge and opens the way which Kant pursues in his *Critique of Practical Reason*.

Kant is, at this point, considering the proper nature and employment of metaphysical thinking. And what he wants to point out is that metaphysics is illegitimate if it is taken to give us knowledge about matters of fact. At the same time, he also wants to defend the proper understanding of metaphysical speculation and assign it its proper role. The way in which he proceeds may be illustrated by his discussion of the Ideas of the soul, the world, and God.

In our experience we are aware of the unity of apperception, and this involves a constantly present " I." This ego or self we know only in conjunction with the objects of experience, and to attempt to think of the self as isolated from this experience is to become the victim of fundamental fallacies, or "paralogisms" as Kant designates them. Both those who attempt to prove the immortality of the soul, as though it were some type of single, unitary, and immortal substance, and those who deny the immortality of the ego or self are unjustified. Strictly speaking, we can have no knowledge about this issue. What we can say is that the Idea of the soul functions always in a regulative fashion and thus gives cohesion to our thinking about ourselves as knowing subjects.

A second Idea of reason is the world. Again, there is a persistent tendency to so isolate the material objects of our experience that we come to see them as a "world" which exists independently of our experience and as a thing in itself. But such reasoning is fallacious, Kant argues, and he exposes its inadequacy by pointing to four "antinomies" in which each of two contradictory propositions seems to be established by the refutation of the other.

The first antinomy can be posed by showing that it may be argued that the material world which exists independent of experience must either have a beginning in time and be limited in space or else have no beginning in time and no limits in space. According to Kant it is absurd to argue the first alternative, for then there must have been a time before the time of creation, and therefore there would have been an absolutely empty time in which there would have been nothing to produce the world. The second alternative is also absurd, he contends (though some modern physicists might disagree), for if there is no beginning in time and no limitation in space, then an eternity must have elapsed at the present moment and at every moment in the past; and space must be infinite in extent from every point in space. The fact of this antinomy, he believes, corroborates his position that space and time are the forms of our perception and may not be projected as characteristics of an independent world.

The second antinomy indicates that it is impossible to argue that the matter of the independently existing world is either infinitely divisible or is composed of simple, unextended parts (atoms or monads). But, he argues, any particle is at least mathematically divisible, for we cannot conceive of any particle, no matter how small, which does not have a right and left side; consequently, all matter it would seem is composite and infinitely divisible. At the same time, it would seem that every particle would still have to be composed of an infinite number of smaller parts, each of which would be absolutely simple and unextended. But if space and time are merely forms of our perception we are again talking about how we perceive and understand these objects and not about the objects in themselves.

The third antinomy may be stated in the form that either all events in the world must be mechanically determined or else that to some extent there must be freedom. If the first alternative is taken, this would imply that there is an infinite series of causes, and this, Kant argues, is unthinkable. If the second alternative is taken, this would imply either that there is no cause or that there is a cause which is itself not caused, and this also is not tenable. The point, once again, is that we cannot attribute either determinism or freedom to the objective world because we have constructed the world according to the nature of our own mind.

The final antinomy is put in this way: there may exist an absolutely necessary Being or God belonging to the world either as a part or cause of it, or there may not exist such a necessary Being. Neither conclusion can be established on the basis of our perceptual experience, and therefore they form an irreconcilable antinomy for reason. It should be noted that in his second *Critique* Kant will discuss the possibility of *postulating* both freedom and God on moral grounds, but in terms of pure or theoretical reason one cannot justify such a conclusion. And it should also be noted that the antinomies which Kant thinks are irreconcilable are not convincing for many philosophers, though they have remained valid antinomies for others. We shall see various reactions to this type of argumentation in some of the subsequent philosophers.

The third Idea of reason which Kant mentions is God. Sometimes he refers to this as the "Ideal" of the reason. This is the culminating metaphysical Idea, for in the Idea of God the first two Ideas find their common ground. But, as in the other cases, the Idea of God is simply a regulating conception which our minds logically construct, but whose actual existence as a thing in itself we can never confirm in our ex-

perience. Since we can neither appeal to our experience (the cosmological argument and the teleological or physico-theological argument)
nor move from a definition of God to his existence by logical deduction
(the ontological argument) we can only conclude that the arguments
do not establish the conclusion they intend. Again, later philosophers
will react variously to this type of argument; but Kant himself later
goes beyond the conclusion of his analysis of pure reason and will
indicate how the Idea of God may be understood as an implication of
moral awareness.

Critique of Practical Reason

In his first Critique Kant discusses scientific knowledge or our
knowledge of the world of sense perception, and in his discussion he
attempts to show the valid and invalid functions of the pure reason.
In his second *Critique* he continues his analysis of human knowing by
investigating our moral knowledge. It should be clear that for Kant this
is also "knowledge," though of a different type than scientific knowledge; therefore it has its own legitimacy. Indeed, in his preface to the
second *Critique* he indicates that practical or moral reason is to be
given primacy over scientific knowledge. In any case, we are still
dealing with valid knowledge and not with faith or belief. Kant's
discussion of this subject may also be found in his book *Fundamental
Principles of the Metaphysics of Morals*.

Professor C. D. Broad has drawn together the emphases in Kant's
moral reason in a clear fashion (*Five Types of Ethical Theory*, pp. 117 f).
Kant is endeavoring to discover an *a priori* principle which ought to
govern the will and thereby place ethics upon an absolutely certain
foundation. Kant begins his argument by asserting that there is nothing
intrinsically good but a good will. A good will is one which knows
what duty is and which acts dutifully. It should be clear that to "will"
is not merely to desire; it is to decide upon a course of action. In
other words, a good will is one which habitually decides rightly.
The rightness or wrongness of a volition depends wholly on the nature
of its motive; consequently, if the motive is right the volition is right
also. But what is the criterion for the rightness of a motive? A right
motive, it is contended, is one which is in accord with some accepted
general principle. But what is the right kind of an accepted general
principle? The answer is that a categorical imperative is this type of
principle (a categorical imperative is to be distinguished from a hypothetical general principle, which is a principle of conduct not accepted
on its own merits but rather regarded as an extrinsic rule which enables

one to gain some desired end). This categorical principle must be formal, that is, it must be a rule such that anyone who accepts it can consistently desire that everyone else make it the principle of their conduct and act upon it.

Every man is aware of this moral demand, Kant maintains, and he formulates this categorical imperative in three different ways. First, "Act solely on that principle which you would be willing might become universal law of nature on which every other person would also always act." Illustrations which Kant uses to make this clear are those of suicide or refusal to pay a loan; both of these are wrong because to universalize them would be a formal self-contradiction. Second, "Treat every human being, including yourself, as an end in himself and not as a means to the advantage of anyone else." And, third, one should always act as if one were a member of an ideal "kingdom of ends" in which everyone would be at the same time sovereign and subject. As a member of such a kingdom of ends every individual would act in accordance with the categorical imperative, and this means that he would act in a manner which is in accord with the rational consensus of his fellow citizens.

On the basis of this analysis of the moral conscience, Kant now proceeds to argue that while no positive proofs can be given, it is possible to postulate as implications of this moral conscience the reality of God, freedom, and immortality. Consequently, while pure reason ends in antinomies in spite of its drive for comprehensiveness, the practical reason can affirm these postulates.

Freedom is implied in the fact that the oughtness of the moral imperative implies that man is able to respond obediently. However, no man does his duty with perfection in this life; nevertheless, one should in some sense be able to do what is categorically demanded of him. If ought implies can, then there must be some freedom for obedience. Further, the complete good would be complete obedience to duty and happiness in doing that duty. At the same time, in the ordinary mortal lifespan man is not completely free, completely virtuous, or completely happy. Yet, once again, he ought to be all three. Indeed, the closer one comes to fulfilling his duty in this life, the more extensive he recognizes his duty to be. The more one develops his abilities, the more he increases his capacities and the more responsible he is for utilizing these abilities in accordance with the categorical imperative. Only an infinite time (immortality) would insure that one is able to continue to gain competence and fulfil its consequent responsibilities. Consequently, if this ought has any rational meaning at all, then it must imply that there is sufficient time for the achievement of this supreme good. On the basis of this ought one can postulate immortality as well as freedom; and finally, one can also postulate God as the one who provides freedom and provides for the actualization of this freedom in virtue and happiness. The reality of God is postulated, according to Kant, because in this life we find that happiness does not automatically follow the fulfillment of duty. Thus, there can be an assurance of the coincidence of these two only if we can also postulate a just Judge who ultimately rewards the virtuous and punishes the wicked. Because the postulate of God insures the appropriate award for obedience to duty it seems to Kant to be reasonable. To act rationally, therefore, is to act *as if* there were a God, *as if* man was an immortal soul, *as if* man was free and morally responsible for his choices. In this sense, reason tells us how we ought to behave and what reality ought to be like.

Philosophy of Religion

Kant's ethical theory and philosophy of religion are closely related. The moral conscience has religious implications. As we have seen, belief in God and belief in immortality were regarded by Kant as postulates of morality. In his book, *Religion Within the Limits of Reason Alone*, published in 1793, we have an interpretation of central Christian beliefs from the perspective of his own philosophical position. As a philosopher of religion, Kant wants to explore the meaning of religion as an advocate of human reason, as one who intends to assess religion as a cultural manifestation and as a phenomenon of reason. He does not intend to imply that religion exists solely within the limits of reason; but he does argue that it is of value to see what may be discovered about religion by looking at it through rational categories. By a contemplation of religion within the limits of reason, he means to look at this phenomenon in terms of practical or moral reason. Consequently, his first contention is that religion is the attitude of acceptance of all of our duties as divine commandments. To say this is not to discuss the nature of God, or the metaphysical content of religious ideas, but solely to analyze the way in which the practical reason speaks of religion and what it says.

In his discussion, Kant holds that morality leads ineluctably to religion, through which it extends itself to the idea of a powerful, moral Lawgiver. The will of this Sovereign sets the final end of creation and this ought, at the same time, to be man's final end. The proposition that one should make the highest good in the world one's own final end is a synthetic *a priori* proposition which is introduced by the moral law itself. In order to pursue his investigation of the moral law, Kant begins by an analysis of human nature. He chooses to discuss the categories of sin and atonement, doctrines which held little interest for most philosophers of Enlightenment.

Every man is recipient of the demands of the categorical imperative, but he remains free to obey or deny this demand. The source of obedience or disobedience, Kant maintains, is found in the will and in the use it makes of its freedom. We cannot probe deeply enough to establish the ultimate grounds for these choices, but we can refer to these dispositions as a property of the will belonging to it by nature.

In every person there is to be found an original predisposition to good as well as a propensity to evil. The predisposition to good is the more basic of these inclinations and is an ingredient in the life of every man. The propensity to evil may be regarded as having been acquired. Consequently, when one actualizes a propensity he must accept responsibility for so doing; he cannot excuse himself on the grounds that his action was necessary. In other words, Kant sees human life as being lived in the tension between man's original predisposition to good and his propensity to evil. Man's moral character is structured precisely by the use of his freedom as he meets these contrary claims.

Following an analysis of the biblical account of man's fall, Kant concludes that men do habitually adopt the maxim of self-love, rather than moral law, as the primary guide to action. This evil, he claims, is "radical" because it corrupts the ground of all maxims and therefore becomes a pervasive inclination to reverse the moral order. Why man tends to respond in this manner is rationally inscrutable, but Kant does take this to be a true description of man's nature.

On the other hand, he also maintains that since man is responsible for this misorientation, and since he still is aware of the ought of the categorical imperative, man has the ability to reverse the direction of his will and adopt the good maxim. Throughout this discussion it is assumed that there is still a seed of goodness which remains in man and that this "seed" may be brought to fruition by man's acquiring new habits of obedience to the highest maxim. While it seems to be most difficult to bring about such a revolution, it must be remembered that duty demands this, and duty demands nothing we cannot do. Such a redirection of the will is not undertaken for any utilitarian purpose, such as winning favors from God. Quite the contrary, religion is moral when man is obedient to duty because it is his duty.

Jesus is taken to be the archetype of the moral disposition in man; Jesus is the guide and example of what every man ought to be. But we cannot on rational-moral grounds speak about his nature as it is in itself. Thus, while religion does tend to distinguish Jesus from other men, this is rationally valid only in so far as he serves as the prime example for our own activity and obedience. Kant does at times speak as though there is a kind of indirect equation of divine justification with the event of the good will and man may attribute his change of will in part to divine assistance. But he always insists that each man must do as much as is in his power to become a better man, and the possibility for this resides fundamentally in his ability to follow his original predisposition to good.

The Critique of Judgment

Kant's third major section of his theory of knowledge deals with aesthetic teleological knowledge; the over-all title of this study is *The Critique of Judgment*. In the critique of aesthetic judgment, he examines the feelings of beauty and the sublime. Once again Kant begins with the attempt to ascertain the *a priori* element in this judgment. He recognizes that it is impossible to establish absolute standards for beauty and that no criterion such as the categorical imperative can be invoked. Consequently, he appeals to a feeling which he argues is disinterested, which is to say it is not a matter of selfish or individual interest. The most characteristic response to beauty is that of release to the object; there is a feeling of harmony in our mental processes which has no further end beyond the aesthetic enjoyment of the contemplated object. We do not seek to gain some advantage by the contemplation of beauty nor do we ask what our duty is in regard to beauty; rather there is a submission to the harmony it evokes and an enjoyment of its intrinsic qualities.

Our response to the sublime is one of wonder and awe. The awareness of the immensity of structures and of the seeming unmeasurableness of the mathematically sublime are examples of this experience. But there is also the dynamically sublime which is found in nature when we view its power as seen in an ocean storm or a volcanic eruption. In each of these experiences something unique is intimated. In the mathematically sublime the limitations of our categories of understanding are made evident, and in the dynamically sublime the superiority of our moral worth over nature is revealed. Consequently, in all such experiences we feel ourselves to be much greater than the world of experience which our understanding has made.

In this final critique Kant attempts to push the range of rational experience to its most comprehensive and most humane dimensions. He closes by showing the inadequacy of the mechanistic view of nature, especially when it is applied to living organisms, and argues for the purposefulness of life. In every living being there is a purpose which is manifest in the mutual interdependence and teleology of each part in relation to the whole and of the whole to each part. While this is uniquely true of living organisms, Kant suggests that it may also be postulated of nature as a whole. This, of course, cannot be proven in an apodictic fashion, we cannot, in terms of pure reason, "know" this. But the experience of beauty and sublimity as well as the idea of purposefulness do suggest that the world may be the production of an infinite Artist, and it is reasonable to postulate this possibility.

In surveying the work of Immanuel Kant, one cannot help but be impressed. Using almost any reasonable criterion, he must be judged as one of the very greatest philosophers. Whether one evaluates him in terms of the originality, strength, and range of his thought or in terms of his influence upon subsequent thinkers, he stands among the most significant philosophers in western civilization. He set the course for recent and contemporary philosophical discussion as has no other thinker.

Following upon his initiation, German philosophy came to its most abundant flowering. Fichte, Schelling, and Hegel followed in close order and together with Kant they established the German philosophical tradition as the pathfinder in philosophical exploration, as well as the impetus for many of the most impressive philosophical constructions. Even beyond these successors, the long reach of his thought has provoked renewal and fresh reflection. Consequently, the full impact of Kant cannot yet be ascertained, for it continues as a living influence.

Immanuel Kant: Suggested Additional Reading

Abernethy, George L. and Thomas A. Langford, eds., *History of Philosophy: Selected Readings*. Belmont, Calif.: Dickenson, 1965, pp. 491–528.*

Beck, Lewis W., *Studies in the Philosophy of Kant*. Indianapolis: Bobbs-Merrill, 1965.*

Beck, Lewis W., *Commentary on Kant's Critique of Practical Reason*. Chicago: University of Chicago paperback, 1960.

Duncan, Alistair R. C., *Practical Reason and Morality*. New York: Thomas Nelson and Sons, 1957.*

Ewing, A. C., *A Short Commentary on Kant's Critique of Pure Reason*. Chicago: University of Chicago, Phoenix Books, 1950.

Heidegger, Martin, *Kant and the Problem of Metaphysics*. Translated by J. S. Churchill. Bloomington, Ill.: University of Illinois Press, 1962.*

Jones, William T., *Morality and Freedom in the Philosophy of Immanuel Kant*. London: Oxford University Press, 1940.*

Kant, *The Critique of Pure Reason*. Translated by Norman Kemp Smith. New York: St. Martin's Press, 1963.

Kant, *Critique of Practical Reason*. Edited and translated by Lewis W. Beck. Indianapolis: Bobbs-Merrill, Liberal Arts Press, 1956.

Kant, *Critique of Judgment*. Translated by J. H. Bernard. New York: Hafner, 1951.

Kant, *Perpetual Peace*. Translated by L. W. Beck. Indianapolis: Bobbs-Merrill, Liberal Arts Press, 1957.

Kant, *Religion within the Limits of Reason Alone*. Translated by T. M. Greene and H. H. Hudson. New York: Harper Torchbook, 1960.

Kaufmann, Walter, *Philosophic Classics*. Englewood Cliffs, N.J.: Prentice-Hall, 1961, II, 415–584.*

Kemp, J., *The Philosophy of Kant*. New York: Oxford University Press, 1968.

Körner, S., *Kant*. Baltimore: Penguin, 1955.

Lindsay, A. D., *Kant*. London: E. Benn, 1944.*

Paton, Herbert J., *Categorical Imperative: A Study in Kant's Moral Philosophy*. New York: Harper and Row, Torchbook, 1967.

Scott-Taggert, M. J., "Recent Work on the Philosophy of Kant," *American Philosophical Quarterly*, 3 (1966), pp. 171 f.

Smith, Norman Kemp, *A Commentary to Kant's Critique of Pure Reason*. Second edition, revised and enlarged. New York: Humanites Press, 1962.*

Teale, A. E., *Kantian Ethics*. London: Oxford University Press, 1951.*

Wolff, Robert P., ed., *Kant—A Collection of Critical Essays*. Garden City: Doubleday, Anchor, 1967.

Chapter Twenty

Fichte and Schelling

Fichte

Johann Gottlieb Fichte (1762–1814) was born at Rammenau in Saxony. The son of a poor peasant weaver, he earned money as a child herding geese. A local nobleman who had missed the Sunday sermon was referred to the young gooseherd, who repeated it to him verbatim. Visibly impressed, the nobleman undertook to arrange for the young Fichte's education. He studied first theology and philosophy in Leipzig and Vienna, and at the age of sixteen went to Zurich where be became a private tutor. In the course of tutoring a student in the philosophy of Kant, Fichte experienced something of a philosophical conversion to the moral philosophy of duty. In 1791 he met Kant, then an old man, who was not at first particularly impressed by Fichte. The next year Fichte published his *Essay on the Critique of All Revelation* in which Kant showed some friendly interest. Through some slip, the author's name failed to appear on the published book. Many mistakenly attributed the book to Kant, who immediately set the record straight and thus assured Fichte's fame in philosophical circles. As a result, Fichte in 1794 was named professor of philosophy at Jena to be the successor to Reinhold. He proved to be a brilliant lecturer and a productive scholar, but his radical criticisms of theology provoked charges of atheism from clerics and his moral rigorism annoyed easy-going students and colleagues. In 1795 he was summarily dismissed from his position. He then moved to Berlin, where he was associated with Romantic writers, including Schleiermacher and the Schlegel brothers. During the Napoleonic occupation, Fichte's moral idealism led him to fulfill the role of public orator and popular essayist in seeking to arouse the German people to spiritual self-affirmation in his famed *Addresses to the German People*. In this period he taught briefly at Erlangen and Koenigsberg, and finally became a professor and the first Rector at the new university in Berlin. In 1814, at the age of 52, he died of a virulent hospital fever, possibly typhus, which he caught from his wife, who had been nursing wounded soldiers.

Fichte's writing was extensive. His chief technical works were basically a series of increasingly subtle elaborations of his *Science of Knowl-*

edge (Wissenschaftslehre). His moral idealism and his lively and expressive literary style are most evident in such works as *The Vocation of Man, The Vocation of the Scholar, Way to a Blessed Life, Characteristics of the Present Age,* and *Addresses to the German Nation.*

Fichte began his philosophical career as a devoted disciple of Kant, having found the Kantian primacy of practical reason decisive for both metaphysics and ethics. When Mme. de Staël asked him for a brief exposition of his philosophy, he is reported to have told her: "Grasp my metaphysics, Madame; you will then understand my ethics." Yet the specific emphases to which Fichte was led came out of his own situation rather than that of Kant. For Kant, the basic problem was doing one's duty, which was obvious to every man of sound reason. In a period of cultural confusion, Fichte's generation had the problem of finding or creating some new meaning for human experience. It is not surprising that Fichte and his generation did concentrate on the relations of the Self to the world and to other selves in the effort to formulate a meaningful connection between the Self and the apparently alien "Not-Self."

At the beginning Fichte was confronted by a fundamental dualism in philosophical thinking. One group of philosophers emphasized the external world composed of substances, mental or material, bound together by necessity, from which our knowledge of ultimate reality is supposed to derive. This view Fichte calls dogmatism. To it he opposes idealism, which recognizes the primacy of the activity of consciousness and the real value of the individual. Thus idealism is a source of freedom, for it insists that nature is contingent and teleological. Which philosophical orientation should a man choose? A choice involves an act of faith, but Fichte insists the choice of idealism is rationally justified, for we know our own inner experience better than the external world and in moral striving we gain an insight into the noumenal world or ultimate reality. If we begin with mechanical necessity, we make human nature unintelligible; if we start with consciousness and our moral ideals, we impart meaning to that within which our action occurs. "The kind of philosophy which one adopts," he maintains, "depends upon the sort of man one is, for a philosophical system is not a lifeless piece of furniture that one might take or discard . . . but it is animated by soul of the man who has it" (*Werke,* Vol. I, p. 434). If a man is a free, moral, sensitive person pursuing his ultimate interests, there is no doubt that he will choose the idealistic faith. In choosing his philosophy a man makes his character manifest in thinking and doing, for the moral law governs the will and the thinking mind. A man can become truly free only by obeying the moral law and the dictate of moral reason.

St. Augustine and Descartes began with the indubitable act of thinking and the implied reality of the thinking self. Fichte begins in his *Foundation of the Entire Science of Knowledge* (1794) with the effort to deduce all experience from the undifferentiated primary-ultimate activity. It is not a *thing-in-itself*, not a process distinguishable from others. It is the basic principle of active self-affirmation which is the foundation of all reality. For Fichte, "I am," "I act," "The Ego posits itself as acting" all have essentially the same meaning.

Fichte begins his dialectic with the assertion, "The Self posits itself as infinite activity." The absolute and infinite activity evokes and sets for itself a field of operation in which it is to act. This Fichte states as a second principle or antithesis, "The Self posits a Not-Self"; thus opposition to a Self or Subject characterizes the essence of all objects. The Self has, then, bound itself by its reciprocal relation to the Not-Self. Hence, Fichte's third principle: "The Self posits a limited self in opposition to a limited not-self." Here we have the familiar conscious self of everyday empirical knowledge.

The question naturally arises as to why self-opposition arises in the infinite activity and later as to how it gets itself a world. Fichte argues that there is no higher reason by which we can demonstrate logically that the Absolute Self posits or negates itself, and hence there is no theoretical answer to such questions. There is only the answer of practical reason. In immediate intuition we perceive that striving is the essence of practical reason. An independent Self that is to strive and conquer must create a world of objects that can be known by theoretical reason if it is to have a Not-Self. The will, in its struggling and unceasing pursuit, is the ideal; it reveals its own limited nature as an empirical self, and also, in activity in accord with duty, reveals its essential unity with the infinite Self. In the course of time Fichte gave this an increasingly religious interpretation, until late in his career he reached a form of Christian Platonism in which the perfect will transcends freedom and attains union with God.

Fichte's philosophy gives metaphysical emphasis to Kant's doctrine of the primacy of practical reason. In it the Kantian postulates become facts. Freedom, immortality of the soul, and the existence of God are the metaphysical foundations which make comprehensible man's status in the universe. Man's true vocation is to attain in increasing freedom an expanding loyal devotion to spiritual ideals. The duty to which I am devoted is my duty. The effort to fulfill it reveals my true being and destiny. Yet Fichte's concern is not a narrow one. It is not merely personal and private. Although he assumes a political role, he does not equate freedom with politics. It has basically a moral quality and involves a genuine religious commitment to striving for the good of mankind. Individuality and freedom are necessary for the achievement of self-consciousness, but they can be attained only when men cooperate for the same basic ends. Thus moral freedom is a social enterprise in which men cooperate to provide the ends and means to further cooperation for the welfare of all. Fichte, in maintaining that duties and rights are fundamentally social, moves beyond Kant's moral individualism and the Enlightenment's economic and political version of it.

In Fichte's moral philosophy continuous striving is virtuous, while laziness and complacency are the roots of evil, which often manifests itself as falseness. Fichte places himself squarely on the side of truth-telling: "I positively owe every man absolute frankness and truthfulness." Nature always limits man, but nature's obstacles provide the challenges for moral striving, the conquering of evils, and the movement to higher spiritual levels. This is our career as moral beings; in which we discover and recognize what we were meant to be. It should be noted that sheer activity is the highest activity only if it is actually an activity of the Self. All action determined from within through desire for a specific object, or from some need or impulse, is not genuine activity, but mere passivity and bondage. Only action that arises from the duty and free expression of the Self is really activity. The truly free man, then, acts not from specific wants or desires, but for the sake of acting and creating—ultimate self-affirmation. One is not to disavow his duty as beyond ability. Rather, "If I ought, I can."

Fichte's religious views underwent considerable modification and development during his career. Early in his thought he claimed that the moral order was God. The "living and operative moral order is itself God. We need no other God, and we cannot conceive any other." He was unable to describe God as personal, for personality implied to him finiteness. In response to his critics, Fichte asserted that God is a living and active moral order, not just something constructed by man. It is a moral world-order which fulfills itself in and through rational beings and unites them in itself.

With the appearance of *The Vocation of Man* (1800) Fichte's religious views took a new turn. The moral order appears as the eternal and infinite will which "finds me in union with all finite beings like myself and is the common mediator between us all." Thus he fuses the idea of doing one's duty and fulfilling his moral vocation with the spirit of devout commitment to and trust in the divine will. This remains a question of practical moral faith rather than of knowledge.

In *The Way to the Blessed Life or The Doctrine of Religion* (1806) he presents a fuller working out of his religious speculations in which he comes to terms with Christian Platonism and the Johannine Gospel. Here he recognizes in the Logos the timeless image of God mani- festing itself in the human consciousness as the living incarnation of the Divine in the human. Love is the heart of life. Man may either follow the love of the finite and changeable directed toward the grati- fication of natural impulses, or he can rise to true life and love the infinite and eternal which is "the innermost root of all finite existence." The Self seeks its own source; it seeks the awareness of its reality in God. On the level of rational morality in which the Self knows its duties, it becomes conscious of its own nature. In creative moral acts in which it undertakes to subdue the sense perceptions for moral purposes, the Self finds communion with mankind in the active love of man for others. At a still higher level beyond freedom and striving lies the sacrifice of freedom in unity with the Divine will. This immedi- ate awareness of union is supplemented by the knowledge that God is the one true reality and that the infinite divine life is immanent in man. Obviously he cannot take the path of traditional theism. He re- jects the view that God created the world out of nothing, insisting that we are only modes of God's eternal order, for our life is His, our finite reason only exists in and through the Absolute Reason, our strength is His strength, our moral will is His. God's true nature is love which transcends all our rational predications. It is our destiny to enact the eternal in our finite existence and thus to realize our immor- tality. In this view man works for human betterment by seeking to con- trol nature for moral ends and to unite fellow selves in brotherly love and cooperation. Power, happiness, peace, and quiet are the goals of life. Striving is its own reward, and one who loses his desires in the great movement of the divine will truly finds his life. When one achieves union with God, he will know the peace that passeth understanding.

Fichte pressed beyond the limitations Kant had placed on human knowledge. He prepared the way for Hegel's rationalism and dia- lectic. His later writings anticipated much that appeared in Schopen- hauer's work. The anti-rationalistic and mystical elements, which accompanied Fichte's rationalism, influenced Romantic writers like the two Schlegels, Tieck and Novalis. His stirring, patriotic appeals for German national unity and for a state based on equality and justice commanded wide popular interest. His emphases on action, will, and moral purpose were prophetic.

Schelling

Although his influence has waned in the twentieth century, Schelling (1775–1854) was the leader of the German Romantic Movement and a man with considerable impact in the nineteenth century. Among his fellow Romanticists were the literary historian Tieck, the poets Hölderin and Novalis, the theologian Schleiermacher, and the Schlegel brothers, the translators of Shakespeare. Their interests were predominantly literary, so they stressed not so much moral freedom as aesthetic freedom and artistic creation. In this movement Schelling played an important role.

Friedrich Wilhelm Joseph von Schelling, son of an erudite Lutheran pastor, was born in Württemberg in 1775. He was precocious and at 15 was admitted to theological studies at the University of Tübingen. Here he became a friend of Hegel and Hölderin, who were five years his senior. At 17 he published a dissertation which he soon followed with essays. In 1795 he published his first book, *On the Ego as a Principle of Philosophy*, as a disciple of Fichte. Kant, Spinoza, Boehme, and the Neoplatonic writers were to influence his subsequent writings. From 1803 to 1806 Schelling was a professor at the new university of Würzburg. In 1806 he moved to Munich where he held a number of government appointments which did not interfere with his lecturing at Stuttgart and Erlangen. In 1807 Hegel, Schelling's friend of earlier years, published his first important work, *The Phenomenology of Spirit*. This work marked the first step in Hegel's rise to philosophical fame and his rejection of Schelling's doctrine of the Absolute. This was a bitter pill for Schelling to swallow, and his resentment of it contributed to the diminution of his interest in publishing. Ten years after Hegel's death in 1831 Frederick William IV appointed Schelling to the chair of philosophy at the University of Berlin to combat the views of the left-wing Hegelians. Although many distinguished men attended, his lectures were not very successful. In 1846 he gave up lecturing, except for occasional appearances at the Berlin Academy. He died in 1854 in Switzerland. Subsequently his lectures were published as the *Philosophy of Revelation* and the *Philosophy of Mythology*.

There is in Schelling no single system of philosophy which we can label Schelling's system. He was engaged in a process of philosophizing in which both continuities and discontinuities are apparent. Historians of philosophy have disagreed as to the precise number of stages or phases which should be delineated in his development. It is convenient to note stages, but these should not be interpreted as discrete or independent systems. His philosophizing ranged from the ego-philosophy of Fichte through the philosophy of Nature and art, the philosophy of the religious consciousness, and a version of speculative theism, all bound together by his concern with the relation between the finite and the infinite.

Schelling began as a disciple of Fichte, but soon became dissatisfied with the reduced, and even ignored, status of Nature in Fichte's system and was led to protest the sacrifice of Nature to ethics. He insisted that Nature has value in its own right regardless of man's moral good. In fact, Nature is a form of the same activity whose purest expression is the human self. Nature is not simply a passive limit to the activities of the ego, but contains within herself an activity of self-limitation, resembling the self-limitation found in self-consciousness. This activity is controlled by a fundamental law of polarity, revealed in a conflict between the forces of attraction and repulsion and the consequent equilibrium. As attraction, Nature is objective and material; as repulsion, it is subjective, ego, and spirit. Schelling not only overcomes the Cartesian dualism; he also overcomes the division between the organic and inorganic, between mechanism and vitalism by an organic conception of physics in which all natural phenomena are instances of the same basic kind of structure. In this view Nature is seen as a living universal organism endowed with a creative organizing principle or world soul, as Plato taught.

In his *System of Transcendental Idealism* (1800), Schelling employs Kantian and Fichtean perspectives to present his philosophy of consciousness. In order to obtain the world of objects from the world of the ego, consciousness is directed on itself as the only object of which we have immediate knowledge. When we abstract from all objects of knowledge, internal or external, we experience the pure activity of abstracting, which is pure self-activity. Viewed in this way, the consciousness of the not-self is the limit of self-activity. Building on this, Schelling offers an interpretation of three stages in knowledge. He sees knowledge advancing from sensation to perception, from perception to reflection, and from reflection to will. All sensation involves the feeling of one's self as limited. Hence we become aware of the force (gravity) of the consciousness of the real objective world in space, and of intensity, or the immediate consciousness of the self and its own activity in time. Reflection comes from the perception of the external world, and will comes from reflection on the internal world.

For Schelling, the self is not simply one of the objects of knowledge, but the condition of all knowledge. Since the ultimate nature of the self is pure self-activity, knowledge finally depends upon willing, which is the action of the self.

Moving from the theoretical to the practical, Schelling offers a philosophy of history, for self-determination can be achieved only through concrete action in the world. He deduces the system of rights and the state as conditions for moral action. He views history as both the expression of human liberty and the progressive revelation of God. Liberty is possible only under law providing for a harmonious realization of freedom by many individuals through the recognition of mutual rights. The goal of history is the steady realization of human freedom under a world constitution. Only under such a constitution can a stable and moral political order, or second Nature, be achieved to overcome the unpredictable and selfish wills of individual states. But man can move in the direction of such a world order only to the extent that there is an identity between man's free acts and the workings of a higher spirit, a Fate or Providence operating in history that necessarily brings them to pass. This absolute unity between freedom and necessity in an unconscious intelligence lies beyond the reach of human knowledge and is always the object of faith. Thus the totality of history is the continuing revelation of God and our evidence for His existence. There is a sense in which men are not only the actors, but also the playwrights in the drama of history even when they are not fully aware of what motivates their work.

Schelling provides one bridge over the gap between Nature and Spirit by his use of the unconscious intelligence operating in history. But in the third part of his system of transcendental philosophy he moves beyond Fichte and shifts his emphasis from the moral life to artistic creation, from action for its own sake to aesthetic contemplation. Leaning heavily on Kant's *Critique of Judgment*, Schelling declares that in artistic creation the Self reveals a more basic activity of the Self than in knowledge or will—that of the Absolute becoming finally aware of itself as productive activity. Here we see the ultimate reason for all existence in man's conscious creation of beauty. Thus in the artistic attitude the philosopher finds the metaphysical synthesis of necessity and freedom, the real and ideal, nature and thought, the conscious and the unconscious. "The Self is conscious in its production, unconscious in its product." The true art work or product is unconscious and infinite, so that the artist never completely understands his work. In such a view, the purpose of art is not to be understood as utility, pleasure, knowledge, or morality; rather it is beauty or the realization of the infinite in the finite. This finite incarnation of the infinite is a combination of free activity and the unlimited resources of Nature.

Both in his system of transcendental philosophy and in his *Philosophy of Art* (1804) Schelling follows the aesthetic theories of Friedrich Schlegel in proclaiming the artist as the inspired revealer of God and art itself as the eternal Idea itself grasped and made vivid in imagination. This does not make the artist a philosopher, since he lacks theoretical understanding of his work. But the artist feels in artistic intuition the meaning of the whole universe working in and through his own artistic creation. In the decades that followed such theories stimulated the development of many other aesthetic theories.

In his works *Exposition of My System of Philosophy* (1801), *Bruno* (1802), and *Lectures on the Method of Academic Study* (1803) Schelling reveals the influence of Spinoza and Neoplatonism on his thought. In fact, his exposition was written in a geometrical form. "The standpoint of philosophy is the standpoint of reason." Philosophical knowledge is a "knowledge of things as they are in themselves, that is, as they are in Reason." Philosophy, then, is a knowledge of the relations between things and the Absolute, or between the finite and the infinite. The Absolute is to be thought of as pure identity or indifference (the lack of difference) to the distinction between subjective and objective. There is no subject, no object, no time, no space in reason. Subject and object deal only with form and are indifferent to essence. Schelling believes that his theory of identity enabled him to overcome the dispute between realism and idealism and the difficulties in the derivation of the Many from the One, but his critics are not satisfied. Hegel refers to this phase of Schelling's thought in his famous quip about Schelling's Absolute as "the night in which . . . all cows are black."

In the lectures of his final period, posthumously published as the *Philosophy of Revelation* and the *Philosophy of Mythology*, Schelling still maintains the rationalism of his philosophy of Identity. But he continues to insist that from ideas we can deduce only ideas and to emphasize the distinction between negative philosophy, which is limited to the world of concepts and essences, and positive philosophy, which stresses existence. Positive philosophy does not begin merely with God as Idea, as a what or essence, but with God "as a pure that" in an existential sense. Schelling takes pains to assert that God is not an impersonal Idea but a creative personal being, the Lord of creation. He asserts that in the religions of mankind there can be discovered an immediate self-manifestation of the essence of existence, in divine revelation. The myths of religion, primitive or sophisticated, are not to be explained rationally as Hegel attempted, but interpreted as answers to the ultimate problems rational thought cannot solve. The religious man demands a God who reveals Himself and brings about man's redemption. Thus Schelling's empirical studies in the history of mythology and revelation seek to show God's progressive self-revelation to man and the progressive work of divine redemption. Reason cannot cross the gulf between the universal and the particular, the possible and the actual, without the help of more concrete experience. Schelling's religious views are interesting and complex but cannot be easily summarized here. They reveal his eagerness to persist in the search for truth and his willingness to re-examine older positions in the effort to achieve syntheses. They have aroused some interest among existentialists in the twentieth century; and have greatly influenced the thought of the twentieth-century theologian Paul Tillich.

Fichte and Schelling: Suggested Additional Reading

Adamson, Robert, *Fichte*. London: William Blackwood & Sons, 1881.*

Copleston, Frederick C., *A History of Philosophy*, Vol. 7, Part I: Fichte to Hegel. Garden City: Doubleday, Image, 1965.

Fackenheim, Emil L., "Schelling's Philosophy of Religion," *University of Toronto Quarterly*, Vol. XXII (1952), pp. 1–17.

Fichte, *Addresses to the German Nation*. Edited by George Kelly. New York: Harper Torchbook, 1968.

Fichte, *The Popular Works of Johann Gottlieb Fichte*. Translated by William Smith. London: Trübner, 1889.*

Fichte, *The Science of Ethics as Based on the Science of Knowledge*. Translated by A. E. Kroeger. New York: Appleton, 1897.*

Fichte, *The Science of Rights*. Translated by A. E. Kroeger. London: Trübner, 1889.*

Fichte, *The Vocation of Man*. Translated by William Smith. La Salle, Ill.: Open Court, 1965.

Fichte, *The Way towards the Blessed Life: Or the Doctrine of Religion*. Translated by William Smith. London: J. Chapman, 1849.*

Gray-Smith, Rowland, *God in the Philosophy of Schelling*. Philadelphia: University of Pennsylvania, 1933.*

Hayner, Paul C., *Reason and Existence: Schelling's Philosophy of History*. Leiden: E. J. Brill, 1967.*

Hirsch, Eric D., *Wordsworth and Schelling*. New Haven: Yale University Press, 1960.*

Schelling, *The Ages of the World*. Translated by F. de W. Bolman, Jr. New York: Columbia University Press, 1942.*

Schelling, *Schelling: Of Human Freedom*. Translated by James Gutmann. La Salle, Ill.: Open Court, 1936.

Stein, R. W., *The Doctrine of God in the Philosophy of Fichte*. Philadelphia: University of Pennsylvania, 1945.*

Watson, John, *Schelling's Transcendental Idealism*. Chicago: S. C. Griggs, 1882.*

Chapter Twenty-One

Hegel

Georg Wilhelm Friedrich Hegel (1770–1831), the greatest of the German idealist philosophers and one of the most influential philosophers of the modern world, was born into the home of a minor civil servant in Stuttgart in southern Germany. He was reared in the atmosphere of eighteenth-century rationalism, steeped in the Enlightenment, and developed a genuine enthusiasm for Greek thought. In 1788 he entered the Protestant theological seminary at the University of Tübingen, where he became a friend of the younger Schelling and the poet Hölderin. He soon became a religious radical and an advocate of higher criticism of the Bible while studying Rousseau with his new friends and sharing their enthusiasm for the ideals of the French Revolution. As a student, Hegel did not demonstrate unusual ability. After his graduation in 1793, he took up residence as a tutor in an aristocratic family in Berne. He moved on in 1796 to Frankfurt where he accepted a similar post.

In 1801 Hegel became an instructor at the University of Jena and published his first book, *The Difference between the Philosophical Systems of Fichte and Schelling*, which strengthened the impression that Hegel was a disciple of Schelling. In the following year he assisted Schelling in editing the *Critical Journal of Philosophy*. But Hegel was already reaching for a new position which the subsequent publication (1807) of his major work, *The Phenomenology of Spirit*, made clear to Schelling's profound disappointment. The battle of Jena abruptly closed the University, leaving Hegel practically destitute. He then edited a newspaper at Bamberg for two years, after which he became the rector or headmaster of a *Gymnasium* in Nuremberg for six years. In his spare time he continued to work on his most elaborate treatise, the *Science of Logic* (1812–1816). In 1816 he was appointed to a professorship at Heidelberg, where he soon published his *Encyclopedia of the Philosophical Sciences in Outline*, the work in which he presented his philosophy in the triad of logic, philosophy of nature, and philosophy of mind. In 1818 Hegel was called to the University of Berlin to fill the chair left vacant since the death of Fichte. He published his *Out-*

lines of the Philosophy of Right in 1821. In his years at Berlin he gave an extended series of lectures on fine arts, history, and religion, which were published posthumously; they run to more than a dozen volumes in English translation. Hegel was the dominant figure in German philosophical thought until his death in 1831 during a cholera epidemic.

Hegel is quite a different personality from his immediate predecessors. He does not possess the evangelical urge to make converts like Fichte, nor does he lose himself in the enthusiasms of Schelling and his fellow Romanticists. The impression he gives is one of great objectivity—a real concern for dispassionate and logical understanding of the universe. Even when he deals with the expressions of the emotional in life, his approach is coolly analytic and detached in description. He is a thoroughgoing rationalist with exemplary qualities; he is painstaking, methodical, and conscientious. He reacts negatively to appeals to feelings and mystical intuitions in the writings of others. The rational expressed in systematic and conceptual form is his ideal, for he believes the real to be rational and the rational real. On many occasions he indulges his love of paradoxes and seeks in one way or another to reconcile them. Some critical readers of his erudite writings have seen Hegel as arrogant, as though God had no secrets which Hegel's mind could not decode, and as egocentric, implying that past work was but prologue to Hegel's philosophy. Hegel's lectures provoked vigorous reactions from his listeners. Consequently, the works of Marx and Kierkegaard can be partially understood as efforts to correct what they viewed as errors in Hegel's philosophy. Hegel's idealism had a continuing impact on American and British philosophy well into the twentieth century, but as logical empiricists and analytical philosophers have turned away from traditional metaphysics, his works have suffered from increasing neglect. The recent appearance of J. N. Findlay's *Hegel: A Re-examination* and Walter Kaufmann's *Hegel: A Re-interpretation* suggest that Hegel's writings may in time receive the careful, critical analysis they deserve.

Hegel shares with Fichte and Schelling the responsibility for transforming Kant's critical philosophy into a metaphysical idealism, although each did it in a different way. All three agree in rejecting the unknowable thing-in-itself of Kant. If things-in-themselves lie beyond the range of reason, then they are nothing at all for Hegel. Reality is independent of individual minds, but it cannot be independent of mind altogether. Hegel insisted that the real is rational and the rational is real. The universe is not an expression of blind will, as Schopenhauer asserted, nor is it a thing-in-itself forever beyond the reach of man's mind. Reason governs all aspects of life and is the key to unlock reality. Because the universe is governed by definite laws, it can be understood dialectically.

Hegel's thought is complex and detailed and cannot be adequately summarized in a single chapter. It is possible to state some of the basic conceptions which shape his thought and provide some brief description of the major segments of his philosophy. A more adequate understanding awaits the student's careful reading of Hegel's actual writings with assistance from the excellent commentaries now available.

Basic in Hegel's philosophy is what has come to be known as the organic theory of truth and reality. In human life, we are familiar with the fact that each organ functions in a particular way because it is an interrelated part of the whole organism. Cut off from these relations it cannot be sustained. Hegel applies and extends this point about the relation of parts in the whole organism to all truth and reality. For him, every truth or fact depends upon and, in turn, helps to determine every other truth or fact in the system. Within the system everything is said to be internally related.

It follows that any organic whole is more than the mathematical sum of its parts. This is true of men and animals, but it is also true of contrived wholes like a painting, a novel, or a symphony. The whole does not exist independent of or without parts. It is these parts taken in their unity. The whole logically determines the nature of each of the parts, while the parts in turn contribute to the nature of each other and to the whole. In Hegel's view, Reality, or the Absolute, is an infinite whole which logically determines all its finite parts, which, in turn, contribute to the Absolute.

The Absolute, for Hegel, is not a being set over against the world as a first or final cause. The Absolute is the cosmos in its unity as an inclusive historical process gradually unfolding itself while moving toward complete fulfillment of itself. Although Hegel is willing to call the Absolute Mind God, it is obvious that Hegel's God is very different from the traditional conceptions of God in Judaism and Christianity. The Absolute has come to consciousness of itself in man, especially in the philosophy of Hegel. But Reality is an endless process, and only the Absolute can have complete knowledge. What we do know at any given stage of the Absolute is real and adequate so far as that stage goes. Thus Hegel can speak of degrees of reality and degrees of knowledge. We can see that he influenced some to think of all knowledge as relative and others to maintain skepticism about the possibility of man's achieving real or adequate knowledge.

It should be noted that Hegel used the two terms *concrete* and *abstract* in a special way. When you try to see something by itself, stripped of its interrelationships, you are viewing it *abstractly*. When you consider it in terms of its organic relationships, you are viewing it *concretely*. In the Hegelian sense, only the Absolute is completely concrete. Hegel criticized the systems of Fichte and Schelling for being abstract, while insisting that his own system was concrete. He distinguished between *abstract* and *concrete* universals. For example, "man is a rational animal" is an abstract definition of man, since it omits all the characteristics which differentiate one man from another. On the other hand, Hegel insists that his logical categories are concrete universals containing all specific differences within themselves. They are involved in organic relationships and imply each other. None of them can exist without the others and without the Absolute. The concept and status of the concrete universal have been matters of dispute between Hegel's followers and critics ever since Hegel first enunciated the concept.

The all-inclusive conception in Hegel's system of thought is the *Absolute Idea*, often referred to simply as the *Absolute* or the *Idea*. The Absolute Idea is the living out or the making explicit of a plan or nature inherent in the world process. The Absolute Idea is conceived of as a process of evolving self-consciousness, culminating in complete self-knowledge or comprehension of the Idea. The structure of the world is harmonious with our minds, which are organic constituents of it, so that the Idea is knowable by human minds. In asserting that human reason can disclose the nature and processes of ultimate reality, Hegel has taken the metaphysical leap beyond Kant's critical philosophy. He finds in dialectic the key to absolute knowledge.

The Absolute Idea moves through a dialectic of numerous triads, each of which involves a thesis, antithesis, and synthesis. At any point we begin with a thesis which reveals or affirms a certain aspect of reality. The thesis implies a negation which is the antithesis. Both thesis and antithesis are subsequently united and transcended (*aufgehoben*) in a higher synthesis. This synthesis, in turn, is the beginning of a new triad which leads in its turn to still another triad. There are triads within triads. The triad constitutes the basic pattern of a universal dialectical movement in which all experience and the knowledge rooted in it are finally transformed into a system of truth, the elements of which are seen in all their necessary connections. The Hegelian dialectic is objective since it is the actual order which the thought of the Absolute follows.

The most general triad reveals Logic as thesis, Nature as antithesis, and Mind or Spirit (*Geist*) as synthesis. The Absolute Idea *in itself* (*an sich*) as pure reason, independent of the world, is the categories of Logic. The Idea moves *for itself* (*für sich*), or out of itself, into the external world of Nature, as disclosed by the natural sciences. The Idea then turns back to itself in a synthesis of Logic and Nature as Mind. In human experience it becomes self-conscious of its own activity.

Hegel's Logic

In his *Critique of Pure Reason* Kant demonstrated that the reason is able to attain universal and necessary knowledge of the objects of experience by imposing upon sense impressions certain categories or forms of the understanding for the purpose of synthesizing them into a structured whole. As we have seen, Fichte, Schelling, and Hegel tried to derive the categories needed for an interpretation of experience, but they declined to restrict themselves to Kant's twelve categories and rejected Kant's limitation of knowledge in terms of the categories to the phenomenal world. Hegel specifically rejects Schelling's version of the Absolute as an absolute self-identity which in itself is the vanishing point or effacement of all differences and can be described only in negative terms. If it can be apprehended at all, it will be in mystical intuition. Hegel is confident that speculative reason can know directly the inner reality of the Absolute, which discloses itself in Nature and in the history of the human spirit, for the rational is real and the real is rational. Obviously Hegel's *Logic* is different from formal logic as we ordinarily conceive it. Hegel is concerned not only with the form of thought, but also with its content. Thus his *Logic* is basically a metaphysics, for he believes his categories to be objective realities inherent in the structure of the universe. They are not human inventions designed for utilitarian purposes, nor are they innate structures of the human understanding inapplicable to the thing in itself, as Kant maintained.

Hegel recognizes that the views of reality and knowledge which he advocates necessitate a new logic. Aristotelian logic taught that there are permanent substances and fixed types, that all propositions are either true or false, and that when they are true, they are finally true. This either-or logic Hegel rejects because he wants a logic that will be faithful to continuity and disclose the pattern of dynamic processes in the progressive unfolding of the Absolute.

The method by which Reason advances from lower to higher categories of thought is *dialectic*, which employs three stages found in every phase of life: thesis, antithesis, and synthesis. In the first stage is set forth a "thesis," ordinarily some definite statement embodying a partial truth about the cosmic situation. In the second stage criticism suggests the inadequacy and one-sidedness of the thesis, thus leading to the consideration of an "antithesis," which in turn reveals its limitations. Hence Reason is compelled to go beyond the inadequate thesis and antithesis to preserve and incorporate the partial truths into a higher and more concrete "synthesis." But this "synthesis" proves to be as inadequate and one-sided as a thesis, again provoking an antithesis, both of which are caught up into a higher synthesis. Hegel believes this triadic pattern in both cosmic history and human reflection goes on endlessly.

One basic triad Hegel employs is that of Being, Nothing, and Becoming. He believes that the movement of thought is from the more general and abstract to the specific and concrete. Pure being is the most general concept or category with which we begin. It is void of determinate form, but all things share it. When the mind tries to think being without any determination, it finds it is thinking nothing. The mind oscillates from being to not-being and back to being. Each apparently dissolves the other. But from the synthesis of the two comes Becoming or Change in their unity and truth. Change or Becoming is Being and Not-Being. To treat each in isolation is to land in a contradiction. In Change Nothing passes into Being or Being passes into Nothing. This double passage is what is caught up in the concept of Becoming and held without destruction. This is identity-in-difference.

In the second major portion of the *Logic*, the logic of essence, Hegel deduces, in pairs, related concepts: essence and existence, substance and accident, cause and effect, action and reaction, force and expression. These he designates as categories of reflection. He introduces the concept of actuality as "the unity of essence and existence." Being as actuality is the union of the inner and the outer. It is one-sided and abstract to interpret Being as unattached, external appearance or as a hidden featureless essence underlying appearances.

In the third section of his work, Hegel moves from the logic of essence to the logic of the Concept (*Begriff*) or Notion, which subjectively considered is a mediated being that organically relates the differences to which it gives rise, so that on becoming differentiated it reveals its more basic and concrete unity. The universal "man" is not an abstraction; it reveals itself in particular men like Socrates and

Plato, and these men in turn exist in it. Such an organic relationship between universals and individuals is made more explicit in *Judgments* and reestablished in a formal way and at a higher level in the syllogism, which is not an artificial device but part of the logical structure that really constitutes the universe.

The Notion objectively considered involves specific elements assembled mechanically and chemically. Yet, despite their reality, chemistry and mechanics have a more comprehensive meaning in teleology, since all things have a final purpose. Here he focuses on the concept of the objective rather than on Nature as an empirically given existing reality to be probed.

As one would expect, the third stage of the logic of the Concept will be the synthesis on a higher plane of subjectivity and objectivity. As such the Concept of Notion is called the Idea. In the Idea the inadequate and one-sided elements of the subjective and objective, the formal and the material, are brought together and enriched in rational life with purpose, will, and value. The Absolute Idea is now seen as the concept of self-consciousness, personality, and self-thinking thought which knows itself in its object and its object in itself. As Hegel puts it, "The Absolute Idea alone is *being, eternal life, self-knowing truth*, and it is *all truth*. It is the one subject matter and content of philosophy" (*Science of Logic*, translated by W. H. Johnston and L. G. Struthers, II, p. 466).

Philosophy of Nature

In the comprehensive view of the Hegelian system, logic in its totality is to be seen as the thesis of a final, all-inclusive triad: Idea-Nature-Spirit. Just as Nothing and Being are the same and different with Becoming as their synthesis, so Idea passes over into Nature, and Nature into Idea, with Spirit as their synthesis. Having presented logic as the analysis of the rational Idea of reality, Hegel seeks to deduce the unfolding material existence of Nature.

Nature, the system of sense-perceived things and processes, is the antithesis of the rational Idea. From, and to, all eternity the Idea is expressed in Nature. Thus the Idea is not prior in time to its manifestation in Nature. Nature, as the enactment of the Idea, has no beginning or end in time. Hegel divides Nature into three realms: (1) the inorganic, (2) the chemical, (3) the organic.

In Nature objects and events are related externally and display quantitative qualities. The basic formulations and changes of matter can be described in purely quantitative and mathematical terms like mass, velocity, and gravitation, which are subject to the laws of mechanics and astronomy, themselves "externalizations" of the laws of thinking. In the inorganic realm he stresses the significance of the law of gravity, which he interprets as the symbolic expression of his dialectic, since it represents the synthesis of opposing forces. Hegel is very critical of the Newtonian system for regarding Nature as a mechanical whole.

Hegel notes the appearance of qualitative changes which direct our attention from alterations in the external relations among objects to internal transformations occurring within particular objects. Thus we pass from processes like abstract motion, inertia, and gravitation to sound, heat, light, electricity, and chemical reaction. At this stage we find more triadic patterns. Everywhere we discover repulsion and attraction, separation and combination, and reconciliation of a sort as parts are fused into new wholes.

At a higher level we find that organic bodies are both objects and subjects. The parts that comprise the whole become elements in a synthesis that exists in and for itself and displays a guiding role for the constituent elements. Organisms are individuals in the sense that they maintain their essential identities throughout their careers. In them the Idea reveals itself as a living matter.

At the level of life we can distinguish again three stages in the career of the earth as an organization of a sort. There is the geological or mineral stage, transitional between physical-chemical existence and the realm of the vegetable and animal, in which the universal characteristics of life are foreshadowed. In the next stage we find plants and living bodies assimilating eternal material for their processes and forms, and reproducing according to their kind. At the third and higher level of animal life, Nature extends these formative, assimilative, and reproductive processes so that the organism can become a self-conscious soul. Consciousness appears first in animals, but only human beings have the power of self-consciousness.

It is of course obvious that Hegel's philosophy of Nature is teleological. Nature is not self-existent and cannot be adequately understood through the study of quantitative relations. In the Hegelian system Nature is the prelude to the true individuality which self-consciousness makes possible. Hegel is not writing science, nor is he equipped to. He is not hostile to the empirical work of scientists, although he "looks down" on it from a higher viewpoint and often unwisely takes positions in controversies among scientists. It is generally recognized that his work in the Philosophy of Nature is not of the same stature as that in the Philosophy of Mind, the third major part of Hegel's system.

In the Philosophy of Mind or Spirit Hegel deals with the cultural experiences of man. Many readers feel this is the best part of Hegel, for he introduces a wealth of detailed applications and illustrations which have some familiarity. Here the major triad consists of Subjective Mind, Objective Mind, and Absolute Mind.

Under the heading Subjective Mind Hegel deals with three subdivisions: (1) anthropology, (2) phenomenology of Mind, and (3) psychology. (1) In anthropology Hegel treats the soul as a natural entity in the physical world—a sensing and feeling subject. On one hand, the soul enjoys self-feeling, but, on the other, it lacks reflective self-consciousness. The upright body, the hand, the mouth, and the power of weeping and laughing all enable man to externalize his thoughts and feelings. The world makes impacts upon a man's body that are internalized by him. (2) Under phenomenology of Mind Hegel discusses some of the topics treated earlier in his book of the same title, among which are perception, sense experience, desire, reason, and self-consciousness. He depicts the subject's reaching universal self-consciousness and recognizing other selves both as distinct from and one with itself. (3) The third section, psychology, does not describe an empirical psychology, but rather a dialectical deduction of concepts in the various stages of the activity of the finite spirit in itself. He treats intention, recollection, imagination, and memory, as well as the practical drives, impulses, and will. He concludes that "The actual free will is the unity of the theoretical and practical spirit; *free will which exists for itself as free will.*"

Just as the Absolute in itself objectifies or reveals itself in Nature, so does the Mind or Spirit objectify or reveal itself in the Objective Mind consisting of the triad of Law (*Recht*), personal or subjective morality, and social morality.

The first stage of Objective Mind or Spirit is the realm of Law (*Recht*) in which the individual subject, aware of his freedom, expresses his will in the realm of material things by effectively appropriating and using material things as tools or instruments for a rational will. Since they, in contrast to things, have rights, wills, and moral dignity, persons cannot become the property of another. Thus slavery, even if voluntary, is ruled out as immoral. A man cannot hand over his total freedom to another as something external to himself. Private property is the initial phase in the objective realization of personal character. But a person can withdraw his will from a thing in which he has previously embodied his will. Thus he alienates the thing since it is external to him. This leads to the concept of contract, for two or more persons may agree to exchange, sell, or donate property. The union of will reached in a contract may be willfully or unintentionally repudiated, but such action is wrong. If it is unintended repudiation, it requires restoration or compensation. If it is willful and involves fraud or crime, it will require penalty or punishment provided by the legal system.

Hegel does not justify punishment as a deterrent to possible crimes in the future nor as a part of therapy to reform the offender. He thinks of the offender as having negated right and the rational free will as such. Punishment thus should not be imposed by the aggrieved parties, but should be the expression of the general will as embodied in the state. In such a theory, the criminal as a rational free being not only acquiesces in his punishment but in some sense is held to demand his punishment to annul the wrong of his crime.

The antithesis of Law (*Recht*) is personal or subjective morality (*Moralität*), for there is more to goodness than merely obeying the law or fulfilling contracts. There is indeed the subjective inwardness of purpose, intention, and the attitude of a person's conscience. Unlike Kant, Hegel recognizes that when the rational moral will confronts choice it must consider all of the relevant consequences and implications of a proposed act. A man therefore may include goods other than the fulfillment of duty, but nothing that violates duty. As a man reflects subjectively upon his purposes and intentions, his conscience appears. Without its employment and overriding authority, true morality does not emerge. A person may act in an intelligent and generous fashion without acting virtuously. Yet the conscience is not infallible and may even fall into expediency or fanaticism. To will what is rational and productive of the social good one needs the wisdom of the reasoned ethics embodied in institutions of society. Here we find the synthesis of Law (*Recht*) and personal morality (*Moralität*) in social morality (*Sittlichkeit*).

The synthesis and reconciliation of the "subjective and objective Good existing *an und für sich*" is for Hegel *Sittlichkeit*, social morality or the ethical life. It includes the ethical institutions of the family, civil society, and the state. It is an ethical community organized in terms of laws and institutions which made it possible for a man to achieve his true nature and actually exercise rational freedom.

Hegel viewed the family as the basic institution in which individuals attain their freedom. Marriage is more than a sexual relation or a civil contract, for two persons freely give up their individual wills to enter into a more inclusive life of mutual love and common purposes. Since it is a social institution, the family should be initiated by a civil ceremony and terminated only by procedures determined by law. Parents see in their children the objective realization of their love, which previously had been only subjective feeling for each other. Children are integrated into a complex ethical interaction within the family. While the family imposes restrictions on its members, these are not to be interpreted as interferences with one's nature but as ways in which individuals freely determine their growth and that of others in a living, organic whole. Hegel stresses the importance of family as an ethical institution in contrast to the Romanticists, who had more sympathy for casual unions and free love as expressions of individuality.

The family contains its own antithesis, namely its members who mature, leave the family circle, and join with similar individuals in what Hegel calls civil society (*bürgerliche Gesellschaft*). Individuals and groups of individuals have wants and interests which they pursue in the economic order. The particularity, interdependence, cooperation, and competition of these interests point to the need for their organization in a more inclusive community, the state.

In Hegel's ideal sense, the state is the whole which absorbs and synthesizes all other human institutions. It is the highest level of organized society and thus the most complex and concrete. Just as the natural order manifests the Idea or Absolute on the physical level, so the state manifests the Idea or Absolute on the social level. "The state is the actuality of the ethical idea." It is only in the state as a citizen that the individual becomes actually free and possesses rights that can be rationally defined and defended. But this should not be read as the glorification of any existing national state. Hegel is offering within the context of his metaphysics the Idea of a rationally organized society—a sort of Platonic ideal.

Like all institutions, the institution of the state is continually developing. Hegel takes the fully developed state to be a hereditary constitutional monarchy with an appointed system of state officials or highly trained bureaucrats and a bicameral legislature representing both the landed "estate" and the commercial "estate." Both the monarch and bureaucracy participate in the legislative function, but the monarch is bound by the constitution and the advice of his officials. Hegel does not favor universal suffrage. Although he believes that government should carry out the rational will of the nation, Hegel does not think you can derive the rational will by counting the votes of the ignorant and irrational. He favors liberty of thought and speech for matters of general interest, but he warns that such liberty must not be abused.

Unlike Kant and other thinkers of the Enlightenment, Hegel does not view a league of nations and perpetual peace as realistic possibilities. He sees the state as the ultimate unit of social organization with no real competitor for man's political loyalties. There is then no political force that can moderate strife among nations and prevent wars. This does not mean that Hegel justifies aggression.

Hegel concludes his treatment of objective mind with a section on universal history, which he expands in his popular *Lectures on the Philosophy of History*. He sees history as the expression of the finite spirit for freedom. The Absolute Idea reveals itself in the succession of dominant states, each of which loses its eminence once its role has been carried out. He repeats Schiller's words: "The history of the world is the world's court of judgment."

We have sketched Hegel's account of the development of the Absolute Idea: first, in itself as revealed in the categories of Logic; secondly, externalized for itself in physical nature; and thirdly, become self-conscious in and for itself in the psychological processes of Subjective Mind, and revealed as Objective Mind in social institutions. But the final culmination is attained in *Absolute Mind*, in which the totality of reality is apprehended in its organic unity and completeness. In Art, this is accomplished through the medium of a sensuous form of some kind; in Religion, the unity of human and divine is found in worship; in Philosophy, the Absolute is discovered in the conceptions of pure thought. Obviously there is the closest kind of relation among these three achievements of the Spirit, which fulfill the system.

Although he does not deny the existence of beauty in nature, Hegel maintains that beauty in art is superior to nature. Man creates more adequate forms of beauty than those he discovers in Nature. Hegel has left behind him the philosophy of Nature and is elucidating his philosophy of Spirit in which a work of art is held to express the unity of spiritual content with material embodiment. Much exists in nature that involves unresolved contradictions and is basically disagreeable. The Spirit, working through the artist, provides a fuller sensuous embodiment of the Idea than found in Nature, and thus brings *ideal beauty* into being. In symbolic art, the material embodiment is dominant; in romantic art the spiritual content predominates, while in classical art the two are evenly balanced. In symbolic art the artist only suggests, rather than expresses, his meaning in ambiguity and mystery. Hegel feels that symbolic art is more appropriate to the early stages of humanity. He admires classical art in which there is harmony or balance between content and form. In the great works of Greek sculpture he sees the perfect union of Spirit and matter when the Greek gods are portrayed as immortal beings clad in perfect human bodies. Yet this does not altogether satisfy the Spirit, so we have romantic art in which the Spirit, felt as infinite, overflows its finite sensuous embodiment. Romantic art is concerned with the movement, action, and conflict of the life of the Spirit. Painting, music, and poetry are better adapted for revealing the inner life of the Spirit than architecture and sculpture. It is not possible to summarize briefly the richness of detail, the imaginative theories, and the breadth of interest which Hegel reveals in the more than fifteen hundred pages in which he discusses art. The reader can only be directed to them.

In Hegel's system, as we have already noted, religion is a form of Absolute Mind, along with art and philosophy. The content of religion is representation (Vorstellung), in which pure thought is clothed in some kind of imagery. Philosophy conceives or thinks the Absolute. But Hegel does not reject the representations or pictures of religion as being only popular delusions. He views them instead as actual revelations of the Absolute which express the truth as adequately as the popular mind is able to embrace it. Thus the same truth is expressed in quasi-imaginative form in religion, and in conceptual form in philosophy.

Hegel finds in Christianity, which he calls the absolute religion, the most adequate representation of truth that is possible for a religion. He sees it as the symbolic expression of his own Absolute Idealism. He has only scorn for those German Romanticists who take "feeling" rather than reason as the foundation of the religious life. With a dig at Schleiermacher, Hegel says that if feeling is the basis of the religious life, then the dog's dumb adoration of his master is the highest kind of religion. Men cannot get at the Absolute through intuition or feeling, but only through sustained logical thought.

God is the Absolute for Hegel, and so he begins with God, in contrast to Schleiermacher who began with human experience. God is subject and object, and the reconciliation of the two. His activity is seen in his creating and revealing himself. The world is God as object. God reveals himself as an object to attain self-consciousness through the world. Thus God can become and truly be God only through revealing himself in the finite, in the world, and in man.

All other religions are steps leading up to Christianity, which is a perfect revelation of the Absolute. Christianity is distinguished from the other religions of the world by its doctrine of incarnation, which Hegel takes as the religious expression of the philosophical truth that the Infinite Being is necessarily manifest in the finite and not differentiated from it. Hegel also treats the doctrine of the Trinity in philosophical terms. The Father is the thesis, the Son is the antithesis (the

Absolute objectified), and the Holy Spirit is the return of the Spirit upon itself. In the "Science of God," God is viewed as he is before the creation of the world; in the "Philosophy of Nature," as his material embodiment; and in the "Philosophy of Mind," as reconciling the finite and the Infinite. The particular finite self feels itself out of harmony with the Absolute Spirit, with its own nature, and with the world. Hence the finite, estranged spirit manifests the need for reconciliation or atonement, which is possible only through the atoning activity of the Absolute Spirit. Hegel indicates that the reconciliation of the human spirit with the Divine Spirit could become actual to all men only if it was manifested in the visible form of a particular man who was simultaneously known to be "the Absolute Idea, the Son of God" (*Philosophy of Religion*, Vol. III, p. 73). But the atonement is not merely an historical event, for it is true at all times and may be appropriated by any man in a subjective process. In the Church and in the activity of the Holy Spirit Christians can continue to experience the atonement as a present reality and to continue to believe that the universe is good and is the work of God, despite the presence of seeming evil and discord.

Hegel gave lectures on the traditional proofs for the existence of God. He recognized the force of Kant's criticisms of these proofs, but sought to reformulate the arguments to escape the chief criticisms. Like Anselm, he tried to vindicate by reason the truth of the Christian faith and the validity of the ontological argument for God's existence.

More than any other philosopher in the nineteenth century, Hegel studied sympathetically the actual literature of the various world religions and recognized what he considered contributions and degrees of truth. He took religion seriously and acknowledged that it brings man into relationship with the divine. But still philosophy provides the final synthesis in which man knows his own position in a universe that is organic and rational. The universe in its turn becomes conscious of itself in the cultural life of man.

Hegel: Suggested Additional Reading

Abernethy, George L. and Thomas A. Langford, eds. *History of Philosophy: Selected Readings*. Belmont, Calif.: Dickenson, 1965, pp. 529–549.*

Copleston, Frederick C., *A History of Philosophy*, Vol. 7, Part I: Fichte to Hegel. Garden City: Doubleday, Image, 1963.

Fackenheim, Emil. H. *The Religious Dimension in Hegel's Thought*. Bloomington: University of Indiana Press, 1967.*

Findlay, J. N., *Philosophy of Hegel: An Introduction and Reexamination.* New York: Macmillan, Collier paperback, 1962.

Hegel, *Early Theological Writings.* Translated by T. M. Knox. Introduction by Richard Kroner. New York: Harper Torchbook, 1961.

Hegel, *The Philosophy of History.* Translated by J. Silbres. New York: Dover, 1956.

Hegel, *The Logic of Hegel.* Translated from the *Encyclopaedia of the Philosophical Sciences* by William Wallace. Oxford: Clarendon Press, 1892.*

Hegel, *Hegel's Philosophy of Right.* Translated by T. M. Knox. New York: Oxford University Press, paper, 1942.

Hegel, *The Philosophy of Hegel.* Edited by Carl J. Friedrich. New York: The Modern Library, 1953.*

Hegel, *Phenomenology of Mind.* Translated by J. B. Baillie. New York: Harper and Row, Torchbook, 1967.

Kaufmann, Walter, ed. and trans., Vol. I: *A Re-Interpretation*, Vol. II: *Hegel: Texts and Commentary.* New York: Doubleday, Anchor, 1966.

Löwith, Karl, *From Hegel to Nietzsche: The Revolution in Nineteenth Century Thought.* Translated by David E. Green. New York: Doubleday, Anchor, 1967.

McTaggert, J. McT. E., *Studies in the Hegelian Dialectic.* Cambridge: Cambridge University Press, 1922.*

Mure, G. R. G., *The Philosophy of Hegel.* London and New York: Oxford University Press, 1965.*

Reyburn, Hugh Adams, *The Ethical Theory of Hegel.* Oxford: Clarendon Press, 1921.*

Stace, Walter T., *Philosophy of Hegel.* New York: Dover, 1955.

Walsh, W. H., *Hegelian Ethics.* New York: St. Martin's Press, 1969.

Chapter Twenty-Two

Schopenhauer

Arthur Schopenhauer was born in 1788 into one of the rich banking and merchant families that composed the aristocracy of the free city of Danzig. In 1793, after the second partition of Poland and the Prussian seizure of Danzig, his father moved the family to Hamburg, where he continued his commercial interests. He was determined that his son Arthur should follow him in a commercial career, so he planned for him what he considered to be a useful, if unconventional, education. At the age of nine Arthur was placed in the home of a business friend in Le Havre, France, where in a two-year period he acquired a good knowledge of French. When he was fifteen his parent took him on an extensive tour, during which they left him for three months at Wimbledon, England, in a conservative boarding school conducted by a strict clergyman. This experience left him with a strong distaste for the stuffy atmosphere of Anglo-Saxon cant and old-fashioned religiosity, although later in life he did express appreciation for individual English writers.

On the return trip from England the young Schopenhauer was upset by his observations of the squalid conditions in which the lower classes lived in southern France and Austria. His mother referred to this sensitivity as a morbid tendency to "brood over the misery of things." The death of the older Schopenhauer by suicide in 1805 undoubtedly shocked the son and reminded him of the family history of emotional instability. Out of loyalty to his father he worked for two years with a business firm in Hamburg, but, finding this life increasingly distasteful, he resigned to undertake the systematic study of Greek and Latin. Meanwhile his mother had established a *salon* in Weimar which attracted many brilliant and popular intellectuals. Her interests and style of life repelled him to the point that he left home and never became reconciled with her.

Reaching age twenty-one, Schopenhauer received his share of his father's estate and became financially independent. He promptly enrolled as a medical student at the University of Göttingen, but in his second year he began the serious study of Plato and Kant. In 1811 he transferred to the University of Berlin to attend the lectures of Fichte and Schleiermacher. His notes on their lectures were studded with sarcastic and savage comments which reveal the origins of his lifelong contempt for university professors of philosophy. While other scholars, under the influence of nationalistic sentiment, were deserting their books for the sword during the Franco-Prussian War, Schopenhauer retired to work on his doctoral dissertation, *On the Fourfold Root of the Principle of Sufficient Reason*, which was accepted by the University of Jena in 1813. He had it published at his own expense, but except for some appreciative comments by Goethe it attracted no attention in intellectual circles. Later he received an appointment as lecturer at the University of Berlin, where he intended to refute the philosophy of the immensely popular Hegel, but with customary audacity he scheduled his lectures at the same hours at which Hegel lectured. He wound up without an audience and quickly gave up his university career, more convinced than ever of the shallowness and ingrown nature of professional philosophical circles.

Schopenhauer completed his masterpiece, *The World as Will and Idea*, at age thirty. It was published at the end of 1818, but like Hume's *Treatise* it was ignored by philosophers and a second edition, twenty-six years later, met with scarcely more notice. Despite rejection by the academic world, Schopenhauer continued to write philosophical works in the tranquil city of Frankfurt, where he found life congenial to his tastes. In 1836 he published *On the Will in Nature*, and three years later he was awarded a prize by the Scientific Society at Trondheim in Norway for an essay on the freedom of the will. This work, together with an unsuccessful prize essay entitled *On the Foundation of Morality*, was published in 1841 as *The Two Fundamental Problems of Ethics*. It was only in 1851, with the publication of a collection of essays on various topics under the title of *Parerga and Paralipomena*, which came to be widely read when the influence of Hegelianism was waning and liberals in Germany were ripe for pessimism following the failure of the revolution of 1848, that attention at home and abroad was directed to his earlier writings. Thus in his declining years Schopenhauer came to enjoy his belated fame, which had many cultic overtones. Army officers were attracted to him and women flocked about him despite the savage comments he had made in his famed essay, "On Women." On the occasion of his seventieth birthday, congratulatory letters came from all over the world and appreciative articles on his work appeared in many journals. He died quietly in 1860.

Schopenhauer's Theory of Knowledge

Schopenhauer's doctoral thesis, *On the Fourfold Root of the Principle of Sufficient Reason,* and the first book of *The World as Will and Idea* contain his treatment of the theory of knowledge and perception. Although the distinction between what is and what is rationally knowable is an old one in the history of philosophy, Schopenhauer thought it had not been properly made until Kant elaborated it. Kant had shown how the metaphysical claims of dogmatic rationalism exceed the limits of the human mind's competence. Schopenhauer endorses his doctrine that the world of experience is the phenomenal world, an intellectual construction which is limited by the knower's sense, reason, and understanding. Thus the knower can never know reality as it is in itself, but only as it is conditioned by these three faculties. Here we have the distinction between the *phenomenal* world as it is experienced and rationally understood and the *noumenal* world as it stands independently of the knower's effort to apprehend it rationally. When Schopenhauer enunciates "The World is my idea," he is emphasizing that physics is our version of nature conditioned by all the limitations of human knowing and therefore incapable of penetrating into the nature of reality as it is in itself.

In all our ordinary dealings with the world, Schopenhauer believes, we bring with us the idea of a principle which justifies our efforts to seek the *why* of anything. This principle he calls "the principle of sufficient reason" and identifies it initially as "Nothing is without a reason why it is." It is the responsibility of philosophy and science to discover a sufficient reason for everything. The principle of sufficient reason does not require a logical demonstration, for Schopenhauer views it as a self-evident proposition which is presupposed in all thought. In his analysis he discloses four chief classes of objects and four chief kinds of relatedness. He concludes there are four basic forms of the principle of sufficient reason. Hence the title of his doctoral dissertation, *On the Fourfold Root of the Principle of Sufficient Reason.*

The first class of objects is subject to the law of sufficient reason of becoming or change; each change involves a cause, which it repeatedly follows as its effect. Such changes are capable of being perceived, for example, in physics and chemistry under the *a priori* forms of space, which makes coexistence and succession possible. Here he is following Kant.

The second class of objects, abstract concepts, are subject to the law of sufficient reason of knowing which asserts that a judgment does not express knowledge unless it is true, and "truth is the relation of a judgment to something different from it, which can be called its ground." This ground may be found in a formal argument, sense observations, *a priori* principles, or even in the traditional laws of thought.

The third class of objects consists of "the *a priori* intuitions of the forms of outer and inner sense, space and time," whose relations are governed by what Schopenhauer formulates as the principle of sufficient reason of being. Geometry rests on the law governing positions in space in three dimensions, and arithmetic deals with succession in time in one dimension. Again Schopenhauer follows Kant in asserting that space and time are *a priori* forms presupposed in any perception whatever and imposed upon the sensations by the mind.

The fourth class of objects is subject to the law of sufficient reason of action or the law of motivation. A man acts because of motives which have their ground in his character. Since Schopenhauer believes that each conscious action has a physical correlate, he is led to claim that when I move my hand I view it as a physical act with a physical cause if I apprehend it externally; the same act apprehended internally is viewed as being set in motion by a motive. The implications of this position can be seen fully only in his treatment of the world as Will.

It should be noted that the principle of sufficient reason only holds within the world of phenomena and here nothing occurs without a sufficient reason, which is in principle knowable. The principle of sufficient reason does not apply to the noumenal world beyond the sphere of phenomena. It does not even apply to the totality of the world of phenomena, for it governs the relations between phenomena. In this respect Schopenhauer follows Kant's rejection of the cosmological argument for the existence of God, which sought to argue from the world as a totality to God as the sufficient ground or reason for phenomena.

Schopenhauer's Metaphysics

Despite his frequent and severe criticisms of Fichte, Schelling, and Hegel, Schopenhauer's metaphysical system is in many respects an integral part of German speculative idealism. His system may properly be described as transcendental voluntaristic idealism. To the extent that he says the world is our idea we may classify his view as idealism. It is voluntaristic in that he makes Will rather than Reason ultimate reality. It is transcendental in that one individual Will is an overriding absolute Will which individuates itself in the various phenomena of experience.

In the second book of *The World as Will and Idea*, Schopenhauer elaborates his theory of the Will as objectified in nature. We have seen how, in his theory of knowledge, neither perception nor the scientific conceptualization of perception gives us any insight into the real or noumenal world. Like Descartes and Kant before him, Schopenhauer turns to the self for something more promising. Although we *perceive* ourselves as bodies, governed by spatio-temporal relations with other bodies, we immediately *intuit* one noumenal object—ourselves as Will. Will is not to be understood in Kant's sense as primarily moral and rational, but as endless striving for what one is not and has not. Not only are we basically Will, but, Schopenhauer asserts, the entire world may by analogy be understood to be basically Will in the same sense we are. He states his doctrine of the objectification of the Will in these words: "The act of will and the movement of the body are not two different things objectively known, which the bond of causality unites; . . . they are one and the same, but they are given in different ways,— immediately and again in perception. . . . The action of the body is nothing but the act of will objectified, i.e., passed into perception. . . . The whole body is nothing but objectified will, i.e., will become idea" (*The World as Will and Idea*, Bk. II, sec. 18).

Body and will, then, are the same thing experienced in different ways. We perceive our bodies as objects subject to the same scientific laws as other spatio-temporal objects. A bodily action thus is nothing more than an act of will objectified, or "passed into perception." We can know ourselves in two ways: (1) externally as physical objects which are merely the phenomenal manifestation of, or objectification of, the Will, (2) internally as the Will which is ultimate and real. Hunger is "objectified" as teeth and stomach; our eyes are the phenomenal manifestation of the Will to see. In the same sense the gravitational pull of the earth on our bodies, the ceaseless tides of the ocean, and the movement of the iron filings toward the magnet are all phenomenal manifestations or objectifications of the Will. How, in Schopenhauer's theory, the judgment that bodily action and Will are one and the same thing can be justified is never made clear. If they are both the same, Schopenhauer leaves us with the problem of justifying his preference for the Will as against phenomenal manifestations.

In underlining Will rather than Reason as ultimate, Schopenhauer emphasizes the irrational character of reality. Reason is not the ultimate creative power in the universe. He regards it as something practical, like a dog's keen scent, which becomes an effective biological tool or instrument in the struggle for existence. Nevertheless, reason through conceptualization falsifies reality and may inhibit feeling, immediacy, and intuition. In this side of his thought Schopenhauer reveals his affinities with the reaction of Romanticism against Kantianism.

On the animal level the striving of the Will is entirely blind and without plan. It is an intense urge to live, feed, and procreate. It is a ceaseless proliferation of life which involves never-ending struggle and pain. The Will perpetuates itself through procreation; it cares nothing for the individual but seeks only the perpetuation of the species. Thus Schopenhauer describes the satisfaction of the sexual impulse as "the strongest and most powerful of motives" next to "the love of life" and the one that intrudes itself, often in the most devious ways, into all aspects of life. Man's egoism is tricked by passion, temporary female beauty, romantic song and story, and a bondage to something he does not understand, and leads him to desert his individual interests and undertake the perpetuation of the species without concern for the cost. Some lower creatures perish in the act of procreation or soon thereafter, while others devote the major portion of life's energy to its demands. Every living thing, including the human being, is moved by the irrational impulse to perpetuate itself.

Although Schopenhauer's pessimism is closely bound up with his voluntaristic idealism, it is not a logical consequence of it. One could maintain either position without the other. His pessimism rests on his analysis of desire, which, he held, could appear only when some lack or deficiency was felt as pain. When man's effort removes the deficiency and fulfills the desire, he then is restored to his former state with the possible addition of a little ennui or boredom. The repetition in an endless cycle of desire and fulfillment without positive pleasure or happiness beyond the removal of pain points up the futility and "burden of existence." The genius sees most clearly the miserable and ceaseless round of human existence. As Gautama Buddha expressed it, the cardinal truth of existence is the universality of misery. Schopenhauer provides empirical data from both history and contemporary society to support his claims about misery and the state of many men who in society appear to be only muzzled wolves and tigers. If anything, this is the worst of all possible worlds. But at every stage Schopenhauer shows the Will individuated into an immense diversity and multiplicity of particular phenomena as seething against itself in a ceaseless and devouring conflict, for "The Will must live on itself, for there exists nothing beside it, and it is a hungry Will" (*ibid.*, I, p. 201).

Schopenhauer's Theory of Art

Schopenhauer's grim and pessimistic picture of the reasonless sway of existence and of the debasing nature of human evil prepares the way for Schopenhauer's theory of art, which he develops in the third book of *The World as Will and Idea*. Unlike many previous philosophers who had assigned to art an ornamental or minor role in life, Schopenhauer assigns to art a preeminent role in his system. In fact, he offers two methods of escape from the tyranny of the Will: the way of art and aesthetic contemplation and the way of salvation as seen in asceticism.

Schopenhauer's theory of art is to be classified as a cognitive one, for he presents art as a form of knowledge. "Its one source is the knowledge of the Ideas, its one aim the communication of this knowledge" (*ibid.*, I, p. 239). He leans on a metaphysical theory of what he terms Platonic Ideas. He asserts that the Will objectifies itself immediately in eternal Ideas, which are related to the individual natural things in the fashion of archetypes to copies. The question immediately arises as to how a "knowing individual" with an intellect that is the subservient tool of a blind Will of endless striving can achieve a kind of knowledge which is so different from the ordinary kinds of knowledge for which Schopenhauer's theory of knowledge provides. Basically, Schopenhauer maintains there is a sharp difference between the aesthetic and scientific attitudes toward experience. In the scientific attitude we are concerned with the uses and effects of particular objects, so we summarize the available data about their properties and relations. In so doing we are giving expression to desires proceeding from the Will, and thus knowledge continues to be subordinated to the Will. However, man can, in momentary aesthetic experiences, transcend or abolish this subservience to the Will and direct his contemplation upon the Ideas themselves without reference to the satisfaction of desires. Thus the aesthetic attitude enables us to penetrate to the inner nature and meaning of the art object. Although we cannot summarize this experience in concepts and words, we can know what the object really is. In this experience the individual loses himself in contemplation, so that the distinction between subject and object disappears for him. The distinction between subject and object or between the perceiver and his perception arises only in individuals differentiated from one another through the principle of sufficient reason and is not found in the Ideas prior to such differentiation. Thus "the knowing individual as such" together with "the particular things known by him" are always "in a particular place, at a particular time, and are links in the chain of

causes and effects," while the "pure, will-less, painless, timeless subject of knowledge" of aesthetic perception and its correlate the "Idea"
have on the other hand "passed out of all these forms of the principle of sufficient reason" (*ibid.*, I, p. 232).

Schopenhauer's glorification of the role of artistic genius reveals
the impact of Romanticism on his thought. To be able to forget the
practical bearings of the phenomenal world upon oneself and to penetrate, recognize, and produce the eternal Ideas in a work of art is the
mark of artistic genius. Since art objects are often very imperfect
copies of the Idea, it takes a certain amount of artistic genius to grasp
the Ideas in them and to share them with us in order to provide us with
peace and temporary cessation from desire. Schopenhauer distinguishes
the sense of beauty from the sublime. The sense of beauty is associated
with delight in perceptual knowledge as such, without one feeling any
struggle with the Will, without being aware of the unfriendly and
disagreeable aspects of existence. The sense of the sublime, by contrast,
involves the sense of victory over the hostile and unfriendly phenomena
of the Will in achieving the contemplation of Ideas, as when in a violent
storm at sea we transcend the immediate desires and fears of the Will
to contemplate the infinite greatness of the universe.

Schopenhauer drew up a hierarchy of the principal arts according to
ascending grades of the objectification of the Will in the following
order: architecture, sculpture, painting, poetry, music. The Ideas
which architecture presents to our contemplation, "gravity, cohesion
and rigidity," are the universal qualities of stone and the simplest
and most inarticulate manifestations of the Will. To observe the roof
press the earth through its columns and the arch support itself is to
witness in counteraction the opposed forces which constitute the
essence of architectural perfection. In the milder climates of India,
Egypt, Greece, and Rome the architect had more freedom in dealing
with these forces than in the harsher climates of northern Europe where
snow and rain make necessary high-pointed roofs and vaultings.

A level above architecture is found in animal paintings and sculpture,
like the horses at Venice and the Elgin marbles, which express the free
and naive strength of the Will uncontrolled by the intellect. Next we
find painting and sculpture of the human form. Sculpture captures the
outward beauty and grace of the human form, while painting is better
adapted for expressing the character and passion in the effort to portray
the Idea of the individual, in so far as this is possible within the limited
materials of the artist.

But poetry is a much higher art, for it can represent Ideas of all
levels. Through the use of epithets the poet is able to communicate

images that stimulate the hearer or reader to contemplate the eternal Idea in the perceptible object. The poet holds up a "clarifying mirror" in which "all that is essential and significant appears to us as collected together and placed in the brightest light, and what is accidental and foreign excluded" (*ibid.*, I, p. 321). The chief aim of poetry is the representation of man revealing himself through a series of actions accompanied by thoughts and emotions. Schopenhauer maintains that poetry gave the poet a freedom in the choice of situations and treatments of them not available to the historian and painter, whose materials impose more obvious restrictions on their work. Moreover, the poet can give full expression to his inner feelings and illumine the feelings of millions of other human beings. Thus the poet can bring to consciousness the actions and feelings of mankind.

The highest form of poetry is tragedy, for it presents most directly and intimately the blind strivings of the Will and the pain, suffering, and evil with which its objectifications are infected. In tragedy the hero atones, not for his own particular sin, but for the breaking of the Will into separate persons. Yet, for Schopenhauer, the highest of all the arts is not tragedy but music. All the other arts enable us to contemplate the various levels of objectification of the Will, but Music is unique in penetrating behind the Ideas and revealing the Will itself, the inner nature of the thing-in-itself. "We might, therefore, just as well call the world embodied music as embodied will," so that if one could express precisely in concepts all that music expresses without concepts, we should possess the one true philosophy.

All the arts provide us, then, with beauty and consolation that momentarily permit us to become absorbed in the work of art and forget the individuality of our concerns. To lose our individuality in this way gives us temporary relief from the pain and frustration of the individual's desires. Although there is much in Schopenhauer's views on aesthetics that is suggestive and can even be accepted while rejecting Schopenhauer's pessimism and metaphysics, it would appear that he stresses too much the interests of the spectator or listener rather than those of the creator of art objects.

Schopenhauer's Ethics and Morality

In the fourth book of *The World as Will and Idea* and in the *Basis of Morality*, Schopenhauer presents his views on ethics and religion. The idealists after Kant were basically optimists and stressed perfectionism or the normal fulfillment of personality. This emphasis was, of course, inconsistent with Schopenhauer's pessimism and irrationalism, in which the best that morality could provide a man was not a practical guide to conduct or success, but some relief or escape from the miserable lot of human existence. At first glance, it might appear that Schopenhauer would have little to offer a man wishing to escape from his slavery to desires and the Will. He has a deterministic theory of human action in which whatever a man does inevitably expresses his inner will, which is fixed and unchangeable. The common-sense belief in the freedom of the will is an illusion, for across the spans of experience, however remote or complex, the causal chain remains unbroken. Schopenhauer also rejects the "theological morals" of previous philosophers who grounded their systems of ethics in God's will or some form of transcendent Absolutes. He feels that Kant's criticisms of the various proofs of God's existence banished Theism from philosophy and that Kant should have been aware that he was trying indirectly and erroneously to salvage the spirit of the Bible by founding morality on the categorical imperative. He also rejects the Socratic identification of knowledge and virtue, since he believes egoism to be the fundamental drive in man.

"Egoism is, from its nature, limitless. The individual is filled with the unqualified desire of preserving his life and of keeping it free from all pain, under which is included all want and privation" (*Basis of Morality*, p. 151). Anyone who understands egoism will know that human nature cannot be reformed by social institutions. Neither will he accept the romantic illusion that one should seek positive happiness. When men are worn out by the endless cycle of struggle and frustration, they discover that the search for the avoidance of pain has more meaning than the quest for pleasure. In Schopenhauer's view the egoist is intent on his own advantage and does not harm other people unless they get in his way. The malicious man, however, derives his basic satisfactions from hurting others. All the vices and depravity of human conduct spring from egoism and malice.

How can one find within human nature a motive strong enough to defy the demands of egoism and malice? Schopenhauer nominates compassion, or sympathy, as the true virtue with which to oppose the evil incentive of life. Compassion, or sympathy, requires a curbing of the will-to-live and the development of a disinterested self-identification with others so that their suffering becomes ours. This expresses itself in a double aspect: (1) as *justice* in the restraint of personal advantage so that one does not exploit or oppress others who need impartial treatment; (2) as *love* (*caritas* or *agape* in distinction from *eros*, which is self-directed) like that which is taught in the purer forms of Christianity and Buddhism, where love returns good for evil, bears all things, and is unmindful of the claims of the self.

Schopenhauer's insistence that compassion is the only true virtue underlines his pessimism. The performance of altruistic acts prompted by justice or love does not end the frustration and pain of existence. Schopenhauer's morality thus bears a tragic outlook and a firm conviction that happiness and wellbeing are beyond human achievement.

If the world is as miserable and evil as he depicts it, why does not Schopenhauer advocate suicide? Although he does not view it as a crime or an act of cowardice, he sees suicide as a mistake since it does not destroy the Will, but only its bodily manifestation. Instead Schopenhauer thinks it better to deny the Will completely so that the human individual ceases to become attached to anything and thus cannot manifest the Will. He finds the way of salvation clearly marked by the Hindu philosophy of Maya and the Buddhist ethic. We must renounce the Will to live and all its works and virtues, no matter how much we value them as good, progressive, or comfortable. In other words, we must somehow will not to will. Along this path Schopenhauer finds asceticism and celibacy important steps. The universal practice of celibacy would, he argues, guarantee that there would be no more individual human beings in existence and thus eliminate human sin, evil, frustration, and the more complicated objectifications of the Will like human knowledge and the Platonic Ideas. Fasting and scourging have their place, for they help to reduce desires of all sorts. So Schopenhauer praises the saint who has a body (the Will made manifest) which no longer does the bidding of the Will. He believes that primitive Christianity and Buddhism originally stressed celibacy, universal suffering, the duty of charity, and the effort to subdue the claims of the self before these religions were corrupted by efforts to come to terms with the world.

The peace that comes from the denial of the Will-to-live surpasses, according to Schopenhauer, everything else in life. In concluding *The World as Will and Idea* he writes: "What remains after the entire abolition of the Will is for all those who are still full of Will certainly nothing; but, conversely, to those in whom the Will has turned and denied itself, this our world, which is so real, with all its suns and milky-ways is nothing." Of course there are many difficulties in Schopenhauer's views. How is the Will's denial of itself possible? It is an exception to Schopenhauer's theory of determinism? Would the universal Will in all its manifestations really be conquered if universal celibacy were to prevail? Perhaps these and other critical

questions should not be pressed too closely, for Schopenhauer is trying
to communicate some insights that transcend conceptual analysis
much in the fashion of the Hindu Vedas and the writings of some of the
Christian mystics.

Arthur Schopenhauer: Suggested Additional Reading

Abernethy, George L. and Thomas A. Langford, eds., *History of Philosophy:
Selected Readings*. Belmont, Calif.: Dickenson, 1965, pp. 568–586.*

Barnes, Hazel E., *The Pessimistic Handbook*. Lincoln: University of Neb-
raska Press, 1964.*

Copleston, Frederick C., *Arthur Schopenhauer: Philosopher of Pessimism*.
London: Burns, Oates and Washburne, 1946.*

Gardiner, Patrick, *Schopenhauer*. Baltimore: Penguin, 1963.

Knox, I., *The Aesthetic Theories of Kant, Hegel and Schopenhauer*. New York:
Humanities Press, 1936.*

Schopenhauer, *The Art of Literature*. Ann Arbor: University of Michigan
Press, paper, 1960.

Schopenhauer, *The World as Will and Representation*. Translated by E. F.
Payne. 2 vols. New York: Dover, 1966.

Schopenhauer, *The Philosophy of Schopenhauer*, Edited, with an introduction
by I. Edman. New York: The Modern Library, 1928.*

Schopenhauer, *On the Basis of Morality*. Translated by E. F. Payne.
Indianapolis: Bobbs-Merrill, Liberal Arts Press, 1965.

Schopenhauer, *Essays On Freedom of the Will*. Translated by Konstantin
Kolenda. Indianapolis: Bobbs-Merrill, Liberal Arts Press, 1960.

Schopenhauer, *The Will to Live: Selected Writings*. Edited by Richard
Taylor. Garden City: Doubleday Anchor, 1962.

Taylor, Richard, "Schopenhauer" in D. J. O'Connor, ed., *A Critical
History of Western Philosophy*. New York: Free Press of Glencoe, 1964,
pp. 365–383.

Wallace, William, *Life of Arthur Schopenhauer*. London: W. Scott, 1890.*

Zimmern, Helen, *Schopenhauer: His Life and Philosophy*. London: Allen
and Unwin, 1932.*

Chapter Twenty-Three
Søren Kierkegaard

Søren Kierkegaard (1813–1855), Danish philosopher and theologian, was born in Copenhagen, the son of a wealthy businessman. Physically Kierkegaard was a frail child, born with a hunched back and uneven legs, but his brilliance was recognized early and his family encouraged his intellectual maturation. In his autobiography (*The Point of View of My Work as an Author*, 1848, published posthumously) he mentions three things which he inherited from his father: imagination, dialectic skill, and religious melancholy; and, according to his account, his father deliberately cultivated these powers in his son.

In 1830 Søren entered the University of Copenhagen in the theological course, although he reports that during his first years in the university his primary interest was in literature and philosophy. Through his undergraduate years he enjoyed the theater and good food and was known for his cleverness and gourmet tastes, but he neglected his studies and only poorly fulfilled his intellectual promise.

Sometime around the year 1835 Kierkegaard experienced a convulsive inner turmoil. He became poignantly aware of his relation to his father, and in assessing his father's emotional condition and unusual influence he became convinced that his parent had suffered some secret moral defection and that his gaining of wealth was a way by which God was ironically punishing him. Further, Søren was persuaded that a divine curse had been placed upon the entire family; this suspicion gnawed at him until he reached a point of profound melancholy or despair which issued, for a time, in complete estrangement from his father. Through the initiative of the father, however, the relationship was renewed and a closer and newly creative bond was established between them.

As a result of this alienation and renewal of relationship the young man not only learned to better understand his father but again found a consoling belief in God's fatherly love. In May 1838, just a few months before his father's death, the young Kierkegaard had a profound religious experience which issued in his acceptance of the study and interpretation of religious existence as his vocation. With renewed energy he returned to his academic work and in 1841 graduated from the university in the theological course.

Another part of Kierkegaard's biography is also important for understanding his work as a writer and his sensitivity to human pathos. For several years Søren courted a young girl, Regina Olsen; subsequently he proposed and in due time their engagement was announced. Almost immediately after the announcement he became distressed, convinced that he had done the wrong thing; consequently, in 1841, a year after he had given her a ring, he broke the engagement. His own accounts of this relationship reveal a deep love for Regina, and great agony over the broken engagement, but there was a dominant awareness that his own vocational dedication would not allow this love to come to fruition in marriage. He was persuaded that he must give her up in order to surrender himself with a single devotion to the writing which he believed to be his peculiar vocation.

In the period from 1841 until 1847 Kierkegaard wrote an impressive number of books: *Either/Or, Repetition, Fear and Trembling* (1843); *Philosophical Fragments* and *The Concept of Dread* (1844); *Stages on Life's Way* (1845); *Concluding Unscientific Postscript to the Philosophical Fragments* (1846); *Edifying Discourses In Various Spirits* and *Works of Love* (1847).

In 1848 occurred his second great religious experience, an overwhelming conviction that he should openly and radically attack the "official" Christianity of his homeland. Thus he moved into his period of renunciation of culture-Christianity or "Christendom" as he preferred to call it. The last years of his life were dedicated to this attack upon Christendom, by which he intended to distinguish between the requirements of authentic Christian discipleship and the Christian faith and life as it was nominally exemplified in the Church of Denmark. His writing of this time illustrates his concerns: *Training in Christianity, For Self-Examination,* and *Judge for Yourselves!* (1850–1852). When Bishop Munster (a former friend of Søren's father and a frequent visitor in their home) died in 1854 and was succeeded by Hans Martensen, who had been Søren's tutor briefly during his undergraduate days and a man whom Kierkegaard greatly disliked, a renewed attack on the state church was launched. In the period between December 1854 and September 1855 he wrote some twenty-one articles in the *Fatherland* as well as a number of other pamphlets. The battle was soon transferred from the arena of the scholars to the public forum, popular outcries were heard, and counter attacks occurred as adversaries entered the debate. Kierkegaard held his lonely vigil, but the exertion proved to be too much, and in October 1855 he was stricken with a paralysis from which he died a month later.

The Spheres of Existence

Kierkegaard has often been called the "Father of modern existentialism." And while existentialist philosophers have been radically different in their emphases, so that many might not want to trace their genealogy to him, it is basically true to say that Søren Kierkegaard inaugurated or at least gave new life to this philosophical approach. To understand some of the basic emphases of this type of thinking we should begin by looking carefully at Kierkegaard's description of man in existence.

The group of books which he wrote between 1843 and 1845 he described as his "aesthetic works." In these writings he consistently used pseudonyms for himself. It is not possible to indicate exactly why he used these "false names," but certainly one of the reasons prominent in his own thinking was that these writings represented something of his own intellectual search and maturation and that in these early works he was exploring ground which he was not sure he would himself be willing to stand upon.

According to Kierkegaard, there are three stages on life's way: the aesthetic, the ethical, and the religious. These three stages are set forth both in his *Stages On Life's Way* and in the *Postscript*, and they represent the fundamental choices which are given to man in his existence. That is to say, man organizes his life around one of these alternative possibilities, each of which makes an absolute claim upon man.

Kierkegaard does not mean to suggest that there is a necessary progression from one of these stages to the next, so that every man can be described as moving from the aesthetic to the moral to the religious stage. Nor are these stages viewed as being temporally distinct even when found within the single life. But in spite of the mixture of these spheres in the life of the concrete, existing individual, he still contends that each man basically organizes his life around one of these commitments, which then becomes the dominant determinant in his life. In the last analysis, no compromise between the radical counter claimants is possible; man fundamentally sees himself as an aesthetic, moral, or religious being. While the radical differentia between the variant modes of existence are retained through his thought, there is also an awareness that once the absoluteness of the religious stance is affirmed it is possible to transform or reinterpret the ethical and aesthetic claims in such a manner as to make them participants in the religious stance in life.

Underlying the discussion of these three stances which the concrete individual may take in life are two assumptions which are basic to all of Kierkegaard's thought. In the first place, there is an emphasis upon man in existence. As opposed to Hegel and his endeavor to understand man as a part of the Absolute and therefore to understand the "essential" nature of man, Kierkegaard intends to interpret man in regard to the individuality and uniqueness of his existence. The individual, *qua* individual, is the main concern of this thinker. Man is not to be subsumed under some more inclusive category; individual men are not to be understood only in terms of their representation of some essential nature of reality. Existence takes precedence over essence, and to come to a valid interpretation of human existence we must look at man in his existence, in his historical way of life, and in terms of his own distinctive way of living. Throughout, there is an uncompromising antagonism with Hegelianism with its inclusive, all-encompassing interpretation of man and history, an interpretation which seemed to him to deny the uniqueness of the individual man and his context. In the second place, Kierkegaard also insists upon the freedom of man. The individual in his freedom rather than the individual as an expression of universal and necessary laws is the responsible agent who determines his own mode of existence.

Aesthetic Stage

The aesthetic sphere of existence Kierkegaard represents by reference to three characters who are well known in literature: Don Juan, Faust, and Ahasuerus (the wandering Jew). The character of the aesthete as a Don Juan is to be found in the accentuation of man's passionate sensate nature. For instance, in his description of Johannes the Seducer in *Either/Or* he explores, with great sensitivity, the various ways in which a man may heighten and titillate his feelings, and enjoy his skill in being passionately related to a girl. This story, despite its title, is not in the style of contemporary seduction stories; rather it is the account of how a sensitive, clever young man, Johannes, becomes engaged to an intriguing girl, deriving the greatest pleasure from every encounter, every conversation, and every look, and how he plans and executes every nuance of the relationship; then, once he has won her, he reverses the process and, again enjoying the passionate qualities of the involvement, slowly and carefully brings the relationship to a conclusion. At no point is the passion sensual in crude terms; it is the story of an aesthete who has developed his passionate awareness to an unusually keen point of sensitivity, who relishes every moment and every movement, and who holds each taste for enjoyable reflection.

The story of Faust is used to indicate the possibility in aesthetic experience of moving from the confidence and buoyancy of Don Juan to skepticism and the radical need to search for truth. Faust knows that the human spirit cannot be satisfied by passionate involvement in transient experience, and a Faustian man is sure that he has not found the true meaning of existence even though his entire living is an attempt to find meaning. Nevertheless, this search is the search of the aesthete: negatively, because he refuses to view himself in the light of moral standards or religious demands which are imposed on his existence and, positively, because he attempts to derive his meaning and his pleasure from the search as search. Yet, the pleasure must also be examined and its foundation explored. Faust represents the man who has the insatiable hunger of the doubter of truth but who also refuses to acknowledge the hopelessness of his mode of existence or the depths of his own despair. He lives by and for his unending search, always with a hopeful reach.

It is the wandering Jew, Ahasuerus, who brings the recognition of despair to its keenest focus. In the symbol of Ahasuerus Kierkegaard sees the man who accepts the necessity of an endless and indifferent wandering through the world, and who accepts the complete absence of hope whether it be placed in God or men. It is typical of man to attempt to hide or deny this despair, and indeed much of the intensity of the aesthetic search is precisely for this purpose, but in the wandering Jew the conclusion of aesthetic existence is made clear: he is man in despair, without hope, seeing his existence for what it is and accepting his fate—a wanderer on the earth who finally resorts to irony to explain his position.

Ethical Stage

Next Kierkegaard turns to the ethical stage or sphere of existence. In this sphere man lives by the rules which are set down by some society or by some tradition. At every turn he appeals to an unconditional standard of moral perfection, and he measures his own actions against that norm. The chief character who is used to represent this attitude is named Judge William. In the second part of *Either/Or* (the "either" representing aesthetic existence and the "or" moral existence), the Judge describes this way of life. The way of wisdom, as the Judge understands it, is expressed in one precept: *Choose Thyself*.

The act of decision separates the ethical from the aesthetic sphere. In his discussion of the aesthete, Kierkegaard has said that to live in the aesthetic sphere does not involve a choice; it is rather an immediate response which might also be called a "natural reaction" or a following of the desires of the heart. There is always a transient character to the aesthetic existence, for, since no absolute judgement or decision is made, one lives only moment by moment and what is done in one moment may be changed in another. On the other hand, the act of choice is an expression of the ethical sphere. Thus, whenever in a strict or radical sense there is an awareness of an absolute either/or and a decision is made about this juncture in life, such a decision is evidence of the ethical dimension. This means that the ethical sphere is dominated by the will, by conscious and deliberate decision.

But what is ethical existence? Judge William calls the ethical the "universal and as such divine." In contrast to aesthetic existence, the ethical has continuity, it ties the past to the future. Hence, Judge William argues that the great thing is not to be this or that, but *to be oneself*, and this is something which every man can be if he wills. In this choice of himself, man acknowledges an absolute either/or and an absolute distinction between good and evil, and he makes a decision in the light of this acknowledgment. Here, then, is ethical existence, it is the act of choosing, of exhorting one's freedom or capacity for significant decision.

Religious Stage

Kierkegaard is convinced that neither the aesthetic nor the ethical sphere is representative of authentic life and that in the last analysis if man is to find his true self and his true destiny he must move on to the religious sphere. The aesthetic realm leaves man without a continuing self and the ethical sphere leaves man with an incomplete understanding of himself. The latter contention Kierkegaard supports by arguing that although the ethical reaches out toward the universal, the ethical man either has to disregard sin in human life, or, if he probes this dimension of his existence, he is immediately carried beyond the point at which an ethical interpretation is any longer viable.

To move to the religious stage of life is to find one's existential fulfillment in the transcendent reality. The man who is living authentically is responsible not only to himself and to his neighbor but also, and above all, he is responsible to God. The ethical stage is surpassed when man recognizes (chooses) himself as guilty and hopes for divine forgiveness. In the concluding pages of the *Postscript* a distinction is drawn between "religion A" and "religion B." When a man stands aware of the self-annihilation of his sinfulness before God, he is in the state of "religion A." In this condition he is capable of experiencing the crisis of existential despair, the "sickness unto death." This sickness is found in the man who "despairingly . . . wants to be himself; but with the despair cannot get rid of the self." Consequently, to be sick unto death is to know that there is an authentic selfhood and yet not be able to realize that selfhood. "Religion B" is the designation for the mode of existence which is expressed in faith. For Kierkegaard, it is in faith that man finds his authentic selfhood, but such affirmation requires the risk of everything; it is a leap. However, the risk is necessary if man is to be himself and is to live his life with an awareness of its singular as well as its infinite and eternal significance.

In the book which Kierkegaard regards as his best, *Fear and Trembling*, he describes a man who became a "Knight of faith" and who therefore fulfilled the promise of the religious stage of existence. This man is Abraham, and as Kierkegaard retells the Old Testament story he emphasizes the qualities of the deciding, unique, free person. The focus of the story is upon Abraham's willingness to sacrifice his son Isaac. According to all general ethical standards, this is a foolish act; it fits no embracing objective criterion for human activity, and it has no place in a rationally ordered (Hegelian) world scheme. Yet Abraham is willing to do this singular act. The poignancy of the sacrifice is emphasized by the fact that the hope for immortality in the story is through one's progeny; consequently it is through Isaac that Abraham and his hopes should live. The temptation which Abraham most immediately faces is that of taking his own life, for by so doing he would be performing a heroic act and might be acclaimed. But he is unreserved in his commitment to the commandment of God; he goes up on Mount Moriah, draws the knife, and is ready to offer his son—that is, everything, his future, his plans, even God's promises. To do this act would not make him a hero, but, according to Kierkegaard, it is the sign of his saintliness. Here is one man who is willing to set aside the common standards and decisively act upon his own unique calling and follow his own singular path. As used by our author, this story is a parable of what all Christians should be, but each man can become a knight of faith only as he goes through the same existential threat and makes an affirmation like that of Abraham.

For each man there is a crisis experience which begins when a man faces the nothingness of his present mode of existence and senses fear or, more exactly, an anxiety which is the beginning of despair. At this moment, man must make a leap into faith. In *Postscript*, in his section on "What it is to Become a Christian," Kierkegaard states that real Christian faith is found in a decision made by the person. Thus, "The thing of being a Christian is not determined by the *what* of

Christianity but by the *how* of the Christian." Faith is neither rational assurance nor assent to certain dogmatic formulae; rather it is an affective appropriation. Faith cannot be reduced by indicating its reasonableness or its objective certainty. Rather it is a holding fast with an inward passion for God, a radical trust in God, and it is a commitment which is only validated in the process of life.

In the last analysis, according to Kierkegaard, the religious man or the man of faith is one who has become contemporaneous with Jesus Christ; that is, he has taken this singular historical figure as his guide and the maelstrom of existence. Consistently, he uses phrases which refer to becoming, in contrast to arrival, in order to stress the fact that existential truth has continuous consequences in one's daily conduct and thought. To become contemporaneous with this particular past figure is both to believe in the importance of the past (in this case the historical Jesus) and to identify with its implications for one who would follow the way of a knight of faith.

Truth as Subjectivity

One of the most fundamental antipathies in Kierkegaard's thought is his reaction to the philosophy of Hegel, though it should be noted that he holds his most caustic comments for Hegelianism as a widespread attitude rather than for Hegel himself. He does not attempt to counter particular points of Hegel's own philosophical statement; rather he rejects every system which assumes an essentialistic or pantheistic base. The basic argument he proposes is that Hegelianism gives primacy to essence over existence; therefore, it speaks in universal, inclusive terms about man and his meaning. Since in Hegel's system thought and being must be regarded as fundamentally identical, Hegelianism attempts to subsume all men under its "system of world history." Hence, Hegel's theory of world history is inimical to Kierkegaard's understanding of man's life as a responsible individual. In other words, for the Hegelian, existence is deduced from essence as the individual human existents are submerged in the larger category of "mankind."

In opposition to this philosophy, Kierkegaard proposes to follow out the "logic" of subjectivism or man's inwardness. Truth obtained by means of such "objectively" oriented research is "hypothetical" and "approximate." What must be found is a way of approaching and interpreting life which emphasizes the existential attitude of the individual person. In the discussion in the *Postscript*, it is insisted that truth is always practical, always incomplete, and essentially paradoxical. In simpler language, subjective truth is to be found in the free exercise of judgment and action. Truth is found by participation, personal involvement, and intense engagement. He writes, "Christianity protests every form of objectivity; it desires that the subject should be infinitely concerned about himself. It is subjectivity that Christianity is concerned with, and it is only in subjectivity that its truth exists." And in this sense, "Faith is the highest passion in the sphere of human subjectivity."

When the truth is approached in an objective manner, the concern is with the object to which the subject is related. If the object is understood to be true, then the one who knows that object may be said to be in the truth. But when the question of truth is approached in a subjective manner, the reflection is focused upon the relationship of the knower to that which is known. If the mode of this relationship is true, then the individual is in the truth. In this latter approach the emphasis is clearly upon the knower and how he is related to that which is known.

Kierkegaard takes as an illustration of this method of knowing the question of man's knowledge of God. From an objective point of view, the primary interrogation is whether or not the object of attention is the true God, and whether or not he can determine the approximate truth of the God-idea. From the subjective point of view "The question (is) whether the individual is related to something *in such a manner* that his relationship is in truth a God-relationship." God cannot be approached as an object. He is always subject and can only be found through subjective interinvolvement. The man who knows God in inward passion is driven by his infinite need of God and feels an infinite concern for his relation to God. According to this interpretation it is better to pray to an idol with infinite passion than to pray to the "true God" with a false spirit. " *The objective accent falls on WHAT is said, the subjective accent on HOW it is said.*"

Kierkegaard rejects every attempt to mediate between these two approaches, though he argues that such an attempt represents the continual effort of Hegelian philosophy. One is forced to a choice and brought to the point where he must make a confession of faith. For faith is found precisely in the contradiction between the objective questioning and uncertainty and the infinite passion of the individual's inwardness. If one can grasp God objectively he does not believe, but if one believes he must do so in the face of the fact that he cannot grasp God with certainty.

Becoming a Christian in Christendom

The final period of Kierkegaard's life found him involved in a struggle against what he took to be the false interpretation of Christianity perpetuated by the state church in Denmark. His primary charge against the "official" Christianity of the nation is that it undermines both the moral seriousness of genuine Christianity and undercuts the transcendent element in Christian faith so that the church and the world are identified. In a parable, which he tells twice in his writings, Kierkegaard recounts the story of a young clergyman who is searching for a position. In his search he is concerned to find a church which will give him the values prized by society at large, while at the same time allowing him to serve God. He abides by the government regulations; he seeks a wife and a well-paying parish and wants to impress the Bishop. Then he preaches on the text, "Seek ye first the Kingdom of God." This young man is typical of people within Christendom in general; they do not seek the Absolute, they seek absolutely everything.

What authentic Christianity demands is purity of heart, which comes only through the willing of one thing. But this is precisely what the established religious and social order will not allow. Therefore the problem is how can one become a Christian in Christendom? How can one express radical faith in a situation where moderate, compromised, culturally conformed faith is the way of life? How can one be a Christian in a culture where everyone claims to be a Christian and where Christian faith no longer has any distinctive character? Kierkegaard attempts to formulate answers to this problem in terms of what it means to become a Christian, as we have seen, but he is aware of the tremendous resistance which the institutional structures will express.

In the face of this opposition, Kierkegaard took the offensive and carried the battle to his opponents. It cannot be claimed that his influence was very largely felt during his own lifetime even in his own country. But his approach to philosophical problems was to become more influential, especially in the twentieth century when both theistic and nontheistic thinkers would utilize his approach to questions of life and thought.

For the first several decades after Kierkegaard's death the regnancy of Hegelian idealism retarded his impact. But after the turn of the century he was being read with interest both on the continent and among English-speaking people, and his influence became extensive. A divergence of interests gave rise to two distinct movements among existentialist thinkers. Some philosophers, notably Martin Heidegger, Karl Jaspers, and Jean-Paul Sartre, developed this philosophy in terms of an exclusive interest in its anthropological implications. Others, such as Gabriel Marcel, along with theologians Paul Tillich, Rudolf Bultmann, and Carl Michalson, concentrated upon and explicated theistic aspects of the position.

In the period between the two World Wars, existentialism became prominent, especially in France and Germany, and was widely espoused as a new style of philosophical thought and action. Since the second world war, many commentators feel its influence has waned among philosophers and its popular following has declined. But the existentialists' emphases upon the primacy of existence over essence and the participation of the knower in the process of gaining knowledge continue to be important factors in epistemological and ethical study.

Søren Kierkegaard: Suggested Additional Reading

Abernethy, George L. and Thomas A. Langford, eds., *History of Philosophy: Selected Readings*. Belmont, Calif.: Dickenson, 1965, pp. 550–567.*

Bonifazi, Conrad, *Christendom Attacked: A Comparison of Kierkegaard and Nietzsche*. London: Rockliff, 1953.*

Brown, James D., *Kierkegaard, Heidegger, Barth, Brunner*. New York: Macmillan, Collier, 1962.

Collins, James D., *The Mind of Kierkegaard*. Chicago: Henry Regnery, Gateway paperback, 1965.

Grene, Majorie, *Introduction to Existentialism*. Chicago: University of Chicago, Phoenix Books, 1959.

Hanna, Thomas, *The Lyrical Existentialists*. New York: Atheneum, 1962.*

Hohlenburg, Johannes E., *Søren Kierkegaard*. Translated by T. H. Croxall. New York: Pantheon, 1954.*

Jolivet, R., *Introduction to Kierkegaard*. Translated by W. H. Barber. New York: Dutton, 1952.*

Kaufmann, Walter, *Existentialism from Dostoevsky to Sartre*. New York: World Publishing Company, Meridian, 1962.

Kierkegaard, *The Concluding Unscientific Postscript*. Translated by D. F. Swenson and Walter Lowrie. Princeton: Princeton University Press, 1944.*

Kierkegaard, *Stages on Life's Way*. Translated by Walter Lowrie. New York: Schocken, 1967.

Kierkegaard, *Kierkegaard's The Concept of Dread*. Translated by Walter Lowrie. 2nd edition. Princeton: Princeton University Press, 1967.

Kierkegaard, *A Kierkegaard Anthology*. Edited by Robert Bretall. New York: Modern Library, 1959.

Kierkegaard, *Fear and Trembling and the Sickness unto Death*. New York: Doubleday, Anchor, 1954.

Kierkegaard, *Either/Or*. Translated by Walter Lowrie and D. F. and Lillian M. Swenson. 2 vols. New York: Doubleday, Anchor, 1959.

Kierkegaard, *Edifying Discourses*. Introduction by Paul Holmer. New York: Harper and Row, Torchbook, 1958.

Kierkegaard, *Philosophical Fragments*, 2nd edition. Originally translated and introduced by Lillian Swenson. New Introduction and commentary by Neils Thulstrup. Translation revised and commentary translated by Howard V. Hong. Princeton: Princeton University Press, 1967.

Lowrie, Walter, *Kierkegaard: A Life*. 2 vols. New York: Harper and Row, Torchbook, 1962.

Chapter Twenty-Four

Bentham and Mill

The philosophical situation in nineteenth-century England differed quite markedly from that which prevailed in the preceding two centuries in both England and Europe. It produced neither front rank speculative metaphysicians like Descartes or Berkeley nor thinkers as persistent as Locke and Hume in pursuing basic epistemological questions. Instead it was a century in which thoughtful men turned their attention to more limited fields of inquiry within an urgent social context. In the main, British philosophers revealed very little acquaintance with German philosophical developments, although Caird and Bradley were exceptions in the latter part of the century. In the field of science they deferred to the working scientists for knowledge about the physical world.

The English philosophers of the nineteenth century were preoccupied with the pressing problems of social reform occasioned by the application of machine technology to the production of goods in a traditional rural society. This Industrial Revolution produced an urban proletariat living in the midst of unbelievable squalor, illness, ignorance, child labor, low pay, and long hours of work. Writers, philosophers, and many generous spirits took the initiative in reporting the misery of the workers, the complacency of the owners, and the injustices of the political and legal system which reinforced the status quo. Among these persons was a loosely organized group of left-wing Whigs who came to be called "Philosophical Radicals." The most conspicuous of the leaders of this reform group were the philosophers Jeremy Bentham, James Mill, and John Stuart Mill. In a day when journals were widely read and influential they founded the *Westminster Review* in 1824 and the *London Review* in 1835 for the promulgation of their doctrines. They rejected the slogans and doctrinaire ideas of the French Revolution, and fought the post-Napoleonic tendency to reaction and the blind support of the status quo. They concerned themselves with the development of basic theories, broadly empirical and hedonistic, in psychology, logic, ethics, and politics in the optimistic hope that once these theories were formulated and understood there would soon follow the appropriate applications to specific social problems.

Jeremy Bentham

Jeremy Bentham (1748–1832) was the precocious son of a wealthy lawyer. He gave himself to the study of Latin at the age of four and soon thereafter to French and the violin. At the age of twelve he entered Queens College, Oxford, and received his B.A. at age fifteen and his M.A. three years later. To please his father he studied law and attended Blackstone's lectures (which later he subjected to severe criticism), but he never practiced law although he became an outstanding legal critic and reformer. A legacy from his father enabled Bentham to give full time to writing and study, so that his published works ran to eleven volumes. He led an austere life, never marrying and never consenting to see anyone save for "some specific purpose." He did not imbibe wine and had no taste for poetry: "Prose," he asserted, "is when all the lines except the last go on to the margin. Poetry is when some of them fall short of it." Nevertheless, he attracted many sensitive and able intellectuals as disciples and friends. One would have to go all the way back to the ancient Epicureans and Stoics to find so dedicated a group of thinkers committed to a common viewpoint as a strategy for dealing with the world's ills.

Bentham scornfully rejected Blackstone's views on natural rights and the appeals to the "moral sense" doctrines of English and Scotch philosophers. Locke's ideas on social contract, natural rights, and natural law he held to be unwarranted and *a priori*. He judged the American Declaration of Independence and the French Declaration of the Rights of Man and the Citizen to be meaningless documents. He held the English Common Law to be a jungle of contradictory notions which were valuable for enabling greedy lawyers to charge exhorbitant, and often completely unnecessary, fees.

In his first work, *Fragment on Government*, Bentham maintains that political obligation and obedience to law are dependent on the welfare of the people whom they protect. The ultimate basis of organized political society rests upon the principle of utility. Later he was to call this the greatest happiness principle, although the school of thought continued to be known as utilitarianism. Bentham states the principle in the following terms:

By the principle of utility is meant that principle which approves or disapproves of every action whatsoever, according to the tendency which it appears to have to augment or diminish the happiness of the party whose interest is in question: or, what is the same thing in other words, to promote or to oppose that happiness. I say of every action whatsoever; and therefore not only of every action of a private individual, but of every measure of government (*Principles of Morals and Legislation*, Ch. 1, sec. 2).

Happiness is used here to mean the same as pleasure. Unhappiness is the same as pain. Men seek the greatest possible happiness for themselves. The function of law and its sanction is to see that a man, in seeking his own greatest possible happiness, should not thwart this pursuit for others. Bentham does not attempt to prove the principle of utility (which he takes from Hume), since he holds it to be a self-evident principle and the proof of it unnecessary on the basis that whatever is employed to prove everything else cannot itself be demonstrated.

In Bentham's view, the purpose of government and its system of law is to provide the citizenry with the greatest possible amount of happiness. In order to accomplish this, the legislators need to choose among acts which please one person and those which bring happiness to others. As a precise scientific method of appraising pleasures and pains, Bentham proposes a "hedonistic calculus" which would scrutinize pleasures and pains in the light of the following seven basic considerations: (1) the intensity of the pleasure or pain, (2) its duration or length, (3) its certainty of occurrence, (4) its nearness or remoteness, (5) its fecundity or likelihood of being followed by sensations of the same kind, (6) its purity or likelihood of not being followed by sensations of the opposite kind, and (7) its extent or the number of persons it may affect. He tells us: "Sum up all the values of all the *pleasures* on the one side and those of all the *pains* on the other. The balance, if it be on the side of pleasure, will give the *good* tendency of the act upon the whole, with respect to the interests of the *individual* person; if on the side of pain, the *bad* tendency of it upon the whole." Thus he believes one has only to add these sum-totals for each individual to determine the tendency of any act to affect the community's happiness. Bentham is chiefly interested in the quantitative aspects of pleasure. For him all actions are equally good if they produce the same amount of pleasure. He appears unaware of the difficulties encountered by any theory that seeks to combine additive and nonadditive qualities. Critics have dealt harshly with his hedonistic calculus. Yet the seven measures he proposes do involve basic considerations which must be investigated in any serious act of decision-making.

It is clear that the concept of government in Bentham's philosophy is not a positive one involving a preconceived plan or absolute goal. The function of government is simply to maximize pleasure and minimize pain. This the legislators can accomplish mainly by the use of punishments. Bentham delineates four "sanctions," or pains and pleasures, which guided actions. These are (1) the "physical or natural," (2) "political," (3) "moral or popular," and (4) "religious." Only the political sanction is the concern of the legislator who, by providing punishments in the form of taxes, penalties, and jail sentences, can add to the costs of an action judged to impair the greatest happiness of the greatest number. This might inhibit the proposed action on the part of any individual or group of individuals. The legislators, then, are to confine themselves to the allocation and enactment of these punishments.

Critics of Bentham were quick to point out that if he were correct in suggesting that everyone pursues his own greatest happiness, his theory would have considerable difficulty in accounting for the altruism of legislators in voting for political sanctions that would motivate behavior in the direction of the greatest happiness of the greatest number when such voting appeared to run counter to the immediate interests of specific legislators. Bentham defended his altruistic hedonism by asserting that there is an ultimate identity of interests such that a man following enlightened self-interest can see altruism as following from egoism. As for himself, he found his own personal pleasure in promoting the happiness of others. But the integration of egoism and altruism is more difficult to establish than Bentham acknowledged.

James Mill

Although Bentham remained the intellectual leader, James Mill (1773–1836) was the driving force behind utilitarianism. The son of a poor Scotch farmer, James Mill managed to obtain a degree at the University of Edinburgh in 1790, after which he took a four-year course in the divinity school and was licensed to preach. Growing agnosticism forced him to give up a career in the ministry to follow an even more precarious life in London as a freelance writer in philosophy and economics. His famed work, *History of India*, was published in 1817. Subsequently he held many important administrative posts in the India House. In 1808 he became a close friend and disciple of Bentham, whom he influenced in many ways.

The chief philosophical contribution of James Mill was his two-volume *Analysis of the Phenomena of the Human Mind*, which carried to great extremes the theory of associationism, a view shared by most of the early utilitarians. He acknowledged the roots of his empiricism in the thought of Hume and Hartley in England and of Condillac and Helvétius in France. Consciously following what he took to be the example of the science of physics, Mill argued that psychology should begin with its primary or simplest elements in sense perception and then trace the manner in which these elements combine, according to the laws of association, to form more complex ideas and related mental phenomena. All association, he held, is to be interpreted as contiguity in time or place. The strength of any association will depend on the frequency with which it has been repeated and the vividness of the accompanying feelings and sensations. As a reformer, Mill believes that men's behavior and desires can be changed if the proper psychological arrangements are made to destroy the old associations and replace them with new associations. Although as a social reformer he might use this associationism in several ways, he tends to stress mainly its connection with a form of individualism which believed that under ideal conditions the less government we have the better off we will be.

John Stuart Mill

To the lay reader, James Mill is more likely to be known for the strict educational program he laid out for his son, John Stuart Mill (1806–1873), who later in his classic *Autobiography* referred to it as "a course in Benthamism." As an infant prodigy, John Stuart Mill overshadowed even Bentham. He began the study of Greek at the age of three and of Latin at eight, together with algebra and geometry. By the age of eight he had read in the original Aesop's *Fables*, Xenophon's *Anabasis*, and the whole of Herodotus. By age ten he could read Plato and Demosthenes with ease. It is safe to say that before adolescence he had worked his way through most of the ancient classics and made a good start of calculus and economics. But art and religious instruction were systematically excluded from his course of study by his father. James Mill never sent his son to school, but heard his lessons on walks in the late afternoon. He appointed him teacher of the younger children in the family and compelled him to write criticisms of every author he read. Years later John Stuart Mill complained that he had never been a boy or played cricket. At age twenty he had a severe depression. Apparently Wordsworth's poetry was influential in stimulating his return to a normal participation in the utilitarian movement and a new interest in the "cultivation of the feelings" through poetry and art.

In 1823 John Stuart Mill entered the service of the East India Company as a clerk in his father's department and subsequently held positions of increasing responsibility until the company was dissolved in 1858. He had a long attachment of love with Mrs. Harriet Taylor, whom he married after her first husband's death. Mill generously attributed to her many of his ideas. There is evidence to indicate that she moderated the influence upon him of the extreme individualists among the Utilitarians and interested him in a form of socialism more akin to the cooperative and syndicalist versions than the Marxian. Whatever concessions he may have made to socialism under Mrs. Taylor's influence, it is still accurate to characterize him as a liberal in a capitalist society. Among his many works are *A System of Logic* (1843), *Principles of Political Economy* (1848), *On Liberty* (1859), *Considerations on Representative Government* (1861), *Utilitarianism* (1863), *Examination of Sir William Hamilton's Philosophy* (1865), *Autobiography* (1873), and *Three Essays on Religion* (1874). He wrote countless book reviews and essays. It is remarkable that most of this writing was done in Mill's spare time in evenings and on weekends. In 1865 he served a term as a member of the House of Commons. In 1873 he died in Avignon, France, where he had lived in retirement.

Mill's Experimental Logic

A System of Logic (1843) is the book which first firmly established John Stuart Mill's reputation in philosophical circles. This was due to the clear statement and examination of what Mill called the five canons of inductive proof. He refined Francis Bacon's earlier statement of inductive procedure, but he did not repeat Bacon's mistake of over-looking the significance of deduction.

Logic, for Mill, is "the science of the operations of the understanding which are subservient to the estimation of evidence" (*System of Logic*, Introd., sec. 7). It is a philosophy of evidence, an explanation of the use of reason for the discovery of causes. Thus deductive logic or "the logic of consistency" is a "smaller logic" within the "larger logic" of the empirical ascertainment of truth. Deduction does not lead to new truth. It merely enables us to develop formally the implications of any generalization we have already accepted. Human thinking begins and ends in observations of particular facts. Mill thus gives major attention in his *System of Logic* to describing in a meticulous fashion inductive methods and consequently relegating deduction to a subsidiary role.

Mill delineates four inductive methods and adds a combination of two of them as a fifth: (1) the method of agreement, (2) the method of difference, (3) the method of concomitant variations, (4) the method of residues, and (5) the joint method of agreement and difference.

This type of causal analysis assumes that the sole invariable antecedent of an event is its cause, and the sole invariable consequent of an event is its effect. The method of difference is basic, for the inclusion or exclusion of a given factor is accompanied by the presence or absence of a specific condition or type of behavior. When the method of difference cannot be used altogether, the method of concomitant variation may still be employed for inductive proof and provide correlation. Critics of Mill have argued that the five methods are not laws for discovering causality, but are at most methods of eliminating candidates which have been proposed as causes.

One of the perennial problems of inductive logic has been to find a satisfactory justification for arguing inductively. It is still a problem for contemporary logicians. Mill deserves credit for attacking the problem directly and for his candor in stating his difficulties. Although much of his work has been superseded, logicians still return to it as material for useful critical analysis. Mill tends to claim that what justifies inductive arguments is the observed constancy of nature, which is itself a supreme induction. This circular reasoning does not satisfy him and leads him to reexamine the evidence for the law of universal causation. As an empiricist he has special difficulties in distinguishing between a subjective psychological sequence and an objective natural sequence.

Mill's Ethics

Mill's *Utilitarianism* provides a striking example of his efforts to blend new ideas with the basic principles of Benthamite thought as taught to him by his father. He was always intensely loyal to his father and Bentham. Yet in the light of his own experiences he came to feel that there were specific values which Bentham had ignored or even rejected. Mill felt that utilitarianism could be made more adequate and generous and therefore more defensible without sacrificing any essential principle of Benthamism. This is what he undertook to do in his now classic essay *Utilitarianism*.

Mill sums up the basic position of his ethical system in these words:

The creed which accepts as the foundation of morals, *Utility*, or the Greatest Happiness Principle, holds that actions are right in proportion as they tend to promote happiness, wrong as they tend to produce the reverse of happiness. By happiness is intended pleasure, and the absence of pain; by unhappiness, pain, and the privation of pleasure (*Utilitarianism*, Ch. 2, par. 2).

This is orthodox Benthamism, but Mill does not leave it here. The Benthamites have no room in the hedonistic calculus for anything but quantitative distinctions in happiness. If the simple game of push-pin provides men as large a quantity of pleasure as reading a page of poetry, then for Bentham push-pin is as valuable as poetry. But Mill contends that pleasure differs in kind or quality as well as in amount. The higher intellectual and aesthetic pleasures are greatly superior to the crude physical pleasures. "It is better to be a human being dissatisfied than a pig satisfied; better to be a Socrates dissatisfied than a fool satisfied." Essentially he is proposing the addition of an eighth criterion, quality, to the seven criteria of Bentham's hedonistic calculus. Mill argues:

It is quite compatible with the principle of utility to recognize the fact, that some *kinds* of pleasure are more desirable and more valuable than others. It would be absurd that while, in estimating all other things, quality is considered as well as quantity, the estimation of pleasures should be supposed to depend on quantity alone (*Utilitarianism*, Ch. 2, par. 4).

In arguing for this distinction Mill seeks the support of sensitive people who might otherwise be repelled by hedonism as a crude ethical materialism or "pig philosophy." It is unthinkable, for Mill, that a man would sacrifice his human dignity to join the animals in a round of uninterrupted pleasures. One who knows the pleasures of both poetry and push-pin will always prefer the pleasures of poetry.

It is easy to see why Mill's revision of Utilitarianism should appear to Benthamites as a heresy. Mill is going beyond the basic happiness principle in proposing another criterion of value in terms of which pleasures are to be judged. Yet Mill does not make clear how we are to decide what quality makes a nobler or better pleasure. Benthamites naturally accuse him of rejecting the hedonistic calculus as a sufficient measure of pleasure and of opening the door to subjectivists who believed in a variety of moral sentiments. Although he continued publicly and loyally to call himself a utilitarian, Mill's letters reveal that he recognized some of the difficulties of his position and that he was moving in the direction of perfectionism and Kantianism.

Although he joins Bentham in asserting the teleological position in ethics that the moral value of actions depends on their consequences, Mill does not follow Bentham in his insistence that the motive of an act has no bearing on the moral evaluation of the act. Mill maintains that whenever the motive makes a difference in the act, it also makes a difference in the morality of the act. Mill also moves beyond Bentham's professedly selfish pleasure in promoting altruistic hedonism. He has a more social conception of personality and maintains that people have a deeply rooted benevolent and sympathetic regard for their fellows. Thus altruistic hedonism has a fundamental empirical origin which does not have to be accounted for in terms of individualism or egoism.

In contrast to other utilitarians, Mill emphasizes that the minimization of pain is more significant than the maximizing of pleasure. Nearly everyone admits the duty of responding to an SOS call is more imperative than the duty to continue to enjoy the pleasures of smoking a pipe full of tobacco, that the duty of the government to provide fire, police, and emergency health protection against the pains which threaten one's existence takes precedence over the government's duty to provide recreational swimming. The traditional Benthamite hedonistic calculus appears to deny this moral priority. Mill urges the recognition that "utility includes not solely the pursuit of happiness, but the prevention or mitigation of unhappiness, and if the former aim be chimerical, there will be all the greater scope and more imperative need for the latter."

Mill is such a lucid writer that certain logical defects in his presentation of utilitarianism are more obvious than in less able writers. Consequently, he has provided the authors of logic textbooks with several of their best examples of logical fallacies. Whatever may be the logical inconsistencies in theory or his lack of success in blending the new with the old, he does provide a more subtle and generous ethical theory. This theory is still accepted by many ordinary people who, for one reason or another, have given up the theological and metaphysical sanctions of older moral theories and who may even be ignorant of the term "utilitarianism."

Mill's Social Philosophy

Mill's social philosophy is likewise important for the practical impact which it had on liberalism in the period between the social revolutions of 1848 and the outbreak of World War I in 1914. Here again Mill struggles vigorously to remain a Benthamite while making concessions which will render his social philosophy more adequate and relevant. He calls himself a democrat, but the system of government he favors in *Representative Government* (1861) has strong aristocratic emphases. He places a high evaluation on intellectual culture and tends to depreciate those who lack it. He wants to confine the right to vote to taxpayers for fear of legislation in the interests of the poor at the expense of the rich. This should be set against some of the concessions Mill makes to non-Marxian socialism. He acknowledges that the ultimate source of political authority lays in the people, but he cautions, "The people ought to be masters, but they are masters who must employ servants more skilful than themselves." He is really advocating the expert guidance of an *élite* of trained administrators and bureau-crats like those of his colleagues at the India Company. He does not believe that democratic institutions provided automatic safeguards against the majority's abuse of power over the minority. He feels the ordinary citizens do not require political rights to govern, but rather need them to avoid being misgoverned. He recognizes that the demand for universal suffrage will ultimately be irresistible. He thus wishes to include workers in the class of responsible, direct tax payers and sees universal education as the best possible preparation for universal suffrage. In *Representative Government* he abandons, for all practical purposes, the Benthamite assumption of *Utilitarianism* that each in-dividual's pursuit of his own good will automatically lead to the common pursuit of the common good.

Mill's most famous and influential work, *On Liberty*, was published in 1859—the same year as Darwin's *Origin of Species*. Earlier liberals had identified freedom with political freedom and defended the in-dividual against the tyranny of temporal and spiritual rulers. While embracing this view of freedom, Mill moves beyond it. He writes:

... when society is itself the tyrant—society collectively over the separate individuals who compose it . . . it practices a social tyranny more formidable than many kinds of political oppression, since, though not usually upheld by such extreme penalties, it leaves fewer means of escape, penetrating more deeply into the details of life, and enslaving the soul itself. Protection there-fore against the tyranny of the magistrate is not enough; there needs pro-tection also against the tyranny of the prevailing opinion and feeling; against the tendency of society to impose, by other means than civil penal-ties, its own ideas and practices as rules of conduct on those who dissent from them. . . . (*On Liberty*, Ch. I).

For Mill the purpose of good government is to protect and advance the common welfare. The government has a right to interfere with the acts of individuals only to prevent harm to others. In his own personal life, where he does not harm others, the individual should have the fullest liberty of thought and expression, of choice and action. Mill asserts: "If a person possesses any tolerable amount of common sense and experience, his own mode of laying out his existence is the best, not because it is the best in itself, but because it is his own mode." He argues against the limitation or suppression of the free discussion of any idea on several grounds. If the heterodox opinion is true, this is an added reason for its expression. If it is false, we gain by having it exposed mercilessly in the full glare of free discussion and we may be led to other truth in the process. If the heterodox belief is partly true and partly false, society needs free discussion to sift out the true from the false. In eloquent words which are still frequently quoted, Mill says:

If all mankind minus one were of one opinion, and only one person were of contrary opinion, mankind would be no more justified in silencing that one person, than he, if he had the power, would be justified in silencing mankind. Were an opinion a personal possession of no value except to its owner; if to be obstructed in the enjoyment of it were simply a private inquiry, it would make some difference whether the injury were inflicted on only a few persons or on many. But the peculiar evil of silencing the expression of an opinion is, that it is robbing the human race; posterity as well as the existing generation; those who dissent from the opinion still more than those who hold it. (*On Liberty*, Ch. II).

Mill does not allow as much liberty to men in their actions as in their opinions. He retains, however, the utilitarian bias in favor of the least government for society. In the free market of ideas he favors the unorganized, informal pressure of public opinion to the organized coercion of the formal police power. But more than either he favors free rational discussion, which he optimistically feels will in the long run prevail and do less harm and more good than any other conceivable alternative. Mill wrote before Freud, modern advertising, motivational research, drug-induced confessions, refined terror, "brain washing," and wire-tapping. Obviously our contemporary situation, a century later, is more complex and presents problems with which Mill did not and could not grapple. But many of the problems with which he dealt remain relevant as we seek today to define the limits of liberty. The fact is that, although we may find him too optimistic and too rational, we continue to read him because many of his arguments remain as urgent and compelling as when they were first written.

John Stuart Mill: Suggested Additional Reading

Abernethy, George L. and Thomas A. Langford, eds., *History of Philosophy: Selected Readings*. Belmont, Calif.: Dickenson, 1965, pp. 606–620.*

Anschutz, Richard Paul, *The Philosophy of John Stuart Mill*. Oxford: Clarendon Press, 1953.*

Britton, Karl, *John Stuart Mill*. Baltimore: Penguin, 1953.

Halévy, E., *The Growth of Philosophical Radicalism*. Boston: Beacon Press, paperback, 1955.

Jackson, Reginald, *An Examination of the Deductive Logic of John Stuart Mill*. London: Oxford University Press, 1941.*

Kubitz, Oskar, *Development of John Stuart Mill's System of Logic*. Urbana, Ill.: University of Illinois, 1932.*

Levi, Albert W., ed., *The Six Great Humanistic Essays of John Stuart Mill*. Edited by A. W. Levi. New York: Washington Square Press, 1963.

Mill, *Collected Works*. Vols. 1, 2. Toronto: University of Toronto, 1963.*

Mill, *The Philosophy of John Stuart Mill*. Edited by Marshall Cohen. New York: Random House, Modern Library, 1961.*

Mill, *On Liberty*. Indianapolis: Bobbs-Merrill, Liberal Arts Press, 1956.

Mill, *On the Logic of the Moral Sciences*. Edited, with an introduction by Henry M. Magid. Indianapolis: Bobbs-Merrill, Liberal Arts Press, 1965.

Mill, *Autobiography*. Indianapolis: Bobbs-Merrill, Liberal Arts Press, 1958.

Mill, *Theism*. Edited by Richard Taylor. Indianapolis: Bobbs-Merrill, Liberal Arts Press, 1957.

Nagel, E., *John Stuart Mill's Philosophy of Scientific Method*. New York: Hafner, 1950.

Packe, M. St. J., *John Stuart Mill*. London: Secker and Warburg, 1964.*

Stephens, L., *The English Utilitarians*. Vol. III. London: Duckworth, 1900.*

Epilogue

We have come to the end of our survey, but not to the end of philosophy. The reader may properly ask himself at this point what he has gained from the study. Obviously we have presented only a small fraction of the history of Western philosophy, for many volumes have been written on the individual philosophers and topics we have discussed. Nevertheless, we have attempted to provide a sense of the richness of the philosophical tradition by introducing the reader to major thinkers and problems. If he has been stimulated to engage in serious reflection or has been led to systematic reading in the writings of the philosophers, if he has gained insights into the cultural traditions of the West, and if he is propelled beyond the confines of this survey and is convinced that there is more to learn than we have provided, then our effort has been successful.

Our book ends with the treatments of Kierkegaard and Mill, but there is no implication that subsequent developments are insignificant or anticlimactic. Our decision to terminate the history at this point is based on such practical considerations as the time available in a two-semester course and the most convenient point of historical division. In fact, the last century of Western philosophy offers more than sufficient materials for a full-length book, which it surely deserves. The twentieth century provides a great diversity of philosophical movements and thinkers. Analytical philosophy, phenomenology, existentialism, pragmatism, positivism, the revival of Neothomism, the varieties of idealism and realism and the writings of such independent thinkers as Bergson, Moore, Whitehead, Wittgenstein, Merleau-Ponty, and Heidegger invite systematic examination. Even such a selective list indicates the wide range and the specialization of philosophy as it continues its development. The student who has been through a history of philosophy should be in a better position to undertake further study. He should not be surprised if he finds himself returning again and again to these seminal figures and ideas in the effort to decide whether some current doctrine has validity or originality. So the work of philosophy continues, and as long as men remain reasonable and share their views and criticisms philosophy will have a history.

Index